Fodor's

PRAGUE

Second Edition

Where to Stay and Eat for All Budgets

Must-See Sights and Local Secrets

Ratings You Can Trust

Fodor's Travel Publications   New York, Toronto, London, Sydney, Auckland
www.fodors.com

FODOR'S PRAGUE

Editor: Maria Teresa Burwell

Editorial Production: Evangelos Vasilakis
Editorial Contributors: Mark Baker, Mindy Kay Bricker, Raymond Johnston, and Evan Rail
Maps: David Lindroth, *cartographer;* Bob Blake and Rebecca Baer, *map editors*
Design: Fabrizio La Rocca, *creative director;* Moon Sun Kim, *cover designer;* Guido Caroti, *art director;* Melanie Marin, *senior photo editor*
Production/Manufacturing: Colleen Ziemba
Cover Photo (Charles Bridge): David Zimmerman/Masterfile

SPECIAL SALES

This book is available for special discounts for bulk purchases for sales promotions or premiums. Special editions, including personalized covers, excerpts of existing books, and corporate imprints, can be created in large quantities for special needs. For more information, write to Special Markets/Premium Sales, 1745 Broadway, MD 6-2, New York, New York 10019, or e-mail specialmarkets@randomhouse.com.

AN IMPORTANT TIP & AN INVITATION

Although all prices, opening times, and other details in this book are based on information supplied to us at press time, changes occur all the time in the travel world, and Fodor's cannot accept responsibility for facts that become outdated or for inadvertent errors or omissions. So **always confirm information when it matters,** especially if you're making a detour to visit a specific place. Your experiences—positive and negative—matter to us. If we have missed or misstated something, **please write to us.** We follow up on all suggestions. Contact the Prague editor at editors@fodors.com or c/o Fodor's at 1745 Broadway, New York, New York 10019.

PRINTED IN THE UNITED STATES OF AMERICA

10 9 8 7 6 5 4 3 2 1

Be a Fodor's Correspondent

Your opinion matters. It matters to us. It matters to your fellow Fodor's travelers, too. And we'd like to hear it. In fact, we *need* to hear it.

When you share your experiences and opinions, you become an active member of the Fodor's community. That means we'll not only use your feedback to make our books better, but we'll publish your names and comments whenever possible. Throughout our guides, look for "Word of Mouth," excerpts of your unvarnished feedback.

Here's how you can help improve Fodor's for all of us.

Tell us when we're right. We rely on local writers to give you an insider's perspective. But our writers and staff editors—who are the best in the business—depend on you. Your positive feedback is a vote to renew our recommendations for the next edition.

Tell us when we're wrong. We're proud that we update most of our guides every year. But we're not perfect. Things change. Hotels cut services. Museums change hours. Charming cafés lose charm. If our writer didn't quite capture the essence of a place, tell us how you'd do it differently. If any of our descriptions are inaccurate or inadequate, we'll incorporate your changes in the next edition and will correct factual errors at fodors.com *immediately.*

Tell us what to include. You probably have had fantastic travel experiences that aren't yet in Fodor's. Why not share them with a community of like-minded travelers? Maybe you chanced upon a beach or bistro or B&B that you don't want to keep to yourself. Tell us why we should include it. And share your discoveries and experiences with everyone directly at fodors.com. Your input may lead us to add a new listing or highlight a place we cover with a "Highly Recommended" star or with our highest rating, "Fodor's Choice."

Send your nominations, comments, and complaints by mail to Prague Editor, Fodor's, 1745 Broadway, New York, NY 10019. Or e-mail editors@fodors.com with the subject line "Prague Editor."

You and travelers like you are the heart of the Fodor's community. Make our community richer by sharing your experiences. Be a Fodor's correspondent.

Happy traveling!

Tim Jarrell, Publisher

CONTENTS

MAPS

CLOSEUPS

ABOUT THIS BOOK

Our Ratings

Sometimes you find terrific travel experiences and sometimes they just find you. But usually the burden is on you to select the right combination of experiences. That's where our ratings come in.

As travelers we've all discovered a place so wonderful that its worthiness is obvious. And sometimes that place is so unique that superlatives don't do it justice: you just have to be there to know. These sights, properties, and experiences get our highest rating, **Fodor's Choice,** indicated by orange stars throughout this book.

Black stars highlight sights and properties we deem **Highly Recommended,** places that our writers, editors, and readers praise again and again for consistency and excellence.

By default, there's another category: any place we include in this book is by definition worth your time, unless we say otherwise. And we will.

Disagree with any of our choices? Care to nominate a place or suggest that we rate one more highly? Visit our feedback center at www.fodors.com/feedback.

Budget Well

Hotel and restaurant price categories from ¢ to $$$$ are defined in the opening pages of each chapter. For attractions, we always give standard adult admission fees; reductions are usually available for children, students, and senior citizens. Want to pay with plastic? **AE, D, DC, MC, V** following restaurant and hotel listings indicate whether American Express, Discover, Diner's Club, MasterCard, and Visa are accepted.

Restaurants

Unless we state otherwise, restaurants are open for lunch and dinner daily. We mention dress only when there's a specific requirement and reservations only when they're essential or not accepted—it's always best to book ahead.

Hotels

Hotels have private bath, phone, TV, and air-conditioning and operate on the European Plan (aka EP, meaning without meals), unless we specify that they use the Continental Plan (CP, with a continental breakfast), Breakfast Plan (BP, with a full breakfast), or Modified American Plan (MAP, with breakfast and dinner) or are all-inclusive (including all meals and most activities). We always

list facilities but not whether you'll be charged an extra fee to use them, so when pricing accommodations, find out what's included.

Many Listings
- ★ Fodor's Choice
- ★ Highly recommended
- ⊠ Physical address
- ✛ Directions
- ⌖ Mailing address
- ☎ Telephone
- 🖷 Fax
- ⊕ On the Web
- ✉ E-mail
- 🎫 Admission fee
- ◷ Open/closed times
- ⏵ Start of walk/itinerary
- Ⓜ Metro stations
- ▭ Credit cards

Hotels & Restaurants
- 🏨 Hotel
- ⤸ Number of rooms
- ♨ Facilities
- 🍽 Meal plans
- ✕ Restaurant
- ✍ Reservations
- 🏛 Dress code
- ⭦ Smoking
- 🍷 BYOB
- ✕🏨 Hotel with restaurant that warrants a visit

Outdoors
- 🏌 Golf
- ⛺ Camping

Other
- ☕ Family-friendly
- 🛈 Contact information
- ⇨ See also
- ⊠ Branch address
- ☞ Take note

WHEN TO GO

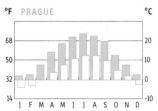

°F PRAGUE °C

68 — 20
50 — 10
32 — 0
14 — -10

J F M A M J J A S O N D

Prague is beautiful year-round, but it's busiest in summer and during the Christmas and Easter holidays. Spring offers generally good weather with a more relaxed level of tourism, as flowers are blossoming, historical sights are open longer, and the Prague Spring Music Festival is in full swing. During the busy Easter season you can watch an unusual fertility ritual with pagan roots, in which boys with willow branches whip the girls in order to keep them fertile; the girls reply by splashing their tormentors with water. When fall arrives, trees take on red-and-gold hues, and Czechs head to the woods to pick their beloved mushrooms. In winter you encounter fewer visitors and find much cheaper hotels; you also have the opportunity to see Prague breathtakingly covered in snow, but it can get very cold and dark, as the sun tends to set by 5 and many days are overcast. Also, some castles and museums, especially those outside of Prague, close for the season. January and February generally bring the best skiing in Bohemia's mountains—and there's great difficulty in finding a room at the ski resorts. If you're not a skier, try visiting the mountains in late spring (April or May) or fall, when the colors are dazzling and you have the hotels and restaurants nearly to yourself. In much of the rest of Bohemia and Moravia, even in midsummer, the number of visitors is far smaller than in Prague, and trips to the towns that dot the countryside can be a welcome break from the long lines and crowded areas of the Golden City.

Climate

Winters can be bone-chillingly cold, with dark, overcast days. The maximum average temperature in December and January is 32° F, and temperatures frequently drop to the low 20s F. Things brighten up considerably in the spring and summer seasons. The days peak in July with around 10 hours of sunshine per day. Showers are infrequent and usually light and short, while temperatures hover in the high 70s F. Fall brings with it fewer crowds and slightly cooler temperatures in the 60s F, as well as a riotous display of color on the foliage in parts of the city and countryside.

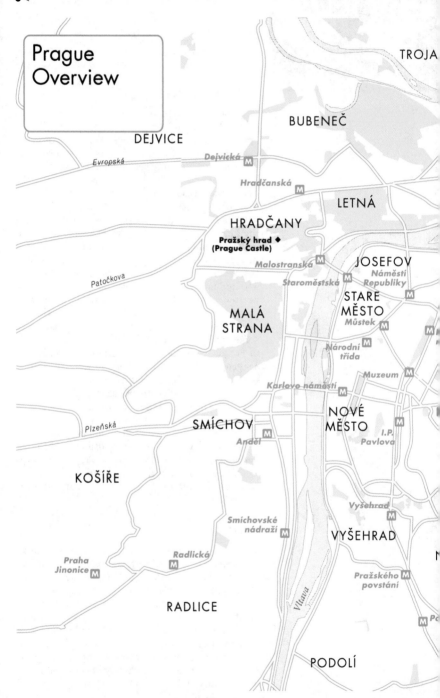

Prague Overview

TROJA

BUBENEČ

DEJVICE

Evropská

Dejvická Ⓜ

Hradčanská Ⓜ

LETNÁ

HRADČANY

Pražský hrad ◆ (Prague Castle)

Malostranská Ⓜ

JOSEFOV

Náměstí Republiky Ⓜ

Staroměstská Ⓜ

STARE MĚSTO

Patočkova

Můstek Ⓜ

Ⓜ

MALÁ STRANA

Národní třída Ⓜ

Muzeum Ⓜ

Karlovo náměstí Ⓜ

NOVÉ MĚSTO

Plzeňská

SMÍCHOV

Anděl Ⓜ

I.P. Pavlova

KOŠÍŘE

Vyšehrad Ⓜ

Smíchovské nádraží Ⓜ

VYŠEHRAD

Praha Jinonice Ⓜ

Radlická Ⓜ

Pražského povstání Ⓜ

RADLICE

Ⓜ

Vltava

PODOLÍ

WHAT'S WHERE

PRAGUE	Simply put, Prague is one of Europe's most beautiful cities. An evening stroll across the Charles Bridge—as the sun sets behind the castle and the last rays are reflected by the Old Town's golden spires—has become one of those European "musts."
STARÉ MĚSTO	On a sunny summer weekend, Old Town Square will be so packed with revelers you might think a rock concert was coming up. The 15th-century astronomical clock, which is on one side of the town hall, has a procession of 12 apostles that make their rounds when certain hours strike. From another side, the Church of Our Lady before Týn's Gothic spires and the solid gold effigy of the Virgin Mary keep watch over onlookers.
MALÁ STRANA	The "Lesser Quarter" is full of winding cobblestone streets and baroque buildings, including numerous foreign embassies and stately palaces, virtually untouched since the 18th century. Go left and you will find sculpted house signs, which are works of art in their own right; go right, and you will be greeted by a statue of a saint holding a golden staff at the entrance to a church. For a break, look for one of the many gardens that are tucked into the neighborhood.
HRADČANY	The Castle district is known for being the seat of Prague Castle, and its sights can easily take up most of a day. St. Vitus's Cathedral, which sits in the castle proper, with its buttresses, gargoyles, spires, and towers, looms high over the area. The history of Prague is irrevocably intertwined with that of the castle, which was founded in the 9th century. At night, floodlights light up the area, giving the impression to riverside onlookers that the castle is floating above the city.
JOSEFOV	The history of the Jewish Quarter's ghetto is revealed in the Old Jewish Cemetery, packed with thousands of tilting headstones, and in the synagogues that still dot the neighborhood. The Old-New Synagogue, constructed around 1270, is the oldest in Europe. The Jewish Museum, which comprises five different buildings, has collections of Eastern European Jewish property confiscated and preserved. Today art nouveau structures have replaced the former ghetto buildings, and some of the city's finest shopping can be had along Pařížská Street.

NOVÉ MĚSTO	"New" is a relative term, and that's the case for Prague's "New Town," which was first planned out by Charles IV in the 14th century. Wenceslas Square, a commercial boulevard lined with shops, restaurants, and hotels, forms the backbone of New Town. It's worth seeing not only for its scale, but also for the National Museum, which sits at the top of the square like a king on his throne. Two doors over is the State Opera House with its intense red plush gilding and original interior artwork. Back down the square, follow Národní třída to reach the blue- and gold-top National Theater, a source of Czech cultural pride.
VYŠEHRAD	Upriver from the Charles Bridge, the compact district Vyšehrad is known for its ancient castle that sits perched above the Vltava's waters. A cemetery holding the nation's finest writers, composers, and artists is on the grounds, as is a castle; views from its ramparts are stunning. Below the walls, near the waterfront, are several Cubist homes.
VINOHRADY	True to its name—which means vineyards—Vinohrady began as a wine-growing region. Although the area has been transformed into an upscale, residential neighborhood with tree-lined streets and several parks, it offers *vino*-lovers plenty of wine bars and shops. Walk over to Náměstí Míru (Peace Square) for a peek at the neo-Gothic Church of St. Ludmila and its twin 200-foot-high octagonal spires. Just to the left of the front doors of the church is the Vinohrady Theater, topped by two massive statues symbolizing drama and opera.
LETNÁ	Known for its sprawling park that overlooks the eastern half of the city and a bend of the Vltava River, this area is where some of the largest demonstrations that led to 1989's "Velvet Revolution" took place. Now citizens happily rollerblade, ride bicycles, and walk their dogs around the pathways in the park.
HOLEŠOVICE	This gritty, workaday part of town, across the Vlatva River from and northeast of the Old Town, holds the Veletržní palác (Trade Fair Palace), which contains the National Gallery's Collection of Modern & Contemporary Art.
SMÍCHOV	A former industrial center, Smíchov is now home to several large office buildings, multiplex cinemas, and a major shopping mall. Still, it betrays hints of what it used to be in days long gone by in Bertramka, a villa that once hosted Wolfgang Amadeus Mozart.

WHAT'S WHERE

ŽIŽKOV	This working-class area supposedly has more bars or clubs than any other Prague neighborhood. Check out the rocketlike TV tower and its enormous metal babies, constructed by a local artist.
BEYOND PRAGUE	Day trips outside the capital. It's nice—if you are not planning on traveling elsewhere in the Czech Republic—to see how the "other half" lives outside Prague. The best castles can be found at Karlštejn, Konopiště, Český Šternberk, and Křivoklát, all within an hour's drive or bus ride. The former Nazi concentration camp at Terezín is a dark day trip, but highly recommended.
WESTERN BOHEMIA	Western Bohemia is spa country, and Karlovy Vary is clearly the king of the three main spas. But the other two, Mariánské Lázně and Františkovy Lázně, have their charm. Don't come expecting hot stones, aromatherapies, and exfoliations with orange rinds. Spas in these parts are serious medical treatments. Come instead to stroll through another era of history and enjoy the beautiful grounds.
SOUTHERN BOHEMIA	If Western Bohemia means spas, Southern Bohemia equals castle territory. And the undisputed must is Český Krumlov. It's hard to imagine a more scenic town—embraced by the Vltava River on three sides with its majestic castle rising above it all. Yes it's touristy, but Český Krumlov lives up to the hype. Plan at least a day and night here to enjoy the painfully picturesque streets, and the excellent restaurants and hotels. If hiking and biking is your thing, Třeboň has well-marked bike trails fan out all along the border area with Austria.
MORAVIA	Lacking a world-class tourist attraction, Moravia doesn't make it onto too many itineraries. Its industrial capital Brno can't hold a candle to Prague. Wine-lovers, though, may want to make their way to southern Moravia, where most of the country's wine is produced. Several new wineries have opened up, and towns like Valtice, Mikulov, and Znojmo all make for good bases of exploration. Even if you don't travel extensively in Moravia, you should at least try to get to Telč. Its gorgeous central square, lined with its baroque and Renaissance façades, is not to be missed.

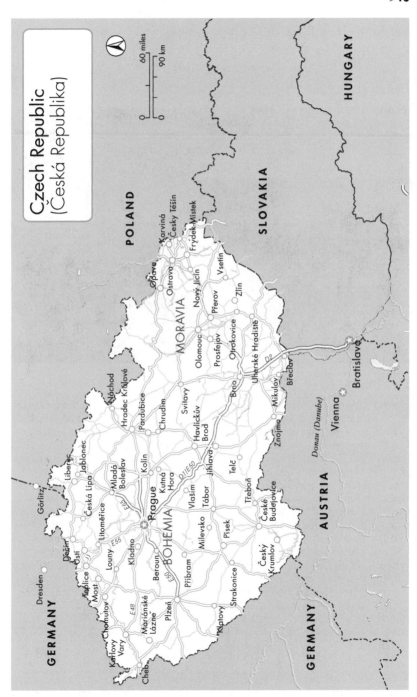

Czech Republic
(Česká Republika)

60 miles
90 km

GERMANY

POLAND

SLOVAKIA

HUNGARY

AUSTRIA

GERMANY

MORAVIA

BOHEMIA

Dresden
Görlitz
Děčín
Ústí
Teplice
Most
Chomutov
Karlovy Vary
Cheb
Mariánské Lázně
Plzeň
Klatovy
Strakonice
Český Krumlov
Písek
Milevsko
Příbram
Beroun
Kladno
Louny
Litoměřice
Česká Lípa
Liberec
Jablonec
Mladá Boleslav
Kolín
Kutná Hora
Prague
Vlašim
Tábor
Třeboň
České Budějovice
Jihlava
Telč
Havlíčkův Brod
Chrudim
Pardubice
Hradec Králové
Náchod
Svitavy
Brno
Znojmo
Mikulov
Břeclav
Uherské Hradiště
Otrokovice
Prostějov
Olomouc
Přerov
Zlín
Vsetín
Nový Jičín
Ostrava
Opava
Karviná
Český Těšín
Frýdek-Místek

Vienna
Bratislava
Donau (Danube)

E55
E50
E48
D1/E50
D2

QUINTESSENTIAL PRAGUE

Pivo (Beer)

Every discussion about the Czech Republic begins and ends with beer: Czechs are the world's largest consumers of beer per capita, they invented modern pilsener, (named after the town, Plzeň) and Czech beer is still considered the best in the world. It's so good, in fact, that it commands the type of reverence usually reserved for wine. But if you really want to chug it down like a local, don't drink from a bottle or a can. Head to the nearest "pivnice," or pub, find a seat at a table, wipe the inevitable cigarette ash off the table cloth, and wait for the waiter to plunk down a mug in front of you. Turn to your neighbor, raise your glass, and say "Na zdraví," "To your health!" (any pronunciation will work). Congratulations. Now you can apply for citizenship.

Parks

Czechs are nature-lovers at heart. On summer weekends, they beat a trail to their vacation cottages to tend the garden and, yes, drink beer in the countryside. During the week, though, the only natural outlets available are the city's parks. Letná, across the river from Old Town, and Riegrovy Sady in Vinohrady are two of the most popular. Bring a book, blanket, and a picnic, stroll the walks, or snag some Rollerblades and glide around like a native. Around 5 or 6 PM the leisure ends and the real party starts. Both parks have huge beer gardens and some evenings it seems the whole city is slightly tipsy, laughing merrily under the stars.

With Prague so full of visitors from other countries, it can be a little hard to find what makes the city "Czech." A good way to start is by doing some of the things that Czechs like to do.

Culture

Czechs are culture vultures, and performance art of all stripes is the biggest draw. Live theater, musicals, concerts, and clubs—especially featuring local performers—are normally booked solid. Eschew, at least for one day, the impromptu classical church concerts you see all over town. These are put on for the tourists with nary a local in sight. The weekly *Prague Post* carries a full listing of authentic rock concerts, music club acts, and classical music performances aimed at Czechs and where language is not likely to be a problem. Here the performances are genuine and the audience reaction is heartfelt. The Czechs survived three centuries of Austrian occupation—from 1620 to 1918—with only a shared culture to unite them. And that cultural bond endures.

Cafés

The café tradition dates from the 19th century, and played a strong role in both the Germanic and Czech cultures here through the ages. Until recently cafés were on the decline, as historical properties folded and banks opened branches in their place. Happily, cafés appear to be making a modest comeback—traditional coffeehouses, modern Seattle-style coffee bars, and a sort of new-age teahouse (known locally as a "čajovna") all have their niche. Whatever the type, they remain great places to kick back, relax, chat, and people-watch. Prague is filled with cafés of all sorts, but the best-known remains Kavárna Slavia. The "Slavia" nurtured the souls of dissident writers and musicians during a dark Communist period; it's no wonder, since it has one of the best views in town. The food's good, too, which is an added bonus.

IF YOU LIKE

Castles

More than 2,000 castles, manor houses, and châteaux dot the Czech Republic forming a precious and not-to-be-missed part of the country's cultural and historical heritage. Grim ruins glower from craggy hilltops, and fantastical Gothic castles guard ancient trade routes. Hundreds of noble houses—Renaissance, baroque, and empire—are sprinkled throughout the countryside. Their former bourgeois and aristocratic owners were expelled in the anti-German reaction of 1945–46 or forced out by the Communists. Today some of their valuable old seats stand in near ruin, but just as many have been returned to the care of the original owners. Others remain in state hands as museums, homes for the elderly, or conference centers. More sights than ever are now open to the public. Picture galleries, rooms full of historic furniture, exquisite medieval stonework, and baroque chapels—all speak of a vanished way of life whose remnants survive in every town and village of Bohemia and Moravia.

- Zámek Konopiště (Konopiště Castle) is an easy drive from Prague. The former residence of Franz Ferdinand, this castle is packed with paintings, statues, and a compulsive collection of hunting trophies.

- Český Šternberk's castle has a dark beauty that is almost ominous at night. It's easy to picture scenes from the Thirty Years' War here.

- Hrad Krumlov (Krumlov Castle) completes the fairytale look of the town, and two black bears romping in the castle's moat animate the tableau.

Fine Dining

Not long ago a trip to this part of the world meant enjoying the history and natural beauty in spite of the indifferent food. A solidly meat-and-potatoes country, the Czech Republic has opened its arms to fusion cuisine and exotic new flavors. If restaurant standards keep improving at their present pace, it won't be long before people are coming to Prague because of the food. In most ways, that's good news. New chefs are arriving and new ideas are reinvigorating the standard roast pork or duck with dumplings, or broiled meat with sauce. Grilled pond trout appears on most menus and is often excellent. Prague diners have also welcomed Indian, Brazilian, Mexican, and Thai restaurants with gusto. This culinary revolution, however, doesn't come cheap and prices at the best places easily meet or exceed their counterparts in Western Europe or North America.

- Allegro at Prague's Four Seasons hotel is a worthy splurge where the expatriate chef has fused the best of Italian and Central Europe cooking.

- Pravda features a globe-trotting menu in a sleek, minimalist setting. Wasabi and truffles are no strangers here.

- C'est La Vie on Kampa Island lets you dine on beautifully prepared fish while watching the boats pass through the locks on the Vltava river.

- Kampa Park's sensory assault begins with the view of the Charles Bridge and carries through with the seasonal ingredients artfully prepared on your plate.

Hiking & Biking

The Czech Republic has 40,000 km (25,000 mi) of well-kept, -marked, and -signposted trails both in the mountainous regions and leading through beautiful countryside from town to town encouraging outdoor enthusiasts and avid hikers to leave Prague and retreat to nature. The most scenic areas are the Beskydy range in northern Moravia and the Krkonoše range (Giant Mountains) in northern Bohemia. If you make your way to the spa towns, both Mariánské Lázně and Karlovy Vary are surrounded by beautiful forest. In Karlovy Vary, an easy day walk takes you up to Jelení Skok (stag's leap)—with a gorgeous overview of the spa. Around the country, you will find colored markings denoting trails on trees, fences, walls, rocks, and elsewhere. The main paths are marked in red, others in blue and green, while the least important trails are marked in yellow. Hiking maps can be found in almost any bookstore; look for the large-scale *Soubor turistických* maps. Within Prague, parks such as Stromovka or Divoká Šárka offer numerous trails and beautiful, tree-laden scenery; the latter contains a swimming pool as well.

Czechs are also avid cyclists, and it's not uncommon to see a cyclist, dressed in a store-bought team jersey, pedaling like mad to stay out of the way of Prague's notoriously bad drivers. The flatter areas of southern Bohemia and Moravia are ideal for biking. Outside the larger towns, quiet roads stretch for miles. The hillier terrain of northern Bohemia makes it popular with mountain-biking enthusiasts. Not many places rent bikes, though.

Beer & Wine

The king of beers in this part of the world is not Budweiser—though Czech Budvar runs a close second, but world-famous Plzeňský Prazdroj (Pilsner Urquell). The word "prazdroj" means "source" and you can tour the source of modern beer at the Pilsener Urquell Brewery in Plzeň. Some other beers to watch for and try include: the slightly bitter Krušovice; the fruity Radegast; and the bolder, Prague-brewed Staropramen. Prague hosts a galaxy of pubs where local hops can be sampled.

- Pivovarský dům serves seasonal micro-brewed beers that have beer-lovers draining their glasses.

- Pivovary Staropramen offers a variety of beers and tours of the brewery.

Czechs also produce quite drinkable wines: peppy, fruity whites and mild, versatile reds. Southern Moravia, with comparatively warm summers and rich soil, grows the bulk of the wine harvest. Look for the Mikulov and Znojmo regional designations. Favorite white varietals are Müller-Thurgau, with a muscat bouquet and light flavor, and Neuburské, yellow-green in color and with a dry, smoky scent. Rulandské bílé, a semidry burgundylike white, has a flowery bouquet and full-bodied flavor. As for reds, Frankovka runs to fiery and slightly acidic, while the cherry-red Rulandské červené is a very drinkable, drier choice. Plenty of restaurants in Prague serve fine Czech wines.

- Perpetuum offers Czech's best vintages along with traditional cuisine with a French twist.

GREAT ITINERARY

Day 1: Arrival, Prague Castle

On the first day—particularly if your plane lands early—get yourself situated in your hotel and shoot for at least one great site before hitting the sack. That site has got to be Prague Castle, whose grounds contain the towering St. Vitus's Cathedral and the Golden Lane, a row of minuscule cottages built along one of the Castle's walls. Later relax in the nearby Royal Gardens. Take a leisurely stroll down through Malá Strana to the Charles Bridge before returning to your hotel.

Day 2: Josefov & Staré Město (Old Town)

On the second day, hit Josefov, the Jewish Quarter, in the morning before the crowds. Then walk over to Old Town Square, to see the Astronomical Clock and the Gothic Church of Our Lady before Týn. If you have time afterward, explore the streets that radiate from the square to Wenceslas Square.

Day 3: Malá Strana

On the third day walk across the baroque, statue-adorned Charles Bridge on your way to Malá Strana, home to numerous embassies and palaces; the bridge is less busy early in the morning. In the Church of Our Lady Victorious be sure to catch the odd effigy of the Holy Infant of Prague, a wax doll dressed in ceremonial garb.

Day 4: Day Trip to Kutná Hora

For an easy day trip, visit the well-preserved medieval mining town of Kutná Hora, whose rich deposits of silver put it on the map in the 13th century. The St. Barbara Church, built with the miners' donations and named after their patron saint, has many colorful murals depicting mining scenes; outside, the Gothic structure's three tent-shape spires rise above lines of buttresses. Be sure to save time either before or after Kutná Hora to visit the suburb of Sedlec to see the eerie Bone Church. If castles are more your thing, substitute a quick visit to Karlštejn or Konopiště.

Day 5: Český Krumlov

Take a trip to southern Bohemia to soak up the Renaissance charm of Český Krumlov, which is surely one of the most beautiful cities in this part of the world. Built around loops of the Vltava River, the town is listed as second in importance on UNESCO's list of World Heritage Sites, behind only Venice. Plan on spending the night here.

Day 6: Karlovy Vary

Make your way back to České Budějovice and then westward in the direction of Plzeň and eventually to Karlovy Vary. If you have got the time, make a pit stop to tour the famous Pilsner Urquell Brewery in Plzeň. If you want to drink, it might be wise to plan an overnight here. Otherwise, continue on to the lovely spa town of Karlovy Vary. This is the king of Bohemia's spa resorts with winding hillside walks and cooling pools for taking a dip. Check out the historic city center and don't pass up a romantic dinner at the Embassy restaurant atop one of the bridges over the tiny Tepla river. Plan on spending the night.

Day 7: Return to Prague

Complete any unfinished itinerary from previous days, or go exploring in a new neighborhood: Nové Město, Vyšehrad, or Vinohrady. In the evening treat yourself to a fine performance at the National Theater or the Rudolfinum, to end your trip on a high note.

ON THE
CALENDAR

The top seasonal events in Prague and the rest of the Czech Republic are listed below, and any one of them could provide the stuff of lasting memories. For contact information about most of these festivals, inquire at the Prague Tourist office or the local visitor information centers.

ONGOING Late Feb.– late Mar.	Prague holds the St. Matthew's Fair, an annual children's fair at the Výstaviště exhibition grounds. It opens on St. Matthew's day (February 24) and runs for most of the next four weeks. An ancient traditional fair has now been replaced by a giant fun fair, which occupies a large space in the Prague exhibition grounds. Come here for every variety of noisy mechanical fairground attraction. The flashing lights and volume of noise will satisfy the most demanding of children who will also want to buy from the eye-catching selection of sweet and refreshment stalls.
July–Sept.	The old stone walls and ramparts surrounding the courtyard of the Old Burgrave's Hall in Prague Castle create the perfect backdrop for the Letní shakespearovské slavnosti (Summer Shakespeare Festival), which includes several evenings of open-air Shakespeare performances. Drawing on the talents of many performers from Prague's professional theaters, the festival company usually presents two plays during the three-month season. Performances begin at 8:30.
WINTER Dec. 5	One of the most important celebrations in Prague is the Eve of the Festival of St. Nicolas. Beginning in the late afternoon and continuing throughout the rest of the evening, this is one of the main Christmas-season celebrations in Prague. Although activities are focused mainly around the Old Town Square, you can find that Mikuláš and his entourage will also be at most of the Christmas markets, street corners, and even on the metro. This is the evening when small children are brought out to meet the jolly, white-bearded saint himself and his accompanying angels and sometimes terrifying devils. If they have been good, then the angels reward them with some sweets from their baskets, but if they have been bad, a devil may well try to take them away in a sack. All this provides as much fun for the grown-ups as it does for the kids, and the surrounding cacophony of fire crackers and the intoxicating bouquet of mulled wine helps make it a festive evening.
Late Jan.	Prague hosts the FebioFest International Film, Television & Video Festival at the end of January, which lasts for about 10 days. The festival has grown into an extremely popular and wide-ranging celebration of international film. Special prices at several main

ON THE CALENDAR

		cinemas pull in the crowds to every event. Throughout the festival, films are shown from mid-morning to well past midnight. The range of genres is vast: from Third-World art films to cult blockbusters, you find just about every kind of movie. Most venues offer a simultaneous translation into English at each showing. A detailed guide is available, and advance booking is a good idea because lines can be long.
	Feb.	The Best of Czech Opera Festival, a biannual festival in odd-numbered years, provides opera lovers with an unparalleled opportunity to experience the full range of Czech operatic theater productions. For two weeks Prague's opera houses play host to the country's many regional companies, which relish this chance to bring their best productions and artists to the capital. This gives a chance to everybody to shine, and the final concert evening sees the presentation of several respected awards for operatic achievement. The repertoire varies from the familiar to the frankly obscure.
SPRING Mar.		Prague and Brno jointly host the Days of European Film, an 11-day film festival focusing on the latest European releases.
Late Mar.		English-language and world authors appear at the Prague Writers' Festival, a four-day celebration of the written word that draws international writers for a series of readings and literary discussions.
Apr.		Eastertime brings two festivals of sacred music to Prague, Musica Ecumenica and Musica Sacra Praga.
Apr.		Brno puts on an Easter Spiritual Music Festival each year during Easter week.
May		The annual Prague Spring International Music Festival is undoubtedly the most significant cultural festival of the year. Opening with the customary performance of Smetana's "Má vlast" on the anniversary of the composer's death, the festival presents three weeks of world-class music making throughout Prague. Internationally renowned performers gather in Prague's magnificent concert halls and churches to play music from the entire classical repertoire. Tickets are in high demand, but prices are relatively modest, and there are usually some seats available on most performance days.
Late May		Thousands of runners fill the city's streets for the Prague Marathon, which tends to draw a wide, international group of long-distance runners.

SUMMER June	The international dance festival Tanec Praha hits the capital and brings together important representatives in European contemporary dance to a variety of venues throughout the city. This gathering of young dancers creates a heady atmosphere for those whose interest is in the modern dance form and it's a chance to compare the various styles of performances now in vogue.
Mid-June– mid-Aug.	The Janáček Festival of Music takes place in Olomouc each summer at Hukvaldy Castle. Janáček's birthplace (still preserved) provides the peg on which to hang a richly varied annual festival of music making. Naturally enough, the Master's own works are a chief feature, but performers are drawn from around the country. In addition to concerts, there are visiting drama and opera companies.
Early July	Karlovy Vary hosts its annual Karlovy Vary International Film Festival in early July. It's the biggest film festival in the Czech Republic and compares favorably to Cannes, Venice, and Berlin. The focus is often on new Central European offerings, giving it a kind of fringe caché. Plan ahead if you want to take part. Day passes are available for visitors to see the movies, but many shows sell out. Hotel rooms need to be booked in advance.
Late Aug.	Prague's two-week Verdi Festival is always staged at the State Opera and showcases performances of several of the master's operas during a two-week period starting in mid-August.
FALL Mid-Sept.	The two-week Prague Autumn International Music Festival is the last major European music festival of the summer season. It's a chance to see a wide range of international performers and orchestras perform a range of Czech and international music.
Late Oct.	An early fall highlight is always the International Jazz Festival, a week-long series of performances by international jazz artists.
Nov.	Prague stokes the cultural fires against the approach of winter with the Czech Press Photo Exhibition. An exciting variety of work from the professional lenses of the many Czech photographers is always on display at this large photography exhibition. The aim is to stimulate press photographers to do work beyond their normal realm, and the results are usually well worth watching. A jury of top professionals awards prizes.
Nov.	Jewish musical groups gather from all over the world for the month-long Musica Iudaica International Music Festival, a festival of Jewish music.

Exploring Prague

WORD OF MOUTH

"My favorite places in Prague happen to be the most touristy—the Charles Bridge and Old Town Square. They may be touristy, but they are very beautiful."
—isabel

"If you are at all into baroque and gold leaf adornment, the church interiors are a real treat. The Astrological clock draws crowds about every hour of the waking day and into the evening."
—TopMan

"The clock itself is a marvel, but I found it and the circle of 365 names below it more interesting than the anticlimactic conga line of Apostles."
—AHaugeto

By Mark Baker   **THE BACKBONE OF PRAGUE IS THE VLTAVA RIVER** (also sometimes known by its German name, Moldau), which runs from south to north with a single sharp turn to the east. The city was originally composed of five independent towns that today represents the historic district: Hradčany (Castle Area), Malá Strana (Lesser Quarter), Staré Město (Old Town), Nové Město (New Town), and Josefov (Jewish Quarter).

Hradčany, the seat of Czech royalty for hundreds of years, centers around the Pražský hrad (Prague Castle). A cluster of white buildings yoked around the pointed steeples of a chapel, the Prague Castle overlooks the city from a hilltop west of the Vltava River. Steps lead down from Hradčany to the Lesser Quarter, an area dense with ornate mansions built for the 17th- and 18th-century nobility.

Karlův most (Charles Bridge) connects the Lesser Quarter with the Old Town, which is hemmed in by the curving Vltava River and three large commercial avenues: Revoluční to the east, Na příkopě to the southeast, and Národní třída to the south. A few blocks east of the bridge is the district's focal point Staroměstské náměstí (Old Town Square), a former medieval marketplace laced with pastel-color baroque houses. To the north of Old Town Square, the diminutive Jewish Quarter fans out around a wide avenue called Pařížská.

> **MARK'S TOP 5 THINGS TO DO IN PRAGUE**
>
> 1. Walk across the Charles Bridge at night drinking in the dramatic city skyline.
> 2. Have a drink at the Letna beer garden at sunset, enjoying the breathtaking backdrop of the Old Town's spires.
> 3. Hike the high-altitude meadow from Hradčany to Petřin Hill with stunning vistas over the city.
> 4. Get lost in the Old Town. Stow your map at the hotel and leave the masses behind on Karlova, choosing instead the labyrinth of little cobblestoned alleyways.
> 5. Stroll the river on the Malá Strana side while feeding the swans.

Beyond the former walls of the Old Town, the New Town fills in the south and east. The name "new" is a misnomer—New Town was laid out in the 14th century. (It's only new when compared to the neighboring Old Town.) Today this mostly commercial district includes the city's largest squares, Karlovo náměstí (Charles Square) and Václavské náměstí (Wenceslas Square). Roughly 1 km (½ mi) south of Karlovo náměstí, along the Vltava, is the ancient castle of Vyšehrad high above the river.

On a promontory to the east of Václavské náměstí stretches Vinohrady, one of Prague's well-heeled residential districts. Bordering Vinohrady are the working-class neighborhoods of Žižkov to the north and Nusle to the south. On the west bank of the Vltava lie many older residential neighborhoods and several parks. About 3 km (2 mi) from the center in every direction, Communist-era housing projects begin their unsightly sprawl.

STARÉ MĚSTO (OLD TOWN)

A GOOD WALK

Numbers in the text correspond to numbers in the margin and on the Central Prague map.

The north end of Wenceslas Square, which ends in a "T" intersection with a wide pedestrian walkway and an upscale shopping strip, is a good place to begin a tour of Old Town. This intersection marks the border between the old and new worlds in Prague. A quick glance around shows the often-jarring juxtaposition: centuries-old buildings sit side by side with modern retail names like United Colors of Benetton and McDonald's.

Start on the perimeter of Old Town by turning right at the tall, art deco Koruna complex onto **Na příkopě** ❶ ▶. A short detour down the first street on your left, Havířská ulice, takes you to the 18th-century **Stavovské divadlo** ❷ (Estates Theater). Part of the National Theater complex, this theater appears relatively plain outside, but it glitters with refurbished baroque beauty inside.

Return to Na příkopě, turn left, and continue to the street's end. On weekdays between 8 AM and 5 PM, it's worth stepping into the stunning interior of the Živnostenská banka (Merchant's Bank), at No. 20. A little farther on, crane your neck at the Česká národní banka (No. 28), where a Central European version of Lady Liberty running with a lion graces the rooftop.

Na příkopě ends abruptly at náměstí Republiky (Republic Square), an important New Town transportation hub (with a busy metro stop) undergoing a massive facelift in the summer of 2006 that is likely to continue into 2007. Two buildings, constructed centuries apart but both monumental and stunning, anchor the area. Hundreds of years of grime have not diminished the majesty of the Gothic **Prašná brána** ❸, with its stately spires looming above the square. Adjacent to this tower, the rapturous art nouveau **Obecní dům** ❹ concert hall and municipal center looks like a brightly decorated confection.

Walk through the archway of the massive Prašná brána and down the formal **Celetná ulice** ❺, the first leg of the "Royal Way." Monarchs favored this route primarily because the houses along Celetná were among the city's finest, providing a suitable backdrop to the coronation procession. The cubist building at Celetná No. 34 is **Dům U černé Matky boží** ❻, the House of the Black Madonna, and now a museum of cubism. You can see the Madonna mounted in a niche cut into the corner of the building.

After a few blocks, Celetná opens onto **Staroměstské náměstí** ❼, a busy hub of Old Town, surrounded by dazzling architecture on all sides. On the east side of the square, the double-spired church **Kostel Panny Marie před Týnem** ❽, rises from behind a row of patrician houses. To the immediate left of this, at No. 13, is Dům U Kamenného zvonu (House at the Stone Bell), a baroque town house that has been stripped down to its original Gothic elements and now contains a small art museum.

Next door, at No. 12, stands the gorgeous pink-and-ocher **Palác Kinských** ❾, considered the most prominent example of late baroque–rococo in the area. At this end of the square, you can't help noticing the expressive **Jan Hus monument** ⑩.

At this point you can take a detour to see the National Gallery's Gothic art collection at **Klášter svaté Anežky České** ⑪. Go northeast from the square up Dlouha Street, and then straight along Kozi Street all the way until it ends at U Milosrdných. If you're more in the mood for commerce than art, take a stroll up Pařížská Street out of the north end of the square, which has some of the most glamorous stores—and storefronts—in the city.

Return to Staroměstské náměstí, and beyond the Jan Hus monument is the Gothic **Staroměstská radnice** ⑫, with its impressive 200-foot tower that gives the square its sense of importance. As the hour approaches, join the people milling below the tower's 15th-century astronomical clock for a brief but spooky spectacle taken straight from the Middle Ages involving a skeleton, the 12 apostles, and a fierce-looking Turk; this happens every hour on the hour and tends to draw large crowds of onlookers.

> **WHAT'S FREE**
>
> ■ Watching the animated figures chime the hour at the Astronomical Clock.
>
> ■ Strolling the grounds and gardens of Prague Castle, including the Královský letohrádek (Royal Summer Palace, also known as the Belvedere).
>
> ■ Visiting the western third of St. Vitus's Cathedral, inside the Prague Castle walls, including the façade and the two towers you can see from outside.
>
> ■ Visiting the grave of Franz Kafka in Vinohrady, Nový židovský hřbitov, in the New Jewish Cemetery.

The square's second church, the baroque **Kostel svatého Mikuláše** ⑬, can be confused with the Lesser Quarter's similarly named Chrám svatého Mikuláše on the other side of the river.

You'll find the **Franz Kafka Exposition** ⑭ adjoining Kostel svatého Mikuláše on náměstí Franze Kafky, a little square that used to be part of U Radnice Street. Turn left and continue along U Radnice proper a few yards until you come to **Malé náměstí** ⑮, a mini-square with arcades on one side. Look for tiny Karlova ulice, which begins in the southwest corner of the square, and take another quick right to stay on it (watch the signs—this medieval street seems designed to confound the visitor). The České muzeum výtvarných umění (Czech Museum of Fine Arts) attracts tried-and-true fans of 20th-century Czech art, but you may find yourself lured away by the exotic **Clam-Gallas palác** ⑯, at Husova 20. Recognizing it is easy: look for the Titans in the doorway holding up what must be a very heavy baroque façade.

A block north, the street opens onto Mariánské náměstí, where you'll find the entrance to the mammoth **Clementinum** ⑰, a grouping of historic buildings once used as a Jesuit stronghold.

Head the other way down Husova for a glimpse of ecstatic baroque style stuffed inside a somber Gothic church at the **Kostel svatého Jiljí** ⑱, at

No. 8. Continue walking along Husova to Na perštýně, and look up. You can see a sculpture of a man hanging from a building. "Hanging Out" is by David Černý, the art prankster also responsible for the upside-down horse suspended in the Lucerna pasáž on Wenceslas Square. A right turn puts you on a quiet square, Betlémské náměstí, where you'll find the most revered of all Hussite churches in Prague, the **Betlémská kaple** ⑲.

Return to Na perštýně and continue walking to the right. As you near the back of the buildings on the busy Národní třída (National Boulevard), turn left at Martinská ulice. At the end of the street, the forlorn but majestic church **Kostel svatého Martina ve zdi** ⑳ looks as if it got lost. Walk around the church to the left, through a little archway of apartments and a courtyard with shops and restaurants, onto the bustling Národní třída. To the left, a five-minute walk away, lies Wenceslas Square and the starting point of this walk.

There's little public transit in the Old Town, so walking is really the most practical way to get around; you could take a cab, but it's not worth the trouble. It takes about 15 minutes to walk from náměstí Republiky to Staroměstská. If you're coming to the Old Town from another part of Prague, three metro stops circumscribe the area: Staroměstská on the west, náměstí Republiky on the east, and Můstek on the south, at the point where Old Town and Wenceslas Square meet.

TIMING Wenceslas Square and Old Town Square teem with activity around the clock almost year-round. If you're in search of a little peace and quiet, you can find the streets at their most subdued on early weekend mornings or when it's cold. The streets in this walking tour are reasonably close together and can be covered in a half-day. Remember to be in the Old Town Square just before the hour if you want to see the astronomical clock in action.

What to See

⑲ **Betlémská kaple** (Bethlehem Chapel). The original church was built at the end of the 14th century, and the Czech religious reformer Jan Hus was a regular preacher here from 1402 until his exile in 1412. Here he gave the mass in Czech—not in Latin as the church in Rome demanded. After the Thirty Years' War in the 17th century, the church fell into the hands of the Jesuits and was finally demolished in 1786. Excavations carried out after World War I uncovered the original portal and three windows, and the entire church was reconstructed during the 1950s. Although little remains of the first church, some rem-

> ## PRAGUE BY NUMBERS
>
> Prague neighborhoods are sometimes referred to by number, which corresponds to its postal district. There are 10 postal districts, but most of the popular tourist attractions are in Prague 1. Typically, visitors explore the following areas:
> **Prague 1:** Staré Město (Old Town), Josefov (the Jewish Quarter), Hradčany (the Castle Area), Malá Strana (the Lesser Quarter), Nové Město (New Town)
> **Prague 2:** Southern Nové Město (New Town), Vysehrad, western Vinohrady
> **Prague 3:** Eastern Vinohrady, Žižkov

nants of Hus's teachings can still be read on the inside walls. A word of warning: even though regular hours are posted, the church is not always open at those times. ⊠ *Betlémské nám. 5, Staré Město* 🔳 *50 Kč* ⊙ *Tues.–Sun. 10–6:30.*

⑤ Celetná ulice. Most of this street's façades indicate the buildings are from the 17th or 18th century, but appearances are deceiving: many of the houses in fact have parts that date back to the 12th century. Be sure to look above the street-level storefronts to see the fine examples of baroque detail.

⑯ Clam-Gallas palác (Clam-Gallas Palace). The work of Johann Bernhard Fischer von Erlach, the famed Viennese architectural virtuoso of the day, is showcased in this beige-and-brown palace. Construction began in 1713 and finally finished in 1729. Enter the building to glimpse at the battered but finely carved staircase, done by the master himself, and the Italian frescoes depicting Apollo. Clam-Gallas palác is now used for art exhibitions and concerts. If you don't see anyone selling tickets at a table on the street, go inside and up to the desk on the second floor. ⊠ *Husova 20, Staré Město* 🔳 *No phone* ⊕ *www.ahmp.cz/eng* ⊙ *Tues.–Sun. 10–6.*

⑰ Clementinum. The origins of this massive complex—now part of a university—dates back to the 12th and 13th centuries, but it's best known as the stronghold of the Jesuits, who occupied it for more than 200 years beginning in the early 1600s. Despite many buildings being closed to the public, the sites here are well worth a visit. The Jesuits built a resplendent library, displaying fabulous ceiling murals that portray the three levels of knowledge, with the "Dome of Wisdom" as a centerpiece. Next door, the Mirror Chapel is a dazzling symphony of reflective surfaces, with acoustics to match. Mozart played here, and the space still hosts occasional chamber music concerts. The Astronomical Tower in the middle of the complex was used by Johannes Kepler, and afterward functioned as the "Prague Meridian" where the time was set each day. At high noon, a timekeeper would appear on the balcony and wave a flag that could be seen from the castle, where a cannon was fired to mark the hour. ⊠ *Mariánské náměstí 4, Staré Město* 🔳 *224–813–892* 🔳 *90 Kč* ⊙ *Mar.–Dec., weekdays 2–7, weekends 10–7.*

⑥ Dům U černé Matky boží (House of the Black Madonna). In the second decade of the 20th century, young Czech architects boldly applied cubism's radical reworking of visual space to architecture and design. This museum, refurbished and now run by the National Gallery, showcases fine examples of every genre.

> **WORD OF MOUTH**
>
> "Gosh! How to do justice to Prague? What an amazingly beautiful city! It's called Golden Prague for a reason. In other cities we visited . . . I would find myself wasting "foot capital" and energy navigating not-so-interesting stretches between things I wanted to see. In Prague, however, at least on the castle side, there is no wasted time: virtually everything is beautiful and interesting, so I got a lot of bang for my foot-capital buck." —Mary_Fran

The building itself is cubist, designed by Josef Gočár. Inside there are three floors of paintings, sculptures, drawings, furniture, and other "applied arts" in the cubist style. And don't miss the gift shop, which, while pricey, is worth discovering for some of the oddest-looking home furnishings you've ever seen. ☒ *Celetná 34, Staré Město* ☎ *224–211–732* ⊕ *www.ngprague.cz* ▦ *100 Kč* ⊙ *Tues.–Sun. 10–6.*

⑭ Franz Kafka Exposition. Though only the portal of the original house remains, inside the building is a fascinating little exhibit (mostly photographs) on Kafka's life, with commentary in English. Kafka came into the world on July 3, 1883, in a house next to the Kostel svatého Mikuláše (Church of St. Nicholas). For years the writer was only grudgingly acknowledged by the Communist cultural bureaucrats, reflecting the traditionally ambiguous attitude of the Czech government toward his work. As a German and a Jew, moreover, Kafka could easily be dismissed as standing outside the mainstream of Czech literature. Following the 1989 revolution, however, Kafka's popularity soared, and his works are now widely available in Czech. ☒ *Náměstí Franze Kafky 3, Staré Město* ▦ *50 Kč* ⊙ *Tues.–Fri. 10–6, Sat. 10–5, Sun. 10–6.*

> **CAFÉ CULTURE**
>
> Coffee culture in the Czech Republic is evolving quickly. It used to be that the standard coffee drink was called "turecko" (literally "Turkish"), a spoonful of coffee grounds with hot water poured on top and usually served in a dreary plastic cup. But these days Czechs are more in step with modern times. The standard cup is an espresso, often called "<u>presso</u>," served with sugar and a little plastic cup of milk on the side. If you want something bigger, say "dvojité presso" (double espresso). Most places will also have cappuccino and sometimes drinks like lattes.

NEED A BREAK? A few doors south of the Kafka house, tucked under the portico, **Bar U Radnice** (☒ *U Radnice 2*) offers a comfortable nook serving coffee, tea, hot chocolate, and soft drinks along with a nice selection of cakes, baguettes, and salads.

⑩ Jan Hus monument. Few memorials in Prague have elicited as much controversy as this one, which was dedicated in July 1915, exactly 500 years after Hus was burned at the stake in Constance, Germany. Some maintain that the monument's Secessionist style (the inscription seems to come right from turn-of-the-20th-century Vienna) clashes with the Gothic and baroque style of the square. Others dispute the romantic depiction of Hus, who appears here as tall and bearded in flowing garb. The real Hus, historians maintain, was short and had a baby face. Still, no one can take issue with this fiery preacher's influence. His ability to transform doctrinal disputes, both literally and metaphorically, into the language of the common man made him into a religious and national symbol for the Czechs. ☒ *Staroměstské náměstí, Staré Město.*

⑪ Klášter svaté Anežky České (St. Agnes's Convent). Near the river between Pařížská and Revoluční streets, this peaceful complex has Prague's first buildings in the Gothic style, built between the 1230s and the 1280s. The convent now provides a fitting home for the National Gallery's marvelous collection of Czech Gothic art, including altarpieces, portraits, and statues. ⊠ *U Milosrdných 17, Staré Město* ☎ *224–810–628* ⊕ *www.ngprague.cz* ⊡ *100 Kč* ⊗ *Tues.–Sun. 10–6.*

★ ❽ **Kostel Panny Marie před Týnem** (Church of the Virgin Mary Before Týn). One of the best examples of Prague Gothic, this church's exterior is in part the work of Peter Parler, architect of the Charles Bridge and Chrám svatého Víta (St. Vitus's Cathedral). Construction of its twin black-spire towers was begun later, by King Jiří of Poděbrad in 1461, during the heyday of the Hussites. Jiří had a gilded chalice, the symbol of the Hussites, proudly displayed on the front gable between the two towers. Following the defeat of the Czech Protestants by the Catholic Hapsburgs, the chalice was removed and eventually replaced by a Madonna. As a final blow, the chalice was melted down and made into the Madonna's glimmering halo (you can still see it by walking into the center of the square and looking up between the spires). The entrance to the church is through the arcades on Old Town Square, under the house at No. 604.

> **SAVING FACE**
>
> In the Church of the Virgin Mary Before Týn find the grave marker (tucked away to the right of the main altar) of the great Danish astronomer Tycho Brahe. Tycho had a firm place in history: Johannes Kepler used Tycho's observations to formulate his laws of planetary motion. But it is legend that has endeared Tycho to the hearts of Prague residents. The robust Dane, who was fond of duels, supposedly lost part of his nose in one (take a closer look at the marker that features a relief of his face). He quickly had a wax nose fashioned for everyday use but preferred to parade around on holidays and festive occasions sporting a bright metal one.

Much of the interior, including the tall nave, was rebuilt in the baroque style in the 17th century. Some Gothic pieces remain, however: look to the left of the main altar for a beautifully preserved set of early Gothic carvings. The main altar itself was painted by Karel Škréta, a luminary of the Czech baroque. ⊠ *Staroměstské náměstí, between Celetná and Týnská, Staré Město* ⊗ *Weekdays 10–1, 3–5.*

❶❽ **Kostel svatého Jiljí** (Church of St. Giles). A powerful example of Gothic architecture, including buttresses and a characteristic portal, is displayed in this church's exterior. Considered an important outpost of Czech Protestantism in the 16th century, the church reflects baroque style inside, with a design by Johann Bernhard Fischer von Erlach and sweeping frescoes by Václav Reiner. The interior can be viewed during the day from the vestibule or at the evening concerts held several times a week. ⊠ *Husova 8, Staré Město* ⊗ *Weekdays 9–5.*

❷❶ **Kostel svatého Martina ve zdi** (Church of St. Martin-in-the-Wall). It was here in 1414 that Holy Communion was first given to the Bohemian laity in the form of both bread and wine, defying the Catholic custom of the time that dictated only bread would be offered to the masses, with wine reserved for priests and clergy. From then on, the chalice came to symbolize the Hussite movement. The church is open for evening concerts, held several times each week, but that's the only way to see the rather plain interior. ✉ *Martinská ulice, Staré Město.*

NEED A BREAK?

In the Platýz courtyard immediately east of the church (also accessible from Národní), **Káva Káva Káva** (✉ Národní třída 37) offers one of the best selections of coffee in town, along with a small assortment of pastries and desserts. You can pay extra to access the Internet on the computers downstairs, or use Wi-Fi for free if you spend 60 Kč or more.

🔞 **Kostel svatého Mikuláše** (Church of St. Nicholas). Designed in the 18th century by Prague's own master of late baroque, Kilian Ignaz Dientzenhofer, this church is probably less successful in capturing the style's lyric exuberance than its namesake across town, the Chrám svatého Mikuláše. Still, Dientzenhofer utilized the limited space to create a well-balanced structure. The interior is compact, with a beautiful, small chandelier and an enormous black organ that overwhelms the rear of the church. Afternoon and evening concerts for visitors are held almost continuously. ✉ *Staroměstské náměstí, Staré Město* ◷ *Apr.–Oct., Mon. noon–4, Tues.–Sat. 10–4, Sun. noon–3; Nov.–Mar., Tues., Fri., and Sun. 10–noon, Wed. 10–4.*

🔞 **Malé náměstí** (Small Square). Note the iron fountain dating from around 1560 in the center of the square. The colorfully painted house at No. 3, originally a hardware store, is not as old as it looks, but here and there you can find authentic Gothic portals and Renaissance *sgraffiti* that reflects the square's true age.

❶ **Na příkopě.** The name means "At the Moat" and harks back to the time when the street was indeed a moat separating the Old Town from the New Town. Today the pedestrian zone Na příkopě is prime shopping territory. Sleek modern buildings have been sandwiched between baroque palaces, with the latter cut up inside to accommodate casinos, boutiques, and fast-food restaurants. The new structures are fairly identical inside, but at the end of the block, Slovanský dům (No. 22) is worth a look. This late-18th-century structure has been tastefully refurbished and now houses fashionable boutiques, stylish restaurants, and one of the city's better multiplex cinemas.

❹ **Obecní dům** (Municipal House). The city's art nouveau showpiece still fills the role it had when it was completed in 1911 as a center for

FodorśChoice
★

> **PRAGUE PLAYS WITH PLASTER**
>
> *Sgraffiti*, plural for *sgraffito*, is a process where two contrasting shades of plaster are used on the façade of a building. Often the *sgraffiti* serves to highlight the original architecture, other times it can produce an optical illusion, painting brickwork and balconies from thin air. Walls can also be covered with lively classical pictures, which make houses resemble enormous Grecian vases. One of the best examples of *sgraffiti* is Kafka's former residence, U Minuty, just next to the clock tower on Old Town Square.

concerts, rotating art exhibits, and café society. The mature art nouveau style recalls the lengths the Czech middle class went to at the turn of the 20th century to imitate Paris. Much of the interior bears the work of Alfons Mucha, Max Švabinský, and other leading Czech artists. Mucha decorated the Hall of the Lord Mayor upstairs with impressive, magical frescoes depicting Czech history; unfortunately it's closed to the public. The beautiful **Smetanova síň** (Smetana Hall), which hosts concerts by the Prague Symphony Orchestra as well as international players, is on the second floor. The ground-floor restaurants are overcrowded with foreigners but still lovely, with glimmering chandeliers and exquisite woodwork. There's also a beer hall in the cellar with decent food and superbly executed ceramic murals on the walls. ⊠ *Nám. Republiky 5, Staré Město* ☎ *222–002–100* ⊕ *www.obecnidum.cz* ☉ *Information center and box office daily 10–6.*

NEED A BREAK?

If you prefer subtle elegance, head around the corner from Obecní dům to the café at the **Hotel Paříž** (⊠ U Obecního domu 1, Staré Město ☎ 224–222–151), a Jugendstil jewel tucked away on a relatively quiet street. Excellent cakes and coffee.

❾ **Palác Kinských** (Kinský Palace). With its exaggerated pink overlay and numerous statues, this exuberant building, built in 1765 from Kilian Ignaz Dientzenhofer's design, is considered one of Prague's finest rococo, late-baroque structures. The façade looks extravagant when contrasted with the somber baroque elements of other nearby buildings. (The interior, however, was "modernized" under Communism.) The palace once contained a German school—where Franz Kafka studied for nine misery-laden years—and presently holds the National Gallery's graphics collection. Communist leader Klement Gottwald, flanked by comrade Vladimír Clementis, first addressed the crowds after seizing power in February 1948 from this building—an event recounted in the first chapter of Milan Kundera's novel *The Book of Laughter and Forgetting.* ⊠ *Staroměstské náměstí 12, Staré Město* ☎ *224–810–758* ⊕ *www. ngprague.cz* ▧ *100 Kč* ☉ *Tues.–Sun. 10–6.*

❸ **Prašná brána** (Powder Tower). Once used as storage space for gunpowder, this imposing dark tower—covered in a web of carvings—offers a striking view of the Old Town and Prague Castle from the top. Construction of the tower, which replaced one of the city's 13 original gates, was begun by King Vladislav II of Jagiello in 1475. At the time, the kings of Bohemia maintained their royal residence next door, on the site of the current Obecní dům, and the tower was intended to be the grandest gate of all. But Vladislav was Polish and heartily disliked by the rebellious Czech citizens of Prague. Nine years after he assumed power, fearing for his life, he moved the royal court across the river to Prague Castle. Work on the tower was abandoned, and the half-finished structure remained a depository for gunpowder until the end of the 17th century. The oldest part of the tower is the base. The golden spires were not added until the end of the 19th century. ⊠ *Nám. Republiky, Staré Město* ▧ *40 Kč* ☉ *Apr.–Oct., daily 10–6.*

**OFF THE
BEATEN
PATH**

MUZEUM HLAVNÍHO MěSTA PRAHY (Museum of the City of Prague) – The high point of this museum is a paper model of Prague that shows what the city looked like before the Jewish ghetto was destroyed in a massive fire in 1689. Display boards—not all are in English—trace the history of the city from its origins through the 17th century. Though technically situated in Nové Město, the trek over to this out-of-the-way museum is easy from Old Town, since it's near the Florenc metro station. ⊠ *Na Poříčí 52, Nové Město* ☎ *224–816–772* ⊕ *www.muzeumprahy.cz* ⊠ *40 Kč* ☉ *Tues.–Sun. 9–6* Ⓜ *Lines B & C: Florenc.*

★ ⑫ **Staroměstská radnice** (Old Town Hall). This is one of Prague's magnets: hundreds of people gravitate here throughout the day to see the hour struck by the mechanical figures of the **astronomical clock.** Before the hour, look to the upper part of the clock, where a skeleton begins by tolling a death knell and turning an hourglass upside down. The Twelve Apostles promenade by, and then a cockerel flaps its wings and screeches as the hour finally strikes. To the right of the skeleton, the dreaded Turk nods his head, almost hinting at another invasion like those of the 16th and 17th centuries. This theatrical spectacle doesn't reveal the way this 15th-century marvel indicates the time—by the season, the zodiac sign, and the positions of the sun and moon. The calendar under the clock dates from the mid-19th century.

The Old Town Hall served as the center of administration for Old Town beginning in 1338, when King John of Luxembourg first granted the city council the right to a permanent location. The impressive 200-foot **Town Hall Tower,** where the clock is mounted, was first built in the 14th century. For a rare view of the Old Town and its maze of crooked streets and alleyways, climb the ramp or ride the elevator to the top of the tower.

Walking around the hall to the left, you can see it's actually a series of houses jutting into the square; they were purchased over the years and successively added to the complex. On the other side, jagged stonework reveals where a large, neo-Gothic wing once adjoined the tower until it was destroyed by fleeing Nazi troops in May 1945.

Guided tours of the Old Town Hall depart from the main desk inside (most guides speak English, and English texts are on hand). Previously unseen parts of the tower were opened to the public in 2002, and you can now see the inside of the famous clock. ⊠ *Staroměstské náměstí, Staré Město* ☉ *May–Sept., Tues.–Sun. 9–6, Mon. 11–6; Oct.–Apr., Tues.–Sun. 9–5, Mon. 11–5* ⊠ *Tower 50 Kč.*

**NEED A
BREAK?**

One of the best rooftop views in the city is at Hotel U Prince (⊠ Staromestká nám. 29), diagonally opposite the astronomical clock. Go in the arched entryway to the right and walk all the way to the back, where a golden angel with a trumpet stands watch over a glass-door elevator. Take the elevator to the rooftop bar, which has covered seating and portable heaters running in cold weather. Be forewarned though, it's a splurge.

❼ Staroměstské náměstí (Old Town Square). There are places that, on first
FodorsChoice glimpse, stop you dead in your tracks with sheer wonder. The unexpect-
★ edly large size of the square, which suddenly opens up from the little
alleyways, and colorful baroque houses contrasting with the sweeping
old-Gothic tower of the Tyne church in the background gives it a majestic presence. Considered the heart of the Old Town, the square grew
to its present proportions when the city's original marketplace was
moved away from the river in the 12th century. Its shape and appearance have changed little since that time. During the day the square is
festive, as musicians vie for the favor of onlookers and artists display
renditions of Prague street scenes. In summer the square's south end is
dominated by sprawling outdoor restaurants. During the Easter and
Christmas seasons, it fills with wooden booths of vendors selling everything from simple wooden toys to fine glassware. At night, the brightly
lighted towers of the Týn church rise gloriously over the glowing baroque
façades.

During the 15th century the square was the focal point of conflict between Czech Hussites and German Catholics. In 1422 the radical Hussite preacher Jan Želivský was executed here for his part in storming
the New Town's town hall three years earlier. In the 1419 uprising, three
Catholic consuls and seven German citizens were thrown out the window—the first of Prague's many famous defenestrations. Within a few
years, the Hussites had taken over the town, expelled the Germans, and
set up their own administration.

Twenty-seven white crosses embedded in the square's paving stones, at
the Old Town Hall's base, mark the spot where 27 Bohemian noblemen were killed by the Austrian Hapsburgs in 1621 during the dark days
following the defeat of the Czechs at the Battle of White Mountain. The
grotesque spectacle, designed to quash any further national or religious
opposition, took about five hours to complete, as the men were put to
the sword or hanged one by one.

One of the most interesting houses on the Old Town Square juts out
into the small extension leading into Malé náměstí. Trimmed with elegant cream-color 16th-century Renaissance *sgraffiti* of biblical and classical motifs, the house, called **U Minuty** (⊠ 3 Staroměstské náměstí, Staré
Město), was young Franz Kafka's home in the 1890s.

❷ Stavovské divadlo (Estates Theater). Built in the 1780s in the classical
style, this opulent, green palais was for many years a beacon of Czech-
language culture in a city long dominated by German. It's best known
for hosting the world premiere of Mozart's opera *Don Giovanni* in October 1787, with the composer himself conducting. Prague audiences
were quick to acknowledge Mozart's genius: the opera was an instant
hit here, though it flopped nearly everywhere else in Europe. Mozart
wrote some of the opera's second act in Prague at the Villa Bertramka,
where he was a frequent guest. You must attend a performance to see
inside. ⊠ *Ovocný tř. 1, Staré Město* ☎ *224–902–322 box office* ⊕ *www.
narodni-divadlo.cz.*

JOSEFOV (JEWISH QUARTER)

Prague had an active and vital Jewish community for centuries, and much of that activity was concentrated in Josefov, the former Jewish ghetto, just a short walk north of Old Town Square.

The area of the ghetto first became a Jewish settlement around the 12th century, but it didn't actually take on the physical aspects of a ghetto—walled off from the rest of the city—until much later. The history of Prague's Jews follows a rough and insecure path. There were horrible pogroms in the late Middle Ages, followed by a period of relative prosperity under Rudolf II in the late 16th century, though the freedoms of Jews were still tightly restricted. It was Austrian Emperor Josef II—the ghetto's namesake—who did the most to improve the conditions of the city's Jews. His Edict of Tolerance in 1781 removed dress codes for Jews and opened the gates to the rest of the city.

The prosperity of the 19th century lifted the Jews out of poverty and many of them chose to leave the ghetto. By the end of the century, the number of poor gentiles, drunks, and prostitutes in the ghetto was growing, while the number of actual Jews was declining. At this time the city officials decided to clear the slum and raze the buildings. In their place, they built many of the gorgeous turn-of-the-20th century and art nouveau town houses you see today. Only a handful of the synagogues, the town hall, and the cemetery were preserved.

World War II and the Nazi occupation brought profound tragedy to the city's Jews. A staggering percentage were deported—many to Terezín, north of Prague, and then later to Polish death camps. Of the 40,000 Jews living in Prague before World War II, only about 1,200 returned after the war, and merely a few live in the ghetto today.

The Nazi occupation contains a historic irony. Many of the treasures stored away in Prague's Jewish Museum were brought here from across Central Europe on Hitler's orders. His idea was to form a museum dedicated to the extinct Jewish civilization.

Today the ghetto is a must-see. The Old Jewish Cemetery alone, with its incredibly forlorn overlay of headstone on headstone going back centuries, merits the steep admission price the Jewish museum charges to see its treasures. But don't feel compelled to linger long on the ghetto's streets after visiting. Much of it is tourist-trap territory, filled with overpriced T-shirt, trinket, and toy shops—the same cheap souvenirs found everywhere in Prague at even steeper prices.

A ticket to the **Židovské muzeum v Praze** (Prague Jewish Museum) includes admission to the Old Jewish Cemetery and collections installed in four surviving synagogues and the Ceremony Hall. The Staronová synagóga, or Old-New Synagogue, a functioning house of worship, does not technically belong to the museum and requires a separate admissions ticket. All museum sites are closed on Saturday and Jewish holidays.

**A GOOD
WALK**

To reach the Jewish Quarter, leave Old Town Square walking up the handsome Pařížská ulice, a centerpiece of the 19th-century urban renewal effort that cleared the ghetto, and head north toward the river. The sudden appearance of a cluster of ancient buildings marks the beginning of the ghetto. Take a right on Široká and stroll two blocks down to the recently restored **Španělská synagóga** ㉑ ▶. The statue of a man perched on a headless figure to the north side of the traffic circle is Franz Kafka, sculptor Jaroslav Róna's monument to the noted Jewish writer. Head back the other way, past Pařížská, turn right on Maiselova, and you come to the **Židovská radnice** ㉒, which is now the Jewish Community Center. Adjoining it on Červená is the 16th-century High Synagogue. Across

the street, at Červená 2, you see the **Staronová synagóga** ㉓, the oldest surviving synagogue in Prague.

Go west on the little street U starého hřbitova. The main museum ticket office is at the **Klausová synagóga** ㉔ at No. 3A. Separated from the synagogue by the Old Jewish Cemetery's exit gate is the former building of the Jewish Burial Society, Obřadní síň, which exhibits traditional Jewish funeral objects.

Return to Maiselova and follow it to Široká. Turn right to find the **Pinkasova synagóga** ㉕, a handsome Gothic structure. Here also is the entrance to the Jewish ghetto's most astonishing sight, **Starý židovský hřbitov** ㉖, the cemetery.

For a small detour, head down Široká Street to the **Rudolfinum** ㉗ concert hall and gallery; across the street is the Uměleckoprůmyslové muzeum (Museum of Decorative Arts). Both are notable neo-Renaissance buildings.

Return to Maiselova once more and turn right in the direction of the Old Town. Look in at the displays of Czech Jewish history in the **Maiselova synagóga** ㉘.

TIMING The Jewish Quarter is one of the most heavily visited areas in Prague, especially in the height of summer, when its tiny streets are jammed to bursting. The best time for a quieter visit is early morning when the museums and cemetery first open. The area itself is very compact, and a fairly thorough tour should only take half a day, but don't go on the Sabbath (Saturday), when all the museums are closed.

What to See

㉔ Klausová synagóga (Klausen Synagogue). This baroque former synagogue displays objects from Czech Jewish traditions, with an emphasis on celebrations and daily life. In the neo-Romanesque **Obřadní síň** (Ceremony Hall), which adjoins the Klausen Synagogue, the focus is on rather grim subjects: Jewish funeral paraphernalia, old gravestones, and medical instruments. Special attention is paid to the activities of the Jewish Burial Society through many fine objects and paintings. The building was built at the end of the 17th century in place of three small buildings (a synagogue, a school, and a ritual bath) that were destroyed in a fire that devastated the ghetto in 1689. ☒ *U starého hřbitova 3A, Josefov* ☎ *221–711–511* ⊕ *www.jewishmuseum.cz* ☒ *Combined ticket to museums and Old-New Synagogue 500 Kč; museums only, 300 Kč* ☉ *Apr.–Oct., Sun.–Fri. 9–6; Nov.–Mar., Sun.–Fri. 9–4:30.*

㉘ Maiselova synagóga (Maisel Synagogue). The history of Czech Jews from the 10th to the 18th century is illustrated here with the aid of some of the Prague Jewish Museum's most precious objects, including silver Torah shields and pointers, spice boxes, and candelabra; historic tombstones; and fine ceremonial textiles—some donated by Mordechai Maisel to the synagogue he founded. The richest items come from the late 16th and early 17th centuries, a prosperous era for Prague's Jews. ☒ *Maiselova 10, Josefov* ☎ *221–711–511* ⊕ *www.jewishmuseum.cz* ☒ *Combined ticket to museums and Old-New Synagogue 500 Kč; museums only, 300 Kč* ☉ *Apr.–Oct., Sun.–Fri. 9–6; Nov.–Mar., Sun.–Fri. 9–4:30.*

㉕ Pinkasova synagóga (Pinkas Synagogue). Two particularly moving testimonies to the appalling crimes perpetrated against the Jews during World War II are held inside this synagogue. One tribute astounds by sheer numbers: the walls are covered with nearly 80,000 names of Bohemian and Moravian Jews murdered by the Nazis. Among them are the names of the paternal grandparents of former U.S. Secretary of State Madeleine Albright. An exhibition of drawings made by children at the Nazi concentration camp Terezín is the second chilling testimony. The Nazis used the camp for propaganda purposes to demonstrate their "humanity" toward the Jews, and prisoners were given relative freedom to lead "normal" lives. However, transports to death camps in Poland began in earnest in 1944, and many thousands of Terezín prisoners, including most of these children, eventually perished. The entrance to the old Jewish cemetery is through this synagogue. ☒ *Široká 3, Josefov* ☎ *221–711–511* ⊕ *www.jewishmuseum.cz* ☒ *Combined ticket to museums and Old-New Synagogue 500 Kč; museums only, 300 Kč* ☉ *Apr.–Oct., Sun.–Fri. 9–6; Nov.–Mar., Sun.–Fri. 9–4:30.*

㉗ Rudolfinum. Thanks to a thorough makeover and exterior sandblasting, this neo-Renaissance monument, designed by Josef Zítek and Josef Schulz, presents some of the cleanest, brightest stonework in the city. Completed in 1884 and named for then–Hapsburg Crown Prince Rudolf, the rather low-slung sandstone building was meant to be a combination concert hall and exhibition gallery. After 1918 it was converted into the parliament of the newly independent Czechoslovakia until German invaders reinstated the concert hall in 1939. Now the Czech Philharmonic has its home base here. The 1,200-seat **Dvořákova síň** (Dvořák Hall) has superb acoustics (the box office faces 17 Listopadu street). To see the hall, you must attend a concert.

Behind Dvořák Hall sits a set of large exhibition rooms, the **Galerie Rudolfinum** (⊕ www.galerierudolfinum.cz) an innovative, state-supported gallery with rotating shows of contemporary art. Four or five large shows are mounted here annually, showcasing excellent Czech work and occasional international artists. ⊠ *Nám. Jana Palacha, Josefov* ☎ *227–059–111 box office, 227–059–309 gallery* ⊕ *www. czechphilharmonic.cz* ⊠ *Gallery 100 Kč* ⊙ *Gallery Tues.–Sun. 10–6.*

★ ㉑ **Španělská synagóga** (Spanish Synagogue). This domed Moorish-style synagogue was built in 1868 on the site of the city's oldest synagogue, Altschul. Here the historical exposition that begins in the Maisel Synagogue continues until the post–World War II period. The displays are not very compelling, but the building's painstakingly restored interior definitely is. ⊠ *Vězeňská 1, Josefov* ☎ *221–711–511* ⊕ *www. jewishmuseum.cz* ⊠ *Combined ticket to museums and Old-New Synagogue 500 Kč; museums only, 300 Kč* ⊙ *Apr.–Oct., Sun.–Fri. 9–6; Nov.–Mar., Sun.–Fri. 9–4:30.*

NEED A BREAK? For first-rate Czech cuisine and beer, it's hard to beat **Kolkovna** (⊠ V Kolkovné 8), opposite the Spanish synagogue. The front room, with a lively bar and wide doors that open onto the street, feels particularly nice in summer.

★ ㉓ **Staronová synagóga** (Old-New Synagogue, or Altneuschul). Dating from the mid-13th century, this is one of the most important works of early Gothic in Prague. Its name refers to the legend that the synagogue was built on the site of an ancient Jewish temple and the temple's stones were used to build the present structure. The entrance represents the oldest part of the synagogue, with its vault supported by two pillars. Amazingly, the synagogue has survived fires, the razing of the ghetto, and the Nazi occupation intact; it's still in active use. As the oldest functioning synagogue in Europe, it's a living storehouse of Bohemian Jewish life. Note that men are required to cover their heads inside and during services men and women sit apart. ⊠ *Červená 2, Josefov* ☎ *221–711–511* ⊕ *www.jewishmuseum.cz* ⊠ *Combined ticket to Old-New Synagogue and museums 500 Kč; Old-New Synagogue only, 200 Kč* ⊙ *Apr.–Oct., Sun.–Fri. 9–6; Nov.–Mar., Sun.–Fri. 9–4:30.*

㉖ **Starý židovský hřbitov** (Old Jewish Cemetery). An unforgettable sight, and one of the most moving in the city, this cemetery is where all Jews living in Prague from the 15th century to 1787 were laid to rest. The lack of any free space in the tiny ghetto forced graves to be piled on top of one another. Tilted at crazy angles, the 12,000 visible tombstones are but a fraction of countless thousands more buried below. Walk the path amid the gravestones; the relief symbols you see represent the names and professions of the deceased. The oldest marked grave belongs to the poet Avigdor Kara, who died in 1439; the grave is not accessible from the pathway, but the original tombstone can be seen in the Maisel Synagogue.

Fodor'sChoice ★

The best-known marker belongs to Jehuda ben Bezalel, the famed Rabbi Loew (died 1609), a chief rabbi of Prague and a profound scholar, credited with creating the mythical Golem. Even today, small scraps of paper bearing wishes are stuffed into the cracks of the rabbi's tomb with the hope he will grant them. Loew's grave lies near the exit. ⊠ *Široká 3, enter through Pinkasova synagóga, Josefov* ☎ *221–711–511* ⊕ *www.jewishmuseum.cz* ✉ *Combined ticket to museums and Old-New Synagogue 500 Kč; museums only, 300 Kč* ☉ *Apr.–Oct., Sun.–Fri. 9–6; Nov.–Mar., Sun.–Fri. 9–4:30.*

㉒ Židovská radnice (Jewish Town Hall). The hall was the creation of Mordechai Maisel, an influential Jewish leader at the end of the 16th century. Restored in the 18th century, it was given a clock and bell tower at that time. A second clock, with Hebrew numbers, keeps time counterclockwise. Now a Jewish Community Center, the building also houses Shalom, a kosher restaurant. ⊠ *Maiselova 18, Josefov* ☎ *222–319–002.*

MALÁ STRANA (LESSER QUARTER)

Established in 1257, this exquisite neighborhood (also known as Little Town) housed the merchants and craftsmen who served the royal court. Today the area holds many embassies, Czech government offices, historical attractions, and occasional galleries mixed in with the usual glut of pubs, restaurants, and souvenir shops. Though not nearly as confusing as the labyrinth of Old Town, the streets in the Lesser Quarter rise from river level nearly 400 vertical meters to the castle, so be prepared for a climb. Pausing along the way will give you a chance to catch your breath and provide views of the colorful jumble of terra-cotta-tile rooftops and, occasionally, the spires of city center beyond.

A GOOD WALK

Begin on the Old Town side of **Karlův most** ㉙ ► (Charles Bridge), which you can reach by foot in about 10 minutes from the Old Town Square. Rising above it is the majestic Staroměstská mostecká věž, one of the finest medieval towers in Europe. The sides are covered with sculptures of emperors, saints, and above the archway on the eastern side of the tower, a row of carved emblems depicting the territories under the rule of King Charles IV. The climb up 138 steps to the viewing gallery is worth the effort for the view you get of the Old Town, the Lesser Quarter, and Prague Castle.

As you walk across the Karlův most toward the Lesser Quarter, it's worth pausing to take a closer look at some of the statues lining the side of the bridge. As you approach the western end you'll see Kampa Island below on the left, separated from the mainland by an arm of the Vltava known as Čertovka (Devil's Stream).

By now you are almost at the end of the bridge. In front of you is the striking conjunction of the two Malá Strana bridge towers, the lower one Gothic, the taller one Romanesque. Together they frame the baroque flamboyance of Chrám svatého Mikuláše in the distance. A dramatic sight anytime, this is particularly impressive at night. And at nighttime the crowds dwindle and the river shimmers with the reflections of city lights making it an even more favorable time to cross.

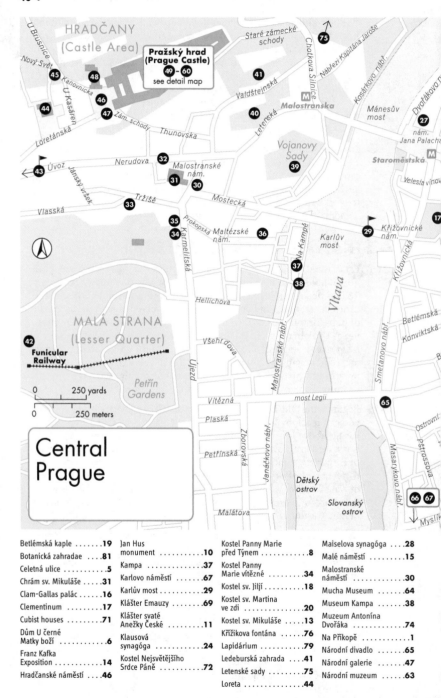

Central Prague

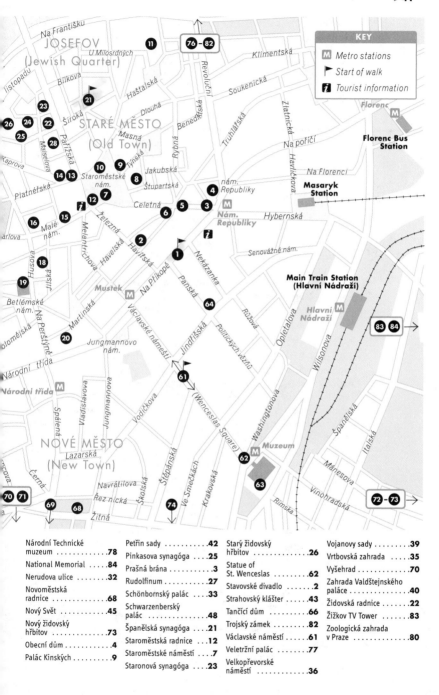

Walk under the gateway of the towers into the little uphill street called Mostecká. You have now entered the Lesser Quarter. There are immediately any number of side streets to explore, each with unexpected discoveries. Making a hairpin turn to the right as soon you get off the bridge will drop you into a charming, less-traveled area where you can follow the Čertovka and, depending on the water level, see big wooden water wheels in action. Or continue up Mostecká to the rectangular **Malostranské náměstí** ㉚, the district's transportation hub. Packed with modern storefronts and restaurants on the street level, the buildings surrounding the square have façades dating back to the Renaissance on the upper levels. Up and slightly behind the square stands the powerfully baroque church **Chrám svatého Mikuláše** ㉛.

Nerudova ulice ㉜ runs up from the square toward Prague Castle. Lined with a mix of shops, restaurants, churches, and a few embassies, it will take you to the huge twin set of staircases that lead up to the castle, or beyond, to Strahovský klášter. A tiny passageway at No. 13, on the left-hand side as you go up, drops you down to Tržiště ulice and the **Schönbornský palác** ㉝, one of Franz Kafka's residences, now the embassy of the United States. Tržiště winds down to the quarter's busy main street, Karmelitská, where the famous Infant Jesus of Prague resides in the **Kostel Panny Marie vítězné** ㉞. A few doors away, closer to Tržiště, lies a meditative garden, the **Vrtbovská zahrada** ㉟. Tiny Prokopská ulice leads off Karmelitská, past the former Church of St. Procopius and into Maltézské náměstí (Maltese Square), a characteristically noble compound.

Take the left just before the square and then an immediate right and you can find **Velkopřevorské náměstí** ㊱ (Grand Priory Square), which is lined with fine baroque buildings. Or continue through Maltese Square, then turn left (before Nebovidská) onto the small side street that becomes a footbridge across the creeklike Čertovka to the island of **Kampa** ㊲, with its broad lawns, river views, and Czech modern-art showcase, **Museum Kampa** ㊳. Head north, keeping the river on your right, and you pass through a small square of shops and restaurants before slipping underneath Karlův most. Continue following the street U lužického semináře and you come to a quiet walled garden, **Vojanovy sady** ㊴. To the northwest, hiding off busy Letenská ulice near the Malostranská metro station, is **Zahrada Valdštejnského paláce** ㊵, a more formal garden with an unbeatable view of Prague Castle looming above. A bit farther north is another garden, the generously shady **Ledeburská zahrada** ㊶.

Another walking option is to take the south entrance out of Kampa park and follow Říční Street back to Karmelitská, putting you at the foot of Petřin Hill, at the top of which is **Petřín sady** ㊷. Cross the street and walk up the short flight of steps, and on your left you see Olbram Zoubek's powerful memorial to the victims of Communism. The broad, steep steps are deliberately difficult to climb as you make your way up to the tortured figure whose body and soul disintegrate in a series of statues receding up the incline. To your right you can find the entrance to the funicular, which you can ride to the top of the hill and the park's attractions.

TIMING The heat builds up during the day in this area—as do the crowds—so it's best visited before noon, or in late afternoon and early evening. The basic walk described here could take anywhere from two hours to the better part of a day, depending on how much dining, shopping, and exploring is done along the way. There are plenty of cafés on literally every block to stop, sip coffee or tea, and people-watch, and a wealth of gardens and parks ideal for resting in cool shade. The trip up Petřín can add two hours to a half-day, depending how much lingering you do at the top and on the hillside. Going to Bertramka will add at least a half day.

What To See

③ Chrám svatého Mikuláše (Church of St. Nicholas). With its dynamic Fodor'sChoice curves, this church is one of the purest and most ambitious examples ★ of high baroque. The celebrated architect Christoph Dientzenhofer began the Jesuit church in 1704 on the site of one of the more active Hussite churches of 15th-century Prague. Work on the building was taken over by his son Kilian Ignaz Dientzenhofer, who built the dome and presbytery. Anselmo Lurago completed the whole thing in 1755 by adding the bell tower. The juxtaposition of the broad, full-bodied dome with the slender bell tower is one of the many striking architectural contrasts that mark the Prague skyline. Inside, the vast pink-and-green space is impossible to take in with a single glance. Every corner bristles with life, guiding the eye first to the dramatic statues, then to the hectic frescoes, and on to the shining faux-marble pillars. Many of the statues are the work of Ignaz Platzer, and in fact they constitute his last blaze of success. Platzer's workshop was forced to declare bankruptcy when the centralizing and secularizing reforms of Joseph II toward the end of the 18th century brought an end to the flamboyant baroque era. The tower, with an entrance on the side of the church, is open in summer. The church also hosts chamber music concerts in summer, which complements this eye-popping setting but does not reflect the true caliber of classical music in Prague. For that, check the schedule posted across the street at **Líchtenšký palác,** where the faculty of HAMU, the city's premier music academy, often give performances.
⊠ *Malostranské náměstí, Malá Strana* 🎫*50 Kč* ⊘ *Daily 9–4:30 for sightseeing, 8:30–9:00 AM for prayer; no admission charge for prayer.*

🕑 **③** **Kampa.** Prague's largest island is cut off from the "mainland" by the narrow Čertovka streamlet. The name Čertovka, or Devil's Stream, reputedly refers to a cranky old lady who once lived on Maltese Square (given the river's present dirty state, the name remains appropriate). During the 2002 floods, the well-kept lawns of the **Kampa Gardens,** which occupy much of

DARK WATERS

In August 2002 the Vltava River swelled to flood Prague. The Charles Bridge closed, so did the metro, the zoo, the Four Seasons, the InterContinental, and the Hilton. By the time the river level dropped, the city was hit with nearly $3 billion in damage. These days, all of these places have been restored and any visitor would be hard-pressed to find evidence of the devastation.

the island, were covered as was much of the lower portion of Malá Strana. The reconstruction is nearly complete, but evidence of flood damage occasionally marks the landscape.

NEED A BREAK?

A brief walk across the footbridge on the west side of Kampa Park will bring you to **Restaurace Nostitz** (⌗ Nosticova 2a), a cozy retreat for coffee or lunch indoors. In warm weather a cold drink on the shaded, spacious patio restores many tired walkers.

▶ **㉙** **Karlův most** (Charles Bridge). The view from the foot of the bridge on FodorsChoice the Old Town side is nothing short of breathtaking, encompassing the ★ towers and domes of the Lesser Quarter and the soaring spires of St. Vitus's Cathedral. This heavenly vision changes subtly in perspective as you walk across the bridge, attended by a host of baroque saints that decorate the bridge's peaceful Gothic stones. At night its drama is spellbinding: St. Vitus's Cathedral lighted in a ghostly green, the castle in monumental yellow, and the Church of St. Nicholas in a voluptuous pink, all viewed through the menacing silhouettes of the bowed statues and the Gothic towers. Night provides the best time to visit the bridge, which is choked with visitors, vendors, and beggars by day. The later the hour, the thinner the crowds—though the bridge is never truly empty, especially in summer. Tourists with flash cameras are there all hours of the night, and as dawn is breaking, revelers from the dance clubs at the east end of the bridge weave their way homeward, singing loudly and talking about where to go for breakfast.

When the Přemyslid princes set up residence in Prague during the 10th century, there was a ford across the Vltava at this point—a vital link along one of Europe's major trading routes. After several wooden bridges and the first stone bridge had washed away in floods, Charles IV appointed the 27-year-old German Peter Parler, the architect of St. Vitus's Cathedral, to build a new structure in 1357. It became one of the wonders of the world in the Middle Ages.

After 1620, following the defeat of Czech Protestants by Catholic Hapsburgs at the Battle of White Mountain, the bridge became a symbol of the Counter-Reformation's vigorous re-Catholicization efforts. The many baroque statues that began to appear in the late 17th century, commissioned by Catholics, eventually came to symbolize the totality of the Austrian (hence Catholic) triumph. The Czech writer Milan Kundera sees the statues from this perspective: "The thousands of saints looking out from all sides, threatening you, following you, hypnotizing you, are the raging hordes of occupiers who invaded Bohemia 350 years ago to tear the people's faith and language from their hearts."

The religious conflict is less obvious nowadays, leaving behind an artistic tension between baroque and Gothic that gives the bridge its allure. Take a closer look at some of the statues while walking toward the Lesser Quarter. The third on the right, a bronze crucifix from the mid-17th century, is the oldest of all. It's mounted on the location of a wooden cross destroyed in a battle with the Swedes (the golden Hebrew inscription was reputedly financed by a Jew accused of defiling the cross). The fifth on the left, which shows St. Frances Xavier carrying four pagan princes (an Indian, Moor, Chinese, and Tartar) ready for conversion, represents an outstanding piece of baroque sculpture. Eighth on the right is the statue of St. John of Nepomuk, who according to legend was wrapped in chains and thrown to his death from this bridge. Touching the statue is supposed to bring good luck or, according to some versions of the story, a return visit to Prague. On the left-hand side, sticking out from the bridge between the 9th and 10th statues (the latter has a wonderfully expressive vanquished Satan), stands a Roland (Bruncvík) statue. This knightly figure, bearing the coat of arms of the Old Town, was once a reminder that this part of the bridge belonged to the Old Town before Prague became a unified city in 1784.

For many art historians, the most valuable statue is the 12th on the left, near the Lesser Quarter end. Mathias Braun's statue of St. Luitgarde depicts the blind saint kissing Christ's wounds. The most compelling grouping, however, is the second from the end on the left, a work of Ferdinand Maxmilian Brokoff (son of Johann) from 1714. Here the saints are incidental; the main attraction is the Turk, his face expressing extreme boredom at guarding the Christians imprisoned in the cage at his side. When the statue was erected, just 31 years after the second Turkish siege of Vienna, it scandalized the Prague public, who smeared it with mud. All but a couple of the bridge's surviving baroque statues, including St. Luitgarde and the Turk, have been replaced by modern copies. Several can be viewed in the Lapidarium museum at the Výstaviště exhibition grounds in Prague 7; a few more occupy a man-made cavern at Vyšehrad.

Staroměstská mostecká věž (Old Town Bridge Tower), at the bridge entrance on the Old Town side, is where Peter Parler, the architect of the Charles Bridge, began his bridge building. The carved façades he designed for the sides of the tower were destroyed by Swedish soldiers in 1648, at the end of the Thirty Years' War. The sculptures facing the Old Town, however, are still intact (although some are recent copies); they depict an old and gout-ridden Charles IV with his son, who later became Wenceslas IV. Above them are two of Bohemia's patron saints, Adalbert of Prague and Sigismund. The top of the tower offers a spectacular view of the city for 50 Kč; it's open daily from 10 to 5, and until 7 in summer.

❸❹ **Kostel Panny Marie vítězné** (Church of Our Lady Victorious). This aging but well-appointed church on the

> **WORD OF MOUTH**
>
> "Please, please, please make the effort to learn even a few words in Czech. Knowing even 'please,' 'thank you,' 'yes,' 'no,' 'excuse me,' and 'I'm sorry,' will make your trip so much more meaningful. I struggled mightily but managed to learn the phrase 'Dinner was wonderful, thank you very much.' Good grief, from the way their faces lit up you'd think I had told them they had just won the lottery. A little consideration can go so far. Czech is not easy to learn but you will be richly rewarded for your efforts."
>
> –turnip

Lesser Quarter's main street is the unlikely home of Prague's most famous religious artifact, the *Pražské Jezulátko* (Infant Jesus of Prague). Originally brought to Prague from Spain in the 16th century, the wax doll holds a reputation for bestowing miracles on many who have prayed for its help. A measure of its widespread attraction is reflected in the prayer books on the kneelers in front of the statue, which have prayers of intercession in 20 different languages. The "Bambino," as he's known locally, has an enormous and incredibly ornate wardrobe, some of which is on display in a museum upstairs. Nuns from a nearby convent change the outfit on the statue regularly. Don't miss the souvenir shop (accessible via a doorway to the right of the main altar), where the Bambino's custodians flex their marketing skills. Alas, the Infant's miraculous powers do not ward off petty theft: as a sign in the vestibule warns, Be Aware of Pickpockets While Praying! ⊠ *Karmelitská 9A, Malá Strana* ✆ *Free* ☉ *Mon.–Sat. 9:30–5:30, Sun. 1–6.*

🔳 **Ledeburská zahrada** (Ledeburg Garden). Rows of steeply banked baroque gardens rise behind the palaces of Valdštejnská ulice. It's a climb if you enter from the street side, but the many shady arbors and niches are worth the exertion. The garden, with its frescoes and statuary, was restored with support from a fund headed by Czech president Václav Havel and Britain's Prince Charles. Renovation seems to be never-ending at the lower entrance, but don't be deterred by the barriers and construction equipment—press on, through the courtyard and up the stairs. You can also enter directly from the upper, south gardens of Prague Castle in summer. ⊠ *Valdštejnské nám. 3, Malá Strana* ✆ *70 Kč* ☉ *Daily 10–6.*

🔳 **Malostranské náměstí** (Lesser Quarter Square). Arcaded houses on the east and south sides of the square date from the 16th and 17th centuries, exhibiting a mix of traditionally curvaceous baroque and Renaissance elements. The Czech Parliament resides partly in the gaudy yellow-and-green palace on the square's north side, partly in a building on Sněmovní street, behind the palace. The huge bulk of the Church of St. Nicholas divides the lower, busier section—buzzing with restaurants, street vendors, clubs, and shops—from the quieter, upper part.

🔳 **Museum Kampa.** The spotlighted jewel on Kampa Island is a remodeled mill house that now displays a private collection of paintings by Czech artist František Kupka and first-rate temporary exhibitions by both Czech and foreign artists. The museum was hit hard by the 2002 flood; waters rose up 6 meters in the building and courtyard. But the museum rebounded quickly and now includes an elegant restaurant with an outdoor patio that offers a splendid view of the river and historic buildings on the opposite bank. ⊠ *U Sovových mlýnů 2, Malá Strana* ☎ *257–286–147* ⊕ *www.museumkampa.cz* ✆ *100 Kč* ☉ *Tues.–Sun. 10–5.*

🔳 **Nerudova ulice.** This steep little street used to be the last leg of the "Royal Way," the king's procession before his coronation, though he made the ascent on horseback, not huffing and puffing on foot like today's visitors. It was named for the 19th-century Czech journalist and poet Jan Neruda (after whom Chilean poet Pablo Neruda renamed himself).

Until Joseph II's administrative reforms in the late 18th century, house numbering was unknown in Prague. Each house bore a name, depicted on the façade, and these are particularly prominent on Nerudova ulice. No. 6, U červeného orla (At the Red Eagle), which proudly displays a faded painting of a crimson eagle. No. 12 is known as U tří housliček (At the Three Fiddles); in the early 18th century, three generations of the Edlinger violin-making family lived here. Joseph II's scheme numbered each house according to its position in its "town" (here the Lesser Quarter) rather than its sequence on the street. The red plates record the original house numbers; the blue ones are the numbers used in addresses today. Many architectural guides refer to the old, red-number plates, much to the confusion of visitors.

Two palaces break the unity of the houses on Nerudova ulice. Both were designed by the adventurous baroque architect Giovanni Santini, one of the popular Italian builders hired by wealthy nobles in the early 18th century. The **Morzin Palace,** on the left at No. 5, is now the Romanian Embassy. The fascinating façade, created in 1713 with an allegory of night and day, is the work of Ferdinand Brokoff, of Charles Bridge statue fame. Across the street at No. 20 is the **Thun-Hohenstein Palace,** now the Italian Embassy. The gateway with two enormous eagles (the emblem of the Kolovrat family, who owned the building at the time) is the work of the other great Charles Bridge statue sculptor, Mathias Braun. Santini himself lived at No. 14, the **Valkoun House.**

The archway at Nerudova No. 13 hides one of the many winding passageways that give the Lesser Quarter its captivatingly ghostly character at night. Higher up the street at No. 33 is the **Bretfeld Palace,** a rococo house on the corner of Jánský vršek. The relief of St. Nicholas on the façade was created by Ignaz Platzer, a sculptor known for his classical and rococo work. But it's the building's historical associations that give it intrigue: Mozart, his lyricist partner Lorenzo da Ponte, and the aging but still infamous philanderer and music lover Casanova stayed here at the time of the world premiere of *Don Giovanni* in 1787.

NEED A BREAK?

Nerudova ulice is filled with little restaurants and snack bars that offers indulgences for everyone's palate. At the bottom of the street, **U Kocoura** (✉ Nerudova 2) is a classic local pub, with long tables, a boisterous clientele, and the original Budweiser (Budvar in Czech) on tap.

For a sensational view of the city, continue up Nerudova ulice until it turns into Úvoz. At No. 40, go through the gateway on your left and follow the path up to **Oz**ivlé Drevo (✉ Úvoz 40), which is in front of Strahovský klášter. The outdoor tables overlook Petrin hill, Malá Strana, and the city beyond. In nice weather, it's one of the most pleasant outdoor spots in the city.

♺ **42** **Petřín sady.** For a superb view of the city—from a slightly more solitary perch—the top of Petřín Hill includes a charming playground for children and adults alike, with a miniature Eiffel Tower. The park is laced with footpaths, with several buildings clustered together near the tower.

Just keep going gradually upward until you reach the base, where you can also find a mirror maze (*bludiště*) in a small structure, and the seemingly abandoned svatý Vavřinec (St. Lawrence) church. The area is beautifully peaceful and an ideal spot for an afternoon of wandering. You can walk up from Karmelitská ulice or Újezd down in the Lesser Quarter or ride the funicular railway from U lanové dráhy ulice, off Újezd; you can also stroll over from Strahov klášter (Strahov Monastery). Regular public-transportation tickets are valid on the funicular. Be aware that lines for the funicular can be long on a clear day, and they move slowly. (If the line is far outside the terminal door, you're in for at least a 30-minute wait, if not longer.) To descend, take the funicular or meander on foot down through the stations of the cross on the pathways leading back to the Lesser Quarter. A number of paths meander down the face of the hillside through fruit orchards, and finally back to Karmelitská; a wide path goes to Strahov Monastery. The funicular, an attraction in itself, is run as an extension of the tram system. The station at the top opens onto a rose garden, a lovely destination in the summer months.

As you exit the funicular at the top of Petřín Hill, the rounded dome to your left is **Štefánik Observatory** (☎ 257–320–540 ⊕ www.observatory.cz), a working astronomical facility with some fine displays (though not many in English). Both day and night telescope viewings are available. A large children's play area in Petřín sady is dominated by the **Petříinská razhelda** (Petřín Tower; ☎ 257–320–112), a smaller replica of the Eiffel Tower with a marvelous view of the city from the top. This is not an attraction for the timid; the only way to the viewing platforms is via a circular stairway that wraps around the outside of the tower, a safe but dizzying ascent. The hardy who make the climb will be rewarded with a dazzlingly view. A stone's throw from the Petřín Tower, the **Bludiste na Petřína** (Mirror Maze; ☎ 257–315–212) is an amusement park attraction with, as the name suggests, a variety of amusingly distorted mirrors. It's great fun for the kids. ⊠ *Petřín Hill* ☜ *Observatory 30 Kč, Tower 50 Kč, Maze 40 Kč* ☉ *Observatory Jan. and Feb., Tues.–Fri. 6–10 PM, weekends 10–noon and 2–8; Mar., Tues.–Fri. 7–9 PM, weekends 10–noon, 2–6, and 7–9; Apr.–Aug., Tues.–Fri. 2–7 and 9–11, weekends 10–noon, 2–7, and 9–11; Sept., Tues.–Fri. 2–7 and 9–11, weekends 10–noon, 2–6, and 8–10; Oct. Tues.–Fri. 7–9, weekends 10–noon, 2–6, and 7–9; Nov. and Dec., Tues.–Fri. 6–8, weekends 10–noon and 2–8. Tower & Maze Jan.–Mar., Nov., and Dec., weekends 10–5; Apr., Sept., and Oct., daily 10–5; May–Aug., daily 10–10.*

㉝ Schönbornský palác (Schönborn Palace). Franz Kafka had an apartment in this massive baroque building at the top of Tržiště ulice in mid-1917, after moving from Zlatá ulička, or Golden Lane. The heavily guarded U.S. Embassy and consular office now occupies this prime location. It's a bad idea to linger here; the Czech police take the threat of terrorist acts against American targets seriously, and if you hang around with no apparent purpose, you could be approached and questioned. ⊠ *Tržiště at Vlašská, Malá Strana.*

㊱ Velkopřevorské náměstí (Grand Priory Square). This square lies south and slightly west of the Charles Bridge, next to the Čertovka. The Grand

Prior's Palace fronting the square is considered one of the finest baroque buildings in the Lesser Quarter, though it's now part of the Embassy of the Sovereign Military Order of Malta—the contemporary (and very real) descendant of the Knights of Malta—and closed to the public. Opposite is the flamboyant orange-and-white stucco façade of the Buquoy Palace, built in 1719 by Giovanni Santini and the present home of the French Embassy. The so-called **John Lennon Peace Wall,** leading to a bridge over the Čertovka, was once a kind of monument to youthful rebellion, emblazoned with a large painted head of the former Beatle. But Lennon's visage is nowhere to be seen these days; the wall is usually covered instead with political and music-related graffiti.

🤚 **39** **Vojanovy sady** (Vojan Park). Once the gardens of the Monastery of the Discalced Carmelites, later taken over by the Order of the English Virgins, and now part of the Ministry of Finance, this walled garden, with its weeping willows, fruit trees, and benches, provides another peaceful haven in summer. The flood of 2002 reached this area, too; lower portions of some walls remain stripped away. Exhibitions of modern sculptures are occasionally held here, contrasting sharply with the two baroque chapels and the graceful Ignaz Platzer statue of John of Nepomuk standing on a fish at the entrance. At the other end of the park you can find a terrace with a formal rose garden and a peacock that likes to preen for visitors. The park is surrounded by the high walls of the old monastery and new Ministry of Finance buildings, with only an occasional glimpse of a tower or spire to remind you of the world beyond. ✉ *U lužického semináře, between Letenská ulice and Míšeňská ulice, Malá Strana* 🕙 *Nov.–Mar., daily 8–5; Apr.–Oct., daily 8–7.*

▌ **NEED A BREAK?**

Immediately north of the entrance to the Vojanovy sady, you can find **Restaurace Vojanův Dvůr** (✉ U ležiokého semináře 23), an admittedly touristy place that nonetheless offers good traditional Czech food with the added bonus of a lovely summer patio. Occasionally the restaurant hosts special beer parties and pig roasts.

35 **Vrtbovská zahrada** (Vrtba Garden). An unobtrusive door on noisy Karmelitská hides the entranceway to a fascinating sanctuary that also has one of the best views over the Lesser Quarter. The street door opens onto the intimate courtyard of the Vrtbovský palác (Vrtba Palace), which is now private housing. Two Renaissance wings flank the courtyard; the left one was built in 1575, the right one in 1591. The original owner of the latter house was one of the 27 Bohemian nobles executed by the Hapsburgs in 1621. The house was given as confiscated property to Count Sezima of Vrtba, who bought the neighboring property and turned the buildings into a late-Renaissance palace. The Vrtba Garden was created a century later. This is the most elegant of the Lesser Quarter's public gardens, built in five levels rising behind the courtyard in a wave of statuary-bedecked staircases and formal terraces reaching toward a seashell-decorated pavilion at the top. In summer it's a popular spot for weddings, receptions, and occasional concerts. (The fenced-off garden immediately behind and above belongs to the U.S. Embassy—hence the U.S. flag that often flies there.) The powerful stone

Fodor's Choice
★

figure of Atlas that caps the entranceway in the courtyard and most of the other classically derived statues are from the workshop of Mathias Braun, perhaps the best of the Czech baroque sculptors. ⊠ *Karmelitská 25, Malá Strana* 🎟 *40 Kč* ☉ *Apr.–Oct., daily 10–6.*

OFF THE
BEATEN
PATH

VILLA BERTRAMKA – Mozart fans should flock to this villa, where the great composer stayed on several occasions as a guest of art patrons Frantisek and Josefina Dusek. The small, well-organized W. A. Mozart Museum is packed with musical memorabilia, including a flyer for a performance of *Don Giovanni* in 1788, only months after the opera's world premiere at the Estates Theater. Also on hand is a handsome collection of period instruments, several purportedly played by the master. Summer concerts here are pricey, but the atmosphere is unbeatable. Take Tram No. 12 from Karmelitská south (or ride metro Line B) to the Anděl metro station. From there a 10-minute walk west on Plzeňská past the shopping malls will bring you within sight of the Hotel Movenpick; Bertramka is up and behind the hotel. ⊠ *Mozartova 169, Smíchov* 🕿 *257–317–465* ⊕ *www.bertramka.com* 🎟 *110 Kč* ☉ *Apr.–Oct., daily 9:30–6; Nov.–Mar., daily 9:30–5.*

★ ☾ ⓰ **Zahrada Valdštejnského paláce** (Wallenstein Palace Gardens). With its idiosyncratic high-walled gardens and superb, vaulted Renaissance *sala terrena* (room opening onto a garden), this palace displays superbly elegant grounds. Walking around the formal paths, you come across numerous fountains and statues depicting figures from classical mythology or warriors dispatching a variety of beasts. But the most amazing piece of sculpture work is "The Grotto," a huge dripstone wall packed with imaginative rock formations and what's billed as "illusory hints of secret corridors." Next to the wall sits an aviary with some rather large owls (look up, they're usually perched in the upper reaches). Albrecht von Wallenstein, onetime owner of the house and gardens, began a meteoric military career in 1622, when the Austrian emperor Ferdinand II retained him to save the empire from the Swedes and Protestants during the Thirty Years' War. Wallenstein, wealthy by marriage, offered to raise an army of 20,000 men at his own cost and lead them personally. Ferdinand II accepted and showered Wallenstein with confiscated land and titles. Wallenstein's first acquisition was this enormous area. Having knocked down 23 houses, a brick factory, and three gardens, in 1623 he began to build his magnificent palace. Most of the palace itself now serves the Czech Senate as meeting chamber and offices. The palace's cavernous former *Jízdárna*, or riding school, now hosts occasional art exhibitions. ⊠ *Letenská 10, Malá Strana* 🎟 *Free* ☉ *Apr. 1–Oct. 31, daily 10–6.*

HRADČANY (CASTLE AREA)

To the west of Prague Castle is the residential Hradčany (Castle Area), the town that during the early 14th century emerged from a collection of monasteries and churches. The concentration of history packed into Prague Castle and Hradčany challenges those not versed in the ups and downs of Bohemian kings, religious uprisings, wars, and oppression. The picturesque area surrounding Prague Castle, with its breathtaking vistas of the Old Town and the Lesser Quarter, can be enjoyed by simply wandering. But the castle itself, with its broad history and architecture, is difficult to fully appreciate without investing a little more time.

A GOOD WALK

Take the metro to Malostranská and then switch to a tram that takes you to Malostranské náměstí. You exit at the Chrám svatého Mikuláše (Church of St. Nicholas; see ⇨ Malá Strana), which fills a large section of the square. To one side of the church is Nerudova ulice, which runs west from the square. Along this slender street are some of the city's best house signs, such as the one for the home of Jan Neruda, a poet and journalist after whom the route is named. Look for his house, At the Two Suns, No. 47. Other notable emblems, among others, are at the White Swan (No. 49), the Green Lobster (No. 43), and the Three Fiddles (No. 12).

At the western (upper) end of the street, look for a flight of stone steps guarded by two saintly statues. Take the stairs up to Loretánská ulice, and enjoy panoramic views of the church and the Lesser Quarter. At the top of the steps, turn left and walk a couple hundred yards until you come to a dusty, elongated square named Pohořelec (Scene of Fire), which suffered tragic fires in 1420, 1541, and 1741. Go through the inconspicuous gateway at No. 8 and up the steps to find the courtyard of one of the city's richest monasteries, the **Strahovský klášter** ㊸ ▶.

Retrace your steps to Loretánské náměstí, the square at the head of Loretánská ulice that's flanked by the feminine curves of the baroque church **Loreta** ㊹. Across the road the 29 half pillars of the Černínský palác (Černín Palace) mask the Czech Ministry of Foreign Affairs. At the bottom of Loretánské náměstí, a little lane trails to the left into the area known as **Nový Svět** ㊺; the name means "New World," though the district is as old-world as they come. Turn right onto the street Nový Svět. Around the corner you get a tantalizing view of the cathedral through the trees. Walk down the winding Kanovnická ulice past the Austrian Embassy and the dignified but melancholy Kostel svatého Jana Nepomuckého (Church of St. John of Nepomuk). At the top of the street on the left, the rounded, Renaissance corner house, Martinický palác, catches the eye with its detailed *sgraffiti* decorations. Martinický palác opens onto **Hradčanské náměstí** ㊻, with its grandiose gathering of Renaissance and baroque palaces. To the left of the bright yellow Arcibiskupský palác (Archbishop's Palace) on the square is an alleyway leading down to the Sternberg Palace, which houses the **Národní galerie** ㊼ and its collections of European art. Across the square the handsome *sgraffito* sweep of **Schwarzenberský palác** ㊽ beckons; this is the building you saw from the back side at the beginning of the tour.

TIMING To do justice to the subtle charms of Hradčany, allow at least two hours just for ambling and admiring the passing buildings and views of the city. The Strahovský klášter halls need about a half-hour to take in, more if you tour the small picture gallery there, and the Loreta and its treasures need an equal length of time at least. The Národní galerie in the Šternberský palác deserves a minimum of a couple of hours. Keep in mind that several places are not open on Monday.

What to See

46 Hradčanské náměstí (Hradčany Square). With its fabulous mixture of baroque and Renaissance houses, topped by the castle itself, this square had a prominent role in the film *Amadeus* (as a substitution for Vienna). Czech director Miloš Forman used the house at No. 7 for Mozart's residence, where the composer was haunted by the masked figure he thought was his father. The flamboyant rococo Arcibiskupský palác (Archbishop's Palace), on the left as you face the castle, was the Viennese archbishop's palace. Sadly the plush interior, shown off in the film, is rarely open to the public. For a brief time after World War II, No. 11 was home to a little girl named Marie Jana Korbelová, who is better known as Madeleine Albright.

★ **44 Loreta** (Loreto Church). The seductive lines built for this church were a conscious move on the part of Counter-Reformation Jesuits in the 17th century who wanted to build up the cult of Mary and attract the largely Protestant Bohemians back to the fold. According to legend, angels had carried Mary's house from Nazareth and dropped it in a patch of laurel trees in Ancona, Italy. Known as *Loreto* (from the Latin for laurel), it immediately became a destination of pilgrimage. The Prague Loreto was one of many symbolic reenactments of this scene across Europe, and it worked: pilgrims came in droves. The graceful façade, with its voluptuous tower, was built in 1720 by Kilian Ignaz Dientzenhofer, the architect of the two St. Nicholas churches in Prague. Most spectacular of all is a small exhibition upstairs displaying the religious treasures presented to Mary in thanks for various services, including a monstrance (a vessel for the consecrated Eucharist) studded with 6,500 diamonds. ⊠ *Loretánské nám. 7, Hradčany* 🎟 *90 Kč* ⊙ *Tues.–Sun. 9–12:15 and 1–4:30.*

★ **47 Národní galerie** (National Gallery). Housed in the 18th-century Šternberský palác (Sternberg Palace), this collection, though impressive, feels fairly limited when compared with nearby museums in Germany and Austria. During the time when Berlin, Dresden, and Vienna were building up superlative old-master galleries, Prague languished, neglected by her Viennese rulers. Works by Rubens and Rembrandt are on display; some other key pieces in the collection wait in the wings. Other branches of the National Gallery are scattered around town. ⊠ *Hradčanské nám. 15, Hradčany* 🕾 *220–514–634* ⊕ *www.ngprague.cz* 🎟 *150 Kč* ⊙ *Tues.–Sun. 10–6.*

★ **45 Nový Svět.** This picturesque, winding little alley, with façades from the 17th and 18th centuries, once housed Prague's poorest residents; now many of the homes are used as artists' studios. The last house on the street, No. 1, was the home of the Danish-born astronomer Tycho Brahe. Living so close to the Loreto, so the story goes, Tycho was constantly disturbed during his nightly stargazing by the church bells. He ended up complaining to his patron, Emperor Rudolf II, who instructed the Capuchin monks to finish their services before the first star appeared in the sky.

48 Schwarzenberský palác (Schwarzenberg Palace). A boxy palace with an extravagant *sgraffito* façade, the **Vojenské historické muzeum** (Military History Museum) is one of the largest of its kind in Europe. Unfortunately the beautifully decorated exterior is all that can be seen while the interior undergoes a long-term renovation that is not expected to be finished until mid-2007. ✉ *Hradčanské nám. 2, Hradčany* ⊕ *www. militarymuseum.cz.*

★ ❸ **Strahovský klášter** (Strahov Monastery). Founded by the Premonstratensian order in 1140, the monastery remained theirs until 1952, when the Communists suppressed all religious orders and turned the entire complex into the **Památník národního písemnictví** (Museum of National Literature). The major building of interest is the **Strahov Library**, with its collection of early Czech manuscripts, the 10th-century Strahov New Testament, and the collected works of famed Danish astronomer Tycho Brahe. Also of note is the late-18th-century **Philosophical Hall.** Its ceilings are engulfed in a startling sky-blue fresco that depicts an unusual cast of characters, including Socrates' nagging wife, Xanthippe; Greek astronomer Thales, with his trusty telescope; and a collection of Greek philosophers mingling with Descartes, Diderot, and Voltaire. On the premises is the order's small art gallery, highlighted by late-Gothic altars and paintings from Rudolf II's time. ✉ *Strahovské nádvoří 1/132, Hradčany* ☎ *220–517–278* ✐ *80 Kč* ☉ *Gallery Tues.–Sun. 9–noon and 12:30–5; library daily 9–noon and 1–5.*

PRAŽSKÝ HRAD (PRAGUE CASTLE)

Numbers in the text correspond to numbers in the margin and on the Prague Castle (Pražský hrad) map.

Despite its monolithic presence, Prague Castle is not a single structure but rather a collection of buildings dating from the 10th to the 20th century, all linked by internal courtyards. The most important structures are the cathedral, the **Chrám svatého Víta** ❺❹, clearly visible soaring above the castle walls, and the **Královský palác** ❺❺, the official residence of kings and presidents and still the center of political power in the Czech Republic. The castle is compact and easily navigated. Be forewarned: in summer the castle, especially Chrám svatého Víta, suffers from huge crowds. **Zlatá ulička** ❺❾ became so packed that in 2002 a separate admission fee was imposed for it.

TIMING The castle is at its best in early morning and late evening when it holds an air of mystery, and it's incomparably beautiful when it snows. The cathedral deserves an hour, as does the Královský palác, while you can easily spend an entire day taking in the museums, the views of the city, and the hidden nooks of the castle. Remember that some sights, such as the Lobkovický palác and the National Gallery branch at Klášter svatého Jiří, are not open on Monday.

What to See

❺❼ **Bazilika svatého Jiří** (St. George's Basilica). Inside, this church looks more or less as it did in the 12th century and is the best-preserved Romanesque relic in the country. The effect is at once barnlike and peaceful, the warm golden yellow of the stone walls and the small arched windows exude a sense of enduring harmony. It was originally built in the 10th century by

Fodor'sChoice
★

Prague Castle (Pražský hrad)

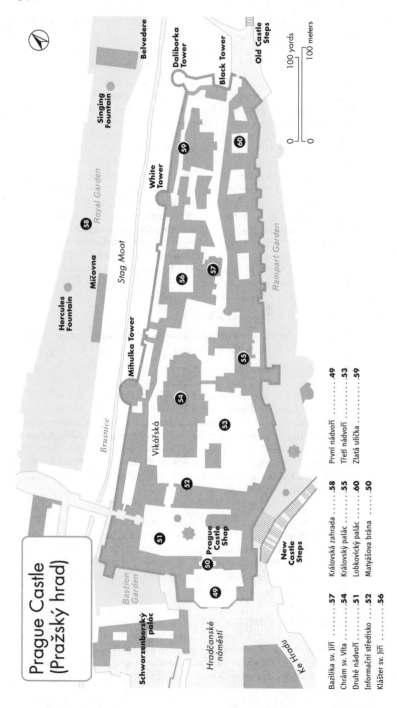

100 yards

100 meters

Prince Vratislav I, the father of Prince (and St.) Wenceslas and dedicated to St. George (of dragon fame), a figure supposedly more agreeable to the still largely pagan people. The outside was remodeled during early baroque times, although the striking rusty-red color is in keeping with the look of the Romanesque edifice. The house-shaped painted tomb at the front of the church holds the remains of the founder, Vratislav I. Up the steps, in a chapel to the right, is the tomb Peter Parler designed for St. Ludmila, the grandmother of St. Wenceslas. ⊠ *Nám. U sv. Jiří, Pražský Hrad* ☎ *257–531–622* ⊕ *www.prague-info.cz* ✆ *50Kč, or included in 2-day castle ticket (350 Kč)* ⊙ *Apr.–Oct., daily 9–5; Nov.–Mar., daily 9–4.*

> ### IT'S BEGINNING TO LOOK A LOT LIKE CHRISTMAS
>
> "We traveled to Prague on Christmas Day. The lights are indeed still lit, and the market stalls are in the square of the Old Town. You can get hot drinks and eat the traditional trdelnik pastries made right in front of your eyes. With all of Prague's spires and amazing architecture, it was entrancing."   –noe847
> "The Christmas markets go on until January 6th, and the atmosphere is wonderful. It was below freezing, even during the day, with a sprinkling of snow on the parks. A cup of hot mead from one of the stalls on the Old Town Square warmed us up, though." –Maria_H

54 **Chrám svatého Víta** (St. Vitus's Cathedral). With its graceful, soaring towers, this Gothic cathedral—among the most beautiful in Europe—is the
Fodor'sChoice
★ spiritual heart of Prague Castle and the entire country. It has a long and complicated history, beginning in the 10th century and continuing to its completion in 1929. To hear its history in depth, English-speaking guided tours of the cathedral and the Královský palác can be arranged at the information office across from the cathedral entrance.

Once you enter the cathedral, pause to take in the vast but delicate beauty of the Gothic and neo-Gothic interior glowing in the colorful light that filters through the brilliant stained-glass windows. This western third of the structure, including the façade and the two towers you can see from outside, was not completed until 1929, following the initiative of the Union for the Completion of the Cathedral. Don't let the neo-Gothic illusion keep you from examining this new section. The six stained-glass windows to your left and right and the large rose window behind are modern masterpieces. Take a good look at the third window up on the left. The familiar art nouveau flamboyance, depicting the blessing of Sts. Cyril and Methodius (9th-century missionaries to the Slavs), is the work of Alfons Mucha, the Czech founder of the style. He achieved the subtle coloring by painting rather than staining the glass.

Walking halfway up the right-hand aisle, you will find the **Svatováclavská kaple** (Chapel of St. Wenceslas). With a tomb holding the saint's remains, walls covered in semi-precious stones, and paintings depicting the life of Wenceslas, this square chapel is the ancient core of the cathedral. Stylistically, it represents a high point of the dense, richly decorated—though rather gloomy—Gothic favored by Charles IV and his successors.

Wenceslas (the "good king" of Christmas-carol fame) was a determined Christian in an era of widespread paganism. Around 925, as prince of Bohemia, he founded a rotunda church dedicated to St. Vitus on this site. But the prince's brother, Boleslav, was impatient to take power, and he ambushed and killed Wenceslas in 935 near a church at Stará Boleslav, northeast of Prague. Wenceslas was originally buried in that church, but so many miracles happened at his grave that he rapidly became a symbol of piety for the common people, something that greatly irritated the new Prince Boleslav. Boleslav was finally forced to honor his brother by reburying the body in the St. Vitus Rotunda. Shortly afterward, Wenceslas was canonized.

The rotunda was replaced by a Romanesque basilica in the late 11th century. Work was begun on the existing building in 1344. For the first few years the chief architect was the Frenchman Mathias d'Arras, but after his death in 1352 the work was continued by the 22-year-old German architect Peter Parler, who went on to build the Charles Bridge and many other Prague treasures.

The small door in the back of the chapel leads to the **Korunní komora** (Crown Chamber), the Bohemian crown jewels' repository. It remains locked with seven keys held by seven important people (including the president) and rarely opens to the public.

A little beyond the Chapel of St. Wenceslas on the same side, stairs lead down to the underground **royal crypt,** interesting primarily for the information it provides about the cathedral's history. As you descend the stairs, you can see parts of the old Romanesque basilica and portions of the foundations of the rotunda. Moving into the second room, you find a rather eclectic group of royal remains ensconced in new sarcophagi dating from the 1930s. In the center is Charles IV, who died in 1378. Rudolf II, patron of Renaissance Prague, is entombed at the rear in the original tin coffin. To his right is Maria Amalia, the only child of Empress Maria Theresa to reside in Prague. Ascending the wooden steps back into the cathedral, brings you to the white-marble **Kralovské mausoleum** (Royal Mausoleum), atop which lie stone statues of the first two Hapsburg kings to rule in Bohemia, Ferdinand I and Maximilian II, and another of Ferdinand's consort, Anne Jagiello.

The cathedral's **Kralovské oratorium** (Royal Oratory) was used by the kings and their families when attending mass. Built in 1493 the work represents a perfect example of late Gothic, laced on the outside with a stone network of gnarled branches similar in pattern to the ceiling vaulting in the Královský palác. The oratory connects to the palace by an elevated covered walkway, which you can see from outside.

A few more steps toward the east end, you can't fail to catch sight of the ornate silver **sarcophagus of St. John of Nepomuk.** According to legend, when Nepomuk's body was exhumed in 1721 to be reinterred, the tongue was found to be still intact and pumping with blood. This strange tale served a highly political purpose. The Catholic Church and the Hapsburgs were seeking a new folk hero to replace the Protestant forerunner Jan Hus, whom they despised. The 14th-century priest Nepomuk,

killed during a power struggle with King Václav IV, was sainted and re-
buried a few years later with great ceremony in a 3,700-pound silver
tomb, replete with angels and cherubim; the tongue was enshrined in
its own reliquary.

The eight chapels around the back of the cathedral are the work of the
original architect, Mathias d'Arras. A number of old tombstones, including some badly worn grave markers of medieval royalty, can be seen
within, amid furnishings from later periods. Opposite the wooden relief, depicting the Protestants looting of the cathedral in 1619, is the
Valdštejnská kaple (Wallenstein Chapel). Since the 19th century the
chapel has housed the Gothic tombstones of its two architects, d'Arras
and Peter Parler, who died in 1352 and 1399, respectively. If you look
up to the balcony, you can just make out the busts of these two men,
designed by Parler's workshop. The other busts around the triforium
depict royalty and other VIPs of the time.

The Hussite wars in the 15th century put an end to the first phase of
the cathedral's construction. During the short era of illusory peace before the Thirty Years' War, the massive south tower was completed, but
lack of money quashed any idea of finishing the building, and the cathedral was closed in by a wall built across from the Chapel of St. Wenceslas. Not until the 20th century was the western side of the cathedral,
with its two towers, completed in the spirit of Parler's conception.

A key element of the cathedral's teeming, rich exterior decoration is the
Last Judgment mosaic above the ceremonial entrance, called the Golden
Portal, on the south side. The use of mosaic is quite rare in countries
north of the Alps; this work, constructed from 1 million glass and stone
chunks, dates from the 1370s. The once-clouded glass now sparkles again
thanks to many years of restoration funded by the Getty Conservation
Institute. The central field shows Christ in glory, adored by Charles IV
and his consort, Elizabeth of Pomerania, as well as several saints; the
risen dead and attendant angels are on the left; and on the right the flames
of Hell lick around the figure of Satan. ⊠ *St. Vitus's Cathedral, Pražský
Hrad* ☎ *257–531–622* ⊕ *www.prague-info.cz* ⊠ *Western section free;
chapels, crypt, and tower require 2-day castle ticket for 350 Kč*
⊙ *Apr.–Oct., daily 9–5; Nov.–Mar., daily 9–4.*

⑤ **Druhé nádvoří** (Second Courtyard). Except for the view of the spires of
St. Vitus's Cathedral, the exterior courtyard offers little for the eye to
feast on. Empress Maria Theresa's court architect, Nicolò Pacassi, received the imperial approval to re-
make the castle in the 1760s, as it
was badly damaged by Prussian
shelling during the Seven Years'
War in 1757. The Second Courtyard was the main victim of
Pacassi's attempts at imparting classical grandeur to what had been a
picturesque collection of Gothic
and Renaissance styles. This court-

> **SIZE MATTERS**
>
> The 18-acre Prague Castle is the
> world's largest ancient castle. Its
> 9th-century polygon design is an
> average of 128 meters (420 feet)
> wide.

yard also houses the rather gaudy **Kaple svatého Kříže** (Chapel of the Holy Cross), with decorations from the 18th and 19th centuries, which now serves as a souvenir and ticket stand.

Built in the late 16th and early 17th century, the Second Courtyard was originally part of a reconstruction program commissioned by Rudolf II. He amassed a large and famed collection of fine and decorative art, scientific instruments, philosophic and alchemical books, natural wonders, coins, and a hodgepodge of other treasures. The bulk of the collection was looted by the Swedes during the Thirty Years' War, removed to Vienna when the imperial capital returned there after Rudolf's death, or auctioned off during the 18th century. Artworks that survived the turmoil, for the most part acquired after Rudolf's time, are displayed in the **Obrazárna** (Picture Gallery), on the courtyard's left side as you face St. Vitus's. In rooms elegantly redecorated by the official castle architect, Bořek Šípek, there are good Renaissance, mannerist, and baroque paintings that demonstrate the luxurious tastes of Rudolf's court. Across the passageway by the gallery entrance is the **Císařská konírna** (Imperial Stable), where temporary exhibitions are held. The passageway at the northern end of the courtyard forms the northern entrance to the castle and leads out over a luxurious ravine known as the **Jelení příkop** (Stag Moat), which can be entered either here or at the lower end via the metal catwalk off Chotkova ulice, when it isn't closed for sporadic renovations. ✉ *Obrazárna: 2nd Courtyard, Pražský Hrad* ☎ *257–531–622* ⊕ *www.prague-info.cz* 🎫 *Courtyard free, Picture Gallery 100 Kč* 🕐 *Picture Gallery daily 10–6.*

⑫ Informační středisko (Castle Information Office). This is the place to come for entrance tickets, guided tours, audio-tour players for listening to recorded tours in English, tickets to cultural events held at the castle, and money changing. You can wander around a great deal of the castle for free, and this offers an enticing opportunity to save money; you can still enter St. Vitus's, though you won't be able to get close to the oldest parts. There are two ticketing options. The cheaper price allows entrance to St. Vitus's Cathedral (the oldest parts and the tower), the Royal Palace, and Golden Lane, and this will provide more than enough castle-visiting for most people; a more expensive ticket includes St. George's Basilica, the powder tower, and an extensive exhibit on the history of the castle. Tickets are valid for two days. You can also pay separately for Golden Lane and St. George's Basilica. Other attractions include the National Gallery and Toy Museum, which have separate admission charges. If you just want to walk through the castle grounds, note that the gates close at midnight from April through October and at 11 PM the rest of the year, while the gardens are open from April through October only. ✉ *Třetí nádvoří, across from entrance to St. Vitus's Cathedral, Pražský Hrad* ☎ *257–531–622* ⊕ *www.prague-info.cz* 🎫 *2-day castle tickets 350 Kč, or Golden Lane 50 Kč, St. George's Basilica 50 Kč; English-language guided tours 400 Kč for up to 5 people, advance booking recommended; grounds and gardens free* 🕐 *Apr.–Oct., daily 9–5; Nov.–Mar., daily 9–4.*

⑯ Klášter svatého Jiří (St. George's Convent). The first convent in Bohemia was founded here in 973 next to the even older St. George's Basilica.

The National Gallery collections of Czech mannerist and baroque art are housed here. Highlights include the voluptuous work of Rudolf II's court painters, the giant baroque religious statuary, and some fine paintings by Karel Škréta and Petr Brandl. Although inside Prague Castle, this museum has a separate admission. ✉ *Jířské nám. 33 Pražský Hrad* ☎ *257–320–536* ⊕ *www.ngprague.cz* 🎫 *100 Kč* ☉ *Tues.–Sun. 10–6.*

⑤⑧ Královská zahrada (Royal Garden). This peaceful swath of greenery affords unusually lovely views of St. Vitus's Cathedral and the castle's walls

Fodor'sChoice
★

and bastions. Originally laid out in the 16th century, it endured devastation in war, neglect in times of peace, and many redesigns, reaching its present parklike form early in the 20th century. Luckily, its Renaissance treasures survived. One of these is the long, narrow **Míčovna** (Ball Game Hall), built by Bonifaz Wohlmut in 1568, its garden front completely covered by a dense tangle of allegorical *sgraffiti*.

The **Královský letohrádek** (Royal Summer Palace, also known as the Belvedere), at the garden's eastern end, deserves its unusual reputation as one of the most beautiful Renaissance structures north of the Alps. Italian architects began it; Wohlmut finished it off in the 1560s with a copper roof like an upturned boat's keel riding above the graceful arcades of the ground floor. During the 18th and 19th centuries, military engineers tested artillery in the interior, which had already lost its rich furnishings to Swedish soldiers during their siege of the city in 1648. The Renaissance-style *giardinetto* (little garden) adjoining the summer palace centers on another masterwork, the Italian-designed, Czech-produced Singing Fountain, which resonates from the sound of falling water. ✉ *U Prašného mostu ulice and Mariánské hradby ulice near Chotkovy Park, Pražský Hrad* ☎ *257–531–622* ⊕ *www.prague-info. cz* ☉ *Apr.–Oct., daily 10–5:45.*

⑤⑤ Královský palác (Royal Palace). A jumble of styles and add-ons from different eras have gathered in this palace. The best way to grasp its size is from within the **Vladislavský sál** (Vladislav Hall), the largest secular Gothic interior space in Central Europe. Benedikt Ried completed this enormous hall in 1493. (He was to late-Bohemian Gothic what Peter Parler was to the earlier version.) The room imparts a sense of space and light, softened by the sensuous lines of the vaulted ceilings and brought to a dignified close by the simple oblong form of the early Renaissance windows. In its heyday, the hall held jousting tournaments, festive markets, banquets, and coronations. In more recent times, it has been used to inaugurate presidents, from the Communist leader

REAR WINDOW

Defenestration (throwing someone out a window) is a peculiarly Bohemian method of protest famously used in the conflict between Hapsburg-backed Catholics and Bohemian Protestants. At one point Protestant nobles stormed the Royal Palace and threw two Catholic officials out the window. Legend has it they landed on a dung pile and escaped unharmed, an event the Jesuits interpreted as a miracle.

Klement Gottwald in 1948 to Václav Havel in 1989, 1993, and 1998, and Václav Klaus in 2003.

From the front of the hall, turn right into the rooms of the **Česká kancelář** (Bohemian Chancellery). This wing was built by Benedikt Ried only 10 years after the hall was completed, but it shows a much stronger Renaissance influence. Pass through the portal into the last chamber of the chancellery. In 1618 this room was the site of the second defenestration of Prague, an event that marked the beginning of the Bohemian rebellion and, ultimately, the Thirty Years' War throughout Europe. The square window used in this protest is on the left as you enter the room.

At the back of the Vladislav Hall, a staircase leads up to a gallery of the **Kaple všech svatých** (All Saints' Chapel). Little remains of Peter Parler's original work, but the church contains some fine works of art. The large room to the left of the staircase is the **Stará sněmovna** (council chamber), where the Bohemian nobles met with the king in a prototype parliament of sorts. The descent from Vladislav Hall toward what remains of the **Romanský palác** (Romanesque Palace) is by way of a wide, shallow set of steps. This **Jezdecké schody** (Riders' Staircase) was the entranceway for knights who came for the jousting tournaments. ⊠ *Royal Palace, Třetí nádvoří, Pražský Hrad* ☎ *257–531–622* ⊕ *www.prague-info.cz* ⊠ *Requires 2-day castle ticket, 350 č* ☉ *Apr.–Oct., daily 9–5; Nov.–Mar., daily 9–4.*

❻⓪ **Lobkovický palác** (Lobkowicz Palace). If you want to get a chronologi-
Fodor'sChoice cal understanding of Czech history from the beginnings of the Great Mora-
★ vian Empire in the 9th century to the Czech national uprising in 1848, this is the place. The building was the residence of the powerful Catholic Lobkowicz family from the beginning of the 17th century until the 1940. During the 1970s the building was restored to its early baroque appearance and now houses the National Museum's permanent exhibition on Czech history. Copies of the crown jewels are on display here, but it's the rich collection of illuminated Bibles, old musical instruments, coins, weapons, royal decrees, paintings, and statues that deserves a visit. Detailed information on the exhibits is available in English. Although inside Prague Castle, this museum has a separate admission. ⊠ *Jiřská 3, Pražský Hrad* ⊕ *www.nm.cz* ⊠ *20 Kč* ☉ *Tues.–Sun. 9–5.*

NEED A BREAK? Break for a coffee, pastry, or even lunch and enjoy one of the loveliest views of the city from the outdoor terrace of the **Lobkowicz Palace Café** (⊠ Lobkovický palác, Jirska 3, Pražský Hrad ☎ 602–595–998). The menu is a touch expensive but full of delicious sandwiches, including ham and cheese, tuna, and smoked salmon, beverages, and desserts. It's a lovely and enchanting place to while away an hour.

❺⓪ **Matyášova brána** (Matthias Gate). Built in 1614, this stone gate once stood alone in front of the moats and bridges that surrounded the castle. Under the Hapsburgs, the gate survived by being grafted as a relief onto the palace building. As you go through it, notice the ceremonial white-marble entrance halls on either side that lead up to the Czech president's reception rooms (which are only rarely open to the public).

49 **První nádvoří** (First Courtyard). The main entrance to Prague Castle from Hradčanské náměstí is a little disappointing. After a formal renovation, many of the grander touches from the earlier years were removed. Going through the wrought-iron gate, guarded at ground level by Czech soldiers and from above by the ferocious *Battling Titans* (a copy of Ignaz Platzer's original 18th-century work), you enter this courtyard, built on the site of old moats and gates that once separated the castle from the surrounding buildings and thus protected the vulnerable western flank. The courtyard is one of the more recent additions to the castle, designed by Maria Theresa's court architect, Nicolò Pacassi, in the 1760s. Today it forms part of the presidential office complex. Pacassi's reconstruction was intended to unify the eclectic collection of buildings that made up the castle, but the effect of his work is somewhat flat.

53 **Třetí nádvoří** (Third Courtyard). The contrast between the cool, dark interior of St. Vitus's Cathedral and the brightly colored Pacassi façades of the Third Courtyard just outside is startling. Noted Slovenian architect Josip Plečnik created the courtyard's clean lines in the 1930s, but the modern look is a deception. Plečnik's paving was intended to cover an underground world of house foundations, streets, and walls dating from the 9th through 12th centuries and rediscovered when the cathedral was completed. (You can see a few archways through a grating in a wall of the cathedral.) Plečnik added a few features to catch the eye: a granite obelisk to commemorate the fallen of World War I, a black-marble pedestal for the Gothic statue of St. George (a copy of the National Gallery's original statue), an inconspicuous entrance to his Bull Staircase leading down to the south garden, and a peculiar golden ball topping the eagle fountain near the eastern end of the courtyard.

59 **Zlatá ulička** (Golden Lane). An enchanting collection of tiny, ancient, brightly colored houses crouched under the fortification wall look remarkably like a set for *Snow White and the Seven Dwarfs*. Rumor has it that these were the lodgings for an international group of alchemists whom Rudolf II brought to the court to produce gold. But the truth is a little less romantic: the houses were built during the 16th century for the castle guards. By the early 20th century Golden Lane had become the home of poor artists and writers. Franz Kafka, who lived at No. 22 in 1916 and 1917, described the house on first sight as "so small, so dirty, impossible to live in, and lacking everything necessary." But he soon came to love the place. As he wrote to his fiancée: "Life here is something special . . . to close out the world not just by shutting the door to a room or apartment but to the whole house, to step out into the snow of the silent lane." The lane now holds tiny stores selling books, music, and crafts and has become so popular that a separate admission fee is now charged. The houses are charming, but crowds can be uncomfortable; and the fact remains that you are actually paying money for the privilege to shop in jostling little stores. This is easier to laugh off if you've purchased a combination ticket to the palace, which always includes Golden Lane, but if you are thinking of paying a separate fee, think hard.

Within the walls above Golden Lane, a timber-roof **corridor** (enter between No. 23 and No. 24) is lined with replica suits of armor and weapons (some of it for sale), mock torture chambers, and the like. A shooting range allows you to fire five bolts from a crossbow for 50 Kč. ⊠ *Pražský Hrad* ☎ *257–531–622* ⊕ *www.prague-info.cz* ⌑ *50 Kč, included in combination 2-day castle ticket for 350 Kč* ⊘ *Golden Lane Apr.–Oct., daily 9–5; Nov.–Mar., daily 9–4. Golden Lane Corridor Apr.–Oct., Tues.–Sun. 10–5, Mon. 1–5; Nov.–Mar., Tues.–Sun. 10–4, Mon. 1–4.*

NOVÉ MĚSTO (NEW TOWN) & VYŠEHRAD

To this day, Charles IV's building projects are tightly woven into the daily lives of Prague citizens. His most extensive scheme, the New Town, is still such a lively, vibrant area you may hardly realize that its streets, Gothic churches, and squares were planned as far back as 1348. When Prague was fast outstripping its Old Town parameters, Charles IV extended the city's fortifications. A high wall surrounded the newly developed 2½ square km (1½ square mi) area south and east of the Old Town, tripling the walled territory on the Vltava's right bank. The wall extended south to link with the fortifications of the citadel called Vyšehrad. In the mid-19th century, construction in the New Town boomed in a welter of Romantic and neo-Renaissance styles, particularly on Wenceslas Square and avenues such as Vodičkova, Na Poříčí, and Spálená. One of the most important structures was the Národní divadlo (National Theater), meant to symbolize in stone the revival of the Czechs' history, language, and sense of national pride. The era of Czechoslovak independence around 1918 ushered in modernist architecture, particularly on the outer fringes of the Old Town and in the New Town. One of modernism's most unexpected products was cubist architecture, a form unique to Prague, which produced four notable examples at the foot of ancient Vyšehrad.

▌ A GOOD
WALK

Václavské náměstí ⑥ ► is a long, gently sloping boulevard rather than an actual square. It's the heart of the modern city and well worth the walk down its length. Hundreds of thousands of Czechs gathered here at the end of November 1989 to demand an end to the then-Communist government. You may remember the image beamed to television sets around the world of thousands of Czechs jangling their keys in protest.

This walk will begin from the top of the boulevard, so first take the metro to the Museum stop, where you will pop out within view of the **Statue of St. Wenceslas** ⑥, a patron saint on horseback, which stands here along with statues of various other saints, including Ludmila, Wenceslas's grandmother. The **Národní muzeum** ⑥, which caps the square, is a massive neo-Renaissance structure finished in 1890; take a tour only if you're interested in viewing dusty stuffed animals and one of Europe's largest collections of rocks. Heading down the square, back toward the Old Town, you can see the Supich Building, built in the early 20th century, at No. 38; note the Assyrian masks on its façade. Across the square, the Hotel Europa, at No. 25, has preserved most of its interior and exterior art nouveau features.

Work by Alfons Mucha, whose name is synonymous with art nouveau, is shown a block off Václavské náměstí, at the **Mucha Museum** ❻❹. To reach the museum, turn right on Jindřišská, and notice the Assicurazioni Generali building on your immediate left. Franz Kafka put in 10 months here in 1906–07 as an insurance clerk. After touring the museum, return to Wenceslas Square via Jindřišská. Back on the square, the Wiehl House, dating from 1896, is a neo-Renaissance building with color-laden *sgraffito* at the corner of Vodičkova and Václavske náměstí.

> ## IN PRAISE OF FLATS
>
> "Wear good walking shoes (the cobblestones are murder)." –Peg
> "I have done dumb things in my life, but few as foolish as running down slippery cobblestone streets, in heels, one hand shielding my eyes from the rain, the other clutching my map, all the while trying not to get ground into goulash under the wheels of the No. 20 tram."   –AHaugeto

At No. 8, you may wish to take a look at the interior of the Adam Pharmacy, which is done in a cubist style.

At the foot of the square, turn left down 28 Řijna to Jungmannovo náměstí, a small square named for the linguist and patriot Josef Jungmann (1773–1847). In the courtyard off the square, at No. 18, have a look at the Kostel Panny Marie Sněžné (Church of the Virgin Mary of the Snows). Building on the church ceased during the Hussite wars, leaving a very high, foreshortened façade that never grew into the monumental structure planned by Charles IV. Beyond it lies a quiet sanctuary, the walled Františkánská zahrada (Franciscan Gardens). From Jungmannovo náměstí, 28 Řijna becomes Národní třída, a busy shopping street that continues about ¾ km (½ mi) to the river. Continue your walk toward the river, stopping for a look at the art nouveau Praha House at No. 7, which displays its name in gilt letters at the top. The **Národní divadlo** ❻❺ (National Theater), a symbol of Czech cultural pride, stands proudly facing the Vltava River. From the theater follow the embankment, Masarykovo nábřeží, south toward Vyšehrad. Note the art nouveau architecture of No. 32, the amazingly eclectic design by Kamil Hilbert at No. 26, and the tile-decorated Hlahol building at No. 16. Opposite, on a narrow island, is a 19th-century, yellow-and-white ballroom-restaurant, Žofín.

Straddling the river at Myslíkova ulice are the modern Galerie Mánes (1928–30) and its attendant 15th-century water tower; it was from a lookout on the sixth floor that Communist-era secret police used to observe Václav Havel's apartment at Rašínovo nábřeží No. 78. This building, still part-owned by the former president, and the adjoining **Tančící dům** ❻❻ are on the far side of a square named Jiráskovo náměstí after the historical novelist Alois Jirásek. From this square, Resslova ulice leads uphill four blocks to a much larger, parklike square, **Karlovo náměstí** ❻❼. On the park's northern end is the **Novoměstská radnice** ❻❽. South of the square is the Benedictine **Klášter Emauzy** ❻❾. For a side trip that encompasses some of the city's cubist architecture, walk to Palackého náměstí via Na Moráni street at the southern end of Karlovo náměstí. The riverfront square has a melodramatic monument to the 19th-century historian František Palacký, *Awakener of the Nation,* and the view from here of the Klášter Emauzy is lovely. The houses grow less attractive south of here, so you may wish to hop a tram (No. 3, 16, or 17 at the stop on Rašínovo nábřeží) and ride one stop to Výtoň, at the base of the **Vyšehrad** ⓲ citadel. Walk under the railroad bridge on Rašínovo nábřeží to find the closest of four nearby **cubist houses** ⓱. Another lies a minute's walk farther along the embankment; two more are on Neklanova, a couple of minutes' walk "inland" on Vnislavova. To get up to the fortress, make a hard left onto Vratislavova (the street right before Neklanova), an ancient road that runs tortuously up into the center of Vyšehrad. If you prefer to go directly to Vyšehrad, take the metro to Vyšehrad from Karlovo náměstí. Following the signs to the castle, you will walk through a small neighborhood before seeing the high stone walls of the citadel.

TIMING You might want to divide the walk into two parts: first take in the busy New Town between Václavské náměstí and Karlovo náměstí, and then doing Vyšehrad and the cubist houses as a separate trip on a different day—or at least after a fortifying lunch. The castle grounds can easily absorb several hours. Vyšehrad is open every day, year-round, and the views are stunning on a day with clear skies.

What to See

★ ⓱ **Cubist houses.** Bordered to the north by Nové Město and to the south by Nusle, the Vyšehrad neighborhood is mostly known and visited for its citadel that sits high above the river on a rocky outcropping. However, fans of 20th-century architecture can find some cubist gems between the area's highwaylike riverfront street and the homes that dot the hills on the other side. Born of zealous modernism, Prague's cubist architecture followed a great Czech tradition: fully embracing new ideas while adapting them to existing artistic and social contexts. Between 1912 and 1914, Josef Chochol (1880–1956) designed several of the city's dozen or so cubist projects. His apartment house **Neklanova No. 30,** on the corner of Neklanova and Přemyslova, is a masterpiece in dingy concrete. The pyramidal, kaleidoscopic window mouldings and roof cornices are completely novel while making an expressive link to baroque forms; the faceted corner balcony column elegantly alludes to Gothic forerunners. On the same street, at **Neklanova No. 2,** is another apartment house attributed to Chochol; like the building at Neklanova No. 30, it uses pyramidal shapes and the suggestion of Gothic columns. Nearby, Chochol's **villa,** on the embankment at Libušina 3, has an undulating effect created by smoothly articulated forms. The wall and gate around the back of the house use triangular moldings and metal grating to create an effect of controlled energy. The **three-family house,** about 100 yards away from the villa at Rašínovo nábřeží 6–10, was completed slightly earlier, when Chochol's cubist style was still developing. Here, the design is touched with baroque and neoclassical influence, with a mansard roof and end gables.

⓺ **Karlovo náměstí** (Charles Square). This square began life as a cattle market, a function chosen by Charles IV when he established the New Town in 1348. The horse market (now Wenceslas Square) quickly overtook it as a livestock-trading center, and an untidy collection of shacks accumulated here until the mid-1800s, when it became a green park named for its patron. ⊠ *Bounded by Řeznická on north, U Nemocnice on south, Karlovo nám. on west, and Vodičkova on east, Nové Město.*

NEED A BREAK?

Tired of goulash? Walk up Ječná Street from Karlovo náměstí a few blocks to Melounová 2. Here you find the Mexican restaurant Banditos (☎ 224–941–096 ▭ No credit cards), offering tasty chicken, beef, and vegetarian dishes, as well as numerous cool cocktails to wash everything down. It doesn't open until noon on weekends.

⑥⑨ Klášter Emauzy (Emmaus Monastery). Another of Charles IV's gifts to the city, the Benedictine monastery sits south of Karlovo náměstí. It's often called Na Slovanech, literally "At the Slavs," which refers to its purpose when established in 1347: the emperor invited Croatian monks here to celebrate mass in Old Slavonic and thus cultivate religion among the Slavs in a city largely controlled by Germans. A faded but substantially complete cycle of Biblical scenes by Charles's court artists lines the four cloister walls. The frescoes, and especially the abbey church, suffered heavy damage from a raid by Allied bombers on February 14, 1945; it's believed they may have mistaken Prague for Dresden, 121 km (75 mi) away. The church lost its spires, and the interior remained a blackened shell until a renovation was begun in 1998; while the reconstruction work is ongoing, the church reopened to the public in 2003. ⊠ *Vyšehradská 49, cloister entrance on left at rear of church, Vyšehrad* 🎫 *20 Kč* ☉ *Weekdays 9–4.*

★ **⑥④ Mucha Museum.** For decades it was almost impossible to find an Alfons Mucha original in his homeland. In 1998 this private museum opened with nearly 100 works from this famous Czech artist's long career. What you expect to see is here—the theater posters of actress Sarah Bernhardt, the magazine covers, and the luscious, sinuous art nouveau designs. But also exhibited are paintings, photographs taken in Mucha's studio (one shows Paul Gauguin playing the piano in his underwear), and even Czechoslovak banknotes designed by the artist. ⊠ *Panská 7, 1 block off Wenceslas Sq., across from Palace Hotel, Nové Město* ☎ *221–451–333* ⊕ *www.mucha.cz* 🎫 *120 Kč* ☉ *Daily 10–6.*

FodorśChoice
★

⑥⑤ Národní divadlo (National Theater). Statues representing Drama and Opera rise above the riverfront side entrances to this theater; two gigantic chariots flank figures of Apollo and the nine Muses above the main façade. The performance space itself is filled with gilding, voluptuous plaster figures and plush upholstery. The idea for a Czech national theater began during the revolutionary decade of the 1840s. In a telling display of national pride, donations to fund the plan poured in from all over the country, from people of every socioeconomic stratum. The cornerstone was laid in 1868, and the "National Theater generation" who built the neo-Renaissance structure became the architectural and artistic establishment for decades to come. Its designer, Josef Zítek, was the leading neo-Renaissance architect in Bohemia. The nearly finished interior was gutted by a fire in 1881, and Zítek's onetime student Josef Schulz saw the reconstruction through to completion two years later. Today, it's still the country's leading dramatic stage. ⊠ *Národní třída 2, Nové Město* ☎ *224–901–377 box office* ⊕ *www.narodni-divadlo.cz.*

❻❸ **Národní muzeum** (National Museum). By day this grandiose edifice seems an inappropriate venue for a musty collection of stones and bones, minerals, and coins. But bathed in nighttime lighting, the building comes into its own displaying an imposing structure, designed by Prague architect Josef Schulz and built between 1885 and 1890. ⊠ *Václavské nám. 68, Nové Město* ☎ *224–497–111* ⊕ *www. nm.cz* ✎ *110 Kč* ☉ *May–Sept., daily 10–6; Oct.–Apr., daily 9–5; except for 1st Tues. of each month, when it's closed.*

TAKING YOU FOR A RIDE

Prague has a reputation for dishonest taxi drivers that jack up the fee on their rides. Many drivers will doctor the meter or fail to turn the meter on and then demand an exorbitant sum at the end of the ride. In an honest cab, the meter starts at about 30 Kč and increases by 25 Kč per km (½ mi) or 4 Kč per minute at rest. Most rides within town should cost no more than 150 Kč to 200 Kč. The best way to avoid getting ripped off is to ask your hotel or restaurant to call a cab for you. And remember that Prague has convenient public transportation that offers an honest alternative.

❻❽ **Novoměstská radnice** (New Town Hall). At the northern edge of Karlovo náměstí, the New Town Hall has a late-Gothic tower similar to that of the Old Town Hall, as well as three tall Renaissance gables. The first defenestration in Prague occurred here on July 30, 1419, when a mob of townspeople, followers of the martyred religious reformer Jan Hus, hurled Catholic town councillors out the windows. Historical exhibitions and contemporary art shows are held regularly in the gallery, and you can climb the tower for a view of the New Town. ⊠ *Karlovo nám. at Vodičkova, Nové Město* ✎ *Tower 40 Kč; gallery admission varies by exhibition* ☉ *Tower May–Sept., Tues.–Sun. 10–6; gallery Tues.–Sun. 10–6.*

★ ❻❷ **Statue of St. Wenceslas.** Josef Václav Myslbek's huge equestrian grouping of St. Wenceslas with other Czech patron saints around him is a traditional meeting place at times of great national peril or rejoicing. In 1939 Praguers gathered to oppose Hitler's takeover of Bohemia and Moravia. It was here also, in 1969, that the student Jan Palach set himself on fire to protest the bloody invasion of his country by the Soviet Union and other Warsaw Pact countries in August of the previous year. The invasion ended the "Prague Spring," a cultural and political movement emphasizing free expression, which was supported by Alexander Dubček, the popular reform-Communist leader at the time. And of course, in November 1989, hundreds of thousands gathered here and all along the square to demand the end of the Communist government. ⊠ *Václavské nám., Nové Město.*

★ ❻❻ **Tančící dům** (Dancing House). This whimsical building was partnered into life in 1996 by architect Frank Gehry (of Guggenheim Museum in Bilbao fame) and his Croatian-Czech collaborator Vlado Milunic. A wasp-waisted glass-and-steel tower sways into the main structure as though

Václav Havel

CLOSE UP

ONE OF THE GREAT MEN to emerge from the anti-Communist revolutions was the Czech playwright and dissident Václav Havel. The author of several anti-Communist, absurdist plays and a series of moving essays on the moral corruption of Communism, Havel captured the support of the students leading the Velvet Revolution and went on to head the country. He quickly assumed the leadership of the anti-Communist opposition and was a crucial force in negotiating the agreement that eventually led the Communists to peacefully relinquish power after 40 years of authoritarian rule.

Havel's rapid ascent from a lowly dissident to the Czech chief executive—in a matter of weeks—proves the weight of his writings. In essays like

"The Power of the Powerless," Havel spoke of the power of ordinary citizens to internally and peacefully resist the Communist authorities. His voice, it's safe to say, became the country's conscience.

Prior to 1989, he was jailed several times for his writings, and when the 1989 events came around, he was one of the few public personalities that was not compromised by the previous regime.

Havel's time as president—from 1990 until 2003, with a some breaks—was a mixed affair. But if there was a success, it was in his image abroad. It's no stretch to say that much of the adoration and attention the Czechs received after 1989 was because of their universally respected president.

they were a couple on the dance floor—a "Fred and Ginger" effect that gave the wacky, yet somehow appropriate, building its nickname. ⊠ *Rašínovo nábř. 80, Nové Město.*

★ **Václavské náměstí** (Wenceslas Square). Some 500,000 students and citizens gathered here in the heady days of November 1989 to protest the policies of the former Communist regime. The government capitulated after a week of demonstrations, without a shot fired or the loss of a single life, bringing to power the first democratic government in 40 years (under playwright-president Václav Havel). Today this peaceful transfer of power is half-ironically referred to as the "Velvet" or "Gentle" Revolution (*něžná revoluce*). It's fitting that the 1989 revolution took place on Wenceslas Square: throughout much of Czech history, the square has served as the focal point for popular discontent. The long "square" was first laid out by Charles IV in 1348 as a horse market at the center of the New Town.

At No. 25, the **Hotel Europa** (⊠ Vaclavske nám. 25) is an art nouveau gem, with elegant stained glass and mosaics in the café and restaurant. The terrace provides an excellent spot for people-watching. Note in particular the ornate sculpture work of two figures supporting a glass egg on top of the building and the exterior mural. In 1906 when the hotel opened, this was a place for the elite; now the dilapidated rooms reflect more a sense of sadly faded grandeur that thankfully hasn't extended to the public spaces.

🐚 **⑳** **Vyšehrad.** Bedřich Smetana's symphonic poem *Vyšehrad* opens with four bardic harp chords that seem to echo the legends surrounding this ancient fortress. Today, the flat-top bluff stands over the right bank of the Vltava as a green, tree-dotted expanse showing few signs that splendid medieval monuments once made it a landmark to rival Prague Castle.

The namesake of Vyšehrad, or the "High Castle," is Vratislav II (ruled 1061–92), a Přemyslid duke who became the first king of Bohemia. He made the fortified hilltop his capital, but under subsequent rulers, it fell into disuse until the 14th century, when Charles IV transformed the site into an ensemble of palaces, the main church, battlements, and a massive gatehouse called *Špička*, whose scant remains are on V Pevnosti ulice. By the 17th century royalty had long since departed, and most of the structures they built were crumbling. Vyšehrad was turned into a fortress.

Vyšehrad's place in the modern Czech imagination is largely thanks to the National Revivalists of the 19th century, particularly writer Alois Jirásek, who mined medieval chronicles for legends and facts to glorify the early Czechs.

Traces of the citadel's distant past can be found at every turn, and are reflected even in the structure chosen for the visitor center, the remains of a Gothic stone fortification wall known as **Špička**, or Peak Gate, at the corner of V Pevnosti and U Podolského Sanatoria. Farther ahead is the sculpture-covered **Leopold Gate,** which stands next to brick walls enlarged during the 1742 occupation by the French. Out of the gate, a heavily restored **Romanesque rotunda,** built by Vratislav II in the 11th century, stands on the corner of K Rotundě and Soběslavova. It's considered the oldest fully intact Romanesque building in the city. Down Soběslavova are the excavated foundations and a few embossed floor tiles from the late-10th-century **Basilika svatého Vavřince** (St. Lawrence Basilica). The foundations, discovered in 1884 while workers were creating a cesspool, are in a baroque structure at Soběslavova 14. The remains are from one of the few early-Medieval buildings to have survived in the area and are worth a look. On the western side of Vyšehrad, part of the fortifications stand next to the surprisingly confined foundation mounds of a medieval palace overlooking a ruined watchtower called **Libuše's Bath,** which precariously juts out of a rocky outcropping over the river. A nearby plot of grass hosts a statue of Libuše and her consort Přemysl, one of four large, sculpted images of couples from Czech legend by J. V. Myslbek (1848–1922), the sculptor of the St. Wenceslas monument.

The military history of the fortress and the city is covered in a small exposition inside the Cihelná brána (Brick Gate), but the real attraction is the **casemates,** a long, dark passageway within the walls that ends at a dank hall used to store several original, pollution-scarred Charles Bridge sculptures. A guided tour into the casemates and the statue storage room starts at the military history exhibit; it has a separate admission fee.

Karel Čapek

WHEN CZECHS ARE ASKED TO NAME THE WRITER WHO'S done the best work with their notoriously difficult language, the name that most often comes up is Karel Čapek. Čapek, who wrote in the first half of the 20th century, is almost unknown today outside his native land. He's perhaps best known for introducing the word *robot* to the world, thanks to his first major success as a playwright in 1921, *R. U. R.* (Rossum's Universal Robots), a satire of the Czech agrarian system. His essay, "Why I Am Not a Communist," was published in 1924, long before Communists took over the Czech Republic. The novel *War with the Newts*—a satire of dictatorships—and a series of interviews with the president of Czechoslovakia, Tomaš Garrique Masaryk, stand out as

Čapek's best work. Čapek earned his master's degree in philosophy and was not only a writer but also an editor of the newspaper *Lidové noviny* (*The People's Paper*).

When France and Britain signed the Munich Agreement, ordering Czechoslovakia to leave its border regions to Germany, Čapek was offered the possibility of exile in England. He chose to remain in Prague even though the decision meant risking his life. During the Nazi occupation, his writings were banned as anti-fascist. Čapek's works later suffered, posthumously, under the Communists as well. Čapek eventually succumbed to pneumonia on December 25, 1938, at the age of 48. His works are still widely translated today.

With its neo-Gothic spires, **Kapitulní kostel svatých Petra a Pavla** (Chapter Church of Sts. Peter and Paul; ✉ K rotundě 10, Vyšehrad ☎ 224–911–353) dominates the plateau as it has since the 11th century. Next to the church lies the burial ground of the nation's revered cultural figures. Most of the buildings still standing are from the 19th century, but scattered among them are a few older structures and some foundation stones of the medieval palaces. Surrounding the ruins are gargantuan, excellently preserved brick fortifications built from the 17th to the mid-19th century; their broad tops allow you to take in sweeping vistas along the riverbank. The church is open daily from 9 to noon and 1 to 5, with an admission charge of 10 Kč.

FodorśChoice ★ A concrete result of the national revival was the establishment of the **Hřbitov** (cemetery) in the 1860s, adjacent to the Church of Sts. Peter and Paul. It filled the fortress with the remains of luminaries from the arts and sciences. The grave of Smetana faces the Slavín, a mausoleum for more than 50 honored men and women including Alfons Mucha, sculptor Jan Štursa, inventor František Křižík, and the opera diva Ema Destinnová. All are guarded by a winged genius who hovers above the inscription AČ ZEMŘELI, JEŠTĚ MLUVÍ ("Although they have died, they yet speak"). Antonín Dvořák (1841–1904) rests in the arcade along the north wall of the cemetery. Among the many writers buried here are Jan Neruda, Božena Němcová, Karel Čapek, and the Romantic poet Karel Hynek Mácha, whose grave was visited by students on their momentous November 17, 1989, protest march. ⊠ *V Pevnosti 159/5b, Vyšehrad* 📞 *241–410–348* ⊕ *www.praha-vysehrad.cz* 🎫 *Grounds and cemetery free, casemates tour 30 Kč, military history exhibit 10 Kč, St. Lawrence Basilica 10 Kč* ☾ *Grounds daily. Casemates, military history exhibit, and St. Lawrence Basilica Apr.–Oct., daily 9:30–5:30; Nov.–Mar., daily 9:30–4:30. Cemetery Apr.–Oct. daily 8–6; Nov.–Mar. daily 8–4* Ⓜ *Line C: Vyšehrad.*

NEED A BREAK?

If you're ready for a beer or soft drink, **U Vyšehradské rotundy** (⊠ K Rotundě 3) provides good, freshly prepared meals of the pork and chicken variety in a normally quiet little pub. In summer there's a small terrace for outside dining. The restaurant stays open seven days a week.

VINOHRADY

From Riegrovy Park the eclectic apartment houses and villas of the elegant residential neighborhood called Vinohrady extend eastward and southward. The pastel-tint formation of turn-of-the-20th-century apartment houses—which not long ago were still crumbling after years of neglect—are slowly but unstoppably being transformed into upscale flats, slick offices, eternally packed restaurants, and all manner of shops. Much of the development lies on or near Vinohradská, the main street, which extends from the top of Wenceslas Square to a belt of enormous cemeteries about 3 km (2 mi) eastward. Yet the flavor of daily life persists: smoky old pubs still ply their trade on the quiet side streets; the stately theater, Divadlo na Vinohradech, keeps putting on excellent shows as it has for decades; and on the squares and in the parks nearly everyone still practices Prague's favorite form of outdoor exercise—walking the dog.

72 **Kostel Nejsvětějšího Srdce Páně** (Church of the Most Sacred Heart). If you had your fill of romanesque, Gothic, and baroque, this church will give you a look at a startling modernist–art deco edifice. Designed in 1927 by Slovenian architect Josip Plečnik (the same architect commissioned to update Prague Castle), the church resembles a luxury ocean liner more than a place of worship. The effect was conscious: during the 1920s and 1930s, the avant-garde imitated mammoth objects of modern technology. Plečnik used many modern elements on the inside. You may be able to find someone at the back entrance of the church who will let you walk up the long ramp into the fascinating glass clock tower. ⊠ *Nám. Jiřího z Poděbrad, Vinohrady* 🎫 *Free* ☾ *Daily 10–5* Ⓜ *Line A: Jiřího z Poděbrad.*

74 **Muzeum Antonína Dvořáka** (Antonín Dvořák Museum). The baroque red-and-yellow villa housing this museum displays the 19th-century Czech composer's scores, photographs, viola, piano, and other memorabilia. The statues in the garden date from about 1735; the house from 1720. Check the schedule for classical performances, as recitals are often held in the first floor of the two-story villa. ⊠ *Ke Karlovu 20, Vinohrady* 📞 *224–918–013* 🎫 *50 Kč* ☾ *Tues.–Sun. 10–1, 2–5* Ⓜ *Line C: I. P. Pavlova.*

73 **Nový židovský hřbitov** (New Jewish Cemetery). Tens of thousands of Czechs found eternal rest in Vinohrady's cemeteries. In this, the newest of the city's half-dozen Jewish burial grounds, you can find the modest **tombstone of Franz Kafka**, which seems grossly inadequate to Kafka's fame but oddly in proportion to his own modest ambitions. The cemetery is usually open, although guards sometimes inexplicably seal off the grounds. Men may be required to wear a yarmulke (you can buy one here if you need to). Turn right at the main cemetery gate and follow the wall for about 100 yards. Kafka's thin white tombstone lies at the front of section 21. City maps may label the cemetery *Židovské hřbitovy.* ⊠ *Vinohradská at Jana Želivského, Vinohrady* ☉ *June–Aug., Sun.–Thurs. 9–5, Fri. 9–1; Sept.–May, Sun.–Thurs. 9–4, Fri. 9–1* Ⓜ *Line A: Želivského.*

LETNÁ & HOLEŠOVICE

From above the Vltava's left bank, the large, grassy plateau called Letná gives you one of the classic views of the Old Town and the many bridges crossing the river. (To get to Letná from the Old Town, take Pařížská Street north, cross the Čechův Bridge, and climb the stairs.) Beer gardens, tennis, and Frisbee attract people of all ages, while amateur soccer players emulate the professionals of Prague's top team, Sparta, which plays in the stadium just across the road. A 10-minute walk from Letná, down into the residential neighborhood of Holešovice, brings you to a massive, gray-blue building, with a cool exterior giving no hint to the Czech and French modern art treasures that honor its corridors. Just north along Dukelských hrdinů Street is Stromovka—a royal hunting preserve turned gracious park.

Numbers in the margin correspond to numbers on the Exploring Prague map.

76 **Křížikova fontána** (Kříž Fountain). Still functioning, this pressurized water and colored-light show was originally built for the Jubilee Industrial Exhibition of 1891. Occasionally, live music accompanies the spectacle of lights, but more often recorded programs of film music, classics, or rock play over the illuminated dancing waters. František Křížik, who built the fountain, was a famous inventor of his day and a friend of Thomas Edison. ⊠ *Výstaviště, exhibition grounds, Holešovice* ☏ *220–103–224* ⊕ *www.krizikovafontana.cz* Ⓜ *Line C: Nádraží Holešovice.*

79 **Lapidárium.** A fascinating display of 11th- to 19th-century sculptures saved from torn-down buildings or the vicissitudes of Prague's weather are sheltered here. Some of the original Charles Bridge statues can be found here as well as a towering bronze monument to Field Marshall Radetsky, a leader of the 19th-century Austrian army. Pieces of a marble fountain that once stood in Old Town Square now occupy most of one room. For horse lovers, there are several fine equestrian statues inside. ⊠ *Výstaviště 422, Holešovice* ☏ *233–375–636* ⊕ *www.nm.cz* 🎟 *40 Kč* ☉ *Tues.–Fri. 12–6, weekends 10–6* Ⓜ *Line C: Vltavská.*

75 **Letenské sady** (Letná Park). Come to this large, shady park for an un-forgettable view of Prague's bridges. From the enormous cement pedestal at the center of the park, the largest statue of Stalin in Eastern Europe once beckoned to citizens on the Old Town Square far below. The statue was ripped down in the early 1960s, when Stalinism was finally discredited. On sunny Sundays expatriates often meet up here to play ultimate Frisbee. Head east on Milady Horáové street after exiting the metro. ☒ *Letná* Ⓜ *Line A: Hradčanská.*

76 **Národní Technické muzeum** (National Technical Museum). Planes, trains, and automobiles dating from the 19th through the 20th century can all be found within this museum's massive Transport Hall. The upper levels showcase technical advancements in cinematography and measuring time and also include a collection of astronomical instruments. Underneath the structure, a reconstruction of a coal mine and its assortment of heavy machinery challenges the claustrophobic. ☒ *Kostelní 42, Holešovice* ☎ *220–399–111* ⊕ *www.ntm.cz* ☒ *70 Kč* ☉ *Tues.–Sun. 9–5* Ⓜ *Line C: Vltavská.*

77 **Veletržní palác** (Trade Fair Palace). The National Gallery's **Sbírka moderního a soucasného umění** (Collection of Modern and Contemporary Art) has become a keystone in the city's visual-arts scene since its opening in 1995. Touring the vast spaces of this 1920s constructivist exposition hall and its comprehensive collection of 20th-century Czech art is the best way to see how Czechs surfed the forefront of the avant-garde wave until the cultural freeze following World War II. Also on display are works by Western European—mostly French—artists from Delacroix to the present. Especially noteworthy are the early cubist paintings by Picasso and Braque. Watch the papers and posters for information on traveling shows and temporary exhibits. The collection is divided into sections, so be sure to get a ticket for exactly what you want to see. ☒ *Dukelských hrdinů 47, Holešovice* ☎ *224–301–024* ⊕ *www.ngprague. cz* ☒ *One floor 100 Kč, 2 floors 150 Kč, 3 floors 200 Kč, 4 floors 250 kč, special exhibits 40 Kč* ☉ *Tues., Wed., and Fri.–Sun. 10–6, Thurs. 10–9* Ⓜ *Line C: Vltavská.*

TROJA

North of Holešovice on the banks of the Vltava, the City Gallery Prague has a branch at Troja Château. Nearby are the Prague Botanical Gardens and the zoo. This area makes a nice half-day trip if you want to get out of the city-center, but it's distant enough from the main part of town that it's bothersome to visit without several free hours.

81 **Botanická zahrada** (Botanical Gardens). The garden's newest addition, a snaking 429-foot greenhouse that simulates three different environments, has been drawing large crowds ever since it opened to visitors in summer 2004. Its path first takes you through a semidesert environment, then through a tunnel beneath a tropical lake and into a rain forest; you end up cooling off in a room devoted to plants found in tropical mountains. Sliding doors and computer-control climate systems help keep it all together. ☒ *Nadvorni 134, Troja* ☎ *234–148–111* ⊕ *www.*

botgarden.cz 💷 *90 Kč* ⊗ *Tues.–Sun. 9–7* Ⓜ *Line C: Nádraží Holešovicé, then Bus 112.*

㊷ Trojský zámek (Troja Château). Built in the late 17th century for the Czech nobleman Count Šternberg, this sprawling summer residence, modeled on a classical Italian villa, had the first French-style gardens in Bohemia. Inside, rich frescoes that took more than 20 years to complete depict the stories of emperors. Outside, a sweeping staircase is adorned with statues of the sons of Mother Earth. ⊠ *U trojského zámku 1, Troja* ☎ *283–851–614* ⊕ *www.citygalleryprague.cz* 💷 *100 Kč* ⊗ *Apr.–Sept. 10–6; Oct.–Mar. 10–5* Ⓜ *Line C: Nádraží Holešovice, then Bus 112.*

㊽ ㊿ Zoologická zahrada v Praze (Prague Zoo). Flora, fauna, and fresh air are the main things you can find in Prague's zoo. Hit hard by the floods in 2002, the zoo has been cleaned up and grants a break from the bustle of the city. Covering 160 acres on a slope overlooking the Vltava River, the zoo has thousands of animals representing 500 species. Take the chairlift for an outstanding view of the area. ⊠ *U trojského zámku 3, Troja* ☎ *296–112–111* ⊕ *www.zoopraha.cz* 💷 *90 Kč* ⊗ *May–Sept. 9–7; Oct.–Apr. 9–4* Ⓜ *Line C: Nádraží Holešovice, then Bus 112.*

ŽIŽKOV

For Prague residents, Žižkov is synonymous with pubs. There are more places to knock back a Pilsener Urquell or a shot of Fernet Stock per square inch here than anywhere else in the city, giving it a kind of seedy reputation that it doesn't deserve. Nowadays the district is starting to recoup. Some of the city's coolest cafés, clubs, and trendy apartments have opened up here. There are still some—in fact lots of—crumbling, rundown areas, but it's also one of the most interesting districts in the city for its nightlight and dining.

㊴ National Memorial. Situated on Vítkov Hill, one of the high points in the city, this stone building contains one outstanding feature: the largest equestrian statue in the world—a 16.5-ton metal structure of Hussite leader Jan Žižka on horseback. In the past the 20th-century memorial was a final resting place for post-war presidents; now, the eerily quiet mausoleum is a popular spot for movie shoots. ⊠ *U Památníku, Žižkov* ☎ *222–781–676* ⊕ *www.nm.cz* 💷 *150 Kč includes tour* ⊗ *By appointment only* Ⓜ *Lines B & C: Florenc.*

㊳ Žižkov TV Tower. Looking like a rocket ready to blast off, the Žižkov TV Tower came under fire from area residents, who claimed it gave their children cancer soon after it began operating in 1990. The eighth-floor platform, reached by a high-speed elevator, gives a bird's-eye view of the numerous courtyards and apartment blocks that make up the city, but in truth, it's almost too tall to give a good view of the low-slung city. Once back down on the ground, look up its 709-foot gray steel legs at the bronze statues of babies crawling on the structure, which were created by local artist David Černy. ⊠ *Mahlerovy sady, Žižkov* ☎ *267–005–778* 💷 *60 Kč* ⊗ *Daily 10 AM–11 PM* Ⓜ *Line A: Jiřího z Poděbrad.*

Where to Eat

WORD OF MOUTH

"Scene: Dark basement restaurant called Amfora. Waitress has just brought dessert menus to our table.

I ask, 'What would you recommend for dessert?'

'We have delicious pancaky for you, yes?'

'Yes, we will have pancaky!!!'

"We now LOVE pancaky? (For those of you who don't understand, pancaky are pancakes stuffed with fruit, whipped cream, ice cream, or chocolate.)" —ThinGorjus

"I have never heard them called that, and I have been to Prague 8 times! The proper way to order them is 'palacinky.' " —amp322

By Evan Rail

HERE'S A BOAST FROM A PRAGUE TRANSPLANT: the best restaurants in this city offer more variety, deeper flavors, and higher culinary quality than anywhere else in this part of the world. In the former Eastern Bloc, only the hippest destinations of what used to be East Berlin and the best addresses in Budapest even come close to comparing. Several movements in Prague contributed to raising the culinary bar. To start, in the years following the Velvet Revolution a sizeable group of foreign restaurateurs—Norwegian, Swedish, French, Korean, Cuban, British, and American—opened eateries like the ones they knew back home. Around the same time, a second group of foreign-trained Czech chefs and returned emigrés started to marry French and Italian culinary notions with local ingredients and the traditional recipes of old Bohemia. And now, a younger, post-'89 generation of Czech chefs and diners are starting to bring a fresh cosmopolitan perspective and an open mind to what was once purely meat-and-potatoes country.

But that kind of good eating comes at a price, and when the quality crescendos, the bill often does as well. Increasingly, real bargains are difficult to find in a city that is becoming less a part of Eastern Europe than a part of, well, just plain Europe.

Moreover, it's easy to be disappointed; many places are only out to make a fast buck on the one-time tourist trade. In the city's center, these pushy restaurants advertise their wares with conspicuously placed menus on the sidewalk and noisy English-language signs of dubious grammar. (When restaurants are serving good food, they don't need to announce AIR CONDITION on the windows to attract business.) Places that use English-speaking touts on the street are rarely good options, and they are often the ones that will add an extra couple of beers to the bill. Sadly, the areas of the city that are the most interesting to travelers—Malá Strana, the Castle Area, Old Town, and Wenceslas Square—are the areas where it can be hardest to find a decent bite at a fair price.

And yet many great places exist, often just around the corner from the rip-offs. Even with so many visitors, Prague still caters to locals and visitors looking for something genuine. Right in the middle of the most touristy areas you can find wonderful options ranging from a boisterous traditional *hospoda* (pub) to an elegant restaurant of international standards.

Service is also improving, though it can be frustratingly inconsistent. And the international trend toward no-smoking restaurants is gaining a foothold in Prague as more and more restaurants offer no-smoking sections.

For the traditional recipes of Bohemia and Moravia, some of the plainest meat and dumplings dishes

---

EVAN'S TOP 5 PRAGUE DISHES

1. Valleta's grilled chicken with goat cheese and avocado
2. Aromi's pasta trio with fresh porcini, veal ragout, and black truffles
3. Allegro's pan-seared *wugyu* beef with grilled asparagus
4. Don Pedro's *bandeja paisa*
5. Cowboys' double-cut grilled rib-eye steak

are being updated with better ingredients—wild duck, goose, and venison—and improved techniques. In fact many chefs don't just look abroad for inspiration, but they mine the rich tradition of Czech cooking for overlooked recipes from the 19th century and earlier.

That said, it can be hard to find typical "Czech" dishes on menus at the better restaurants—especially in the city's center. When Czechs eat out, they want to try something different from the ubiquitous roast pork and dumplings or goulash served at home. In general it's easier finding Czech food at lunch time, when many places offer a two- or three-course *denní lístek* (daily special), usually at sharply discounted prices.

STARÉ MĚSTO (OLD TOWN)

ASIAN
$$$$

✕ **Barock.** As a break from sightseeing, the location can't be beat: Barock's sidewalk tables gaze across at the Old-New Synagogue. Most of the buzz here is for how it looks: walls bathed in matte scarlet, deep-dish orange chairs, and recessed mood lighting make a chic statement, suiting the stylish address on boutique-heavy Pařížská. But Barock remains a popular destination in its own right, in part due to the open-passport approach in the kitchen: crunchy Vietnamese spring rolls, spicy Thai soups and curries, fresh Mediterranean seafood, Continental salads, and hearty Czech classics like roast duck all meet on the same menu. ⊠ *Pařížská 24, Josefov* ☏ *222–329–221* ▭ *AE, DC, MC, V* Ⓜ *Line A: Staroměstská.*

$–$$$

✕ **Orange Moon.** Excellent Burmese, Thai, and Indian dishes draw tourists and locals alike to this reasonably priced spot a short walk from Old Town Square. The two levels are slightly dim and atmospheric, with blond-wood fixtures, orange walls, and photographs of Asian scenes giving a mood-boosting effect. Burmese curried noodles, chicken soup with coconut milk and lemongrass, and beef kebabs with Madras curry represent just three outstanding items from a consistently good menu. ⊠ *Rámova 5, Staré Město* ☏ *222–325–119* ▭ *AE, DC, MC, V* Ⓜ *Line B: Náěstí Republiky.*

BRAZILIAN
$$–$$$

✕ **Brasileiro.** Carnivores, loosen your belts! This busy cellar packs in the crowds with all-you-can-eat *churrasco* (grilled meats) served in the Brazilian *rodizio* style: waiter-chefs carrying overflowing platters of roast beef flank, pork ribs, veal, octopus, prawns, squid, and more constantly proffer portions until you finally signal your submission by turning over the green sign on your table to expose the red "stop" sign underneath. If you're a vegetarian, have no fear: an all-you-can-eat salad buffet is offered at a lower price and includes orange salad with cilantro, couscous with raisins, garlic broccoli, olives, and more. It's fun, fast-paced, and filling, with a cheaper tab if you get the bill before 6 PM. ⊠ *U Radnice 8, Staré Město* ☏ *224–234–474* ▭ *MC, V* Ⓜ *Line A: Staroměstská.*

CONTEMPORARY
★ $$$–$$$$

✕ **La Veranda.** Aphrodisiac menus and seasonal specials are but two of the reasons to consider this elegant dining room and lounge near the Jewish Quarter. A third is Radek David, a culinary juggernaut with an eye for unusual flavor combinations, sending out dishes like foie gras with *gloeg* jelly, sautéed scallops with truffle risotto, goat cheese with eggplant puree, and Parmesan-stuffed cannelloni. Despite the achievements and the acclaim, La Veranda remains somewhat overlooked, making a visit to this stylish, softly lighted room feel like you've been let in on a wonderful secret. ⊠ *Elišky Krásnohorské 2, Staré Město* ☎ *224–814–733* ▤ *AE, DC, MC, V* Ⓜ *Line A: Staroměstská.*

$$$–$$$$ ✕ **Le Terroir.** The finest wines available to humanity can be found here along with cuisine of the extremely haute variety: coq au vin with Beaujolais, Bigorre suckling pig with spaetzle, fresh brioche and rich veal sweetbreads with a sticky dark beer sauce, and poached crayfish with savory caviar. Don't forget the cheese course, as this restaurant has its own cheese room stocking rarities from France and Italy. But wine provides the real lure, and bottles here start around $30 and head off into the upper stratosphere, with the list separated into minute geographic distinctions: the listing for "Bordeaux" has nine subcategories. The clublike cellar is romantic and chic, but open-air dining on the patio is a must in spring and summer. ⊠ *Vejvodova 1, Staré Město* ☎*222–220–260* ▤*AE, MC, V* Ⓜ *Line A or B: Můstek.*

> ### PIVO, PROSÍM (BEER, PLEASE)
>
> *Pivnice* is a Czech beer hall named after *pivo*, meaning beer. Expect a range of beer, usually drunk in high quantities along with simple snacks.

$$$–$$$$ Fodor'sChoice ★ ✕ **Pravda.** Incredibly cosmopolitan, Pravda offers a menu that careens from country to country like a fickle jet pilot. Indonesian sea bass with ginger-coriander sauce, Norwegian salmon with Greenland shrimp, steaming Spanish paella, spicy Moroccan chicken, and rich Alaskan cod with squid-ink risotto are just a few of the intercontinental specialties on the menu. The crowd is multinational as well, including tourists who visit the next-door Old-New Synagogue, Czech and international money men, American expats, and globe-trotting pretty young things. Pravda is slightly more formal in mood than equally slick sister restaurant Barock across the street. ⊠ *Pařížská 17, Josefov* ☎ *222–326–203* ▤ *AE, DC, MC, V* Ⓜ *Line A: Staroměstská.*

$$–$$$ ✕ **Ambiente–Pasta Fresca.** Offering a world beyond mere pasta, the second member of the Ambiente chain has the group's trademark sharp service and a better setting, thanks largely to its location under a high stone-rimmed vaulted ceiling in the cellar of a baroque-era building. It's a mainstay for the business crowd at lunchtime, and the clientele in the evening ranges from locals out on the town to tourists who just wandered in. Whenever you go, soft lighting, candles, and excellent service ensure stress-free dining. ⊠ *Celetná 11, Staré Město* ☎ *224–230–244* ▤ *AE, DC, MC, V* Ⓜ *Line A or B: Můstek.*

CONTINENTAL
$$$$ ✕ **Bellevue.** Come for the setting cast off by the stately 19th-century parlor and elevated by panoramic views of the Vltava River, Prague Castle, and Petřín Hill. The food is similarly sophisticated: homemade pumpkin ravioli with sage butter, venison consommé with veal-liver gnocchi, roast pike-perch with fragrant mushroom risotto, and juicy, herb-encrusted lamb chops with tangy mint sauce are but a few of the seasonal

KNOW-HOW

MEALTIMES

Most restaurants in Prague are open from about 11 AM to 11 PM. This closing time is very regular with traditional Czech restaurants and *hospody* (pubs); their kitchens usually shut down by 10 PM and sometimes earlier if it's a slow night. A small number of restaurants serve the late-night crowd, especially in the city center, but don't put off dinner too long or you may have trouble finding an open kitchen. Some restaurants in neighborhoods outside of the center close on Sunday or open only for dinner, but in the heavily touristed areas, hours remain the same every day. Mealtimes hold to the European standard. Lunch runs from noon until 2 PM; dinner starts at 6 PM and runs until about 8 PM or 9 PM. Czechs don't generally linger over meals, but you'll rarely feel any pressure from the staff to vacate your table.

MENUS

Most restaurants post menus outside. Prix-fixe menus are not popular in the evening, but many restaurants offer a *denní lístek* (daily menu) of three or four items that usually include a soup starter and a simple main course. If you want to try a traditional Czech meal, such as *svíčková* (beef in cream sauce) or *guláš* (a bit thicker and less oily than the Hungarian version), you may find that it's only offered at lunchtime in most restaurants outside of Prague 1.

RESERVATIONS

The need for a reservation varies with the season and the weather—warm summer weather presents the biggest challenge. If you have your heart set on a particular spot, and it's a busy time of day, it's best to drop in or call ahead.

SMOKING

Smoking is popular in Prague. Some of the expensive restaurants have no-smoking sections, but few others do. In traditional Czech establishments, such as *hospody* (pubs) and *pivnice* (beer halls), you may be overwhelmed by the amount of cigarette smoke.

WHAT TO WEAR

At most moderately priced and inexpensive restaurants, casual but neat dress is acceptable. In restaurant listings, dress is mentioned only when men are expected to wear a jacket or a jacket and tie, which is seldom the case.

WINE

Sure, the Czech Republic is more famous for beer than wine, but wines are coming into their own now, especially the whites, which are suited to this relatively northern climate. You can almost always order wines by the glass, though more expensive vintages are usually available by the bottle only. So-called *archivní* (vintage) wines, despite being expensive, are not necessarily better. Moravian wines, such as those from *Valtice*, are often the best bets.

The most popular Czech whites are *Müller-Thurgau* and *Ryzlink* Riesling); of these, domestic Rieslings tend to be the better choice. Czech sauvignon blanc, though harder to find, can be of exceptional quality. After that, four or five varietals can appear on menus, and these are hit and miss.

Two of the most popular reds are frankovka and svatovavřinecké. If you're in an inexpensive restaurant, you may find that the frankovkas are inferior, so try to avoid them. After these, cabernet sauvignon is popular, but regardless of the variety, the Czech reds are generally much lighter in body than the wines of Australia, France, or California.

Most restaurants, aside from pubs, offer a selection of international wines.

PRICES

In better restaurants, prices are slightly lower but generally comparable to what you would find in North America or Western Europe. In traditional Czech restaurants and *hospody*, especially outside the city center, price levels are much lower, and can drop to a rock-bottom 70 Kč on the *denní lístek* (daily menu).

Watch for a *couvert* (cover charge), which may appear in smaller print on a menu. Though a bit annoying, it's legitimate and is meant to cover bread, a caddy of condiments, and/or service. Remember that side orders usually have to be ordered separately and so will be tabulated accordingly. Taxes are included with all meal prices listed in the menu.

PAYING

In a more traditional dining venue, such as a Czech *restaurace* or hospoda, it's possible that the person you ordered from will not be the person who tallies your bill. In that case, you may hear your waiter say *kolega*, meaning a colleague will bring the bill. This situation is less likely in more modern establishments. In the bulk of low- and mid-price restaurants, the waiter or bill person will tally your bill in front of you and stand by while you pull together the money to pay. If you want to do it the Czech way, quickly add on a suitable amount for a tip in your head, and say this new total when you hand over your money. If you need a bit of time, it's best to politely smile and say *moment, prosím* (one moment please). Don't panic if you miss the moment; many people don't make the calculation quickly enough and just leave the money on the table. In the places frequented by tourists, particularly in the city center, the waiter (or a colleague) may expect this already and just leave the bill on the table for you.

Tipping in the Czech Republic has been based traditionally on rounding up the tab to a convenient number rather than calculating a percentage and adding it on, and in the hospody around the city (especially out of the tourist area) this is still how it's done. For example, paying 150 Kč on a bill of 137 Kč would be perfectly acceptable (though locals might stop at 140 Kč). At the better places, a 10% tip is common to recognize good food and service.

WHAT IT COSTS in Czech koruna					
	$$$$	**$$$**	**$$**	**$**	**¢**
AT DINNER	over 500	300–500	150–300	100–150	under 100

Prices are per person for a main course at dinner and include 19% V.A.T.

recipes served here. Be sure to make it clear that you want a seat with a view, as several of the tables have their views blocked by the linden trees along the river. ⊠ *Smetanovo nábř. 18, Staré Město* ☎ *222–221–449* ▭ *AE, MC, V* Ⓜ *Line A: Staroměstská.*

$$$$ ✕ **U Závoje.** This gastronomic beachhead contains a wine bar and wine store, a day café, a cheese shop, a brandy retailer, and this exclusive cellar restaurant—which raids all the best supplies upstairs. Fine wines from around the world are given a place of pride in the restaurant, supported by elaborate cuisine: scallops with Périgord truffles and stewed celery, black lentils with black-pepper tuna, Canadian lobster, roast duck, and venison with cranberries and chanterelles. Be sure to save room—the fig strudel and tarte tatin with walnut ice cream represent a sweet pinnacle for desserts in Central Europe. ⊠ *Havelská 25, Staré Město* ☎ *226–006–111* ▭ *MC, V* Ⓜ *Line A or B: Můstek.*

CZECH ✕ **Kolkovna.** For Czechs and expatriates living in Prague, this is one of
★ **$–$$$** the most popular spots to take visitors for a taste of local cuisine without the stress of tourist rip-offs and dingy neighborhoods. The wood-and-copper decor gives off an appropriate air of a brewery taproom, and you can wash down traditional meals—such as *svíčkova* (beef tenderloin in cream sauce), roast duck, and fried pork cutlets, or upgrades of traditional food, such as turkey steak with Roquefort sauce and walnuts—with a mug of unpasteurized Pilsner Urquell. ⊠ *V Kolkovně, Staré Město* ☎ *224–818–701* ▭ *AE, MC, V* Ⓜ *Line A: Staroměstská.*

$–$$ ✕ **Kavárna Slavia.** Easily the city's best-known café, Slavia serves good
Fodor'sChoice coffee, drinks, and light snacks, as well as the standards of Czech cui-
★ sine: roast duck with potato dumplings and sauerkraut, beef goulash, and roast smoked pork with white cabbage and potato pancakes. Sandwiches and quotidian pasta plates offer lighter, less-expensive options, though aesthetes can make a full meal out of the rich views of the National Theater, the Vltava, and Prague Castle. This spectacular location has a historic air that winds from the days of Viktor Oliva's painting "The Absinth Drinker" (which hangs in the main room), through the era of the playwright and regular patron Václav Havel, and continues into the modern day. ⊠ *Smetanovo nábř. 1012/2, Staré Město* ☎ *224–218–493* ▭ *AE, MC, V* Ⓜ *Line B: Národní Třida.*

DELICATESSENS ✕ **Bohemia Bagel.** This Czech cousin of a college-town bagel shop, de-
¢–$ spite its thick accent, wouldn't feel out of place in Berkeley or Boston. This branch of Bohemia Bagel has a boisterous, morning-after feel. Though they've got nothing on those from the Big Apple, the bagels are a favorite for homesick expats, as are the bottomless cups of filter coffee and the free bulletin board postings, making this place not just a deli but a community center. Offerings include a classic BLT, lox with cream cheese and capers, as well as eggs, pancakes, hash browns, and other usual breakfast staples. ⊠ *Masná 2, Staré Město* ☎ *224–812–560* ▭ *No credit cards* Ⓜ *Line A: Staromětska.*

2

ECLECTIC
$$$–$$$$
✕ **Šípek Bistrot.** Art glass mixes with artful cooking in this surreal salon from designer and architect Bořek Šípek. The glasses, plates, and fixtures are all designed in the artist's whimsical style: bright colors, glossy surfaces, exaggerated angles, and vinelike elongations. The menu is equally quirky: lamb combines with garlic-pepper marinade and rosemary mascarpone, a thick beef steak comes with truffled sabayon sauce, and the sea bass is served with foie gras risotto. Desserts are the ultimate in self-indulgence, such as the baked pear flavored with star anise and dipped in a thick syrup made of sweet Tokay wine. Šípek Bistrot is intimate and truly one-of-a-kind. ⊠ *Valentinská 9, Staré Město* ☏ *222–323–948* ▭ *MC, V* Ⓜ *Line A: Staromětska.*

$–$$$
✕ **Dinitz Café.** The contemporary fusion cuisine of Israel shines at this capacious café and club near Obecní dům. Though it looks old, the Mondrian-inspired design is very much of the moment, matching the hip electronic sound track, and the kitchen strives for a similarly modern approach: the smoky gravlax is made in-house and the chicken liver spread is enriched with goose fat and accompanied by homemade strawberry preserves. Entrées feature inexpensive sandwiches, pastas, and voluminous salads in the Israeli mold: chop up a little bit of everything and throw it in the bowl. Desserts are excellent, too, including the city's best lemon cheesecake. ⊠ *Na poříčí 12, Staré Město* ☏ *222–314–071* ▭ *MC, V* Ⓜ *Line B: Nám. Republiky.*

ITALIAN
$$$$
Fodor'sChoice
★
✕ **Allegro.** The chef Vito Mollica isn't the main draw here: that honor belongs to his cooking. Mr. Mollica serves luscious dishes from around Italy with seasonal menus celebrating artisanal products and rare treats like Alba truffles and 30-year-old balsamic vinegar. To say the chef and the restaurant have raised the bar for Prague dining is an understatement in the extreme. Main courses have included such delights as monkfish saltimbocca, yellowfin tuna carpaccio, and house-made gnocchi with rabbit. Regularly recognized as one of the best Italian kitchens in Central Europe, Allegro is a treat for those who indulge in the top of the line. ⊠ *Four Seasons Prague, Veleslavinova 21, Staré Město* ☏ *221–427–000* ⌞ *Reservations essential* ▭ *AE, DC, MC, V* Ⓜ *Line A: Staroměstska.*

★ $$$–$$$$
✕ **Divinis.** An oenophile's dream, this rough-hewn wine bar and cozy restaurant is hip without being arch, and casual without coming close to slouching on style. Rare delicacies show up on the appetizer menu, including regional Spanish hams and uncommon cured meats from Italy, while main courses are almost always limited to a few seasonal choices, all expertly prepared: prawn ragout, saffron risotto, steamed mussels with cherry tomatoes, Tuscan beef tagliata, and fresh tuna encrusted with fennel seeds. But don't be mistaken: these are all mere accompaniments to the wines, which feature some of the biggest stars from across Italy, including legendary Super-Tuscans, great Barolos, and even Mondavi-Rothschild's budget-busting Opus One. ⊠ *Týnská 19, Staré Město* ☏ *224–808–318* ▭ *AE, DC, MC, V* Ⓜ *Line B: Náěstí Republiky.*

☼ $–$$
✕ **Pizzeria Rugantino.** This family-friendly pizzeria dishes out good, thin-crust pies, large salads and delicious Italian-style bread, along with fresh Bernard beer, a favorite of aficionados. Sunday afternoons are often filled with both Czech and expatriate moms and kids, giving it a circus

On the Menu

TRADITIONAL CZECH FOOD is hearty, with big portions of meat and something starchy on the side, such as dumplings or potatoes. Herbs and spices are not used heavily, though dill, marjoram, and caraway make frequent appearances, and garlic is a mainstay. Aside from these, the flavor comes from the meat. The Czechs know what they're doing when it comes to smoking meat—the natural way—and smoked *uzený* (pork) makes its way into many meals.

Dumplings filled with smoked meat.

Bramborák (*bram*-bohr-ahk). Available from fast-food stands throughout the city as well as in restaurants, this large (six- to eight-inch) potato pancake is flavored with marjoram and deep-fried.

Bezmasá jídla. This section of the menu lists dishes without meat. Listings often include *čočka* (stewed lentils), *smažený sýr* (fried cheese), and *rizoto se zeleninou* (risotto with vegetables).

Česnečka (*ches*-netch-kah). A Czech standby, this garlic soup is a thin—usually meatless—garlic-laced broth containing small pieces of potato, served with fried bread cubes.

Čočky (*choch*-kee). In this traditional dish, green lentils are stewed with or without smoked meat. An egg and pickle are usually served with the meatless version.

Cibulačka (*tsi*-boo-latch-kah). A close relative of česnečka—though a little less potent—this onion soup is usually served with bread, and cheese is sprinkled on top. Unlike the French version, it's not made from meat broth, so it's usually quite light.

Ďábelské toasty (*dya*-bel-skeh). Devil's toasts are a mixture of cooked ground beef, tomatoes, onions, and peppers served on fried or toasted white bread.

Guláš (*goo*-laush). Less oily than its Hungarian counterpart, Czech goulash is cubes of beef or pork, stewed and served in thin gravy. It's usually served with *houskové knedlíky* (bread dumplings) and chopped onions on top.

Hotová jídla (*ho*-to-vah *yee*'dla). This section of the menu contains dishes that are premade and ready to be served. Listed here you can find the most traditional favorites *svíčkova* stewed beef and goulash.

Jídla na objednávku (*yee*'dla na *ob*-yeh'd-nahv-koo). This section of the menu lists dishes that are cooked to order, including a selection of chicken and pork cutlets, as well as beef steak, prepared in various ways. Usually, they differ in their use of ingredients, such as onions, garlic, mushrooms, or cheese.

Klobása (kloh-*bah*-sa). A mainstay of the *občerstveni* (fast-food stand), this smoked sausage is also served in restaurants as an addition to certain types of guláš and soups or by itself.

Kulajda (koo-*lie*-dah). This traditional creamy soup with fresh or dried forest mushrooms is flavored with wine vinegar, caraway, and dill.

Moučníky (*moe*-ooch-*nik*kee). The dessert section on any traditional Czech menu is not terribly long, but you might see *palačinky* (sweet pancakes), *zmrzlina* (ice cream), *compot* (fruit compote), or *dort* (cake).

Nakládaný Hermelín (*nah*-kla-den-ee). A favorite snack of cafés and pubs that consists of a small round of *hermelín* (a soft cheese closely resembling Camembert) pickled in oil, onions, and herbs and served with dark rye bread.

Palačinky (pala-*ching*-kee). Usually served with jam or ice cream inside and whipped cream on top, these pancakes resemble crepes, but are made with a thicker batter.

Přílohy (*pr'zhee*-lo-hee). In traditional Czech restaurants, side orders aren't included with main courses, so look for them in this menu section. Regular dishes include *hranolky* (French fries), *Americké brambory* (literally, American potatoes; actually, fried potato wedges), and *ryže* (rice).

Smažený sýr (*sma*-zhe-nee *see*'r). A postwar addition to the traditional Czech diet, this staple is literally translated as fried cheese. A thick slab of an Edamlike cheese is breaded and deep fried, ideally giving it a crusty shell and a warm gooey interior. It's usually served with tartar sauce—for liberally spreading on top—and fries.

Studené předkrmy (*stoo*-den-eh *pr'zhed*-krmy). The section of cold appetizers on a Czech menu is typically a short one and usually includes *utopenec* (pickled pork sandwich), *tlačenka* (head cheese), and *šunkova rolka* (ham roll with horseradish cream).

Svíčková (*svitch*-koh-vah). Though technically this means a tenderloin cut of beef, on menus it's actually a dish consisting of two to four slabs of stewed beef, usually rump roast; in better restaurants you can get real tenderloin covered with a creamy sauce of pureed root vegetables, garnished with a dollop of whipping cream, cranberry sauce, and a slice of lemon. It's served with *houskové knedlíky* (bread dumplings).

Teplé předkrmy (*teh*-pleh *pr'*zhed-kr-mee). Warm appetizers on a Czech menu ordinarily include *topinka* (toasted or fried dark bread, rubbed with garlic cloves), and *ďabělské toasty* (devil's toasts).

Utopenec (*oo*-toe-pen-etts). Literally translated as "drowned man," utopenec is uncooked pork sausage that has been pickled in vinegar. It's not only a common appetizer in Czech restaurants, but it is a ubiquitous beer-snack staple in Czech pubs.

Vepřo-knedlo-zelo (*veh*-pr'zho-*kne*'dlo-*zhe*-lo). An affectionately shortened name for the three foods that appear on one plate, this popular family dish consists of roast pork, dumplings, and cabbage stewed with a bit of caraway.

Zelňačka (zell-*n'yatch*-kah). Cabbage is the main ingredient in this hearty soup whose flavor is accentuated by caraway and smoked pork or sausage. It can be a filling meal by itself when served in a small round loaf of bread.

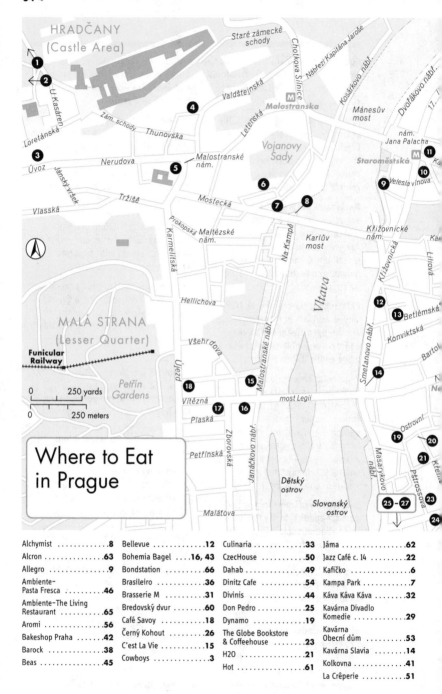

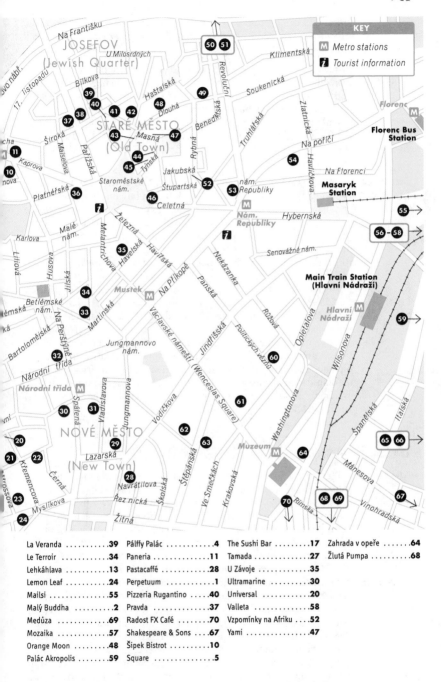

KEY

M Metro stations
i Tourist information

air, and it can get quite loud when full, which is most of the time. ⊠ *Dušní 4, Staré Město* ☎ *222–318–172* ▭ *No credit cards* ☉ *No lunch Sun.* Ⓜ *Line A: Staroměstská.*

JAPANESE   ✕ **Yami.** Korean and Japanese combine with a touch of Tex-Mex in the
$$–$$$$ incredible fusion roll: a burrito-size log of maki sushi filled with unusual ingredients like roast beef, cucumber, and sweet omelets. Traditional sushi recipes are equally good, as are the savory Korean dishes, making this casual eatery in Old Town's bar zone a favorite for those on their way out for the night. Draft Budvar and decent wines are on hand to get you started. ⊠ *Masná 3, Staré Město* ☎ *222–312–756* ▭ *AE, MC, V* Ⓜ *Line A: Starometska.*

VEGETARIAN   ✕ **Beas.** Right behind the soaring spires of Old Town's Týn Cathedral,
★ ¢–$ this simple eatery serves classic North Indian fare on shiny metal trays at a main counter. In other words, don't expect upscale service: you're going to bus your own table. But it's worth the extra work. The flavors of great curries, dhals (stewed lentils), grilled flatbreads, fragrant basmati rice, rich grilled eggplant, and other vegetarian delights make you forget that nothing you're eating contains eggs, meat, or fish. Though meal prices are already exceptionally low, plenty of that local rarity, free tap water, makes it even easier on the wallet. ⊠ *Týnská 19, Staré Město* ☎ *608–035–727* ▭ *No credit cards* Ⓜ *Line B: Náěstí Republiky.*

¢–$ ✕ **Lehkáhlava.** Is this still Prague? Lehká hlava ("Clear head") serves clever vegetarian dishes at bargain-basement prices in a wacky, tripped-out dreamscape that includes an arched blue ceiling with thousands of tiny "stars" and tables that glow from inside. Appetizers like the rich spinach dip and creamy red-lentil soup lead to great veggie stir-fries and a better-than-decent burrito with smoky ratatouille. Kind service and unusual, extremely affordable wines from Spain make it one of the city's new favorites. ⊠ *Boršov 2, Staré Město* ☎ *222–220–665* ▭ *No credit cards* Ⓜ *Line B: Národní Třída.*

MALÁ STRANA (LESSER QUARTER)

CONTEMPORARY   ✕ **C'est La Vie.** The superb spot in a parkside nook on Kampa Island is
$$$$ complemented with food that's every bit as good as the location, served
FodorśChoice   in a semi-formal, yacht-club setting. The menu offers fresh fish and meats
★   prepared with French and Asian influences, both in ingredients and cooking methods, from truffles to Tandoori. Outdoor seating a few steps down on a stone terrace next to the river lets you gaze across to the island or watch tour boats pass through the locks. ⊠ *Říční 1, Malá Strana* ☎ *721–158–403* ▭ *AE, DC, MC, V* Ⓜ *Line B: Národní Třída.*

$$$–$$$$ ✕ **Alchymist.** Like an apartment decorated by Liberace and Count Dracula, Alchymist's ambience goes *way* over-the-top to include zebra-print chairs, crystal chandeliers, scarlet curtains, silver Louis XIV chairs, and ornate gold tables, with random symbols thrown in for good measure. The cuisine is less overstated, though no less confident of its own artistic direction, including such starters as a sweet cheese tart with port wine syrup and a foie gras terrine with dates and pomegranate seeds. Main courses continue the contemporary Continental theme, with a tender beef tagliata, rich duck breast with crisp celery root chips, and a creamy

$$−

saffron risotto, duck breast with seared foie gras, and a coy
tion of fish-and-chips. Seeing and being seen is, naturall
show, and the terrace overlooking the tram stop plays
long, summer afternoons. ⊠ *Malostranské ná*
☎ 257-532-109 ▤ AE, DC, MC, V Ⓜ Line A:

★ $−$$$ ✕ **Café Savoy.** Stellar service and elegant meals
erate prices are de rigueur here. Oh, and kille
a one-time favorite of the city's fin-de-siè
everything from meal-sized split-pea a
Wiener schnitzel, with huge salads
the in-house bakery. The house
properly sweet finish. But if y
the bite-size chocolate truff
cream, rum, green p
☎ 257-311-562 ▤

DELICATESSENS
¢−$ ✕ **Bohemia Bagel**
good bagels, c
branch: frie
gravy. W
Stran

JAPANESE
$$$−$$$$ ✕

an
rior.
in fair weather head up the
labyrinthine staircases to the
rooftop garden, which displays
great views of Old Town and Malá
Strana. The kitchen sends out the
town's best cuts of beef, expertly
prepared, including a killer dou-
ble-cut T-bone. Even vegetarians
have solid options, such as the faux
burger, made of grilled portobello

> Hungry to try your hand at Prague
> cuisine? For serious foodies that
> want to get behind the scenes, the
> Radisson SAS Alcron Hotel offers
> cooking classes. For information
> contact the Radisson at 222-
> 820-000.

mushrooms. An excellent wine list includes top-shelf selections from four
continents, as well as a special collection of single-barrel Bourbons.
⊠ *Nerudova 40, Malá Strana* ☎ 257-535-050 ▤ AE, DC, MC, V
Ⓜ *Line A: Malostranská.*

★ $$−$$$ ✕ **Square.** Once the site of a glimmering café, beloved by artists and writ-
ers from the mid-19th-century onward, this space is now a prime meet-
ing spot for power players in Malá Strana. Excellent bistro foods and
tapas as well as an exceptional selection of wines by the glass make this
a favorite place for the beautiful people and their friends. Dinner takes
it up a notch with tiger prawns and avocado ceviche, lamb steak with

nterpreta-
, part of the
center stage on
m., Malá Strana
Malostranská.

of high quality at mod-
sweets. This restored café,
cle Jewish community, serves
d cream of cauliflower soups to
omplemented by fresh breads from
ake, topped with marzipan, makes a
u can't handle too much more, consider
es, sold individually, with fillings like Irish
pper, and chili. ⊠ *Vitězná 1, Smíchov*
E, DC, MC, V Ⓜ *Line A: Malostranská.*

he second location of Bohemia Bagel serves the same
ffee, and great American-style grill fare as the Old Town
eggs, sweet pancakes, great hash browns, and biscuits with
en hunger strikes, this place is a lifesaver. ⊠ *Újezd 16, Malá*
☎ 257–310–694 ▭ *No credit cards* Ⓜ *Line B: Národní Třida.*

The Sushi Bar. This narrow little room across the river from the National Theater is home to some of the city's best sushi, courtesy of the fish market next door. The selection is first-rate by Central European standards. Beyond sushi, the menu also includes a great seaweed salad and a rich vegetable stew. Though prices for individual pieces of sushi start relatively low, bills can rise quickly depending on how many you order. ⊠ *Zborovská 49, Malá Strana* ☎ 603–244–882 ▭ *DC, MC, V* Ⓜ *Line B: Národní Třida.*

HRADČANY

ASIAN ✕ **Malý Buddha.** Bamboo, wood, paper, incense—and the random creepy
¢–$$ mask on the wall—are all part of the decor at this earthy hilltop hideaway near Prague Castle. Spring rolls, vegetable and mixed stir-fries, fish, and shark steaks come in generous portions. The drink list is unusual, with ginseng wine, herbal drinks, and mystery shots of exotic alcoholic concoctions. The restaurant has a no-smoking policy—a rarity in Prague—so the aromas are pure. If the decorations interest you, you can buy much of what you see, including the colorful Asian ceramics. ⊠ *Úvoz 46, Hradčany* ☎ 220–513–894 ▭ *No credit cards* ⊘ *Closed Mon.* Ⓜ *Line A: Hradčanská.*

CZECH ✕ **Perpetuum.** The country's greatest culinary resources—wild duck and
$$ goose—get a makeover here with improved culinary techniques from France and Italy. Starters include one of the city's best duck *rillettes*, a deliciously greasy spread of slow-cooked duck meat, as well as gratifying salads and soups using seasonal ingredients. But that merely sets the stage for the main courses, such as goose breast with ginger and the stir-fry-like duck fricassee. As if they were competing for a medal in hedonism, Perpetuum also includes one of the city's best wine lists, featuring

Good Food On the Go

THERE WAS A TIME NOT MANY YEARS AGO when a quick bite on the go in Prague was largely limited to the predictable international fast-food chains and the fatty–albeit tasty–fare from the local sausage stands. These are still around, but if you're in the mood for something more flavorful while rushing around, keep an eye out for these specialty shops and bakeries in the downtown area, which offer freshly made sandwiches, salads, prepared meals, and pastries.

Bakeshop Praha (⊠ Kozi 1, Staré Město) has fresh fragrant bread, good salads, and rich brownies. The sandwiches with English bacon have earned a patriotic following. There's seating indoors if you're not looking to take your meal with you.

Culinaria (⊠ Skořepka 9, Staré Město) supplies a wide selection of salads, main courses, and desserts that change regularly. The display is always a painter's palette of vivid color, and the staff is helpful. An herbal juice bar is complemented by a sweeping selection of the best imported soft drinks. You can eat standing up at one of the few tables, or everything is available to go.

Paneria (⊠ Kaprova 3, Staré Město ⊠ Nekázanka 19, Nové Město ⊠ Bělehradská 71, Vinohrady) locations are popping up in almost every district, some within two blocks of each other–there are at least three in Old Town alone. The sandwiches are standardized but made fresh when you order, and they come with toppings such as green olives, mascarpone, and tomato. Desserts include some winners, such as the flan with forest berries.

Czech's best vintages, like the crisp whites from cult producer Dobrá vinice. If you want to see how good Czech food and drink can get, this is it. ⊠ *Na hutích 9, Dejvice* ☎ *222–522–784* ▤ *MC, V* ☉ *Closed Mon.* Ⓜ *Line A: Dejvická.*

NOVÉ MĚSTO (NEW TOWN) & VYŠEHRAD

COLOMBIAN
★ $–$$$

✕ **Don Pedro.** Right on the riverfront, yet overlooked by most tourists, this hip bistro serves authentic dishes from Bogotá, courtesy of the Colombian-Czech couple who owns the place. In large part that means beef: clear beef broth with stewed beef rib known as *caldo de costilla*; white-corn empanadas stuffed with ground beef and rice; and arepas, thick corn pancakes filled with gooey white cheese. Both the 300-gram (10-ounce) beef steak and the grilled beef liver are excellent meals for hearty appetites. ⊠ *Masarykovo nábř. 2, Nové Město* ☎ *224–923–505* ▤ *MC, V* Ⓜ *Line B: Národní Třída.*

CONTEMPORARY
$$–$$$
FodorsChoice
★

✕ **Zahrada v opeře.** Don't be put off by appearances: despite the external harshness of this Communist-era building, it holds an airy, open restaurant inside, with the most innovative and surprising menus in the city. A perfectly balance of creativity and price, the "Garden in the Opera" is an epicurean bull's-eye. Dishes include grilled and roasted fresh fish and regional specialties like the tender rabbit fricassee with mustard sauce. Special events bring in chefs from countries like Nepal and South Africa, making frequent visits a must. It's an exceptional value for the price, and a favorite of many discerning diners. ✉ *Legerova 75, Nové Město* 🕾 *224–239–685* 🖃 *AE, DC, MC, V* Ⓜ *Line C : Muzeum.*

$–$$ ✕ **Ultramarine.** A honeycomb of comfortably lit rooms, all under Gothic-style vaults, Ultramarine is popular with the business-lunch crowd by day and both the preclub clientele and cozy couples in the evening. This restaurant has helped fill an important niche, serving up quality meals in a location that is equal parts pub, café, and restaurant. If you have the midnight munchies, the kitchen is open until 1:30 AM. Beers are a bit pricey by Prague standards, so quaffing is better done elsewhere, but the Thai soup and American-style burgers are local hits. Way, way down, the deep cellar holds even more seating, a bar, and club. ✉ *Ostrovní 32, Nové Město* 🕾 *224–932–249* 🖃 *AE, MC, V* Ⓜ *Line B: Národní Třída.*

CONTINENTAL
$–$$$ ✕ **Universal.** Prices here have doggedly remained unchanged since it opened in the late 1990s. Universal is a Continental cornucopia of excellent salads, classicly European main courses, titanic side orders of scalloped potatoes, luscious lemon tarts, and sweet profiteroles. An affordable midday menu makes it even more alluring at lunchtime, and the cheap house wine draws out after-dinner conversations. Reservations are advisable. ✉ *V Jirchářích 6, Nové Město* 🕾 *224–934–416* 🖃 *MC, V* Ⓜ *Line B: Národní Třída.*

CZECH
$$$–$$$$ ✕ **Černý Kohout.** Cozy, comfortable, and full of European charm, "the Black Rooster" serves classic Czech cuisine in a Continental context, bringing a strong French touch to such traditional fare as Czech lamb from the Šumava national forest and roasted Slovak peppers, as well as adding an Italian influence in the risotto with Czech forest mushrooms. Graceful service with upscale surroundings give the impression of something from a bygone era. Thrifty diners, take note: midweek brings a three-course business lunch of the same high quality for a much lower price. ✉ *Vojtěšská 9, Nové Město* 🕾 *251–681–191* 🖃 *AE, DC, MC, V* Ⓜ *Line B: Národní Třída.*

$$$–$$$$ ✕ **CzecHouse.** On the ground floor of the capacious Hilton Hotel, this renewed restaurant reopened in late 2005 to rave reviews for its upscale interpretations of Czech recipes, including one of the only versions of svíčková *na smetaně* in town to be made from tenderloin, resulting in a radically different version than at your average corner pub. Czech wines are similarly of a higher standard, though beer goes very well with most recipes. Excellent service provides another reason to make the trip to metro station Florenc. ✉ *Pobřezní 1, Karlín* 🕾 *224–842–125* 🖃 *AE, DC, MC, V* Ⓜ *Line B or C: Florenc.*

¢–$$ ✕ **Bredovský dvůr.** Buckets of unpasteurized Pilsner Urquell wash down honey-coated BBQ ribs, massive grilled steaks, thick potato pancakes, and other hearty pub fare prepared with enough sophistication to satisfy discerning foodies. While the arched brick ceilings could easily accommodate a more lavish restaurant, Bredovský dvůr stays true to its roots with simple food and great beer—and lots of it. ✉ *Politickych vězňu 13, Nové Město* 🕾 *224–215–428* 🖃 *MC, V* Ⓜ *Line A or B: Můstek.*

ECLECTIC
$$–$$$$ ✕ **Hot.** Arguably the best meal on Wenceslas Square, this clubby destination mixes pan-Asian, Continental, and Czech dishes with culinary fluency. Basil-oil beef carpaccio competes for attention with *goong phat* (Thai tiger prawns in tamarind sauce) and roast chicken in pandanus leaves with Japanese horseradish—and those are just the appetizers. Main courses include penne *arrabiata*, whole grilled lobster with sweet pineapple-mango salsa, rich Bohemian duck breast with bacon, and a spicy red curry. A separate menu lists made-to-order sushi classics. The attractive staff provides eye candy and the circular room, decorated with bead screens and shimmering surfaces, contradicts its origin as the Soviet-styled dining room of the Hotel Jalta. Patio seating provides an alfresco option, overlooking the throngs on the square. ⊠ *Václavské nám. 45, Nové Město* ☎ *222–247–240* ⊟ *AE, DC, MC, V* Ⓜ *Line A: Muzeum.*

$–$$ ✕ **Dynamo.** Like a manga-inspired diner of the future, Dynamo is tricked out in seafoam-green walls with framed arty posters, lots of glass, and custom-designed wooden benches and booths. The menu seesaws between the vegetarian and the meaty, offering crisp Caesar salads with heaps of croutons, eggplant with grilled vegetables, grilled feta with olives and sun-dried tomatoes, duck breast with honey sauce, and beef liver with marinated celery root. The place is often bustling, occasionally empty before 7 PM, and definitely worth a visit. ⊠ *Pštrossova 29, Nové Město* ☎ *224–932–020* ⊟ *AE, DC, MC, V* Ⓜ *Line B: Národní Třída.*

$–$$ ✕ **Jáma.** American expatriates, Czech politicians, international consultants, and a constant crowd of students make this Czech-American hybrid pub feel like a place where everyone is welcome. Though just hanging out is of primary importance, the menu is leagues ahead of most pubs of this type, with decent Tex-Mex dishes (hearty burritos, crisp nachos, and refreshing taco salads) mixing it up with Czech classics (roast beef with cream sauce and hearty goulash) and international pub standards (big Caesar salads and juicy burgers). Lunchtime brings inexpensive three-course menus. The owner, a sommelier, also has a stash of high-quality French and Italian wines at moderate prices. ⊠ *V Jámě 7, Nové Město* ☎ *224–222–383* ⊟ *AE, DC, MC, V* Ⓜ *Line A or B: Můstek.*

¢–$$ ✕ **H2O.** Trekking through Italian, French, and Asian culinary turf, this creative, spacious diner has a solid following among broke gourmets and students. Stuffed Greek peppers with tzatziki, prosciutto-and-egg sandwiches, stuffed pork belly, and creamy spinach soups are typical dishes on the ever-changing lunch menu; dinners bring more of the same at moderate prices. ⊠ *Opatovická 5, Nové Město* ☎ *776–390–292* ⊟ *AE, DC, MC, V* Ⓜ *Line B: Národní Třída.*

FRENCH
★ $$–$$$$ ✕ **Brasserie M.** When chef Jean-Paul Manzac left the Prague Marriott to open his own shiny bistro, he

> **WORD OF MOUTH**
>
> "We happily dove into our first real hot lunches of pork, kraut, and dumplings . . .This was our initiation into Czech organization, with the little slip of paper tallying our beers and food, and our waiter calculating the bill longhand. (I'd like to see the teens at the local brass 'n' fern try this!)" –AHaugeto

changed the very definition of local French food. Brasserie M. is a spacious restaurant with all the classics from simple *croque* sandwiches to elegant grilled turbot, passing by way of true Alsatian fare, like choucroute garnie (a sort of sauerkraut with meat) and a traditional chocolate mousse (the recipe was passed down from the chef's father). It's all excellent and generally about half the price of fancier French places around town. ⊠ *Vladislavova 17, Nové Město* ☎ *224–054–070* ▤ *AE, MC, V* Ⓜ *Line B: Národní Třída.*

ITALIAN
$–$$
✕ **Pastacaffé.** Great coffees by the Tonino Lamborghini brand and fresh pastas turn this quiet New Town café into a small corner of Milan. Large salads, quick panini, *piadini,* and antipasti round out the menu. Plenty of light and fresh air from the large windows invite all-day loungers, but when the coffee kicks in, people get up and *go.* The cheap, simple dishes are expertly prepared. ⊠ *Vodičkova 8, Nové Město* ☎ *222–231–869* ▤ *AE, DC, MC, V* Ⓜ *Line A or B: Můstek.*

GEORGIAN
¢–$$
✕ **Tamada.** The word *Gruzinská* printed on the sign in the window indicates food from Georgia (the country on the Black Sea coast, not the U.S. state). Georgian dishes carry a bit more tang, spice, and crunch than their Czech counterparts. *Pchali* (a piquant eggplant dish with spinach leaves and walnuts) and *chačapuri* (melted cheese on a soft, fragrant dough), are excellent, and they're only the beginning of an inexpensive and festive meal. A woodsy cabin interior gives a fun relaxed feeling to the space. ⊠ *Jenštejnská 2, Nové Město* ☎ *224–913–810* ▤ *No credit cards* Ⓜ *Line B: Karlovo nám.*

SEAFOOD
★ $$$$
✕ **Alcron.** An intimate salon of just seven tables, Alcron is the city's seafood mecca. Though dating only from 1998, this semicircular room's Jazz-Age murals give it a classic presence. Main courses include creative interpretations of traditional fish recipes from around the world, including seasonal specials such as smoked eel with truffled scrambled eggs, scallops with caviar, lobster bisque and langoustines with seared foie gras. The limited seating arrangements mean reservations are a must. ⊠ *Radisson SAS Alcron Hotel, Štěpáská 40, Nové Město* ☎ *222–820–038* ▤ *AE, DC, MC, V* ⌕ *Reservations essential* Ⓜ *Line A: Můstek.*

THAI
★ $–$$$
✕ **Lemon Leaf.** A front-runner in the city's new crop of Asian places, Lemon Leaf serves a long list of Thai classics to an appreciative, dedicated clientele. Airy and luminous, with big pots of plants, tall windows, and funky lamps, Lemon Leaf provides a solid alternative to European cuisine for lunch or dinner. Crunchy spring rolls and traditional Thai soups reeling with flavor are essential openers to one of the noodle dishes or spicy curries, but keep an eye on the little flame symbols in the menu that denote the hotness of dishes. ⊠ *Myslíkova 14, Nové Město* ☎ *224–919–056* ▤ *AE, MC, V* Ⓜ *Line B: Národní Třída.*

VINOHRADY

ECLECTIC
★ $–$$$
✕ **Mozaika.** Pushing the outer orbits of eclectic, this cellar restaurant in a leafy residential neighborhood offers Thai-style curried mussels, hearty roast beef salads, grilled veal chops, and what some consider to be the city's best (and weirdest) hamburger in Prague, served on a homemade

2

spinach bun and topped with sugary caramelized onions, grilled mushrooms, and rich Swiss cheese. The result? Delicious meals, without the
attitude and the concomitant kick in the wallet from your average pricey
spot. That means it's popular, so reservations are especially recommended. Linger in the modern dining room to view a rotating exhibit
of original art hanging on the walls. ⊠ *Nitranská 13, Vinohrady*
☎ *224–253–011* ▤ *AE, DC, MC, V* Ⓜ *Line A: Jiřího z Poděbrad.*

$–$$ ✕ **Valleta.** Not all of the city's best restaurants are in the center. This ca-
sual, family-run café brings artful cooking to the neighborhood along
the Vinohrady–Vršovice border, thrilling a dedicated crowd of locals.
With a pronounced shabby-chic touch, the setting is decidedly modest,
allowing the food to swing for the stars, courtesy of the well-traveled,
up-and-coming young chef Filip Blažek. Main courses include such flavorful fare as creamy broccoli soup with sweet hazelnut dumplings, spicy
duck tagine with spinach blinis, and roast lamb with tomato chutney,
all in healthy portions, and all served at prices that put the loud touristy
places in the city's center to shame. ⊠ *Mexická 7, Vršovice*
☎ *271–726–548* ▤ *No credit cards* Ⓜ *Line A: Jiřího z Poděbrad.*

ITALIAN ✕ **Aromi.** Gracious, gregarious, and extremely confident, Aromi is ar-
★ $–$$$ guably the city's second-best Italian restaurant and proud of it: it's con-
siderably less stiff than Allegro in Staré Město, but with the same great
service and a festive air, showcasing the overlooked fare of Marche. Clas-
sic pastas made in-house and fresh seafood shown off tableside are two
of the crowd favorites, as are the superb salads and well-chosen Italian
wines. Leave room for after dessert: Aromi stocks an exclusive list of
rare grappas. ⊠ *Mánesova 78, Vinohrady* ☎ *222–713–222* ▤ *MC, V*
Ⓜ *Line A: Jiřího z Poděbrad.*

MEXICAN ✕ **Ambiente—The Living Restaurant.**
$–$$$ The first of what has become a
small chain of successful restau-
rants helped champion the concept
of attentive service, a foreign notion
to Prague waitstaff when it opened
in the 1990s. This branch still retains the original Mexican theme
that made it famous, but pasta and
steaks also figure strongly on the expanded menu. It's a suitable stop before or after a stroll through nearby
Riegrovy sady, one of the city's
grand hilltop parks. ⊠ *Mánesova
59, Vinohrady* ☎ *222–727–851*
▤ *AE, DC, MC, V* Ⓜ *Line A:
Jiřího z Poděbrad.*

¢–$ ✕ **Žlutá Pumpa.** Good eats on the
cheap at the "Yellow Pump," a
popular neighborhood watering
hole, draw the starving artist
crowd, but most people come here

> ## THE SWEET LIFE
>
> There are a few uniquely Czech
> treats around—great as a snack or
> a little gift.
> Tatranka: Delicious wafer candy
> bars, covered with chocolate and
> wrapped in paper. Various flavors
> including vanilla and hazelnut.
> Kofola: A spicy, peppery, far-less-
> sugary Czech-made cola.
> Karlovarske oplatky: These crunchy,
> sweet flat wafer cookies from
> Karlovy Vary come in a square box
> as big as a dinner plate.
> Fidorka: Chocolate-coated wafers
> in coconut, peanut, and other fla-
> vors. Foil-wrapped, about ¼ as
> thick as a hockey puck. Very popu-
> lar with the under-10 set.

to drink. Soak up your beer, cocktail, or high-grade absinthe with decent Mexican-esque dishes. The location is composed of ragtag tables and chairs, crazy murals, smoke, and noise—in a word, fun. ⊠ *Belgická 11, Vinohrady* ☎ *608–184–360* ▤ *No credit cards* Ⓜ *Line A: Nám. Míru.*

VEGETARIAN   ✕ **Radost FX Café.** Rave on: this veg-
★ $–$$ etarian restaurant and café sits right above the venerable Radost FX nightclub. Good filter (aka American-style) coffee, great music, and a chill vibe make this the hipster's choice for weekend brunch. The menu includes extremely satisfying burritos, pasta dishes, and the ever-popular Popeye "burger." The service isn't fast, but really, what's the rush? ⊠ *Bělehradská 120, Nové Město* ☎ *224–254–776* ▤ *No credit cards* Ⓜ *Line C: I. P. Pavlova.*

LETNÁ & HOLEŠOVICE

FRENCH   ✕ **La Crêperie.** Started by a Czech-French couple, this tiny bistro near
¢–$ the Veletržní palác (Trade Fair Palace) is devoted to all manner of crepes, both sweet and savory, using traditional *blé noir* (buckwheat) from France. If you have an extremely hearty appetite, you may need to order several, but save room for the dessert crepe with cinnamon-apple puree layered with lemon cream. The wine list offers both French and Hungarian vintages. La Crêperie is inexpensive, but the honest fare and cool French-rustic atmosphere make it feel like a splurge. ⊠ *Janovského 4, Holešovice* ☎ *220–878–040* ▤ *No credit cards* Ⓜ *Line C: Vltavská.*

ŽIŽKOV

ECLECTIC   ✕ **Palác Akropolis.** Though the concert venue–club downstairs is puls-
$–$$ ing at night, this restaurant is a draw in its own right, in part due to the loopy interior from Czech artist František Skála. Steel-covered menus offer large portions of traditional Czech fare such as pork cutlets and potato pancakes, as well as Mexican-style soups and Buffalo wings, all at reasonable prices. Aquariums containing Skála's industrial sculptures provide something to look at while the food arrives, though sometimes the hipster staff is even more captivating. The music, which ranges from hip-hop to Czech rock, can be quite loud. ⊠ *Kubelíková 27, Žižkov* ☎ *296–330–990* ▤ *No credit cards* Ⓜ *Line A: Jiřího z Poděbrad.*

INDIAN   ✕ **Mailsi.** This modest restaurant serves affordable Pakistani and Indian
★ $$ cuisine beloved by neighborhood denizens. The interior is sometimes criticized for its underdecorated state, save the paintings of *Arabian Nights,* but Mailsi still offers decent vindaloos and kormas at prices lower than in the flashier Indian restaurants downtown, and the owner works to make sure everyone is happy. Take Tram 5, 9, or 26 to the Lipanská

stop, then walk one short block uphill. ⊠ *Lipanská 1, Žižkov*
☎ *222–717–783* 🖃 *No credit cards* Ⓜ *Line A: Jiřiho z Poděbrad.*

CAFÉS

Prague has a rapidly evolving café culture, and finding a good cup of coffee here is now almost as easy as in any large city in Europe. Coffee standards took a beating under communism, but a clutch of new Italian and American-inspired cafés have opened up. These are meshing with the older, traditional coffeehouses from the 19th and 20th centuries, and today's cafés run the gamut from the historical to the literary to the trendy. Most cafés are licensed to sell alcohol, and are open until at least 11 PM, with some transforming into virtual bars by night. In all of the following you can sit down with a small snack and a java, and in most of them you can order simple cocktails and other alcoholic beverages. As a general rule, the old-fashioned-looking cafés serve traditional Czech snacks, such as marinated cheese, while those with splashy new façades carry a selection of more Western-style desserts, such as carrot cake and tiramisu.

Bondstation. For those who like it "shaken, not stirred," this cool café, outfitted with silhouette images of Bond girls and funky molded furniture, pays homage to 007. Stylish people sipping mojitos are a common sight, and occasionally a ringer for one of the Bond girls will drop in. ⊠ *Polská 7, Vinohrady* ☎ *222–733–871* 🖃 *No credit cards.*

Dahab. A tearoom, Middle-Eastern coffeehouse, and full restaurant, Dahab mixes Persian rugs with Bohemian arches. This spot grew from a small couscouserie in the Roxy next door, and there's still a clubby, hip vibe in the air. The food is authentically Middle Eastern, and definitely worth trying for a snack or a full meal. The occasional belly dancer has been sighted as well. ⊠ *Dlouhá 33, Staré Město* ☎ *224–827–375* 🖃 *AE, MC, V.*

The Globe Bookstore & Coffeehouse. Prague's first English-language bookstore with a café draws both foreigners and Czechs for its books, brownies, and brunch—not to mention the bulletin board. The full menu includes marinated cheeses from Greece and the Balkans and other ingredients blended with a light touch. Use the Internet or hook up your own laptop. ⊠ *Pštrossova 6, Nové Město* ☎ *224–934–203* 🖃 *AE, MC, V.*

Jazz Café č. 14. Old-fashioned Parisian charm radiates from marble floors, dim wall lamps, and old oak tables in this large but cozy café. It's frequented by students from nearby Charles University. Marinated *hermelin* cheese makes a good snack, or sometimes a complete meal. ⊠ *Opatovická 14, Nové Město* ☎ *224–934–674* 🖃 *No credit cards.*

Kafíčko. Smoke-free and loving it, the "Little Coffee" grinds freshly roasted beans from Brazil, Kenya, Colombia, and other renowned growing regions. Good cakes and small snacks in a peaceful setting make this a pleasant stop for refueling near Charles Bridge. ⊠ *Míšeňská 10, Malá Strana* ☎ *724–151–795* 🖃 *No credit cards.*

Káva Káva Káva. If you like real Seattle-style arabica, this is your java spot. The beans are custom-roasted, and the baristas know what they are doing, so the coffee is good. You can also surf the Net for a few more crowns downstairs or for free on your own laptop via Wi-Fi. ⊠ *Národní 37, Staré Město* ☏ *224–228–862* ⊟ *No credit cards.*

Kavárna Divadlo Komedie. A smattering of foreigners mingle with Czech performers and other locals at this "Comedy Theater" café while, sipping small coffees or holding big, thick glasses of Hoegaarden beer. The restored functionalist interior features double marble staircases, which lead to the theater downstairs. ⊠ *Jungmannova 1, Nové Město* ☏ *603–148–162* ⊟ *No credit cards.*

Kavárna Obecní dům. This is multitasking made easy: you can relax with a beverage while also drinking in the opulent art nouveau surroundings in this famous building's magnificent café. ⊠ *Nám. Republiky 5, Staré Město* ☏ *222–002–763* ⊟ *AE, DC, MC, V.*

Medúza. The old-fashioned, black-and-white photographs on the walls, burnished chairs, old lacquered tables, and a general "grandma's parlor" feel make this student-y place instantly inviting. The menu offers a selection of mostly vegetarian snacks and *palačinky* (filled pancakes) that go perfectly with a glass of wine. ⊠ *Belgická 17, Vinohrady* ☏ *222–515–107* ⊟ *No credit cards.*

Shakespeare & Sons. Czechs and expats frequent this tranquil bookstore–café out of the city center, which offers Bernard beer, occasional readings, performances, and assorted happenings. The charming book room at the back has the strange power to make hours disappear while browsing. ⊠ *Krymská, 12 Vršovice* ☏ *271–740–839* ⊟ *AE, MC, V.*

Vzpomínky na Afriku. This tiny shop behind the Kotva department store sells the widest selection of premium coffees in town, served here or to go. ⊠ *Templová 7, Staré Město* ☏ *603–544–492* ⊟ *No credit cards.*

Where to Stay

3

WORD OF MOUTH

"On my several trips to Prague, some have found Wenceslas [Square] seedy and unwelcoming, while others have enjoyed the lively, modern, urban feel. If you prefer the quieter, Old-World feel, then Lesser Town area is better. If hanging out in Times Square is your cup of tea, you might find Wenceslas more attractive."

—J63

By Mindy Kay
Bricker

PRAGUE WAS A HOTEL BOOMTOWN IN THE LAST DECADE, trying to catch up with the demands of new visitors. The shortage of rooms that restricted tourism in the first years after the Velvet Revolution has been alleviated, and the good news is that with a little advance preparation, you can find a decent place to stay.

The bad news is that much of the construction has focused on the extreme high and low ends of the market and neglected the middle. Prague—particularly the Old Town and Malá Strana—is awash in lovingly restored palaces, complete with luxurious high-thread-count duvets and the rates to match. Plenty of youth hostels and budget pensions have also sprung up—some of which are miles from the city center. The missing link is decent, mid-price properties.

This means finding a great hotel deal is akin to winning a hotel jackpot. You may have to exceed your lodging budget and save in other areas. If you plan to do some traveling outside of Prague, you'll be happy to know that the price of hotels is much, much lower.

There are some ways to fight the high lodging prices. One is to book online. A hotel Web site often offers rates that are much lower than the walk-in room rate. Some hotels even have a "stay three nights, get a fourth night free" incentive.

Another tip is to travel during the off season—anywhere from November 1 until the end of March (except the Christmas, New Year's, and Easter holidays). Rates drop dramatically and you'll rarely, if ever, need a reservation. The summer and fall seasons, of course, are different stories. Try to book your room at least three months in advance during high season to secure the best rates and quietest rooms.

If you're willing to sacrifice croissants at breakfast or 24-hour room service, consider staying in a private room or a short-term apartment rental. Several agencies now exist to help book rooms in private apartments, and you can find some very nice places at more reasonable prices.

Although Prague does have a number of recognizable Western hotel chains, the vast majority of hotels and pensions are privately owned and operated. There are trade-offs with both. The chains sometimes lack local spirit and a touch of historic architecture. On the other hand they're likely to have air-conditioning in summer and other amenities that smaller hotels cannot afford. On the other hand, private hotels can certainly be quaint and atmospheric, but they can also be run-down—which is a fine line; one person's shabby chic can be another person's just plain shabby.

The most desirable neighborhoods to stay in are the Old Town (Staré Město), the Lesser Quarter (Malá Strana), the Castle Area (Hradčany), and the New Town (Nové Město). Don't despair, though, if you can only find or afford a room outside the center. Prague's public transportation is excellent, and the outlying neighborhoods have the added advantage

KNOW-HOW

FACILITIES

In most cases, cable TV, minibars, breakfast, and some kind of Internet connection are offered in hotels in all price ranges. Wi-Fi Internet access is breaking onto the scene, though Wi-Fi networks can be spotty and usually only function in the lobby and other public areas. Hotels at $$ and $$$ ranges usually have restaurants, cafés, room service, private baths, and hair dryers. At $$$$ hotels you can expect luxury amenities like robes, a sauna, steam bath, pool, concierge, and babysitting—oh, yes, and air-conditioning, which is woefully absent at cheaper hotels. (Many of Prague's older buildings are legally prohibited from installing air-conditioning for architectural reasons, but most of the upscale hotels somehow circumvented the rules.)

RESERVATIONS

During the peak season (May through October, excluding July and August) reservations are a must; reserve 90 days in advance to stay in the hotel and room of your choice. For the remainder of the year, reserve 30 days in advance. If possible, call or e-mail to double check your reservation before you come to avoid any hassles on arrival.

PRICES

Many hotels in Prague go by a three-season system: the lowest rates are charged from November through mid-March, excluding Christmas and New Year's, when high-season rates are charged; the middle season is July and August; the high season, from the end of March through June and also from mid-August through the end of October, brings the highest rates. Easter sees higher-than-high-season rates, and some hotels increase the price for other holidays and trade fairs. Always ask first.

WHAT IT COSTS koruna and euros				
$$$$	**$$$**	**$$**	**$**	**¢**
HOTELS in kč over 6,500	4,000–6,500	2,200–4,000	1,200–2,200	under 1,200
HOTELS in € over 230	140–230	80–140	40–80	under 40

Prices are for two people in a double room with a private bath and breakfast during peak season (March through October, excluding July and August).

of authenticity (real pubs, restaurants, and people), which is harder to come by in the city's center.

A word to star-rating aficionados: unlike many other countries, the Czech Republic doesn't have an official rating system, so hotels rate themselves. They invariably toss on a couple stars more than they actually merit.

LODGING ALTERNATIVES

PRIVATE ROOMS

A private room can be a cheaper and more interesting alternative to a hotel. You can find agencies offering such accommodations all over Prague, including at the main train station (Hlavní nádraží), Holešovice Station (Nádraží Holešovice), and at Ruzyně Airport. These bureaus usually are staffed with people who speak some English, and most can book rooms in hotels and pensions as well as private accommodations. Rates for private rooms start at around 400 Kč per person per night but can go much higher for better quality rooms. In general, there's no fee, but you may need to try several bureaus to find the accommodation you want. Ask to see a photo of the room before accepting it, and be sure to pinpoint its location on a map—you don't want to wind up in an inconvenient location. If you're approached by someone in the stations hawking rooms with a deal, you should be wary of them.

Prague Information Service arranges lodging from all of its central offices, including the branch in the main train station, which is in the booth marked TURISTICKÉ INFORMACE on the left side of the main hall as you exit the station.

APARTMENT RENTALS

Apartment rentals give a fantastic—and cheaper—option for those traveling in a group, or simply for those who prefer to have their own space and actually eat a few meals at home. Gorgeous apartment rentals can be found, from modern with a swimming pool to a more local flair, in other words Ikea bric-a-brac and a bit of Communist kitsch in between. As a fact, many rentals tend to be in the center and remarkably less expensive than surrounding hotels, but you don't get the *International Herald Tribune* brought with your breakfast or someone to turn down your bed in the evening. A longer stay usually guarantees some kind of discount.

If you're looking for an apartment, consider the following agencies:

E-travel. Quick and easy, this Web-based company finds cheap accommodation rates—both in terms of apartments and hotels—in the center of Prague. All of this is done online; you are your own agent. ✉ *Ostrovní 7, Nové Město* ☎ *224-990-990* ⊕ *www.travel.cz.*

Mary's Travel & Tourist Services. Agents have been known to go beyond the call of duty to ensure a safe landing for guests—especially after planes have been delayed past work hours. Their extra efforts have earned this company one of the best reputations in town. Arranging mostly stays in hotels, guesthouses, and apartments, they have a great selection in Old Town, many of which come with cleaning services. They also can arrange out-of-town stays. ✉ *Italská 31, Vinohrady, 120 00* ☎ *222-254-007* 🖨 *222-252-215* ⊕ *www.marys.cz.*

Prague Accommodation Service. A frankly named agency that can help you find a reasonably priced apartment in the center of town for even a short stay. The prices are some of the cheapest around, and many of their apartments are very local when it comes to design, meaning you won't be getting any interior design ideas from them.

✉ *Opatovická 20, Nové Město*
📠 *233-376-638* ⊕ *www.
accommodation-prague-centre.cz.*

Residence Belgicka. For luxury and comfort, you cannot beat this Vinohrady-based apartment complex, excellent for those staying for an extended period of time. The amenities are absolutely first rate compared to other apartments, with DVD players, cable TV, high-speed Internet, Wi-Fi, access to swimming pool, sauna, and gym in another residence, and the list goes on.
✉ *Belgická 12, Vinohrady*
☎ *221-401-800* 📠 *221-401-834*
⊕ *www.mamaison.com.*

Stop City. From rooms to apartments to hotels, this company in Prague 2 can score cheap deals for you in the Prague center. Nothing fancy for the most part, but the rates are some of the best. ✉ *Vinohradská 24, Vinohrady* ☎ *222-521-252*
⊕ *www.stopcity.com.*

Stop In. This company offers private apartments and rooms, many in the more residential areas of the city. If you are visiting relatives or friends, this could be a fun way to be neighbors. ✉ *Nad Bertramkou 11, Smíchov* 📠 *284-680-115*
⊕ *www.stopin.cz.*

HOSTELS

No matter what your age, you can save on lodging costs by staying at hostels. In some 4,500 locations in more than 70 countries around the world, Hostelling International (HI), the umbrella group for a number of national youth-hostel associations, offers single-sex, dorm-style beds and, at many hostels, rooms for couples or family accommodations. Membership in any HI national hostel association, open to travelers of all ages, allows you to stay in HI-

affiliated hostels at member rates; one-year membership is about $28 for adults (C$35 for a two-year minimum membership in Canada, £14 in U.K., A$52 in Australia, and NZ$40 in New Zealand); hostels charge about $10–$30 per night. Members have priority if the hostel is full; they're also eligible for discounts around the world, even on rail and bus travel in some countries. For more information about hosteling, contact your local youth hostel office.

In the Czech Republic hostels are geared to the college crowd. For further information, visit the Web site ⊕ Backpackers.cz.

The **Clown & Bard** (✉ Bořivojova 102, Žižkov, 130 00 ☎ 222-716-453 ⊕ www.clownandbard.com) is a perfect choice if you want to meet other up-all-night travelers. The rates start at 250 Kč for a dorm room and stop at 450 Kč for a two-person double room.

A central favorite close to all of the bars and shopping is the **Golden Sickle** (✉ Vodičkova 12, Nové Město, 110 00 ☎ 222-230-773 ⊕ www.travellers.cz) rates range from 450 Kč for a bed in a dormitory-style room to 3,000 Kč for a four-bed apartment. At the Internet-equipped **Travellers' Hostel** (✉ Dlouhá 33, Staré Město, 110 00 ☎ 224-826-662 ⊕ www.travellers.cz) rates range from 370 Kč for a bed in a dormitory-style room to 1,300 Kč for a single room with a shower. **Hostelling International–USA** (✉ 8401 Colesville Rd., Suite 600, Silver Spring, MD 20910 ☎ 301/495-1240 📠 301/495-6697 ⊕ www.hiusa. org).

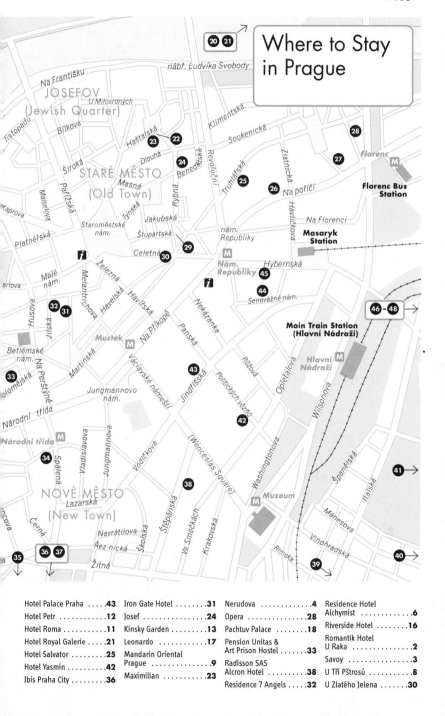

Where to Stay in Prague

STARÉ MĚSTO (OLD TOWN)

Staré Město, Prague's Old Town, is a highly desirable neighborhood to lodge in. The mix of baroque and Gothic buildings creates a storybook feeling. Hotels here are of the old-made-new variety. Don't be surprised to be standing in a hotel lobby that was originally built in the 17th century but looks and smells like a fresh coat of plaster and paint was added a month ago. Trendy restaurants, hip cafés, and the city's best clothing boutiques are all in this area.

$$$$ 🏨 **Four Seasons Prague.** If you love hotels with every small luxury—morning newspapers with your breakfast, in-room massages, and twice-daily maid service, the expense of the rooms will be easier to justify. Sean Connery and Owen Wilson could only agree, having stayed here while they worked in Prague. A baroque house from 1737 and a renovated neoclassical former factory from 1846 are joined together through a contemporary building to form this large luxury hotel with an unbeatable riverside location. Room 234 is the proverbial "room with a view" offering a sweeping vista of the Charles Bridge. Service is consistently excellent and the friendliness of the staff is unbeatable. The in-house restaurant could serve your best meal in Prague. ⊠ *Veleslavinova 21, Staré Město, 110 00* ☎ *221–427–000* 🖶 *221–426–977* ⊕ *www. fourseasons.com* ↪ *141 rooms, 20 suites* ⌂ *Restaurant, in-room safes, minibars, cable TV with movies, health club, massage, sauna, bar, concierge, in-room data ports, business services, meeting rooms, parking (fee), some pets allowed (fee), no-smoking rooms* ⊟ *AE, DC, MC, V* 🍽 *EP* Ⓜ *Line A: Staroměstská.*

$$$$ 🏨 **Grand Hotel Bohemia.** This art nouveau *palais* dominates a picturesque corner near the Prašná brána (Powder Tower). The clean and comfortable hotel was remodeled in the 1990s by its Austrian owners, who opted for a muted, modern look. The overall effect is nice but just shy of elegant. Although the location is unbeatable, and there are little perks, the rooms are a bit overpriced when compared with others. ⊠ *Královdorská 4, Staré Město, 110 00* ☎ *234–608–111* 🖶 *222–329–545* ⊕ *www. grandhotelbohemia.cz* ↪ *73 rooms, 5 suites* ⌂ *Restaurant, café, in-room fax, in-room safes, minibars, cable TV with movies, in-room data ports, bar, meeting rooms, some pets allowed (fee), no-smoking floor* ⊟ *AE, DC, MC, V* 🍽 *BP* Ⓜ *Line B: Nám. Republiky.*

★ **$$$$** 🏨 **Iron Gate Hotel.** An architectural gem offering luxurious details, location, and a peaceful courtyard at a potentially astronomical price (check the hotel's Web site for seasonal deals). The original building dates from the 14th century. During the 16th century, it underwent a major renovation, adding balconies and terraces. And in 2003 it was restored yet again, exposing the original frescoes that had been hidden for years. Expect sleigh beds, tasteful antique touches, and fluffy terry-cloth bathrobes. Public areas have Wi-Fi access. ⊠ *Michalská 19, Staré Město, 110 00* ☎ *225–777–777* 🖶 *225–777–778* ⊕ *www.irongate.cz* ↪ *44 suites* ⌂ *Restaurant, room service, in-room safes, kitchenettes, minibars, cable TV, in-room data ports, concierge, meeting room* ⊟ *AE, MC, V* 🍽 *BP* Ⓜ *Line A: Staroměstská.*

$$$$ ⌂ **Maximilian.** If hotels could be featured on an Oprah makeover show, this would be the result. The transformation is so lovely, it practically brings a tear to the eye. After a renovation in 2005 the Maximilian has become completely modern in the most tasteful way, with classic cherrywood furniture. Comfortable and intimate, it's quiet enough for even the lightest of sleepers and close enough to Old Town Square for the laziest of travelers. ⌂ *Haštalská 14, Staré Město, 110 00* ☎ *225–303–118* ⎙ *225–303–110* ⊕ *www.maximilianhotel.com* ↝ *72 rooms* ⚬ *Restaurant, room service, in-room fax, in-room safes, minibars, cable TV, dry cleaning, laundry service, in-room data ports, business services, meeting rooms, parking (fee), some pets allowed (fee), no-smoking rooms* ▭ *AE, DC, MC, V* ⦿ *BP* Ⓜ *Line A: Staroměstská.*

$$$$
Fodor'sChoice
★ ⌂ **Pachtuv Palace.** Cupped around a historic piece of Staré Město, this palace consists of four buildings: three medieval houses, which were transformed into a baroque palace, and one neoclassicist rooming house built in 1836, offering tremendous views of Prague Castle, Charles Bridge, and the river. The location, view, and beauty of the building are truly unbeatable, not to mention the antique interior design and some of the most comfortable beds around. But what makes this hotel even more alluring is that supposedly Mozart was once locked into one of the rooms here and not let go until he wrote six sonnets for the owner. If you write sonnets, maybe you too can negotiate a deal on the room rate. ⌂ *Karolíny Světlé 34, Staré Město, 110 00* ☎ *234–705–111* ⎙ *234–705–112* ⊕ *www.pachtuvpalace.com* ↝ *50 rooms* ⚬ *In-room safes, minibars, cable TV, in-room DVDs, gym, concierge, room service, in-room data ports, business services, meeting room, parking (fee)* ▭ *AE, DC, MC, V* ⦿ *BP* Ⓜ *Line A: Staroměstská.*

★ **$$$–$$$$** ⌂ **Leonardo.** Apartments are offered here, along with the usual singles, doubles, and suites, at an enviable location: a quiet street, near the Vltava River. The furnishings are clean, with a hint of art deco here and there. The building does beg for a decorative spark, but the helpful staff, comfortable beds, and location make it a nice option. ⌂ *Karolíny Světlé 27, Staré Město, 110 00* ☎ *239–009–239* ⎙ *239–009—238* ⊕ *www.hotelleonardo.cz* ↝ *50 rooms, 11 suites* ⚬ *Restaurant, in-room safes, minibars, cable TV, some pets allowed (fee)* ▭ *AE, DC, MC, V* ⦿ *BP* Ⓜ *Line A: Staroměstská.*

★ **$$$** ⌂ **Josef.** Cool, clean, white lines dominant the decor of this ultra-hip modern boutique hotel designed by London-based Czech architect Eva Jiricna. There are no suites, only single and double rooms, so the sizes range from small to smaller, but Jiricna knows how to manipulate space, glass, and color to make even the smallest space breathable. Wi-Fi is in public areas. ⌂ *Rybná 20, Staré Město, 110 00* ☎ *221–700–111* ⎙ *221–700–999* ⊕ *www.hoteljosef.com* ↝ *110 rooms* ⚬ *Restaurant, café, in-room safes, minibars, cable TV, in-room DVDs, in-room data ports, lobby lounge, dry cleaning, laundry service, in-room data ports, business services, meeting rooms, parking (fee), some pets allowed (fee), no-smoking rooms* ▭ *AE, DC, MC, V* ⦿ *BP* Ⓜ *Line B: Nám. Republiky.*

$$–$$$ ⌂ **Haštal.** The price is great for the location—on a quiet square just a few minutes from the Old Town Square. The building was used as a brewery until the turn of the 20th century. Low on glamour, but nicely appointed. ✉ *Haštalská 16, Staré Město, 110 00* ☎ *222–314–335* 🖷 *222–314–336* ⤳ *24 rooms* ⚄ *Café, minibars, cable TV, parking (fee), some pets allowed (fee); no a/c* ▤ *AE, DC, MC, V* ⦿ *BP* Ⓜ *Line A: Staroměstská.*

$$–$$$ 🏨 **Residence 7 Angels.** Great location, not far from Old Town Square, it's in a residence that originally dates from the 15th century. The rooms differ in decor, with some going for a wrought-iron "country" look and others sporting a sort of overstuffed-sofa "modern" look. A charming restaurant is on-site. Sometimes offers four nights for the price of three out of season. ✉ *Jilská 20, Staré Město, 110 00* ☎ *224–234–381* 🖷 *224–234–381* ⦿ *www.7angels.cz* ⤳ *6 rooms, 4 suites* ⚄ *Restaurant, some kitchenettes, refrigerators, cable TV, laundry service; no a/c* ▤ *AE, MC, V* ⦿ *BP* Ⓜ *Line A: Můstek.*

$$ 🏨 **Hotel Ibis Praha Old Town.** Two words: flower power. That's the design vision for this chain hotel, which opened in 2006. The location is one of the best, putting you right across the street from Obecní dům. Reasonable rates, clean rooms with a modern touch, and Wi-Fi available in public areas and some rooms give this hotel its appeal. ✉ *Na Poříčí 5, Staré Město, 110 00* ☎ *266–000–999* 🖷 *266–000–666* ⦿ *www. ibishotel.com* ⤳ *271 rooms* ⚄ *Restaurant, in-room safes, cable TV, bar, in-room data ports, parking (fee), some pets allowed (fee), no-smoking rooms* ▤ *AE, DC, MC, V* ⦿ *BP* Ⓜ *Line B: Nám. Republiky.*

$$ 🏨 **U Zlatého Jelena.** The simple furnishings may skirt the line on being frumpy, but a killer location, just down from Old Town Square, makes this a nice "budget" choice. If you're curious what most standard Prague apartments are like, this is probably a good example—high ceilings, parquet floors, and brass furniture. And these are probably the largest rooms you will find in the city center without spending a fortune at a four-star hotel. The staff is honest and helpful. ✉ *Celetná 11, Staré Město, 110 00* ☎ *222–317–237* 🖷 *222–318–693* ⦿ *www.beetletour.cz* ⤳ *10 rooms* ⚄ *Café, in-room safes, minibars, cable TV, in-room VCRs, some pets allowed (fee); no a/c* ▤ *AE, DC, MC, V* ⦿ *CP* Ⓜ *Line A: Staroměstská.*

$ 🏨 **Pension Unitas & Art Prison Hostel.** The spartan rooms of this former convent, now operated by the Christian charity Unitas, once served as interrogation cells for the Communist secret police. (Václav Havel was once a "guest.") Today the basement rooms maintain a prison theme, complete with steel bunk beds. The rest of the building is the pension, which is comfortable but not exactly cozy. Expect a shared, but clean, bathroom on each floor and single beds in the

---

DROP ANCHOR

One lodging alternative is "botels": boats moored to the banks of the Vltava that have been fashioned into floating hotels. Prague has several, and what they may lack in comfort, they compensate for in uniqueness. One plus is that you'll probably save a little money over standard hotels. On the downside, you may find yourself spending more trekking to and fro, as the boats tend to be outside the city center. The Admiral (⦿ www. admiral-botel.cz) is the leading botel for the up-market crowd. Budget travelers should take a look at the Racek (⦿ www.botelracek.cz). Always be sure to ask for a room facing the river, rather than the road.

bedrooms. Cheap prices and a great location mean that you need to reserve well in advance, even in the off-season. ☒ *Bartolomějská 9, Staré Město, 110 00* ☏ *224–230–603* 🖷 *224–217–555* ⊕ *www.unitas.cz* 🛏 *40 rooms with shared bath* ⚲ *Restaurant; no a/c, no room TVs, no smoking* 🚬 *AE, DC, MC, V* ⦿ *BP* Ⓜ *Line A: Staroměstská.*

MALÁ STRANA (LESSER QUARTER)

With a bewitching storybook suite of baroque palaces and Renaissance façades, the Lesser Quarter—at the other end of the Charles Bridge from the Old Town—is the darling of Prague. Mostly a quiet area, removed from the bustle across the river, it's also filled with great restaurants and music clubs. Malá Strana provides an excellent location for visiting Prague Castle just up the hill, but may not be the best choice for people with mobility problems. Other cons: access to cars on the narrow cobblestone streets is restricted, parking is difficult, and you'll spend a lot of your time walking on the Charles Bridge to get to the Old Town.

$$$$
FodorsChoice
★

Aria Hotel. In the age of iPod mania, this was Prague's first concept hotel and what a concept it was—a music-themed hotel. Each elegant room is dedicated to a musical genre and equipped with CD/DVD players and speakers. From the outside, you'd never guess that überhipness and gorgeous design lurk within, but few will be disappointed staying here. The rooftop terrace, with its panoramic view of Prague, is simply the best. ☒ *Tržiště 9, Malá Strana, 118 00* ☏ *225–334–111* 🖷 *225–334–666* ⊕ *www. ariahotel.net* 🛏 *52 rooms, 7 suites* ⚲ *Restaurant, café, room service, in-room safes, minibars, cable TV, in-room DVD, gym, massage, sauna, cinema, library, in-room data ports, meeting rooms, parking (fee)* 🚬 *AE, DC, MC, V* ⦿ *BP* Ⓜ *Line A: Malostranská.*

$$$$
FodorsChoice
★

Mandarin Oriental Prague. The picture of understated taste, this outpost of the Mandarin Oriental recently opened in late 2006. Appropriately built in a former monastery, the vaulted ceilings and original 14th century staircases now offer luxurious serenity to guests. Contemporary Asian touches work into a harmonious blend of beige, red, black, and navy. Silk tassels in red or gold indicate to the staff "do not disturb" or "please make up my room." An underground passageway leads to the spa, where a glass floor displays the ruins of a Gothic church uncovered during construction. Here you can receive a Czech specialty, the Linden Blossom scrub, using blossoms long believed to be medicinal in Czech culture. The restaurant serves seasonal dishes that could easily be your best meal in Prague. ☒ *Nebovidská 459, Malá Strana, 118 00* ☏ *233–088–888* 🖷 *233–088–668* ⊕ *www.mandarinoriental.com* 🛏 *99 rooms, 22 suites* ⚲ *Restaurant, in-room safes, minibars, 2 cable TVs, in-room CD and in-room DVDs, in-room data port, gym, spa, massage, sauna, 2 bars, babysitting, dry cleaning, laundry service, Wi-Fi, business services, meeting rooms, fee parking, car rental* 🚬 *AE, DC, MC, V* ⦿ *EP* Ⓜ *Line A: Malostranská.*

$$$$

Nerudova. Built in 1348, this landmark—now a small and modern hotel—is where the author Jan Neruda and his mother lived in 1860. As a tribute, lines from Neruda's *Povidky malostranske (Malá Strana*

Stories) are painted in the stone hallways. The building supposedly has a ghost—you might hear her and her jingling keys in the hallway. Then again, many of the buildings on this street are said to have their own—friendly—ghosts. Try to see a couple of rooms before choosing one as some rooms look out onto a wall. ✉ *Nerudova 44, Malá Strana, 110 00* ☎ *257-535-557* 🖷 *257-531-492* ⊕ *www.hotelneruda-praha.cz* 🛏 *20 rooms* ⚭ *Restaurant, café, in-room safes, minibars, cable TV, parking (fee), some pets allowed (fee)* ▭ *AE, DC, MC, V* ⦿⦿ *BP* Ⓜ *Line A: Malostranská.*

$$$$
FodorsChoice
★
🏨 **Residence Hotel Alchymist.** When dreaming of Prague, this is the hotel that comes to mind. Both the front of the hotel (which is UNESCO-protected) and the squished lobby disguise how large this building actually is. It brings together four Renaissance and baroque houses from the late 15th century. Owned by an Italian and possessing that signature Italian flair, this hotel not only features a 500-year-old staircase, but the imported tiki wood creates a bridge (over a fish-filled pond) that brings together the massage rooms and the sushi bar in the basement. It's truly an embarrassment of riches. ✉ *Tržiště 19, Malá Strana, 118 00* ☎ *257-286-011-016* 🖷 *257-286-017* ⊕ *www.alchymisthotelresidence.com* 🛏 *26 rooms, 20 suites* ⚭ *Restaurant, café, in-room safes, minibars, cable TV, in-room CD and DVD player, in-room data ports, gym, sauna, spa, laundry service, business services* ▭ *AE, DC, MC, V* ⦿⦿ *BP* Ⓜ *Line A: Malostranská.*

$$$-$$$$
🏨 **U Tří Pštrosů.** This inviting inn has had taken a couple licks—first it was flooded, then burned to the ground, and then rebuilt, only to be taken by the Communists. Now it's been restituted to the family owners. But there is beauty in triumph, and the location is so close to the Charles Bridge that you could barter with one of the street vendors from your window. The rooms are spacious and feature a beautifully ornate ceiling. Sadly, there is no air-conditioning, but the rooms do have Wi-Fi, so it's behind the times in some ways and ahead in others. ✉ *Dražického nám. 12, Malá Strana, 118 00* ☎ *257-288-888* 🖷 *257-533-217* ⊕ *www.utripstrosu.cz* 🛏 *14 rooms, 4 suites* ⚭ *Restaurant, minibars, cable TV, laundry service, in-room data ports, meeting room; no a/c* ▭ *AE, DC, MC, V* ⦿⦿ *BP* Ⓜ *Line A: Malostranská.*

$$$
🏨 **Best Western Hotel Kampa.** This early-baroque armory-turned-hotel is tucked away on an abundantly picturesque street at the southern end of Malá Strana, just off Kampa Island. Note the late-Gothic vaulting in the massive dining room. At one time the bucolic setting and proximity to the city center made this lodging option a comparative bargain; now hotels within blocks offer the same, if not better, services and can be a few euros cheaper. But it's a good fallback option if you can't get a room anywhere else in this location. ✉ *Všehrdova 16, Malá Strana, 118 00* ☎ *257-404-444 or 257-404-333* 🖷 *257-404-333* ⊕ *www.bestwestern-ce.com* 🛏 *85 rooms* ⚭ *Restaurant, minibars, cable TV; no a/c* ▭ *AE, MC, V* ⦿⦿ *BP* Ⓜ *Line A: Malostranská.*

★ **$$$**
🏨 **Dům U Červeného Lva** (House at the Red Lion). An intimate, immaculately kept baroque building, dating from the 15th century, this hotel is right on the main thoroughfare in the Lesser Quarter, a five-minute walk from Prague Castle's front gates. Guest rooms have parquet floors

and 17th-century painted-beam ceilings. But a workout is included: there is no elevator, and the stairs are steep. ⊠ *Nerudova 41, Malá Strana, 118 00* ☏*257–533–833* ☒*257–535–131* ⊕*www.hotelredlion.com* ⤳*5 rooms, 3 suites* ⚹ *2 restaurants, in-room safes, minibars, cable TV, bar, some pets allowed; no a/c* ▤ *AE, DC, MC, V* ⏹❘ *BP* Ⓜ *Line A: Malostranská.*

$$$ ▦ **Hotel Roma.** Down the hill from Prague Castle, across the street from Petří hill, and around the corner from Kampa island, this hotel nestles in the middle of some star attractions. The atrium lobby is a bit bland, but a few funky details, including an aquarium window in the lobby wall, give the place some character. Most rooms are simple and spare, with blond-wood furnishings and parquet floors. The Roma also offers suites, eight with real antiques—unfortunately, that also means two single beds with bumping headboards are pushed together. ⊠ *Újezd 24, Malá Strana, 110 00* ☏ *257–326–890* ☒ *257–324–095* ⊕ *www.hotelroma.cz* ⤳ *62 rooms, 25 suites* ⚹ *Restaurant, in-room safes, minibars, cable TV, in-room data ports, gym, sauna, bar, laundry service, Internet room, travel services, parking (fee), some pets allowed (fee); no a/c* ▤ *AE, DC, MC, V* ⏹❘ *BP* Ⓜ *Line A: Malostranská.*

HRADČANY

For some, Prague Castle is the romantic capital in this city. Though it is a hectic spot during the day with a lot of foot traffic, it is quiet and even spacious in the evening, when the starlighted castle grounds open onto hilly parks perfect for long strolls, all the while drinking in a breathtaking panoramic view of the city.

★ **$$$$** ▦ **Savoy.** A modest yellow Jugendstil façade conceals one of the city's most luxurious small hotels. Once a budget hotel, the building was gutted and lavishly refurbished in the mid-1990s. A harmonious maroon-and-mahogany color scheme carries through the public spaces; some rooms are furnished in purely modern style, while others have a 19th-century period look. A tram stop is practically at the front door, making trips into the center quick and easy. ⊠ *Keplerova 6, Hradčany, 118 00* ☏ *224–302–430* ☒ *224–302–128* ⊕ *www.hotel-savoy.cz* ⤳ *55 rooms, 6 suites* ⚹ *Restaurant, café, in-room fax, in-room safes, minibars, cable TV, in-room DVDs, in-room data ports, gym, sauna, concierge, meeting rooms, some pets allowed (fee), no-smoking floor* ▤ *AE, DC, MC, V* ⏹❘ *BP.*

$$$ ▦ **Romantik Hotel U Raka.** With the quaint look of a woodsman's cottage from a bedtime tale, this private guesthouse has a quiet location on the ancient, winding street of Nový Svět, just behind the Loreto Church and a 10-minute walk from Prague Castle. As the name says, the site is saturated with romance. One side of the 18th-century building presents a rare example of half-timbering, and the rooms sustain the country feel. A little luck is needed reserving one of the six rooms, but it does make a wonderful base for exploring Prague. ⊠ *Černínská 10/93, Hradčany, 118 00* ☏ *220–511–100* ☒ *233–358–041* ⊕ *www.romantikhotel-uraka.cz* ⤳ *5 rooms, 1 suite* ⚹ *Cable TV, parking (fee), no-smoking rooms; no kids under 10* ▤ *AE, MC, V* ⏹❘ *BP* Ⓜ *Line A: Hradčanská.*

FodorśChoice
★

NOVÉ MĚSTO (NEW TOWN)

Not exactly, "new," this district dates back to the 14th century and includes the bustling Wenceslas Square. New Town isn't as clean and architecturally fragile as Old Town, but what it loses in baroque curls it makes up for in good location at slightly cheaper prices.

$$$$
Fodor'sChoice
★
Carlo IV. Dripping with glamour, this Italian-owned hotel has an imperial beauty. High ceilings present space for towering palm trees and playful design touches like gargantuan floor lamps and an enormous umbrella lend it an Alice-in-Wonderland quality. A cigar bar is found near the lobby, where you can relax with a cognac inside one of the oldest vauls in Central Europe. Attention to detail trickles down to the cloudlike duvets in the rooms and the fountain in the indoor pool. Old-fashioned rooms are in the original building, which was once used as a bank and have retained the monied feel. Modern rooms are available in the adjoining building. ⊠ *Senovážné nám. 13, Nové Město, 110 00* ☏ *224–593–090* 🖷 *224–593–000* ⊕ *www.boscolohotels.com* ⤳ *130 rooms, 22 suites* ⌂ *Restaurant, in-room safes, minibars, cable TV, indoor pool, gym, hot tub, massage, sauna, steam room, 2 bars, babysitting, dry cleaning, laundry service, in-room data ports, business services, meeting rooms, car rental, parking (fee), some pets allowed (fee), no-smoking rooms* ▤ *AE, DC, MC, V* ⫴◯⫼ *EP* Ⓜ *Line B: Nám. Republiky.*

★ **$$$$**
Hotel Palace Praha. Perched on a busy corner in the city center, this pistachio-green art nouveau building trumpets its Victorian origins. Well-appointed rooms, each with a white-marble bathroom, are dressed in velvety pinks and greens cribbed straight from an Alfons Mucha print. The hotel's restaurant is pure Continental, from the classic garnishes to the creamy sauces. A block from Wenceslas Square, and down the street from Na Příkopě, the advantage here is location, which puts it ahead of other hotels in its class. Children 12 and under stay for free. ⊠ *Panská 12, Nové Město, 111 21* ☏ *224–093–111* 🖷 *224–221–240* ⊕ *www.palacehotel.cz* ⤳ *114 rooms, 10 suites* ⌂ *2 restaurants, in-room safes, minibars, cable TV, in-room data ports, sauna, babysitting, dry cleaning, laundry service, concierge, meeting room, no-smoking floors* ▤ *AE, DC, MC, V* ⫴◯⫼ *BP* Ⓜ *Line A: Můstek.*

$$$–$$$$
Hotel Yasmin. Opened in 2006, the Hotel Yasmin has brought a funky flavor to what, until now, has been a conservative approach to modern in the city's hotels. A

HOME SWAPPING

If you would like to exchange your home for someone else's, join a home-exchange organization. There are two major U.S.-based home exchange organizations. **HomeLink International** (⊠ 2937 NW 9th Terrace, Fort Lauderdale, FL 33311 ☏ 954/566-2687 or 800/638-3841 🖷 954/566-2783 ⊕ www.homelink.org); $110 yearly for a listing, online access, and catalog; $70 without catalog. **Intervac U.S.** (⊠ 30 Corte San Fernando, Tiburon, CA 94920 ☏ 800/756-4663 🖷 415/435-7440 ⊕ www.intervacus.com); $125 yearly for a listing, online access, and a catalog; $65 without catalog.

confluence of classy Asian design and splashy modernism, this hotel is for those who crave übertrendy surroundings in the common areas but prefer clean, breathable, and less flamboyant sleeping rooms. The views are nothing to write home about, but the location—one street over from Václavské náměstí—is. A white lily motif is splashed from floor to ceiling and the decorations—mirrored balls like water drops—add fresh accents. ⊠ *Politickych Veznu 12/913, Nové Město, 110 00* ☎ *221–427–000* 🖷 *221–426–977* ⊕ *www.hotel-yasmin.cz* 📞 *187 rooms, 11 suites* ⚶ *Restaurant, in-room safes, minibars, cable TV, health club, sauna, bar, concierge, in-room data ports, business services, meeting rooms, parking (fee), some pets allowed, no-smoking rooms* ▤ *AE, DC, MC, V* ¶⊙¶ *CP* Ⓜ *Line A: Můstek.*

$$$ 🏨 **Best Western City Hotel Moran.** This renovated 19th-century town house is a comfortable choice for those who want consistency in the quality of their accommodations. A bright, inviting lobby leads to equally bright, clean rooms, with some good views of Prague Castle if you're on an upper floor. ⊠ *Na Moráni 15, Nové Město, 120 00* ☎ *224–915–208* 🖷 *224–920–625* ⊕ *www.bestwestern-ce.com/moran* 📞 *57 rooms* ⚶ *Restaurant, cable TV, in-room data ports, meeting room, some pets allowed, no-smoking floor* ▤ *AE, DC, MC, V* ¶⊙¶ *BP* Ⓜ *Line B: Karlovo nám.*

$$$ 🏨 **Best Western Meteor Plaza.** This hotel is a meeting of two times: modern conveniences in a blue-blooded historic building (Empress Maria Theresa's son, Joseph II, stayed here when he was passing through in the 18th century). The baroque building is five minutes by foot from downtown. Renovations have masked much of the hotel's history behind a modern look. To get a sense of its age, visit the original 14th-century wine cellar. ⊠ *Hybernská 6, Nové Město, 110 00* ☎ *224–192–559 or 224–192–111* 🖷 *224–220–681* ⊕ *www.hotel-meteor.cz* 📞 *90 rooms, 6 suites* ⚶ *Restaurant, minibars, cable TV with movies, gym, sauna, parking (fee); no a/c in some rooms* ▤ *AE, DC, MC, V* ¶⊙¶ *BP* Ⓜ *Line B: Nám. Republiky.*

$$$ 🏨 **Hotel Élite Prague.** A 14th-century Gothic façade and many poetic architectural details have been preserved, thanks to an extensive renovation. Rooms are furnished with antiques, and many have decorated Renaissance-style wooden ceilings. One of the suites is even adorned with a mural ceiling. But rest assured that they did not forsake modern comforts: this is also a Wi-Fi hot spot. ⊠ *Ostrovní 32, Nové Město, 110 00* ☎ *224–932–250* 🖷 *224–930–787* ⊕ *www.hotelelite.cz* 📞 *77 rooms, 2 suites* ⚶ *Restaurant, room service, in-room safes, minibars, cable TV with movies, in-room data ports, hair salon, bar, laundry service, business services, meeting room, parking (fee), some pets allowed (fee)* ▤ *AE, DC, MC, V* ¶⊙¶ *BP* Ⓜ *Line B: Narodní Třida.*

$$$ 🏨 **Opera.** This hotel rejuvenated its grand fin-de-siècle façade with a perky pink-and-white exterior paint job. This exuberance is strictly on the outside though, and the rooms are modern and easier on the eyes. The facilities are frankly overpriced, but the location—close to major tram lines and the Florenc metro—is a plus. Ironically, the opera house itself is not particularly near. ⊠ *Těšnov 13, Nové Město, 110 00* ☎ *222–315–609* 🖷 *222–311–477* ⊕ *www.hotel-opera.cz* 📞 *65 rooms,*

2 suites △ Restaurant, in-room safes, minibars, cable TV, gym, sauna, bar, meeting room, parking (fee), some pets allowed (fee); no a/c ▭ *AE, DC, MC, V* ¶◎¶ *BP* Ⓜ *Line C: Florenc.*

$$$ Ⓗ **Radisson SAS Alcron Hotel.** Opened in 1932, the Alcron was one of Prague's first luxury hotels; a major renovation of the building in 1998 modernized the look but restored the art deco building, the crystal chandeliers, and the milk glass. A dramatic white marble staircase is bound to impress. Rooms are elegant and updated with all the amenities you'd expect in a business-centered hotel. However, the excellent location a block off Wenceslas Square makes it just as attractive to leisure travelers. Both restaurants are excellent, and are consistently rated highly by critics. You get much more comfort for your money here than at a typical chain hotel. ⊠ *Štěpánská 40, Nové Město 110 00* ☎ *222–820–000* 🖷 *222–820–120* ⊕ *www.radissonsas.com* ⟳ *192 rooms, 19 suites* △ *2 restaurants, some in-room faxes, in-room safes, minibars, cable TV with movies, in-room data ports, gym, sauna, bar, dry cleaning, laundry service, in-room data ports, business services, meeting rooms* ▭ *AE, MC, V* ¶◎¶ *BP* Ⓜ *Line A: Můstek.*

$$ Ⓗ **Hotel Harmony.** Looking for that romantic Prague charm? Don't look here. This is for those who want something clean, close, and standard-issue. The stern 1930s façade clashes with the bright 1990s interior, but the cheerful receptionists, comfortably casual rooms, and an easy 10-minute walk to the Old Town compensate for aesthetic flaws. Ask for a room away from the noise of one of Prague's busiest streets. ⊠ *Na Poříčí 31, Nové Město, 110 00* ☎ *222–319–807* 🖷 *222–310–009* ⊕ *www.hotelharmony. cz* ⟳ *60 rooms* △ *2 restaurants, cable TV, meeting rooms, some pets allowed; no a/c* ▭ *AE, DC, MC, V* ¶◎¶ *BP* Ⓜ *Line B: Nám. Republiky.*

★ $–$$ Ⓗ **Hotel Salvator.** The perks here are location and price. This efficiently run establishment just outside the Old Town offers more comforts than most in its class, including cable TV and minibars in all rooms. Rooms are pristine if plain, with standard narrow beds. Two rooms on the top floor have air-conditioning. ⊠ *Truhlářská 10, Nové Město, 110 00 Prague 1* ☎ *222–312–234* 🖷 *222–316–355* ⊕ *www.salvator.cz* ⟳ *28 rooms, 16 with bath; 7 suites* △ *Restaurant, minibars, cable TV, bar, parking (fee), some pets allowed (fee); no a/c in some rooms* ▭ *AE, MC, V* ¶◎¶ *BP* Ⓜ *Line B: Nám. Republiky.*

VINOHRADY

Literally translated to mean "vineyards," as this area was many centuries ago, you can still find vestiges of grapevines in parks like Havlíčkovy sady in Prague 10. Today it's home to some of the city's wealthiest residents, and the values of the town houses here have tripled in value the last decade. For visitors, the wealth means excellent restaurants and pleasant tree-lined streets, perfect for meandering after an exhausting day in the center.

$$$$ Ⓗ **Hotel Le Palais.** Built in 1841 this venerable building served as the home and shop of Prague's main butcher (one of the front rooms was used to produce and sell sausage until 1991). Today you will only find sausage in the distinctive hotel's restaurant. Rooms have original frescoes painted by Bohemian artist Ludek Marold, and a hallway has an original mosaic floor from 1897. Some rooms have fireplaces, making them especially cozy in winter, and all rooms have air-conditioning to make them comfortable in summer. Service is personal and welcoming, and the outstanding gym is a big plus. Public areas and suites are equipped with Wi-Fi. ⊠ *U Zvonařky 1, Vinohrady, 120 00* ☎ *234–634–111* 🖷 *222–634–635* ⊕ *www.palaishotel.cz* 🛏 *60 rooms, 12 suites* ⟏ *Restaurant, minibars, cable TV, in-room DVDs, in-room data ports, gym, hair salon, indoor hot tub, massage, sauna, steam room, lobby lounge, library, meeting rooms, some pets allowed (fee), no-smoking floors, fee parking* ⊟ *AE, DC, MC, V* ⦿ *BP* Ⓜ *Line A: Nám. Miru.*

$$ ⊡ **Hotel Anna.** The bright neoclassical façade and art nouveau details have been lovingly restored on this 19th-century building on a quiet residential street. The suites on the top floors offer a nice view of the historic district. In 2002 the hotel opened an annex, the Dependance Anna, in the central courtyard of the block with 12 cheaper rooms, but you must return to the main hotel for breakfast. In an effort to stay competitive, the hotel has Wi-Fi in its rooms and encourages Internet users to call with questions via Skype. ⊠ *Budečská 17, Vinohrady, 120 21* ☎ *222–513–111* 🖷 *222–515–158* ⊕ *www.hotelanna.cz* 🛏 *22 rooms, 2 suites, 12 annex rooms* ⟏ *Cable TV, Internet, meeting room, some pets allowed (fee); no a/c* ⊟ *AE, MC, V* ⦿ *BP* Ⓜ *Line A: Nám. Miru.*

★ $$ ⊡ **Ibis Praha City.** The price and the location make this hotel a solid pick. A few minutes' walking distance from Wenceslas Square, this is the cheapest air-conditioned place you can find so close to the center. Rooms are without frills but have everything you would expect from an international chain hotel. If you are looking for a reasonably priced place to sleep but little else, it fits the bill quite nicely. ⊠ *Kateřinska 36, Vinohrady, 120 00* ☎ *222–865–777* 🖷 *222–865–666* ⊕ *www.ibishotel.com* 🛏 *181 rooms* ⟏ *Restaurant, minibars, cable TV, some pets allowed (fee), no-smoking rooms* ⊟ *AE, DC, MC, V* ⦿ *EP* Ⓜ *Line C: I. P. Pavlova.*

SMÍCHOV

Smíchov means "mixed neighborhood." When the city had walls, the neighborhood was on the outside and all manner of people could live there. Although it's still a colorful, working-class area, lots of new construction has made it a shopping and entertainment hub as well, with relatively easy access—via tram, metro, or foot—to the city's historical center.

$$$$ ⊡ **Andel's Hotel Prague.** Simply and modernly minimalist, this is where
Fodor'sChoice many of the young, up-and-coming British trendsetters stay. And they
★ should feel right at home, considering the hotel was designed by Britain's Jestico + Whiles. It quickly rose to being the most popular business hotel in the city, offering rooms not only for the in-and-out business person, but luxury apartments for those who feel the pull to stay in Prague longer. With a nod to the Czech glass industry, glass is used liberally for the walls of conference rooms and in the rooms. One of the city's best shopping malls is next door. ⊠ *Stroupežnického 21, Smíchov, 150 00* ☎ *296–889–688* 🖷 *296–889–999* ⊕ *www.andelshotel.com* 🛏 *231 rooms, 8 suites* ⟏ *Restaurant, café, room service, in-room safes, minibars, cable TV, in-room DVDs, in-room data ports, gym, hair salon, mas-*

sage, sauna, bar, laundry service, meeting rooms, no-smoking rooms, fee parking ⊟ *AE, DC, MC, V* ⦿ *BP* Ⓜ *Line B: Anděl.*

$$$$ ▦ **Riverside Hotel.** Most rooms in this small, architectural eye-catcher on the left bank of the Vltava have enviable views of the Fred and Ginger building, the river, or the National Theater—and if the room faces into the courtyard, usually you're compensated with a balcony. The hotel was decorated by French designer Pascale de Montremy, every detail was taken into consideration, down to the plush green bow for room service that reads "Please Make Up My Room." Its wide-striped fabric and French feel inspire cravings for a croissant. Though the hotel does not have room for a full restaurant, a buffet breakfast is included, and sandwiches are offered in the bar or via 24-hour room service. ⊠ *Janáčovo nabřeží 15, Smíchov, 150 00* ☎ *225–994–611* 🖷 *225–994–622* ⊕ *www. riversideprague.com* ⇄ *32 rooms, 13 suites* ⎈ *Restaurant, room service, in-room safes, minibars, cable TV with movies, in-room data ports, bar, dry cleaning, laundry service, meeting room, no-smoking floor* ⊟ *AE, DC, MC, V* ⦿ *BP* Ⓜ *Line B: Anděl.*

$$$ ▦ **Kinsky Garden.** You could walk the mile from this hotel to Prague Castle entirely on the tree-lined paths of Petřín, the hilly park that starts across the street. Opened in 1997 the Best Western hotel takes its name from a garden established by Count Rudolf Kinsky in 1825. The public spaces and rooms are small, but everything is tasteful and comfortable. Aim for a room on one of the upper floors for a view of the park. ⊠ *Holečkova 7, Smíchov, 150 00* ☎ *257–311–173* 🖷 *257–311–184* ⊕ *www.hotelkinskygarden.cz* ⇄ *60 rooms* ⎈ *Restaurant, cable TV with movies, bar, in-room data ports, meeting room, parking (fee), some pets allowed, no-smoking floor* ⊟ *AE, DC, MC, V* ⦿ *BP* Ⓜ *Line B: Anděl.*

$$ ▦ **Arbes Mepro.** Renovations in 2001 added finer furniture and room safes to this hotel. The Smíchov neighborhood has several good restaurants (including the U Mikuláše Dačického wine tavern, across the street from the hotel); shopping at the Nový Smíchov mall (which is behind the hotel); and nice strolls along the river or up the Petřín hill. The wine cellar serves as a breakfast room and can be booked for group dinners. It's a 10-minute walk to the historic center; trams are a block away. ⊠ *Viktora Huga 3, Smíchov, 150 00* ☎ *257–210–410* 🖷 *257–215–263* ⊕ *www.arbes-mepro.cz* ⇄ *27 rooms* ⎈ *In-room safes, cable TV, bar, meeting room, parking (fee), some pets allowed (fee); no a/c* ⊟ *AE, MC, V* ⦿ *BP* Ⓜ *Line B: Anděl.*

$$ ▦ **Hotel Petr.** It is clear from the uninspired interior design that this hotel still holds onto the pant leg of the Communist past. On the plus side, it is set in a quiet part of Smíchov, which is only a few minutes' stroll from the Lesser Quarter. It does not have a full-service restaurant, but it does

---

SAVING ON SUDS

Little extras on your hotel bill–the hot chocolate from room service, that in-house laundry service–can add up. Take your dirty clothes to the local Laundromat and surf the Web at the same time. **Prague Laundromat** (⊠ Korunniæ 14, Vinohrady ☎ 222-510-180 ⊕ www. volny.cz/laundromat/english.htm) has magazines, snacks, and a staff that speaks English if you need to buy soap.

serve breakfast (included in the price). It's a 10-minute walk from the closest metro stop and a five-minute walk from the closest tram stop. ⊠ *Drtinova 17, Smíchov, 150 00* ☎ *257–314–068* 🖷 *257–314–072* ⊕ *www.hotelpetr.cz* 🖙 *37 rooms, 2 suites* ⚴ *Restaurant, cable TV, in-room data ports, parking (fee), some pets allowed (fee); no a/c* ⊟ *AE, MC, V* 📍⊙ *BP* Ⓜ *Line B: Anděl.*

ŽIŽKOV

Though Prague is an unbelievably safe city for anyone to amble about alone, this is one of the seedier parts. It's a bit grittier and louder than other sections. With that said, it is a great neighborhood for extroverts who like student bars, music clubs, and hangouts where a fashion parade of people with piercings, tattoos, dreadlocks, or a dog (and sometimes all of the above) come to socialize. Being an eclectic and punk hood, it may come as little surprise that Žižkov is a popular spot for students or backpackers to stay at a hostel.

$$ 🖾 **Arcotel Teatrino.** The keys to this building have passed through many hands—in 1910 it was the city hall of Žižkov, then a theater, and during Communism a bar (rumor has it, the upstairs rooms were used as a rendezvous point for couples). Today this hotel, which was rebuilt in 2000, has emerged as a beacon of classiness in a neighborhood that is not so classy, but it's still just two tram stops from the city center. The original art nouveau design was kept and paired with modern accoutrements. ⊠ *Bořivojova 53, Žižkov, 130 00* ☎ *221–422–111* 🖷 *221–422–222* ⊕ *www.arcotel.cc* 🖙 *73 rooms* ⚴ *Restaurant, in-room safes, minibars, cable TV with movies, gym, sauna, steam room, meeting rooms, parking (fee), some pets allowed (fee); no a/c* ⊟ *AE, DC, MC, V* 📍⊙ *BP* Ⓜ *Line A: Jiřího z Poděbrad.*

$$ 🖾 **Hotel Ariston.** The staff is proud to say that this hotel is always undergoing some type of renovation, at least every three years that is. The hotel's lobby is decorated in country floral and its rooms are dignified and comfortable. Clean, for sure, but without an inspiring design, you might want to consider this as a fallback in case you can't find something closer at a similar price. The hotel fronts a tram road, so request a room in the back if you're a light sleeper. ⊠ *Seifertova 65, Žižkov, 130 00* ☎ *222–782–517* 🖷 *222–780–347* ⊕ *www.europehotels.cz* 🖙 *61 rooms* ⚴ *Restaurant, in-room safes, cable TV, some pets allowed (fee); no a/c* ⊟ *AE, MC, V* 📍⊙ *BP.*

$$ 🖾 **Hotel Olšanka.** The boxy modern look begs for a makeover, but the main attraction is its outstanding 50-meter swimming pool and updated sports center, which includes a pair of tennis courts and even aerobics classes. Rooms are clean and, though basic, have the expected amenities. A relaxing sauna reserves alternating nights for men, women, or both. The sports facilities can close in August. Although the neighborhood is nondescript, the center is only 10 minutes away by direct tram.

✉ *Táboritská 23, Žižkov, 130 87* ☎ *267–092–202* 🖶 *222–714–320* ⊕ *www.hotelolsanka.cz* 💬 *200 rooms* ⚄ *Restaurant, cable TV, tennis court, pool, health club, bar, in-room data ports, meeting rooms, some pets allowed (fee); no a/c* ▤ *AE, MC, V* ⎮◯⎮ *BP.*

EASTERN SUBURBS

\$\$ 🏨 **Hotel Astra.** This modern hotel is best for drivers coming into town from the east, although the nearby metro station puts it within fairly convenient striking distance from the center (about 15 minutes by metro). The neighborhood is quiet, if ordinary, and the rooms are more comfortable than most in this price range. ✉ *Mukařovská 1740/18, Stodůlky, 100 00* ☎ *274–813–595* 🖶 *274–810–765* ⊕ *www.hotelastra.cz* 💬 *43 rooms, 10 suites* ⚄ *Restaurant, cable TV, nightclub, meeting room, parking (fee), some pets allowed; no a/c* ▤ *AE, DC, MC, V* ⎮◯⎮ *BP* Ⓜ *Line A: Skalka; then walk south on Na padesátém about 5 min to Mukařovská.*

\$\$ 🏨 **Hotel Ibis Karlín.** Minutes from the city center in a peaceful neighborhood with cheap restaurants—not to mention a great wine bar—this hotel offers an excellent way to save money, without sacrificing location or cleanliness. ✉ *Šaldova 54, Karlín, 186 00 Prague 8* ☎ *222–332–800* 🖶 *224–812–681* 💬 *226 rooms* ⚄ *In-room safes, restaurant, cable TV, meeting rooms, parking, pets allowed* ▤ *AE, DC, MC, V* ⎮◯⎮ *BP* Ⓜ *Line B: Křižíkova.*

\$\$ 🏨 **Hotel Royal Galerie.** A decidedly friendly staff will go out of their way to answer any questions you might have regarding your stay or Prague. Rooms are bland but the atrium restaurant is relaxing. The neighborhood, which has made a tremendous comeback after the 2002 floods, is laid-back while being only a few tram stops from the center. ✉ *Křižíkova 87, Karlín, 186 00 Prague 8* ☎ *222–323–340* 🖶 *222–323–340* 💬 *22 rooms* ⚄ *Restaurant, cable TV, meeting room, hot tub, sauna, parking, pets allowed* ▤ *AE, DC, MC, V* ⎮◯⎮ *BP* Ⓜ *Line B: Křižíkova.*

\$ 🏨 **Hotel Arlington.** Ten to 15 minutes outside the city center by metro or tram, this quiet family-owned hotel offers modest rooms in a peaceful neighborhood. It's near the Sazka Arena, for all of the sports and concert fans who don't want to stumble too far to their rooms after a high-energy event. ✉ *Kurta Konráda 22, Vysočany, 190 00 Prague 9* ☎ *226–201–910-13* 💬 *25 rooms* ⚄ *Restaurant, cable TV; no a/c* ▤ *AE, DC, MC, V* ⎮◯⎮ *BP* Ⓜ *Line B: Českomoravská.*

WESTERN SUBURBS

\$\$\$\$ 🏨 **Hotel Diplomat.** This hotel is a popular choice with business travelers thanks to its location between the airport and downtown. From the hotel you can easily reach the city center by metro. The modern rooms have a serious character for the serious traveler, tastefully furnished and quite comfortable. Wi-Fi is available in public areas. ✉ *Evropská 15, Dejvice, 160 00* ☎ *296–559–111* 🖶 *296–559–215* ⊕ *www.diplomatpraha.cz* 💬 *369 rooms, 13 suites* ⚄ *2 restaurants, café, cable TV with movies, gym, sauna, bar, nightclub, in-room data ports, meeting room, parking (fee), no-smoking floors* ▤ *AE, DC, MC, V* ⎮◯⎮ *BP* Ⓜ *Line A: Dejvická.*

Nightlife
& the Arts

4

WORD OF MOUTH

"When I go to the Czech Philharmonic concerts or operas at the National Theater . . . I dress up a lot. The locals are usually VERY dressed up at these events, especially for big concerts. Off-season [events] or smaller venues will be more casual, but older Europeans will almost always be more dressed up than your average tourist. As long as you are neat and presentable and show that you are respectful of the performance, you will fit in. Enjoy!"

—amp322

By Raymond
Johnston

HIGHBROW ENTERTAINMENT IS THE BEST DEAL IN PRAGUE—SECOND ONLY TO THE BEER. The city is home to several well-respected orchestras and opera companies that have their roots in the 19th century, and classical venues that have seen the likes of Mozart and Dvořák conducting their own works. Tickets for highbrow entertainment are reasonably priced compared to other cities. Even if your experience with classical music is limited to old Bugs Bunny cartoons, consider stepping out to the opera or the concert house while you're here. Rarely is high quality culture so accessible.

So too are rock and pop acts. Increasingly Prague is popping up on the touring circuits of old favorites like Bob Dylan and Eric Clapton up through modern acts like Green Day and Pink. Prices for Western shows are high by local standards, which means tickets are often available up to the last minute.

For more intimate evenings, several jazz clubs offer everything from swing to fusion in settings ranging from medieval vaulted basements to cruise boats. House and techno can be found in renovated movie theaters and former factories. In the summer, much of the action moves to outdoor festivals and the clubs in town can be a bit dead.

Czech rock and punk bands are almost unknown outside the country, but they're worth checking out. The most popular bands come and go with the season, but of the local bands with staying power, the Plastic People of the Universe is probably the best known. Be sure to check the times of live rock shows. Many clubs have to start and end early because of noise regulations.

Live theater is rarely in English, although a few venues have been experimenting with simultaneous English supertitles. Czech versions of recent Broadway musicals will probably disappoint those who have seen the originals. There is, however, a wide variety of nonverbal theater and puppet shows tailored for an international audience.

Before 1989, bar offerings were fairly limited to beer and shots of domestic rum or *slivovice* (plum brandy), and most bars closed by 10 PM or so. Now Western-style cocktail bars have come to dominate the downtown area, and traditional Czech pubs, with long wooden tables, early closing hours, and menus that look like they've been run off on mimeograph machines are being pushed out. That's a shame, because nothing beats a good night at the pub for a true Czech experience.

RAYMOND'S TOP 5

1. **State opera.** The productions are solid, and the venue's interior is one of the city's best sights.
2. **Night cruise.** Prague's night skyline is stunning, and cruises provide an opportunity to relax.
3. **Jazz club Agharta.** Lots of cafés offer live music, but the quality is inconsistent. Agharta offers professional acts in a historical vaulted basement.
4. **Pivovarsky dům.** If you're coming to Prague for the beer, this microbrewery serves up the best, and it doesn't employ gimicks.
5. **Laterna magika.** The best theater for those that don't speak Czech.

The cheap beer—combined with the advent of new low-cost airlines—has a downside. Loads of tourists, mostly from Britain, are now arriving on special "stag night" package tours that promise tons of beer combined with sleazy adult entertainment. Weekends are especially bad. Mostly the stags are harmless, but if you happen to run into a gaggle of drunken guys with bad haircuts and silly T-shirts, this is likely a stag, and best avoided. Some bars have banned them altogether. Look for the "No Stag Parties" signs on classier venues for a quiet evening.

A word of caution about adult entertainment. Thanks to the growing popularity of Prague as a stag destination, several dance and strip clubs have sprung up on the sides streets at the upper end of Wenceslas Square. Although these places are legal, they aren't always safe or cheap. Some establishments charge large sums of money for every quarter hour you stay; others simply charge outrageous fees for drinks. Wherever you go, be sure to watch your wallet. Professional thieves frequent the same areas and target those who have had too much to drink.

NIGHTLIFE

Clubbing

The number of clubs in Prague is ever-growing, and the party shows no sign of letting up. Local house, techno, jungle, and trip-hop DJs—not to mention fairly well-known visitors—have made a home in some clubs. Other places specialize in campy Czech pop songs, which are often cheesy Western tunes from '70s and '80s with Czech lyrics. Most dance spots open at 9 or 10 PM, but things don't heat up until after midnight and then keep going until 4 or 5 AM. Unless there's a particularly well-known DJ, the cover charge is usually fairly nominal—30 Kč to 150 Kč.

Abaton. Few signs point the way to this unadorned renovated factory in an industrial area, and the street isn't even named on many maps. The lineup varies from punk to metal and—less often—world music or alternative. This is one of the few venues in town that has live music until really late. ⊠ *Na Košince 8, Libeň* ☎ *No phone* Ⓜ *Line B: Palmovka.*

Double Trouble. If you've got it, flaunt it—that's the mentality at this "no blush music bar" encouraging people to get wild and dance on the tables. A younger crowd flocks to it, but those seeking a mellow joint think the club is aptly named and avoid it. The music varies, often dipping into cheesy pop. ⊠ *Melantrichova 17, Staré Město* ☎ *221–632–414* ⊕ *www.doubletrouble.cz* Ⓜ *Line A: Staroměstská.*

Duplex. Mick Jagger booked this multilevel penthouse nightclub for his 60th birthday party. On weekend evenings, there's dancing and DJs with music that varies widely. Because of the location and aggressive marketing on the street level, the crowd is heavy with tourists who like to travel in packs, and prices are above the norm. ⊠ *Václavské nám. 21,*

Prague Nightlife

KEY
- ● Nightlife
- ① Late-Night Bites
- Ⓜ Metro stations
- 🛈 Tourist information

0 — 250 yards
0 — 250 meters

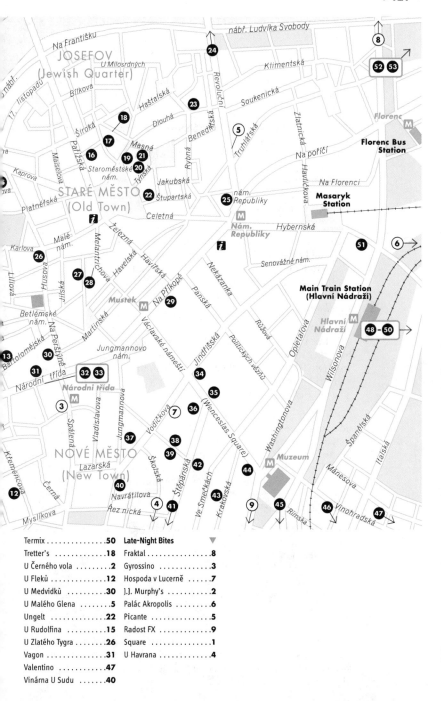

Nové Město ☎ *732–222–111* ⊕ *www.duplexduplex.cz* Ⓜ *Line A or B: Můstek.*

Face to Face. Break-dancing scenes from the film, *Everything Is Illuminated* were shot in this trendy club located on a noisy island. The music varies, usually based on a party of some kind or a theme night. ⊠ *Hlávkův most 1125, Štvanice ostrov* ☎ *242–489–343* ⊕ *www.facetoface.cz* Ⓜ *Line C: Vltavská.*

Karlovy Lázně. Inside a former bathhouse next to the Charles Bridge, this club claims to be the biggest in central Europe. We're not sure about that, but it is pretty big, with four levels of music ranging from house to soul and even old-school disco. The crowd tends to be a mix of young locals and tourists. Lines can be long on weekends. ⊠ *Smetanovo nábřeží 198, Staré Město* ☎ *222–220–502* ⊕ *www.karlovylazne.cz* Ⓜ *Line A: Staroměstská.*

★ **Mecca.** Show off your expensive designer jeans here. This converted factory is *the* place to get down with the überhip. However, if you're not a night owl, be aware that the DJ doesn't usually get going until after midnight. Live acts tend to start around 10 PM. The club has a great lighting, a mirrored disco ball, and a downstairs lounge. ⊠ *U Průhonu 3, Holešovice* ☎ *283–870–522* ⊕ *www.mecca.cz* Ⓜ *Line C: Vltavská.*

Radost FX. A clubbing institution dating from the early '90s, this place still draws a loyal following. The dance floor can be kind of cramped, but other rooms offer lots of seats and couches for hanging out. Those with two left feet can chill upstairs with a drink or eat food late in the vegetarian restaurant. ⊠ *Bělehradská 120, Nové Město* ☎ *603–193–711* ⊕ *www.radostfx.cz* Ⓜ *Line C: I. P. Pavlova.*

Retro. With a location just a bit out of the center, this club provides exodus from the hassle of downtown. The street-level part is a pleasant functionalist-style café with outdoor seating, while the lower level houses a club with a big dance floor. The name is a bit misleading. Although there are some '80's nights and other "retro" music events, the bulk of the schedule is hip-hop and other more modern sounds. ⊠ *Francouzská 4, Vinohrady* ☎ *604–956–272 bar–restaurant* Ⓜ *Line A: Nám. Míru.*

Studio 54. If the party's over, but you're just getting started, this spot specializes in "after-parties" that start at 5 AM, and go on through the early afternoon. Sometimes, usually Friday, there's a headline act at 11 PM or midnight, but normally the place is closed until 4 AM. Most of the clientele are staff finishing their shifts at other bars and clubs. ⊠ *Hybernská 38, Nové Město* ☎ No phone Ⓜ *Line B: Nám. Republiky.*

Jazz Clubs

Jazz gained notoriety under the Communists as a subtle form of protest, and the city still has some great jazz clubs, featuring everything from swing to blues and modern. All listed clubs have a cover charge, usually around 100 Kč to 200 Kč.

Fodor'sChoice **AghaRTA.** Baring the name of an old Miles Davis album, this small but
★ charming vaulted basement is home base for many local jazz acts. The
management also runs a jazz record label and sells their CDs at the club's
store. The place can't handle big acts, so the club's ongoing jazz festival often puts name acts into Lucerna Music Bar (⇨ Rock & Live
Music Clubs, *below*). Music starts around 9 PM, but come an hour earlier to get a seat. ⊠ *Železná 16, Staré Město* ☎ *222–211–275* ⊕ *www.
agharta.cz* Ⓜ *Line A or C: Můstek.*

★ **Jazz Club U staré paní** (USP Jazz Lounge). This club, in a small hotel,
hosts some of the better jazz acts in town, and DJs play after midnight.
Like most of the other clubs, it's too small to handle the business. That
means show up early to get a decent seat. The club also serves a late
dinner. ⊠ *Michalská 9, Staré Město* ☎ *603–551–680* Ⓜ *Line A:
Staroměstská.*

Metropolitan Jazz Club. Old-time swing and some blues are played by
the house bands at this pleasant, unassuming courtyard club. It's great
when you want a cool sound track to enjoy some drinks. ⊠ *Jungmannova 14, Nové Město* ☎ *224–947–777* Ⓜ *Line A or B: Můstek.*

Reduta. This is where President Bill Clinton jammed with Czech President Václav Havel in 1994, and lots of pictures of that night are still
hanging around the joint. Reduta was one of the bigger clubs in the '60s
and '70s, and still feels a little like a dated museum of those glory days.
⊠ *Národní 20, Nové Město* ☎ *224–912–246* ⊕ *www.redutajazzclub.
cz* Ⓜ *Line B: Národní třída.*

U Malého Glena. Patrons are willing to cram into "Little Glen" where
solid house bands and visiting acts come to jam. Get there early to stake
out a seat near the stage; the tunnel-shape vault can be crowded.
⊠ *Karmelitská 23, Malá Strana* ☎ *257–531–717* ⊕ *www.malyglen.cz*
Ⓜ *Line A: Malostranská.*

Ungelt. Hidden in the side streets behind Old Town Square, this basement has been around since the 15th century and has been a club since
2000. The house bands are decent and play jazz, blues, or fusion depending on the night. You won't be among locals, however. The touristy
location and the price keeps them at bay. ⊠ *Týn 2, Staré Město*
☎ *224–895–748* ⊕ *www.jazzblues.cz* Ⓜ *Line A: Staroměstská.*

Pubs & Bars

Cocktail bars and lounges are not traditional Prague fixtures, but several modern-style bars catering to a young crowd have elbowed their
way in over the past few years. Still, the classic Czech experience remains
at the pub (*pivnice* or *hospoda*), social hubs that are liberally sprinkled
throughout the city, sadly disappearing from the town center. Tourists
are welcome to join in the evening ritual of sitting around large tables
and talking, smoking, and—what else?—drinking beer.

Alcohol Bar. Rare rums and 70 types of whiskey round out one of the
largest selections of liquor in Prague in an upscale bar right near Old
Town Square. Small tables and usually unobtrusive music make it a per-

CLOSE UP

Pub Etiquette

BEFORE VENTURING into a Prague pub get familiar with the subtle points of pub etiquette. First, always ask if a chair is free before sitting down (*Je tu volno?*). To order a beer (*pivo*), do not wave the waiter down or shout across the room; he knows you want beer—most pubs serve one brand—and will bring it over to you without asking. Subsequent rounds appear without asking. To refuse, just shake your head or say "no thanks" (*ne, děkuju*). At the end of the evening, usually at around 10:30 or 11, the waiter will come to tally the bill. In a traditional pub, for each beer the waiter will make one mark on a strip of paper. Don't lose the paper or doodle on it. Also, it's a good idea to ask how much each beer costs before ordering and keep track of how many you've had. Some waiters doctor the bills, especially for large groups. For tipping, the common practice is to round up the bill when paying, rather than leaving extra money on the table. Only give a Western-style tip for exceptional service.

fect spot for an intimate conversation. A bouncer by the door discourages large, boisterous groups from trying to enter. ⊠ *Dušní 6, Staré Město* ☎ *224–811–744* Ⓜ *Line A: Staroměstská.*

Bar and Books. Aggressively chasing the cigar set, this sister establishment of two New York bars stocks top-shelf brandies, whiskies, and port wines. Some have rather eye-popping price tags per shot, but they're worth it for those in the know. The dark-wood interior has a formal air suited to whispered discussions of high finance. ⊠ *Tynská 19, Staré Město* ☎ *224–808–250* ⊕ *www.barandbooks.cz* Ⓜ *Line A: Staroměstská.*

Bugsy's. Modern steel-and-glass, lights-in-the-bar design gives this popular American-style cocktail bar a modern look. The list of drinks has all the expected favorites, and sometimes there's live music. Check out the curio rack showing off one of the last Bacardi rum bottles to come from pre-Castro Cuba. ⊠ *Pařížská 10, enter on Kostečna*, Josefov ☎ 224–810–287 ⊕ www.bugsysbar.com Ⓜ Line A: Staroměstská.

Caffrey's Irish Bar. Caffrey's is one of the less rowdy Irish bars in town, probably because it's a touch pricey. The menu offers a full Irish breakfast in addition to burgers and salads. On St. Patrick's Day, this bar is the headquarters of organized celebrations. ⊠ Staroměstské nám., Staré Město ☎ 224–828–031 ⊕ www.caffreys.cz Ⓜ Line A: Staroměstská.

Jágr's Sports Bar. The homegrown star of the New York Rangers hockey team runs this bar with large TV screens and a decent menu. A roulette wheel is available, and the occasional celebrity has been spotted, but watching sports is the main attraction. ⊠ Václavské nám. 56, Nové Město ☎ 224–032–481 Ⓜ Line A or C: Muzeum.

Jáma. (The Hollow). An outdoor beer garden hidden from passersby on the street provides a refuge from the noisy downtown crowds. The indoor bar is decorated with old rock-and-roll posters. Beer and hard cider on tap go with Mexican food and some pretty good burgers. Internet access is available here for a reasonable price, and Wi-Fi access is free. ⊠ V Jámě 7, Nové Město ☎ 224–222–383 ⊕ www.jamapub.cz Ⓜ Line A or B: Můstek.

M1 Secret Lounge. *Movie stars in town for a shoot have been known to stop by this slightly hidden lounge on a side street in Old Town. Fashionistas like to pose in the sleek, underdecorated science fiction–esque setting while sipping their cocktails.* ⊠ Masná 1, Staré Město ☎ 221–874–256 Ⓜ Line A: Staroměstská.

Olympia. *A hot spot from the 1930s, returned to its former glory, provides a somewhat romanticized but enjoyable take on a Czech pub. The interior is quite large, with 250 seats, but still the place gets very busy. Special unpasteurized Pilsner Urquell beer is served.* ⊠ Vitežná 7, Malá Strana ☎ 251–511–079 ⊕ www.olympia-restaurant.cz Ⓜ Line B: Anděl.

FodorśChoice ★ **Pivovarský dům.** This brewpub—which has been around only a decade—may be short on history, but it makes up for that with outstanding beer. The dark, light, and seasonal microbrew beers are stellar. A small menu of routine pub fare is printed on the place mats. The food is good, but a slight letdown when compared to the beer. Fermenting beer can be viewed through a window. ⊠ *Lípová 15, Nové Město* ☎ 296–216–666 Ⓜ *Line A or B: Můstek.*

★ **Pivovary Staropramen** (Staropramen Brewery). For beer, why not go directly to the source? *Staropramen* means "old source," and it's one of the most ubiquitous beers in the city. Two bars inside the brewery, Pivní bar and Restaurace Na verandách–Hospoda, serve several varieties of beer including one that is only sold at the brewery. With advance reservations, tours are available. ⊠ *Nádražní 84, Smíchov* ☎ 257–191–200 *restaurant, 257–191–402 tours* Ⓜ *Line B: Anděl.*

Rocky O'Reillys Irish Pub. Stag parties are welcome—if they keep it down to a roar—at Prague's largest Irish pub, which also shows soccer matches on TV. In the cooler months, there's a burning fireplace. Unless you're a soccer fan, though, it's best not to go when games are being shown on TV; it's mellower at other times. Weekday lunches are also quiet. ⊠ Štepanská 32, Nové Město ☎ 222–231–060 ⊕ *www.rockyoreillys. cz* Ⓜ *Line A or B: Můstek.*

Tretter's. The lost elegance of the 1930s, with clean lines on dark wood, is re-created in a bar that serves Manhattans, martinis, and other classic cocktails, sometimes with live jazz in the background. This was a trendsetter in Prague when it first opened for classic cocktails. ⊠ *V Kolkovně 3, Josefov* ☎ 224–811–165 ⊕ *www.tretters.cz* Ⓜ *Line A: Staroměstská.*

U Černého vola (At the Black Ox). The last old-fashioned pub in the Prague Castle area, this place has cheap beer and the classic long tables. It's almost impossible to find many seats together at any time, though. Terry Jones, of Monty Python fame, is known to be a fan. ⊠ *Loretánské nám. 1, Hradčany* ☎ 220–513–481 Ⓜ *Line A: Hradčandská.*

U Fleků. The oldest brewpub in Europe—open since 1499—makes a tasty, if overpriced, dark beer. The steady stream of tours means it's hard to find a seat. A brewery museum (phone for reservations) opened in 1999. Cabaret shows have been added to the entertainment. Beware of waiters putting unordered shots of liquor on your table. If you don't insist they remove them right away, they'll be on your bill. ⊠ *Křemencova 11, Nové Město* ☎ *224–934–019* ⊕ *www.ufleku.cz* Ⓜ *Line B: Karlovo nám.*

U Medvídků. A former brewery dating as far back as the 15th century, U Medvídků now serves draft Budvar shipped directly from České Budějovice. Reservations are recommended as organized tours often fill the entire bar. The interior, including the tap, have a turn-of-the-20th-century flavor. At times the bar offers exclusive Budvar brews available only at this location. ⊠ *Na Perštýně 7, Staré Město* ☎ *224–211–916* ⊕ *www.umedvidku.cz* Ⓜ *Line B: Národní třída.*

U Rudolfina. Some people claim the way the beer is tapped here makes it the best in town, which probably explains the constant crowds. This was one of the first places in the world to offer unpasteurized beer from tanks, rather than kegs. And the place still retains its old-fashioned charm, making it one of the best authentic Czech pubs in a heavily touristed area. Groups should make reservations—the free table is a rarity. ⊠ *Křížovnická 10, Josefov* ☎ *222–313–088* Ⓜ *Line A: Staroměstská.*

U Zlatého Tygra. The last of the old, smoky, surly pubs in the Old Town is famous for being one of the three best Prague pubs for Pilsner Urquell. It is also renowned as a former hangout of one of the country's best-known and beloved writers, Bohumil Hrabal, who died in 1997. Reservations are not accepted; one option is to show up at 3 PM, when the pub opens, with the rest of the early birds. ⊠ *Husova 17, Staré Město* ☎ *222–221–111* Ⓜ *Line A: Staroměstská.*

Vinárna U Sudu. While Prague is beer territory, this pays homage to that other camp: wine. A mazelike, multilevel cellar forms the large wine bar in a baroque building. This is usually one of the first places during the year to crack open burčák, new wine served shortly after harvest. ⊠ *Vodičkova 10, Nové Město* ☎ *222–232–207* Ⓜ *Line B: Karlovo nám.*

Evening Boat Trips

A relatively new addition to the evening entertainment scene is a scenic boat trip on the Vltava. Several operators now offer two- to three-hour evening floats, usually complete with music and plenty of food and drink.

Dinner Cruise with Music. This "dinner cruise" usually degenerates into a singalong once the beer kicks in, so be prepared for boisterous merriment. The boat is heated and this cruise runs in both winter and summer. The relatively early departure hour—7 PM—means you can catch the sunset during summertime. Entry price includes a buffet dinner and welcome drink, but no additional beverages. ⊠ *Na Františku, under Čechův most Josefov* ☎ *224–810–030* ⊕ *www.evd.cz.*

Evening cruise. Significantly cheaper than trips with live music, the cruises offer some fun pop music, a dance floor, and a bar. Tickets are available at the boats, with departures between 8 and 8:30 PM in the summer. ⊠ *Rašínovo na'břeží, near Palackého bridge* ☎ *224–931–013* ⊕ *www.paroplavba.cz.*

Jazzboat. The Russian-made riverboat *Kotva* was refitted in 2001 and claims to be the fastest on the Vltava. The bands are usually local. Be on time for the shows, as the ship normally leaves at the appointed 8:30 PM departure time. You can also buy food during the cruise, but take cash since credit cards are not accepted. ⊠ *Usually takes off from pier No. 5, under Čechův most, Josefov* ☎ *731–183–180* Ⓜ *Line A: Staroměstská.*

U Bukanýra. The name works out to "At the Buckaneer," but the logo bears more than a passing resemblance to Humphrey Bogart in *The African Queen.* This anchored "house-boat music bar" gives you the feeling of being on the river without having to commit to a three-hour tour. Besides a few life preservers, the nautical theme isn't taken too far. ⊠ *Hořejší nábr., Smíchov* ☎ *608–973–582* Ⓜ *Line B: Karlovo nám.*

Rock & Live Music Clubs

Prague's rock, alternative, and world music scene is thriving. Rock bands on reunion tours find enthusiastic crowds in clubs and arenas. Cover bands are pretty good (Lou Reed once mistook a recording by the local Velvet Underground's cover band for the real thing). World music, especially Romany bands often sell out.

Baráčnická rychta. A former meeting hall in the 19th century, this venue now hosts concerts of world music bands mixed in with local rock and funk. The upstairs has a pleasant beer garden with decent prices for the area. ⊠ *Tržiště 23, Malá Strana* ☎ *257–532–461* Ⓜ *Line A: Malostranská.*

Futurum. Video parties and punk or Goth bands dominate the lineup at this out-of-the-way club with 1950s sci-fi decor, a solid video and sound system, and lots of beer-stained couches. ⊠ *Zborovská 7, Smíchov* ☎ *257–328–571* ⊕ *www.musicbar.cz* Ⓜ *Line B: Anděl.*

Klub Delta. A home for underground Czech bands since the Velvet Revolution, this club is decidedly far from the center. Although it's hard to find, the trip out can be rewarding since new, edgy bands share the program with famous dissident bands from the 1970s. ⊠ *Vlastina 886, Dejvice* ☎ *233–312–443* Ⓜ *Line A: Dejvice, then a tram or bus.*

Lucerna Music Bar. Rock bands on the comeback trail, touring bluesmen like Bo Didley, plus Beatles and Rolling Stones cover bands make up the live schedule. Another big draw are the nights of 1980s or '90s music videos. ⊠ *Vodičkova 36, Nové Město* ☎ *224–217–108* ⊕ *www. musicbar.cz* Ⓜ *Line A or B: Můstek.*

Malostranská Beseda. For a change, here's a club that's upstairs rather than in the basement. The building was a popular meeting place for writers and other artists in the 19th century. Over the years it's been a theater, and since 1971 a folk and country club. Blues, rock, and ska bands make it onto the program these days. ⊠ *Malostranské nám. 21, Malá Strana* ☎ *257–532–092* Ⓜ *Line A: Malostranská.*

★ **Palác Akropolis.** The city's best live music club, and home to an ongoing world-music festival called United Colors of Akropolis. When shows are sold out, though, this place can be pretty packed. The main room closes at 10 PM due to noise concerns. DJs play in the two side bars until late in the evening. ⊠ *Kubelíkova 27, Žižkov* ☎ *299–330–913* Ⓜ *Line A: Nám. Jiřího z Poděbrad.*

Rock Café. This dark little club hosts punk and alternative rock acts with the occasional screening of a movie on video. The bar is painted in orange and yellow, a tribute to the club's whiskey. ⊠ *Národní 20, Nové Město* ☎ *224–914–416* ⊕ *www.rockcafe.cz* Ⓜ *Line B: Národní třída.*

Fodor'sChoice **Roxy.** Part nightclub, part performance space, the Roxy doubles as a residence for DJs and a popular venue for electronica and touring cult bands. The large former theater has a comfortable, lived-in feel. The fun usually ends around 10 PM or so owing to complaints from the neighbors about noise. All exits from the club are final, and patrons are encouraged not to hang around the area. Upstairs, the NoD space has all manner of bizarre acts. Monday is free. ⊠ *Dlouhá 33, Staré Město* ☎ *224–826–296* ⊕ *www.roxy.cz* Ⓜ *Line B: Nám. Republiky.*

Švandovo divadlo Na Smichove. This popular Smíchov night spot does double duty as a concert venue on some nights and a drama stage on others. Interesting avant-garde bands occasionally fill gaps in the schedule. ⊠ *Štefánikova 57, Smíchov* ☎ *234–651–111* ⊕ *www.svandovodivadlo.cz* Ⓜ *Line B: Anděl.*

Vagon. When it fills up, this long and narrow room offers only a few good spots to actually see the band that's playing, so video projectors also show the action on the walls toward the back. The emphasis is on Czech rock acts, with concerts starting at 9 and DJs weekends at midnight. ⊠ *Národní třída 25, Staré Město* ☎ *221–085–599* Ⓜ *Line B: Národní třída.*

Gay & Lesbian

There are a number of good clubs for gays and lesbians, though the scene changes regularly. There are no gay neighborhoods per se, but several clubs have recently opened up in Vinohrady. Clubs—at least on the street level—are fairly discreet, and a rainbow-color sign might be the only clue that a bar caters to gay clientele. For more information, check out the Web sites ⊕ prague.gayguide.net and ⊕ www.gay.cz.

Angel Club. This is a popular Smíchov nightspot for both gay men and women. The music leans toward techno and house. Besides the main room, there are other less-accessible areas for members and VIPs. ⊠ *Kmochova 8, Smíchov* ☎ *777–152–349* ⊕ *www.angel-club.info* Ⓜ *Line B: Anděl.*

Drakes. The admission price allows for multiple visits over 24 hours to this club, which is owned by a gay porn director. Theme parties take place on a regular basis so be sure the check the schedule. The drinks and admission are pricey so most of the clientele are tourists. ✉ *Zborovaská 50, Smíchov* ☎ *257–326–828* ⊕ *www.drakes.cz* Ⓜ *Line B: Anděl.*

Escape to Paradise. Catering primarily to male clientele, this centrally located disco serves dinner from 7 PM. But the dancing and shows with go-go dancers don't really get going until midnight. ✉ *V Jámě 8, Nové Město* ☎ *606–538–111* ⊕ *www.volny.cz/escapeclub* Ⓜ *Line A or B: Můstek.*

Friends. This friendly bar in Old Town serves reasonably priced beer—and Western-priced mixed drinks—in a roomy cellar space. There's plenty of seating most weeknights, but it does get busy on weekends. Videos play every night, and a DJ spins after 10 on weekends, luring people onto a small dance floor. There's no cover. ✉ *Bartolomějská 11, Nové Město* ☎ *224–236–772* ⊕ *www.friends-prague.cz* Ⓜ *Line A or B: Můstek.*

Gay Club Stella. An escape from techno music, here you can find a pleasant, homey bar with a few comfortable places to sit and chat. ✉ *Lužická 10, Vinohrady* ☎ *224–257–869* ⊕ *stellaclub.webpark.cz* Ⓜ *Line A: Nám. Mirú.*

The Saints. This small British-owned pub and cocktail bar is centrally located near several other gay and gay-friendly establishments in Vinohrady. ✉ *Polská 32, Vinohrady* ☎ *222–250–326* ⊕ *www.praguesaints. cz* Ⓜ *Line C: Nám. Míru.*

Termix. This place borders on claustrophobic during the weekends, especially with the decorative automobile sticking out of the bar wall. The street-level door is discreet and easy to miss. The music themes vary from night to night, with Wednesday featuring Czech music. It's closed Monday and Tuesday. ✉ *Třebízského 4a, Vinohrady* ☎ *222–710–462* ⊕ *www.club-termix.cz* Ⓜ *Line C: Nám. Míru.*

Valentino. It claims to be the largest gay club in Prague, and with three floors that's probably right. The former location of the Gejzeer Club is now a similar club with a disco, several bars, and other attractions for a male crowd. There is dancing every night, special parties on weekends, and the occasional fashion show. ✉ *Vinohradská 40, Vinohrady* ☎ *222–513–491* ⊕ *www.club-valentino.cz.*

Casinos

Gambling is legal in Prague. Many bars, especially those open around the clock, have a few slot machines and are marked with a sign that says *herna bar.* For those who want a little more action, most of the big hotels provide some sort of gaming room. A few casinos downtown stand out among the rest.

Casino Palais Savarin. Old-world charm and high betting limits are the trademarks of this gambling hall in a historical rococo palace. For those who wish to go incognito, a private room is also available. Games include roulette and poker, plus slot machines. This one is the destination of choice for local high rollers. ☒ *Na Příkopě 10, Nové Město* ☎ *224–221–636* ⊕ *www.czechcasinos.cz* Ⓜ *Line A or B: Můstek.*

Happy Day Casino. A little piece of Las Vegas lost in the center of Prague, this casino has dozens of slot machines, a few tables, plus blinking lights and bling-bling. ☒ *Václavské nám. 35, Nové Město* ☎ *224–233–506* Ⓜ *Line A or B: Můstek.*

Millennium Casino. At this modern and understated casino near several upscale hotels your gaming choices include video slot machines and table games, including blackjack. ☒ *V Celnici 10, Nové Město* ☎ *224–231–886* ⊕ *www.millenniumcasino.cz* Ⓜ *Line B: Nám. Republiky.*

LATE-NIGHT BITES

When it comes to food, Prague is a city with a curfew. Pubs used to close strictly at 10 PM. Even now, it's hard to find food as early as 10 or 11 PM. Some fast-food branches have late-night windows near major tram stops. Václavské náměstí is lined with all-night food stands selling sausages on paper plates.

Fraktal. Serving fairly good burgers, steaks, Indian, and Mexican food most nights until 11:30 PM, and drinks for a few hours later, this spot remains popular on the city's north side. A number of other bars that also cater to an English-speaking crowd are very close by. ☒ *Šmeralova 1 Holešovice* ☎ *777–794–094* ⊕ *www.fraktalbar.cz.*

Gyrossino (Gyros Rossino). Two side-by-side storefronts without seating sell gyros, falafels, and cold slices of pizza until 5 AM, except Sunday when they close at a more normal hour. All of the late-night trams stop down the street at Lazarská, so it makes a good pit stop. When this joint is closed, it's a hint to go home. ☒ *Spalena 43, Nové Město* Ⓜ *Line B: Národní třída.*

Hospoda v Lucerně (Pub in Lucerna). A somewhat upscale version of the typical Czech pub, but the service can drag. Beer on tap is unpasteurized, and closing time isn't until 3 AM, but the kitchen closes a little earlier. ☒ *Vodičkova 36, Nové Město* ☎ *224–215–186* Ⓜ *Line A or B: Můstek.*

J.J. Murphy's Irish Bar. Decent burgers, pork chops, steaks, and shepherd's pie are served in this Irish sports bar a bit later than most places. Closing time varies, depending on how busy it is. ☒ *Tržiště 4, Malá Strana* ☎ *257–535–575* ⊕ *www.jjmurphys.cz* Ⓜ *Line A: Malostranská.*

Palác Akropolis. Tucked into the corner of a nightclub, this restaurant serves a variety of reasonably priced meals, including a few vegetarian selections, until 12:30 AM. ☒ *Kubelíkova 27, Žižkov* ☎ *299–330–913* Ⓜ *Line A: Nám. Jiřího z Poděbrad.*

Picante. Mexican fast food is served nonstop in a location near several popular nightclubs and bars. Some seating is available. It's the best option in the area, and one of very few places open 24 hours. ☒ *Revoluční 4, Nové Město* ☎ *222–322–022* Ⓜ *Line B: Nám. Republiky.*

Radost FX. The restaurant upstairs from the nightclub of the same name serves international vegetarian food to at least midnight, but seating is limited. ✉ *Bělehradská 120, Nové Město* ☎ *224–254–776* ⊕ *www. radostfx.cz* Ⓜ *Line C: I. P. Pavlova.*

Square. Kafka and Jan Neruda frequented this historical pub, later renovated and turned into an upscale sushi and tapas bar in 2002. The kitchen is open until 12:30 AM and also cooks Mediterranean dishes. The bar stays open even later on weekends. ✉ *Malostranské nám. 5, Malá Strana* ☎ *257–532–109* Ⓜ *Line A: Malostranská.*

U Havrana (The Raven). This is a typical old-school Czech pub with guláš and fried cheese. Although the atmosphere is a bit smoky, it's the only one in town to cook really late. The place used to be nonstop, but now it's open until 4 AM. ✉ *Hálkova 6, Nové Město* ☎ *296–200–020* Ⓜ *Line C: I. P. Pavlova.*

PERFORMING ARTS

Czech composers may be thought of as a footnote in the history of classical music, but in Prague, hardly a program is produced that doesn't include some Dvořák, Smetana, or Martinů; modern music programs often include Petr Eben, a living Czech composer. However tangential the native contribution, Prague played an important role in the development of classical music in Europe. Famous composers including Mozart, Beethoven, Liszt, Chopin, and Haydn all spent time in Prague and presented major works here as well. Places where the composers performed still make note of that fact. The arts got a boost during the late 1800s, when the national-awakening movement inspired the Czechs to build a National Theater (Národní divadlo) to compete with theaters that favored German-language productions. Composers and authors began to explore Czech mythology and history for themes in operas, plays, and classical music.

These days Prague has some of the most impressive venues for classical music in Europe, and they are in remarkably good condition. Prague escaped major damage in both world wars, and has had few other catastrophes. The major classical venues were all built while Prague was part of the Austro-Hungarian Empire, and they reflect the opulence of the era. The cultural year has quite a few predictable highlights in the form of recurring festivals such as the Prague Spring and Prague Autumn festivals.

Live theater has a long history in Prague and remains very popular. You'll see posters in the metros, trams, and all around town advertising what's on at some of the major district theaters. Broadway-style musicals are a relatively new addition to the stage repertoire and are every bit as popular here as they are back home. The drawback for the visitor is that the performances are almost always in Czech, with little provision made for non-Czech speakers.

Dance—both classical ballet and modern dance—is a viable alternative to the stage. Several venues specialize in modern dance and other types

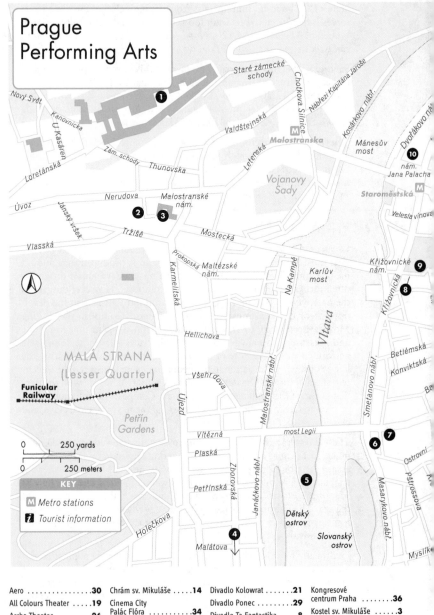

Prague Performing Arts

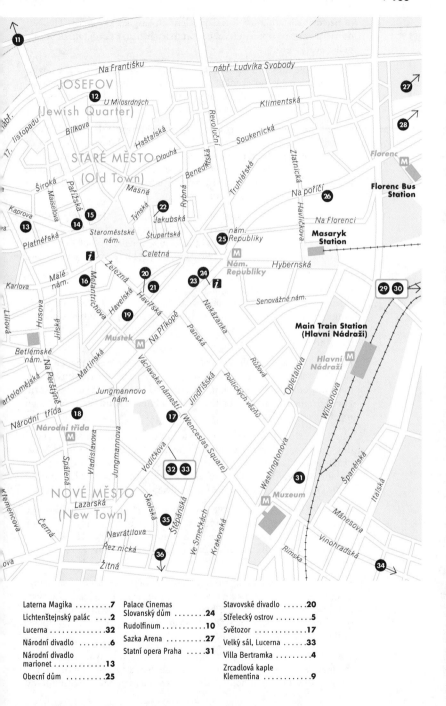

of performance that are less dependent on language to enjoy. The National Theater has made a recent effort to freshen up its program of mostly ballet evergreens.

Most people dress up for major classical concerts and the opera, with a jacket for men and evening attire for women being pretty much expected at most venues except those that cater exclusively to tourists. The Národní divadlo has a no-jeans dress code.

FESTIVALS &
EVENTS One of the largest film festivals in Central Europe, **Febiofest** (⊕ www. febiofest.cz) runs for about a week at the end of January and start of February. Films—both premieres and retrospectives—come from virtually all over the world, and a number of directors and stars, including Roman Polanski, have come to introduce their work. As a side to the festival, world-music bands also perform.

The first sign of the coming of spring is the annual **Matějská pouť** (St. Matthew's Fair; ⊕ www.incheba.cz), which starts on February 24 every year and runs through the middle of April in Výstaviště. Although it started as a religious event in the Middle Ages, now it has carnival rides, food, and other family fun.

Fans of foreign films have a chance to catch up on recent English-subtitled efforts in **Days of European Film,** which happens every March in Prague and Brno. Approximately 10 days of films play at two cinemas; there are also some visiting guests. One highlight is an all-night movie marathon.

Fans of documentary films look forward to the **One World Human Rights Film Festival** (Jeden svět; ⊕ www.oneworld.cz). The festival runs at various theaters, usually including Lucerna and Archa, at the end of April. For convenience, films in English or with English subtitles are grouped together in one theater.

Modern physical theater is showcased in the **4**+4 Days in Motion (4+4 dny v pohybu; ⊕ www.ctyridny.cz), which often has shows in very unusual venues like an old brickworks or disused factories as well as mainstream theaters. The festival usually happens at the end of May, and the name varies depending on the festival length.

Romany (Gypsy) bands have become a hot item in the world-music scene. There's quite a bit of regional diversity in the music, and some groups now play jazz fusion with a Romany influence. The **Khamoro Festival** (⊕ www.khamoro.cz) gathers bands from across Europe at the end of May.

Lots of bands and theater troupes descend on the grounds of a mental health institution for **Mezi ploty** (✉ Ústavní ulice, Bohnice). The two-day festival has some of the best local bands, but be aware that only nonalcoholic beer can be sold on the grounds. The festival takes place at the end of May.

Since 1946 **Prague Spring** (Pražské jaro; ⊕ www.festival.cz) has been the main event of the classical season and usually runs from the end of May to the start of June. Conductors such as Leonard Bernstein and

Sir Charles Mackerras have been among the guests. Important anniversaries of major composers, especially Czech ones, are marked with special concerts. Orchestra concerts, operas, and church recitals make up the bulk of the schedule. Popular music, often in unusual venues, has been added to make the festival accessible to everybody. Bedřich Smetana's *Ma vlást* usually opens the festival. Major events can sell out months in advance.

Prague is known for its tradition of puppet theater, and puppets of various qualities are ubiquitous at street markets. Visiting puppeteers lead shows in the annual **World Festival of Puppet Art** (⊕ www.puppetart.com), which runs from the end of May to the beginning of June at various theaters.

There isn't much English-language theater in Prague. The annual **Prague Fringe Festival** (⊕ www.praguefringe.com), which began in 2002, has visiting acts from Scotland, New Zealand, Australia, and the United States. So far, each year has been bigger in terms of offerings than the one before. The venues change from year to year, but the festival always takes place in early June.

Modern dance is popular in Prague and poses no language barrier. The monthlong **Tanec Praha** (⊕ www.tanecpha.cz) festival takes place in June and brings renowned companies from all over the world to several venues in the city.

The most important film festival in the Czech Republic is in the spa town of Karlovy Vary. The **Karlovy Vary International Film Festival** (⊕ www.kviff.com) ranks with Cannes, Berlin, and Venice among important European festivals. Visitors to the festival, which happens at the start of July, have included Lauren Bacall, Morgan Freeman, Michael Douglas, and Gus van Sant.

The lovely organ in Bazilika sv. Jakuba attracts noted international musicians for the annual **International Organ Festival** (✉ Malá Štuparská, Staré Město ⊕ www.auditeorganum.cz/festival.html), which runs from August to September with weekly concerts.

Young international classical musicians perform at **Mladá Praha** (Young Prague; ⊕ www.mladapraha.cz). A committee in Japan helps search for Asian participants and some musicians come from the Americas and the rest of Europe as well. The festival runs from the end of August through early September, with some events out of town.

Beginning just after the Velvet Revolution, the annual **Prague Autumn** (Pražský podzim; ⊕ www.pragueautumn.cz) emphasizes Czech composers and contemporary music. Visiting orchestras have included the BBC Scottish Symphony and Russian Philharmonia. The festival takes place in the second half of September.

TICKETS The concierge at your hotel may be able to reserve tickets for you. Otherwise, for the cheapest tickets, go directly to the theater box office a few days in advance or immediately before a performance. If all else fails, try one of the ticket agencies below.

Mozart in Prague

CONSIDERING THAT WOLFGANG AMADEUS MOZART visited Prague only four times, it's impressive how deeply he left his stamp on the city. On his first trip, in early 1787, he visited Count Thun and his wife. They lived in what is now the British Embassy in Malá Strana. Mozart stayed at an inn on Celetná Street. During this trip he conducted his *Prague Symphony* and a day later, on January 20, a performance of his opera *The Marriage of Figaro*, which had a more successful run in Prague than in Vienna. One legend from this time has the host of a party inviting him an hour before all the other guests and making him compose new dances for the evening.

His second trip is the most famous. The maestro came to visit composer F. X. Dušek and his new wife, opera singer Josephine, in 1787 at their rural villa, Bertramka (although he also kept rooms at the Uhelný třída Inn). After several missed deadlines, he conducted the world premiere of *Don Giovanni* on October 29 at Stavovské divadlo. He tried out a number of church organs in his spare time.

His third visit was just a pass-through, but the fourth and final trip came just months before he died in 1791. He promised to write a new opera to mark the coronation of Leopold II as king of Bohemia. Unfortunately, *La Clemenza di Tito*, which premiered at the Stavovske divadlo on September 6, was written quickly and was not as well received as *Don Giovanni*. Once news of his death on December 5 reached Prague, his friends staged a memorial service that ended with church bells ringing all over town.

Bohemia Ticket International. This agency specializes in mostly classical music, theater, and black-light theater. ✉ *Na Příkopě 16, Nové Město* ☎ *224–215–031* ⊕ *www.ticketsbti.cz* ✉ *Malé nám. 13, Staré Město* ☎ *224–227–832.*

Sazka Ticket. The owners of Sazka Arena, a major venue for large rock concerts and sporting events, distribute their own tickets exclusively through betting shops and street newspaper stands throughout the city. ✉ *Ocelářská 10, Vysočansky* ☎ *266–121–122* ⊕ *www.sazkaticket.cz.*

Ticketportal. Tickets for major classical and theater venues are for sale through this agency; they also provide tickets through some travel agents. On rare occasion, they have exclusive rights to a show. ✉ *Politických vězňů 15, Nové Město* ☎ *224–091–437* ⊕ *www. ticketportal.cz.*

Ticketpro. This is the main outlet for tickets to all shows and clubs, especially stadium concerts, with several branches across the city. ✉ *Salvátorská 10, Staré Město* ☎ *224–814–020* ✉ *Rytířská 12, Staré Město* ✉ *Václavské nám. 38, Nové Město* ⊕ *www.ticketpro.cz.*

Ticketstream. Hotel desks and some restaurants carry tickets for classical and other events via this agency. ✉ *Koubkova 8, Nové Město* ☎ *224–263–049* ⊕ *www.ticketstream.cz.*

Major Performance Venues

Divadlo Kolowrat. Less significant compared to other National Theater stages, this venue features more experimental works and chamber operas. ⊠ *Ovocný trh 6, Staré Město* ☎ *224–901–487* ⊕ *www.narodni-divadlo.cz* Ⓜ *Line A or B: Můstek.*

Kongresové centrum Praha (Congress Center). The former Palace of Culture, built in 1981, has never found a place in people's hearts. The large, functionalist, multipurpose building has several performance spaces that can seat thousands, but overall it has a very sterile feel. Plays—usually musicals—and special events come here. Bruce Springsteen also played here in the late 1990s. ⊠ *Třída 5 kvetna 65, Nusle* ⊕ *www.kcp.cz* Ⓜ *Line C: Vyšehrad.*

Lichtenštejnský palác (Lichtenstein Palace). Home to the Czech music academy (HAMU), this baroque palace from the 1790s has the large Martinů Hall for professional concerts and a smaller gallery sometimes used for student recitals. The courtyard sometimes has music in the summer months. ⊠ *Malostranské nám. 13, Malá Strana* ☎ *257–534–206* Ⓜ *Line A: Malostranská.*

FodorśChoice ★ **Národní divadlo** (National Theater). This is the main stage in the Czech Republic for drama and dance. Most of the theater performances are in Czech, but some operas have English supertitles. The interior—with its ornate and etched ceilings—is worth the visit alone. ⊠ *Národní třída. 2, Nové Město* ☎ *224–901–448* ⊕ *www.narodni-divadlo.cz* Ⓜ *Line B: Národní třída.*

★ **Obecní dům** (Municipal House). The main concert hall, a true art nouveau gem, is named after composer Bedřich Smetana and is home to the Prague Symphony Orchestra. The Czech Radio Symphony Orchestra also makes occasional use of it. A few smaller halls, all named for famous figures, host chamber concerts. ⊠ *Nám. Republiky 5, Staré Město* ☎ *222–002–100* ⊕ *www.obecnidum.cz* Ⓜ *Line B: Nám. Republiky.*

FodorśChoice ★ **Rudolfinum.** Austrian Crown Prince Rudolf lent his name to this neo-Renaissance concert space and exhibition gallery built in 1884. The large concert hall, named for Antonín Dvořák, who conducted here, hosts concerts by the Czech Philharmonic. The smaller Josef Suk Hall, on the opposite side of the building, is used for chamber concerts. Rivals may have richer interiors, but the acoustics here are excellent. ⊠ *Nám. Jana Palacha, Staré Město* ☎ *227–059–227* ⊕ *www.rudolfinum.cz* Ⓜ *Line A: Staroměstská.*

Sazka Arena. This indoor sports arena often houses big-time rock and pop concerts, like Pink and Green Day. ⊠ *Očálařská 2, Vysočany* ☎ *266–121–122* ⊕ *www.sazkaarena.cz* Ⓜ *Line B: Českomoravská.*

★ **Statní opera Praha** (State Opera House). With the most ornate interior of any venue in Prague, the theater has more than a touch of *Phantom of the Opera*. Marble sculptures support the loges, and a fresco in need a good cleaning adorns the ceiling. The building started life as the German Theater in 1887 and has undergone several name changes since.

4

A rotating stage offers directors a chance to experiment, although the stage can be a bit cramped. ✉ *Wilsonova 4, Nové Město* ☎ *224–227–266* ⊕ *www.opera.cz* Ⓜ *Line A or C: Muzeum.*

Stavovské divadlo (Estates Theater). It's impossible to visit Prague without knowing that Mozart conducted the world premiere of *Don Giovanni* on this stage way back in 1787. Fittingly, the interior was

---

ROCKING PRAGUE

The progressive rock band Yes was the first music act to perform in the Sazka Arena. More recently, Madonna broke the record for the largest audience assembled in Sazka, drawing a crowd of approximately 36,000 to see her concert over two nights.

---

used for scenes in Miloš Forman's movie *Amadeus*. It's stylish and refined without being distracting. Now this is a branch of the National Theater, and high-quality productions of Mozart are usually in the repertoire together with other classic operas and plays. In summer a private company rents the theater for touristy productions of Mozart works. ✉ *Ovocný třída 1, Staré Město* ☎ *224–215–001* ⊕ *www.narodni-divadlo.cz* Ⓜ *Line A: Staroměstská.*

Velký sál, Lucerna (Great Hall, Lucerna). A beautiful art nouveau ballroom with a big main floor and some loges hosts medium-size rock and pop bands like Blackmore's Night, Chuck Berry, and Kraftwerk. Swing orchestras also make use of it. When open, it's one of the more impressive venues. ✉ *Vodičkova 36, Nové Město* ☎ *224–224–537* ⊕ *www.lucerna.cz* Ⓜ *Line A or B: Můstek.*

Villa Bertramka. A bit out of the way, the summer house of the Dušek family, where Mozart composed part of *Don Giovanni*, holds chamber and garden concerts throughout the year with small ensembles playing. ✉ *Mozartova 169, Smíchov* ☎ *257–318–461* ⊕ *www.bertramka.cz* Ⓜ *Line B: Anděl.*

Classical Music

Czechs are spoiled with a string of classical concerts held year-round. In addition to Prague's two major professional orchestras, classical ensembles are the most common finds, and the standard of performance ranges from adequate to superb, though the programs tend to take few risks. Serious fans of baroque music may have the opportunity to hear works of little-known Bohemian composers at these concerts. Some of the best chamber ensembles are the Martinů Ensemble, the Prague Chamber Philharmonic (also known as the Prague Philharmonia), the Wihan Quartet, and the Agon contemporary music group.

Agon Orchestra. Bucking the trend for classical, this group specializes in contemporary music, ranging from John Cage to Frank Zappa. Most often they play at Archa Theatre, but they have been in other venues including Národní divadlo. ⊕ *www.musica.cz/agon.*

ArteMiss Trio. This piano, cello, and violin trio made up of three talented young women has won international competitions and recorded some of Shostakovich work. ⊕ *www.arcodiva.cz.*

Collegium Marianum. Beyond the usual classical standards, members of this group revive seldom-heard works from archives and perform them on period instruments. Performances are usually organized around a historical or geographical theme. ✉ *Melantrichova 971/19, Staré Město* ☎ *224–229–462* ⊕ *www.tynska.cuni.cz* Ⓜ *Line A: Staroměstská.*

Czech National Symphony Orchestra This major full-size orchestra that plays most often at the Rudolfinum. The orchestra has attracted some well-known guest conductors, and has also done some film sound track work.

Czech Philharmonic. Antonín Dvořák conducted the orchestra's first performance back in 1896. Guest conductors have included Gustav Mahler and Leonard Bernstein. Since 1990 there has been a rapid turnover in chief conductors, but the performances have been of consistently high quality. Most programs include some works by Czech composers. ✉ *Rudolfinum, nám. Jana Palacha, Staré Město* ☎ *224–893–111* ⊕ *www.czechphilharmonic.cz* Ⓜ *Line A: Staroměstská.*

Czech Radio Symphony Orchestra. As the name implies, this group started playing live on the radio in 1927. Since the 1960s, it hasn't been directly associated with the national radio system and has fewer concerts than its main rivals. The orchestra makes occasional appearances at Obecní dům and other venues. Besides Czech composers, the orchestra excels in Brahms and Mahler. ⊕ *www2.rozhlas.cz/socr.*

Ensemble Martinů. Domestic and international radio performances and film scores have kept this piano quartet in the spotlight. Formed in 1978 and re-formed in 1993, the group majors in music by the Czech composer Martinů, but also has a wide repertoire of other composers. ⊕ *www.ensemblemartinu.com.*

Nostitz Quartet. Named after a famous 18th-century patron of the arts, this youthful ensemble has won a few prestigious awards. They give excellent performances of works by Mozart and Czech composers and are one of the better groups to appear in various church concerts around town. ⊕ *www.nostitzquartet.com.*

Prague Chamber Orchestra without Conductor. Famous for playing often (but not always) without a conductor, this ensemble covers the classics up through 20th-century composers. Usually they play in the Rudolfinum. ⊕ *www.pko.cz.*

Prague Philharmonia. A relative newcomer established in 1994 concentrates on Classical and Romantic-era pieces plus the work of 20th-century composers. The founding and principal conductor is Jiří Bělohlávek, who also conducted the orchestra when it appeared on BBC World Ser-

CAUTION ⚠

The standards for church concerts vary massively—from world-class to rank amateur. Some of these concerts are blatant scams that depend on the nonrepeat tourist business to make their money. When purchasing tickets, always check that the performance will be played by an established chamber group generally in the bigger and better-known churches.

vice radio with opera singer Magdelena Koená in 2004. Most concerts take place in the Rudolfinum. ⊕ *www.pkf.cz.*

Prague Symphony Orchestra (FOK). The group's nickname stands for Film-Opera-Koncert. They started in 1934, but it wasn't until 1957 that they became the official city orchestra. In the 1930s they did music for many Czech films, although they don't do much opera and film anymore. The ensemble tours extensively and has a large back catalog of recordings. Frenchman Serge Baudo has been the principal conductor since 2001. Programs tend to be quite diverse. One of the guest conductors is Maxim Shostakovich, who conducts his father's works. ⊠ *Obecní dům, Nám. Republiky 5, Staré Město* ☎ *222–002–100* ⊕ *www.fok.cz* Ⓜ *Line B: Nám. Republiky.*

Stamic Quartet. Two members of the quartet were born in the same town as composer J. V. Stamic, so they chose this name. The group often plays some Britten and Bártok along with the usual classics and Czech composers. ⊕ *www.stamicquartet.cz.*

Wihan Quartet. Many quartets borrow names from composers, but few choose the name of a musician. Wihan was a cellist who knew Dvořák. The quartet has won numerous awards since it started in 1985 and has participated in international broadcasts. Most of their sets include at least one Czech composer. ⊕ *www.wihanquartet.cz.*

Church Concerts

Church concerts have become a staple of the Prague classical music scene. The concerts help churches to raise money and also give visitors more of an opportunity to hear classical music, often in an opulent setting. Banners or signs at the churches announce when there's a concert. Listings can also be found in English on the Web site ⊕ www.pis.cz.

Barokní knihovní sál (Baroque Library Hall). Impressive 18th-century frescoes and colorful stucco work in a monastery library hall make for one of the more charming, though lesser-used, concert halls. This is usually a good bet for a quality performance. ⊠ *Melantrichova 971/ 19, Staré Město* ☎ *224–229–462* ⊕ *www.tynska.cuni.cz* Ⓜ *Line A: Staroměstská.*

Bazilika sv. Jakuba (Basilica of St. James). This is an excellent venue for organ concerts due to the church's organ, which finished in 1709 and restored in the early 1980s to its original tone structure. Now it's one of the best in town. ⊠ *Malá Štupartská 6, Staré Město* ☎ *No phone* ⊕ *www.auditeorganum.cz/organ. html* Ⓜ *Line A: Staroměstská.*

> **THE CLASSICS ON ICE**
>
> "I spontaneously decided to take in the 8 PM concert at St. Nicholas Church. The church is pretty and the concert lovely, but it was freezing in there!!! Everybody stayed bundled up and huddled during the concert and I wanted to laugh when the soloist came out in a long wool cape with a fur stole around her neck. Let's have some heaters please!!!!!!!! I would not recommend a concert at this church in the winter or spring, but would instead try the Municipal House. Surely it must be warmer!!"
> —aggiegirl

Bazilika sv. Jiří (Basilica of St. George). Listen to small ensembles playing well-known Mozart tunes and Verdi's *Four Seasons* in a Romanesque setting. The building dates to the 11th century and holds the tombs of some very early princes. ☒ *Nám. U sv. Jiří Pražský Hrad* ☏ *No phone* Ⓜ *Line A: Hradčandská.*

Chrám sv. Mikuláše (Church of St. Nicholas, Staré Město). The chandelier inside this baroque landmark is based on the design for the Czar's crown. Private companies rent out the church for concerts by professional ensembles and visiting amateur choirs and orchestras. The quality and prices vary greatly. ☒ *Staroměstské nám., Staré Město* ☏ *224–190–994* Ⓜ *Line A: Staroměstská.*

Kostel sv. Mikuláše (Church of St. Nicholas). Ballroom scenes in the movie *Van Helsing* used the interior of this beautiful baroque church. The building's dome was one of the last works finished by architect Kilian Ignatz Dientzenhofer before his death in 1751. Local ensembles play concerts of popular classics here throughout the year. ☒ *Malostranské nám., Malá Strana* ☏ *257–534–215* ⊕ *www.psalterium.cz* Ⓜ *Line A: Malostranská.*

Kostel sv. Šimona a Judy (Church of Sts. Simon and Jude). This decommissioned church with a restored organ and frescoes is used by the Prague Symphony Orchestra for chamber concerts and recitals. The baroque altar is actually an elaborate painting on the wall. ☒ *Dušní ulice, Josefov* ☏ *222–002–336 for tickets* Ⓜ *Line A: Staroměstská.*

Zrcadlová kaple Klementina (Mirrored Chapel of the Klementinum). Now part of the National Library, this ornate little chapel in the middle of the Clementinum complex is worth a peek. The music offered is fairly standard selections played with skill if not a lot of enthusiasm. Different concert companies program the space; signs nearby usually have the day's schedule. ☒ *Marianské nám., Staré Město* ☏ *No phone* Ⓜ *Line A: Staroměstská.*

Film

In the arts nothing has changed more in the last few years than the cinema scene. New multiplexes have brought state-of-the-art screens along with popcorn and candy. Small one- and two-screen cinemas are now struggling to stay afloat by offering alternative programming or alternating films with live theater. Most films are shown in their original-language versions, but it pays to check. If a film was made in the United States or Britain, the chances are good that it will be shown with Czech subtitles rather than dubbed. (Film titles, however, are usually translated into Czech.) Movies in the original language are normally indicated with the note *českými titulky* (with Czech subtitles). Prague's English-language publications carry film reviews and full timetables.

Aero. Film junkies make the trek to this out-of-the-way gem of a theater knowing it's worth the trip. The tiny cinema is hidden in the middle of a residential block and keeps an ambitious schedule of two or three different films a day. Festivals and retrospectives sometimes feature films with English subtitles. Czech translations are done to headphones. Visiting guests have included Terry Gilliam, Godfrey Reggio, and Paul Morrisey. The theater also has an outdoor beer garden in the summer months and a lively indoor bar all year-round. ✉ *Biskupcova 31, Žižkov* ☎ *271–771–349* ⊕ *www.kinoaero.cz* Ⓜ *Line A: Želivského.*

Cinema City Palác Flóra. This venue has "Oskar-IMAX," a large-format theater that shows many short films in 3-D and the occasional feature on a very large screen. Most IMAX shows are dubbed. Other screens offer the standard multiplex experience. ✉ *Vinohradská 149, Vinohrady* ☎ *255–742–021* ⊕ *www.cinemacity.cz* Ⓜ *Line A: Flora.*

Evald. A tiny screening room with an adjoining restaurant and wine bar are tucked inside this central cinema. It's a good bet to see new Czech films with English subtitles or offbeat foreign films, sometimes with English subtitles. Popular films sell out quickly so buy your tickets early. ✉ *Národní 28, Nové Město* ☎ *221–105–225* ⊕ *www.cinemart.cz* Ⓜ *Line B: Národní třída.*

Institut Français de Prague. A full-size movie theater is hidden away in the basement here, and most of the programming consists of recent French films and retrospectives of classics (also French). About half of the films have English subtitles, and the admission fee is usually nominal. No food or drinks allowed. "Serious" film watching only. ✉ *Štěpanská 35, Nové Město* ☎ *221–401–011* ⊕ *www.ifp.cz* Ⓜ *Line A or B: Můstek.*

Lucerna. The city's handsomest old movie palace was designed by former President Václav Havel's grandfather and built in 1916. An art nouveau interior harks back to cinema's glory days, but it could use a little more maintenance. The programming tends toward non-blockbuster releases. The café leading to the theater proper sometimes features a live piano player. ✉ *Vodičkova 36, Nové Město* ☎ *224–216–972* Ⓜ *Line A or B: Můstek.*

Palace Cinemas Slovanský dům. Probably the best multiplex in town—certainly the most convenient to downtown—runs about 10 movies at once, with most of these being the latest Hollywood films in English (with Czech subtitles). It occasionally runs Czech films with English subtitles. ✉ *Na Příkopé 22, Nové Město* ☎ *257–181–212* ⊕ *www. palacecinemas.cz* Ⓜ *Line B: Nám. Republiky.*

Střelecký ostrov. The Czech version of a drive-in: an outdoor screen on an island surrounded by the Vltava can be a real treat on a warm summer night. Films start around 9:30 PM and the program features mostly English language films with Czech subtitles (but sometimes Czech films without subtitles). ✉ *Střelecký ostrov, Nové Město* ☎ *777–325–256* ⊕ *www.strelak.cz* Ⓜ *Line B: Národní třída.*

★ **Světozor.** Prague's central art-house cinema has a great central location near the Lucerna shopping passage.

> **WORD OF MOUTH**
>
> "We went to [a marionette show] in Prague . . . It didn't look particularly touristy out front and it was kind of out of the way. We enjoyed it immensely. It was Don Giovanni, too. Funny. Charming. Not London quality. Not New York. But quite delightful, we thought."
>
> –althom1122

Excellent selection of offbeat American films, classic European cinema, and the best of new Czech films. Many films are subtitled in English. ⊠ *Vodičkova 41, Nové Město* ☎ *224–946–824* ⊕ *www.kinosvetozor. cz* Ⓜ *Line A or B: Můstek.*

Opera

The Czech Republic has a strong operatic tradition. Unlike during the Communist period, operas are almost always sung in their original tongue, and the repertoire offers plenty of Italian favorites as well as the Czech national composers Janáček, Dvořák, and Smetana. (Czech operas are supertitled in English.) The major opera houses also often stage ballets. Appropriate attire is recommended for all venues. Suits and ties—or at least a sports coat—for men, and dresses for women are common.

Národní divadlo (National Theater). A slightly bigger budget and three different venues for operas give the National Theater's resident opera company a bit more flexibility than its rival, the Statní opera Praha. Large, ambitious productions are at the main Národní divadlo. Stavovské divadlo runs more mainstream works. And truly experimental or chamber operas wind up in Kolowrat. The productions run from excellent to slightly misconceived, but they are always professional. ⊠ *Národní třída. 2, Nové Město* ☎ *224–901–448* ⊕ *www.narodni-divadlo.cz* Ⓜ *Line B: Národní třída.*

Statní opera Praha (Prague State Opera). With fewer resources than the National Theater, the State Opera is forced to be a bit more creative to compete. The result? More new works and more challenging interpretations of obscure works along with the standard crowd-pleasers. ⊠ *Wilsonova 4, Nové Město* ☎ *224–227–266* ⊕ *www.opera.cz* Ⓜ *Line A or C: Muzeum.*

Puppet Shows & Black Light Theater

Black-light theater, a form of nonverbal theater—melding live acting, mime, video, and stage trickery—was Czechoslovakia's contribution to Expo '58. The name comes from ultraviolet light, which is used to illuminate special makeup and details on the sets, creating optical illusions. Some black-light shows have been running for thousands of performances. Puppetry also has a long tradition, but most of the shows are dialogue-intensive and aimed at a young audience.

All Colours Theater. Since 1993 this small theater has been presenting a small repertoire of nonverbal shows. Faust is the most popular, although they occasionally revive other works. Some legends claim that the real Faust lived in Prague, which gives the show some local significance. ⊠ *Rytířská 31, Staré Město* ☎ *221–610–170* ⊕ *www.blacktheatre. cz* Ⓜ *Line A or B: Můstek.*

Divadlo Broadway. Right off one of the busiest tourist and shopping streets, this former movie theater—the first one to fall victim to the wave of multiplexes—is now home to one of the more recent black-light presentations. *Wow,* which follows a young child facing up to his fears and making choices in a magical, dreamlike realm, had been running for several years in a smaller venue before setting up a permanent home here. ✉ *Na Příkopě 31 Staré Město* ☎ *225–113–307* ⊕ *www. wow-show.com* Ⓜ *Line B: Nám. Republiky.*

Divadlo Image. This is the home of a black-light and pantomime company that has a repertoire of long-running classics of the genre and a "best of" show. ✉ *Pařížská 4, Josefov* ☎ *222–329–191* ⊕ *www. imagetheatre.cz* Ⓜ *Line A: Staroměstská.*

Divadlo Ta Fantastika. A black-light show called *Aspects of Alice,* based loosely on *Alice in Wonderland,* has run here almost daily for more than 2,000 performances. Slightly campy musicals in Czech based on historical themes also play here. The theater was established in New York in 1981 and moved to Prague after the Velvet Revolution. It's been running at its current address, a minor baroque palace, since 1993. ✉ *Karlova 8, Staré Město* ☎ *222–221–366* ⊕ *www.tafantastika.cz* Ⓜ *Line A: Staroměstská.*

Křižíkova fontána. Pressurized water and colored lights keep pace with recorded music that ranges from recent film scores to a tribute to Freddie Mercury and selections of classical music. Live acts share the stage on occasion. Tickets are available at the venue. ✉ *Výstaviště Holešovice* ☎ *220–103–224* ⊕ *www.krizikovafontana.cz* Ⓜ *Nádraži Holešovice.*

★ **Laterna Magika.** The glass-block façade of the Nová scena (New Stage), which opened in 1983, stands out among the ornate 19th-century buildings in the area. The program is almost exclusively made up of black-light and multimedia performances, which are popular with visitors because there's no language barrier. Laterna Magika takes its name from the original black-light presentation at Expo '58. ✉ *Národní třída 4, Nové Město* ☎ *224–931–482* ⊕ *www.laterna.cz* Ⓜ *Line B: Národní třída.*

Národní divadlo marionet (The National Puppet Theater). One puppet company has been presenting Mozart's *Don Giovanni* with string puppets set to recorded music sung in Italian since 1991. The opera is slightly tongue-in-cheek, and Mozart himself makes a guest appearance. A new production of *The Magic Flute,* in German, was added recently. ✉ *Žatecká 1, Staré Město* ☎ *224–819–322* ⊕ *www.mozart.cz* Ⓜ *Line A: Staroměstská.*

Theater & Dance

A dozen or so professional theater companies play in Prague to ever-packed houses. Attending the theater is a vital activity in Czech society, and the language barrier can't obscure the players' artistry. A few English-language theater groups operate sporadically. For complete listings, pick up a copy of the *Prague Post.*

Fodor'sChoice **Archa Theater.** Both for its central location and eclectic programming,
★ Archa is the main venue for modern theater, dance, and avant-garde music. Some visiting troupes perform in English, and other shows are designated as English-friendly in the program. The theater opened in 1994

and had former Velvet Underground member John Cale perform one of its first concerts. ✉ *Na Poříčí 26, Nové Město* ☎ *221–716–333* ⊕ *www.archatheatre.cz* Ⓜ *Line B: Nám. Republiky.*

Divadlo Alfred v dvoře. Most of the programming for this small, out-of-the-way theater is physical, nonverbal theater and dance. Visiting companies come often and take a more modern approach than can be seen in many of the more tourist-oriented nonverbal theaters. ✉ *Fr. Křížka 36, Bubeneč* ☎ *233–376–997* Ⓜ *Line C: Vltavská.*

Divadlo Ponec. A former cylinder factory then a movie theater, this neo-classical building was renovated into a modern dance venue in 2001. The house carries a lot of premieres. Several dance festivals are based here. ✉ *Husitská 24/a, Žižkov* ☎ *224–817–886* ⊕ *www.divadloponec. cz* Ⓜ *Line B or C: Florenc.*

4

Sports & the Outdoors

5

WORD OF MOUTH

"[Consider] renting bicycles and traveling that way around Prague, along the river, stopping at stores, buying a picnic lunch—and sightseeing that way . . . that took the boring out of 'just museums, buildings, and castles.' "

—escargot

By Mark Baker **CZECHS ARE AVID SPORTSMEN AND SPORTSWOMEN.** In the summertime, Prague empties out as residents head to their country cottages to hike or bike in clean air.

In winter the action shifts to the mountains, a few hours to the north and east of the city, for decent downhill and cross-country skiing. If the ponds freeze over in Prague's Stromovka Park, kids nab their skates for pick-up ice hockey games—a national mania.

For short-term visitors, a simple way to stretch your legs is to throw on some running shoes and head to one of the city's many parks. Several shops in Prague now rent Rollerblades or bikes, too—though hills, trams, and cobblestones drain the appeal. Tennis, swimming, and golf are all available and easy to arrange at short notice.

The main ski resorts in the Krkonoše mountains lie about a three-hour bus trip from Prague and are best combined with an overnight stay in the winter. Arrange your accommodation in advance, though, since heavy snows tend to draw skiers from Germany looking for cheaper lift passes than they can find at home or in Austria.

The most popular spectator sport, bar none, is ice hockey. Czechs are world hockey champions, and the Czech gold medal at the Nagano Winter Olympics in 1998 is held up as a national achievement practically on par with the 1989 Velvet Revolution. If you're here in wintertime, witness the fervor by seeking out tickets to a "Extraliga" game. The main Prague teams are Sparta and Slavia; the two met in the Czech championship series in 2006 (Sparta won). Sparta plays its home games at Holešovice's Sportovní Hala, while Slavia plays at the relatively new and luxurious Sazka arena (Metro line B: Českomoravská).

Soccer plays a perennial second fiddle to hockey, although the Czech

> **MARK'S TOP 5 OUTDOOR ACTIVITIES**
>
> 1. Head to T-Mobile or Sazka arena and root for Prague's premier hockey teams. Enjoy NHL-level hockey at a fraction of the cost.
> 2. Check out one of Sparta Praha's soccer matches at Toyota Arena.
> 3. Walk, jog, or, join the rest of the city and rollerblade around Letná Park. Finish off your ride with a beer at the park's beer garden.
> 4. Spend the day lounging, reading, and loafing in Kampa Park in Malá Strana. If you've got a Frisbee, bring that too.
> 5. Beat the heat with a dip at Divoká Šárka's large public pool.

national soccer team ranks among the best in the world. Prague's main professional team, Sparta, hosts its home games at Toyota Arena near Letná. International tournaments attract many of the best clubs in the world to Sparta's home turf. If you're interested in seeing a hockey or soccer game during your stay, the best place to find out what's going on (and where) is the weekly sports page of the *Prague Post,* or inquire at your hotel.

PARKS & PLAYGROUNDS

Praguers are gluttons for a sunny day in the park. A pleasant weekend afternoon brings out plenty of sun-worshippers and Frisbee-tossers, with their blankets, books, and dogs. On weekdays, the Rollerblade crowd cruises the pavements from 5 PM until about 8 PM before retiring for beers at the local beer garden. Two of the city's best beer gardens can be found at Letná and Riegrovy Sady.

Kampa. Under the noses of the throng on Charles Bridge: take the steps off the bridge onto Na Kampě and follow the wide cobbled street to the end; Kampa is a diminutive gem hidden in the heart of Malá Strana. It's a location for lazing in the sunshine and resting your eyes from all the busy baroque architecture, with a playground when the kids grow restless of the endless palaces and churches. ⊠ *Malá Strana* Ⓜ *Tram to Malostranské nám.*

Letná. With killer views of the city across the river, this park is eternally busy. It has a huge restaurant and beer garden, to chill out like a local, located around Letenský zámeček, near the intersection of Kostelní and Muzejní. The large grassy northern plateau sometimes holds concerts or political rallies, but is also a great place to throw a Frisbee or kick a soccer ball. An excellent playground sits in the center near the tennis courts, just to the west of Letenský zámeček. ⊠ *Holešovice* Ⓜ *Tram to Sparta.*

Ⓒ **Riegrovy Sady.** This lush park climbs sharply up the slopes of Vinohrady. On the east side of the park, lovely landscaping surrounds one of the best beer gardens in Prague and a large playground. Lavish views of Prague Castle stand on the distant horizon. ⊠ *Vinohrady* Ⓜ *Line A: Jiřího z Poděbrad.*

Ⓒ **Stromovka.** King of all Prague parks, these lands were formally royal hunting grounds. Today the deer have been usurped by horse-riders and dog-lovers. Remarkably rustic for a city-based park, it's primarily a place for walking rather than loafing about. The racket from the ramshackle amusements at Výstaviště exhibition grounds (found at the park's eastern entrance where Dukelských hrdinů meets U Výstaviště) stresses the fact that you remain city-bound. ⊠ *Holešovice* Ⓜ *Tram to Výstaviště.*

SPORTS & ACTIVITIES

Boating

Given the multitude of locks and weirs on the Vltava, you can't wander too far when boating. It's ideal for the idle and those looking for a view of Charles Bridge from the swans' perspective.

U Kotvy (⊠ Slovanský ostrov, Staré Město ☎ 603–523–371) rents out rowboats (60 Kč per hour, maximum four people per boat) and paddleboats (120 Kč per hour) from Slovanský ostrov, the island in the Vltava just south of the National Theater. It's usually open from 10 AM to sunset from May to September, but in high summer (usually late June through August) lanterns are provided for romantic night cruising.

Day Spas

AS DEEPLY AS PRAGUE CAN NOURISH the mind and the soul with its splendor, intellectual traditions, and arts, it can be also be punishing on the body. Miles of cobblestones pummel your soles while sightseeing, and plates of heavy fried food washed down by a platoon of beers in smoke-filled pubs can make your system protest. Recreational spas are becoming increasingly popular.

Relaxation therapies abound in the soothing spa **Cybex** (⌧ Hilton Prague, Pobřežní 1, Karlín ☎ 224–842–375 ⊕ www.cybexprg.cz Ⓜ Line B or C: Florenc). Treatments leave you feeling like an item on the menu at some posh restaurant: duck in here to be rolled in yogurt and mud, smeared with mint gel or various oils, have your hide rubbed

with salt or pummeled with stones. Prices are steep by Prague standards, starting at 1,200 Kč for a massage, but the range of facilities matches up.

Turn over your jet-lag aches and pains to the hands of experts from southeast Asia at **Sabai Studio** (⌧ Slovanský dům, Na Příkopě 22, Staré Město ☎ 221–451–180 ⊕ www.sabai.cz Ⓜ Line B: Nám. Republiky) inside a shiny shopping center. Thai massage costs 990 Kč an hour; aroma massage, 1,290 Kč.

Overhaul your energy lines in the very center of the city. **Thai World** (⌧ Celetná 6, Staré Město ☎ 224–817–247 ⊕ www.thaiworld.cz Ⓜ Line B: Nám. Republiky) offers Thai (600 Kč per hour), foot (600 Kč), or oil (835 Kč) massages to the weary.

Bowling & Billiards

A newcomer to the Czech Republic, bowling is attracting a following, and it seems that every week a new bowling alley opens up. The lanes tend to be smaller and narrower than back home. Many bars have pool tables, and "Eight Ball" is the game of choice here. The local rules may differ slightly from what you are used to back home—be sure to agree on things like where to spot the cue ball on a scratch before racking up.

Billiard Club Harlequin (⌧ Vinohradská 25, Vinohrady ☎ 224–217–240 ⊕ www.harlequin.zde.cz Ⓜ Line A: Nám. Míru) offers billiards, pool, and snooker on decent tables. Prices are about 110 Kč an hour, slightly higher for snooker.

Six bowling lanes are available in Prague 7 at **Radava SC Praha** (⌧ Milady Horákové 37, Letná ☎ 233–101–213 Ⓜ Tram to Letenské nám.) although booking ahead is advised. Lanes are priced hourly and range from 250 Kč to 420 Kč depending on the time of day.

Cycling

Much of the Czech Republic is a cyclist's dream of gently sloping tracks for peddlers. The capital, however, can be unkind to bicyclers. The ubiquitous tram tracks and cobblestones make for hazardous conditions—as do the legions of tourist groups clogging the roads. Nevertheless, cycling is increasingly popular, and Prague now has several adequate yellow-marked cycling trails that crisscross the city. From April to October, two bike-rental companies provide decent bikes—as well as locks, helmets, and maps. Each runs guided bike tours for around 450 Kč. Ask for a cycling map before you head out, and don't forget to lock up your bike.

City Bike (⊠ Králodvorská 5, Staré Město ☎ 776–180–284 ⊕ www. pragueonline.cz/citybike Ⓜ Line B: Nám. Republiky) runs guided tours leaving at 11, 2, and 5. An additional "sunset" tour requires advance booking. Your English-speaking guides offer fun tidbits of history and point out architecture but do not offer a full tour. The ride's pace is comfortable, for those who haven't taken a spin in a while.

One of the multicultural teams from **Praha Bike** (⊠ Dlouhá 24, Staré Město ☎ 732–388–880 ⊕ www.prahabike.cz Ⓜ Line B: Nám. Republiky) can casually guide you around one of two routes; tours are at 11:30, 2:30, and 5:30.

Golf

Golf is catching on the Czech Republic—but it's definitely seen as an elite sport, not something for the masses. High greens fees and often an old-school "country club" air of formality prevails, even if the facilities don't warrant it. Expect to pay upward of 3,000 Kč for 18 holes, though greens fees drop considerably during the week. Facilities within the city limits are not that great, but Karlštejn has an excellent 18-hole course.

Prague's most central golf course is a 9-holer in the western suburbs at the **Hotel Golf** (⊠ Plzeňská 215, Motol ☎ 257–215–185). Take a taxi to the hotel or Tram 4, 7, or 9 from metro station Anděl to the Hotel Golf stop.

Praha Karlštejn Golf Club (⊠ Bělěc 280, Liteň ☎ 0/724–084–600 ⊕ www. karlstejn-golf.cz) offers a challenging course beside sweeping views of the famous Karlštejn Castle. It's 30 km (18 mi) southwest of Prague, just across the Berounka River from the castle. Trains to Karlštejn, costing about 50 Kč, leave Smíchov nádraží hourly. A short uphill walk or taxi (100 Kč max) can get you to the club.

Health Clubs

For those who like to "feel the burn "there are a number of high-end fitness centers around the city—and cheaper options—all of which you can visit on a day pass. Expect to pay 100 Kč to 300 Kč a visit.

Fodor'sChoice In the Hilton hotel **Cybex** (⊠ Hilton Prague, Pobřežní 1, Karlín ★ ☎ 224–842–375 ⊕ www.cybexprg.cz Ⓜ Line B or C: Florenc) you can work out on superb high-tech fitness machines, then reward yourself with pampering spa services.

Factory Pro (⊠ Nádražní32, Smíchov ☎ 221–420–800 Ⓜ Line B: Smíchovské nádraží) offers numerous machines, squash courts, a swimming pool, sauna, aerobics and yoga classes, and tanning benches.

Inexpensive and sound facilities, including an indoor pool, can be found at the **Hotel Axa** (✉ Na Poříčí 40, Nové Město ☎ 227–072–180 ⊕ www. hotelaxa.com Ⓜ Line B: Nám. Republiky).

Sportcentrum YMCA (✉ Na Poříčí 12, Staré Město ☎ 224–875–811 Ⓜ Line B: Nám. Republiky) is one of the cheaper options in Prague, so expect more crowds; and facilities, although plentiful, may be well-used.

Hockey

A feverish national fixation, ice hockey becomes a full-blown obsession during the World Championships (held every year in late spring) and the Winter Olympics.

The Czech national hockey league, Extraliga, is one of the most competitive in the world, and the best players regularly move on to the North American National Hockey League. Slavia Praha and Sparta are the two best teams, both in Prague. Hockey season runs from September to March. Tickets cost between 50 Kč and 150 Kč and are reasonably easy to get.

> **CHARIOTS OF PRAHA**
>
> Competitors from more than 55 countries run themselves ragged around the city center in May at the Prague International Marathon (www.pim.cz). Should the running bug bite you, there are several noncompetitive races over more reasonable distances. All races start and finish in Old Town Square.

Although a relative giant in the Czech Republic, **HC Slavia Praha** (✉ Sazka Arena Očálařská, Vysočany ☎ 266–121–122 ⊕, www.sazkaarena.cz Ⓜ Line B: Českomoravská) usually finds itself chasing the leaders of the pack in international matches.

Fodor'sChoice ★ **HC Sparta Praha** (✉ T-Mobile Arena, Za Elektrárnou 419, Holešovice ☎ 266–727–443 ⊕ www.hcsparta.cz Ⓜ Line C: Nádraží Holešovice) was the national champion at this writing and is routinely regarded as the premier team in an excellent local league—until players are lured across the Atlantic. Come to spot the next Jágr or Hašek.

Horse Racing

Horse racing has a small but dedicated following in the Czech Republic. If you have a hankering to bet on the ponies—you're in luck.

Prague's horse-racing track, the **Velká Chuchle** (✉ Radotinská 69, Velká Chuchle ☎ 242–447–036 ⊕ www.velka-chuchle.cz Ⓜ Bus 172 from Smíchovské nádraží to Dostihová) is a green plot on the southwestern edge of the city. Each Sunday from April to November—with a rest in July—the course hosts almost all of the country's major prize events; highlights include the Czech Derby in June and the Autumn Racing Festival in September. On race days, trains run regularly from Smíchovské nádraží to Velká Chuchle nádraží, which is right behind the main stands.

The Velká pardubická steeplechase, the most famous race in the Czech Republic—and for many the most dangerous in the world—takes place on the second weekend of October at the **dostihové závodiště Pardubice** (Pardubice Racecourse; ⊠ Pardubice ⊕ www.pardubice-racecourse.cz) in the eastern Bohemia city of Pardubice.

Skateboarding & Rollerblading

Directly above Čechův most on the southern edge of Letná Park, a huge metronome keeps the Vltava flowing to a beat. Behind the timepiece is a paved area known as "Stalin" because a huge statue honoring him stood here until it was removed during a campaign in the early 1960s. The great dictator would have been enraged to know the spot of his former monument is now a favorite hangout for scruffy skateboarders; these flagstones are the city's center stage for skateboarders showing off their ollies.

The rest of Letná is given over to some of the best rollerblading in the city—with awesome views of the Old Town blurring as you whiz by.

In-line skates can be rented at **In-Line pujcovna** (⊠ Milady Horákové 98, Letná ☎ 603–938–328 Ⓜ Line A: Hradčanská) for 50 Kč an hour or 400 Kč a day.

★ Prague hosts the Mystic Skate Cup—part of the World Cup Skateboarding series. It's held annually in July at **Mystic Skatepark** (⊠ Stvanice Island, Holešovice ☎ 222–232–027 off-site office Ⓜ Line C: Vltavská). The park is open to the public year-round. Skateboarders pay 50 Kč; those on a BMX or in-line skates have to cough up 80 Kč.

Skiing

Czechs are enthusiastic and gifted skiers and the country's northern border regions with Germany and Poland hold many small ski resorts. Czechs generally acknowledge the Krkonoše Mountains, which straddle a border with Poland, to be the best. Experienced skiers may find the hills here a little small and the facilities not quite up to international standards. (Hardcore Czech skiers usually head to Austria or France.) Nevertheless, if you're here in midwinter and you get a good snowfall, the Czech resorts can make for a fun overnight trip from the capital. All the area ski resorts are regularly served by buses leaving from Florenc.

Černá Hora (⊠ Cernohorská 265, Janské Lázně ☎ 499–875–186 ⊕ www.cerna-hora.cz) is 180 km (about a four-hour drive) east of Prague. The resort has a cable car, one chairlift, and a couple of drag lifts. The "Black Mountain" is not the biggest of ski resorts, but is often fairly quiet: meaning less waiting and a nice unofficial run, with plenty of forest to explore, directly under the cable car.

On the weekends, when you want to take in some crisp mountain air and clap on a pair of skis, head for **Harrachov** (⊠ Harrachov ☎ 432–529–600 ⊕ www.harrachov.cz). In the west of the Krkonoše, around 120 km (a three-hour drive) from the capital, the resort offers red-and-blue runs served by two chairlifts and 11 rope tows. This small and friendly resort is ideal for beginners and intermediates.

The biggest and most popular ski resort in the Czech Republic is **Skiareal Špindlerův Mlýn** (✉Špindlerův Mlýn ☎499–467–102 ⊕www.skiarealspindl. cz), which is 160 km (about a 3½-hour drive) from Prague. The twin slopes, Svatý Petr and Medvedín, gaze at each other over the small village and offer blue, red, and black runs served by four chairlifts and numerous rope tows. Weekends here are mobbed to a point well past frustration.

Soccer

Games for the domestic Czech league, the Gambrinus liga, run from August to May with a break in December and January. The games and the fans tend to be somewhat lackluster. Tickets are plentiful enough on match days (except for tournaments) at 50 Kč to 150 Kč. Depending on the opposition, it can be tough to secure tickets for European and international matches, which are more expensive (usually between 200 Kč and 500 Kč), but the crowds also gather a bit more verve. The Czech national team has punched well above its weight in the past decade or so, consistently rating in the top 10 in world rankings. Disciplined and carrying strong team ethos, lower-profile Czech-based players form the steely spine that the few world stars dance upon. International matches are hosted at Sparta's stadium.

AC Sparta Praha (✉ Toyota Arena Milady Horákové 98, Letná ☎ 296–111–400 ⊕ www.sparta.cz Ⓜ Line A: Sparta) has an enthusiastic fan base, with the stadium roar to match. Although Sparta has seen its fortunes dip a little recently, the team remains a domestic Goliath and a stone-slinging David in European competition.

Reduced in the early 21st century to bringing up the rear in the capital are second-division **FC Bohemians Praha** (✉ Doliček stadion, Vršovická 31, Vršovice ☎ 271–721–459 ⊕ www.fc-bohemians.cz Ⓜ Tram to Vršovice Nám.).

Sparta's success is much to the chagrin of its bitter rivals **SK Slavia Praha** (✉ Strahov Stadium Diskařská 100, Strahov ☎ 257–213–290 ⊕ www. slavia.cz Ⓜ Bus 176 from Karlovo nám. or bus 217 from Anděl, Metro Line B to Strahov), which has been playing in Strahov stadium while waiting for a new one to be built. The former favorites of the First Republic and their fans have had to be patient thus far. Then again, this team has been the country's underdog since the 1950s.

Swimming

In high summer (primarily in July and August), Prague residents enjoy dipping into "natural" water. Lakes and quarries are variously adopted for bathing, many of them outside the city. However, within the confines of Prague there are a few well-known spots.

★ At **Divoká Šárka** (✉ Nad Lávkou 5, Vokovice ☎ 235–358–554 Ⓜ Tram 20 or 26 to Nad Džbánem [the McDonald's restaurant]) your 50 Kč allows you to swim in the perpetually chilly, constantly flowing water, then warm up with a round of table tennis. When you exit the tram, walk behind McDonald's and take the steps to the right. At the bottom, turn left and walk 1 km through a green valley to find the two pools, fed by the streams you have walked alongside. Or instead of turning left at the bottom of the steps behind the McDonald's, you can also turn right to get to **Džbán,** a murky brown lake surrounded by bars and hot-dog vendors. Those of a delicate nature should avoid the nude sunbathing section.

Hostivař (⊠ K Jezeru, Hostivař ☎ 272–655–546 Ⓜ Line C: Háje then bus 165, 170, 212, 213 to last stop) is a large brown lake that snakes through a forest and fosters sunbathing, refueling, and occasionally, swimming.

Hotel Olšanka (⊠ Táboritská 23, Žižkov ☎ 267–092–202 ⊕ www. hotelolsanka.cz) houses a 25-meter pool open to the public every day. The hotel also offers a sauna (90 minutes for 120 Kč) and massage service (30 minutes for 220 Kč) when you get tired of doing the backstroke.

The busiest summer swimming pool in Prague is **Plavecký Stadión Podolí** (Podolí Swimming Stadium; ⊠ Podolská 74, Podolí ☎ 241–433–952 Ⓜ Tram 3 or 17 to Kublov). The indoor pool is 50 meters long, but when the sun comes out, two open-air pools, with a water slide, draw an army of younger Czechs to sunbathe and frolic on the grass around them. A word of warning: Podolí, for all its attractions, is a notorious hot spot of petty theft. Don't entrust any valuables to the lockers—it's best either to check them in the safe with the *vrátnice* (superintendent), or better yet, don't bring them at all.

Tennis

Tennis is one of the favorite local sports, but the national passion remains at a simmer instead of a rolling boil. The best known Czech players have been Ivan Lendl and, by ethnicity at least, Martina Navratilova. But there are a crop of younger players out there trying to crowd into the top 10. Prague is blessed with several public tennis courts. Most are cinder or clay surface.

At **Bendvík** (⊠ Diskařská 1, Hradčany ☎ 251–611–129 Ⓜ Tram 15, 22, or 23 to Malovanka), indoor courts cost 250 Kč to 430 Kč per hour, outdoor courts 100 Kč to 200 Kč per hour.

Some of the city's best tennis courts are found right next door to the tennis stadium, **Česky Lawn Tennis Klub** (⊠ Ostrov Štvanice 38, Holešovice ☎ 222–316–317 Ⓜ Line C: Vltavská), which in its time has hosted ATP events. Open to the public for 300 Kč to–600 Kč per hour are 10 outdoor courts and 6 indoor courts, all hard surface or clay, despite the name.

Yoga

The mystical atmosphere of Prague, in combination with its reputation as a center for the arts, ensures a steady supply of yoga classes. But for those who don't know the Czech word for "hamstrings," the trick is to find ones taught in English. Good sources for temporary groups and classes are the Internet message boards of http://prague.tv or www.expats.cz.

You can "harmonize your energy systems and manifest the universal law" in English every Monday evening at 10 PM from April to September at **Lotus Centrum** (⊠ Dlouhá 2, Staré Město). You must be over 15; the cost is 100 Kč for 90 minutes.

Shopping

WORD OF MOUTH

"The traditional liquor of the area is Becherovka . . . It's slightly bitter and is rumored (by everyone's grand-mother) to be medicinal. I always bring back a bottle or two . . . I'm a little fuzzy on my liquors, but I know that Slivovice is made from plums (prune plums, to be specific) and Becherovka is made from something else."

—Helena

"I thought Becherovka was made from prunes. I'll double 'czech' on that."

—amp322

By Mindy Kay
Bricker

"I BOUGHT IT IN PRAGUE" HAS A GREAT RING TO IT, and you can find plenty of potential purchases while strolling around town.

Czechs are world famous for their crystal and glassware, and some of the high-end shops have married modern notions of style with traditional Czech glassmaking techniques with beautiful results. It's much the same story with jewelry. Bohemia holds a reputation for quality garnets—the deep red stones are a Prague icon—and the settings and presentation have finally gotten a long awaited update from cheaper metals used in the past.

Also look for traditional handicrafts, whether made of wood, lace, or herbs. One chain to watch for around town is Botanicus, an earthy all-natural emporium selling everything, including candles, soaps, spices, and oils—many made from locally grown products. An ancient craft that Czechs have carried into the modern age is puppet making, which can be adorable or creepy, depending on your taste. Marionettes have a history here that goes back centuries—but be choosy if you want the real deal. Most of the marionettes you see in the souvenir shops are mass produced. Stick to antiques and artisan stores.

Arguably, the more interesting finds are in the city's antiques stores, where you can spot old folk costumes or stunning art deco tea sets stamped with the very retro "Made in Czechoslovakia." Antiquarian booksellers are peppered throughout the city. Many of the books they sell are in Czech or German, but the real finds are the old maps, photographs, and drawings.

The range of clothing stores, especially for women, seems to get better each passing month. And just like anywhere else in the world, the teen sets rules the market—so expect more offerings for trendy Lolitas. The best items are still usually found in the international boutiques, but Czech designers are making their mark. Alas, prices here are higher than you might expect—basically on par with or higher than you would pay back home.

> **MINDY'S TOP 5 BUYS IN PRAGUE**
>
> 1. Crystal wine glasses from Artěl.
> 2. A wearable piece of art from Art Decoratif.
> 3. A fashion-forward dress from Klára Nademlýnská.
> 4. Play it again, Dvořák—a classical CD from Bontonland.
> 5. Massage oil, made from Karlovy Vary's healing waters, from Botanicus.

Disappointingly, vanity sizing doesn't exist, but don't curl up in the fetal position in the dressing room just because your pants size went up by two. Czech women tend to be tall and willowy. Period. Remember those Victoria's Secret models? A good portion of them are Czech. A note on service: shop assistants are notoriously aloof and unhelpful; it's not you, it's them.

Shopping hours in Prague are generous by European standards. Most chains, department stores, and some boutiques are open daily from about 10 AM to 7 PM. Malls are generally open seven days a week from 10 AM to 9 PM or, in some cases, even 10 PM. Some boutiques take a lunch break. (If so, you'll usually see a sign indicating the shop is closed between noon and 2 PM, or whenever the shop assistant decides it's time for lunch.)

In terms of standard souvenirs, Prague is stuffed with shops carrying T-shirts, beer mugs, keychains, spoons, and ashtrays. These provide fodder for the "I was thinking of you" trinkets for friends and family back home. But donning that "Praha Drinking Team" sweatshirt while on vacation will inevitably mark you as a tourist and potential prey for pickpockets.

There is also a tourist market for pseudo-communist kitsch, including Russian-style fur caps bearing a hammer and sickle, and nesting dolls that open up successively from Putin to Stalin. These silly products are shoddily made and have nothing to do with Prague. Don't waste your money.

MAJOR SHOPPING DISTRICTS

Pařížská ulice is the Czech version of the Champs-Élyseés. If you are a high-end shopper looking for Hugo Boss, Dior, Salvatore Ferragamo, Louis Vuitton, and Hermès, this will be your habitat. It's also simply a great tree-lined street to stroll, people-watch, or enjoy an ice-cream cone.

Dlouhá třída, which runs off the Old Town Square, offers a concentrated dose of Czech fashion and interior designers, which has made it the hippest places to shop for local finds. Here you can find local designers such as Tatiana, Klára Nademlýnská, Timoure et Group, and Bohème.

A smorgasbord of clothing and shoe chains awaits you on the centrally located **Na Příkopě**. Zara, Mango, Benetton, and H&M are all here flashing buckled coats, tight jeans, loose skirts, and every other trend down to rocking leather bracelet.

Václavské náměstí, a leafy green boulevard featuring British department stores like Marks & Spencer (with a food section if you have a hankering for some proper English tea) and Debenhams, runs into Na Příkopě and is chock-full of tourist kitsch.

STREET MARKETS

Prague's most central open-air market is on **Havelská** in Staré Město, a few streets away from Václavské náměstí. Here you can find lush produce alongside handmade jewelry and trinkets.

Holešovice, is one of the largest open-air markets in the city, with everything from fruits to cheap denim clothes and antiques lamps. You can find it by taking the metro Line C (red line) to Vltavská station and then catching any tram heading east (running to the left as you exit the metro). Exit at the first stop and follow the crowds.

It's better to hit these two street markets during the week because both are closed Saturday afternoon and all day Sunday.

The annual **Easter Market** sets up shop every year a couple of weeks before and after the Easter holiday at the bottom of Václavské náměstí,

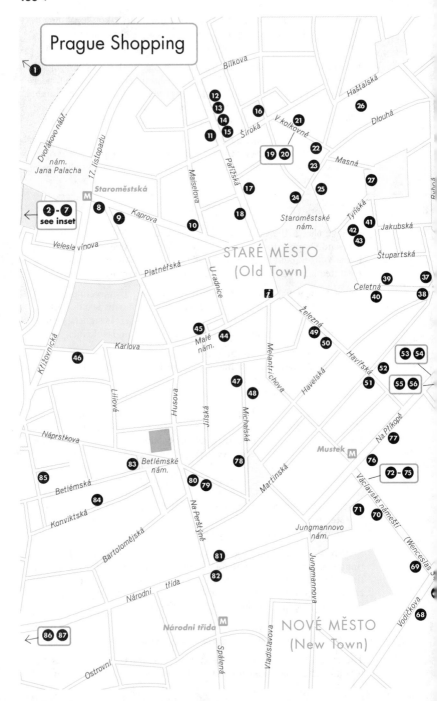

Prague Shopping

Bílkova

Dvořákovo nábř.

nám. Jana Palacha

17. listopadu

Staroměstská

2 - 7 see inset

8

9

Kaprova

Velesla vínova

Platnéřská

Křížovnická

46

Karlova

Náprstkova

85

Betlémská

Konviktská

Bartolomějská

86 87

Ostrovní

Národní třída

Maiselova

11

15

14

13

12

Široká

16

Pařížská

17

18

10

U radnice

Malé nám.

Husova

45

44

47

48

Michalská

Melantrichova

Liliová

Jilská

83

Betlémské nám.

84

80 79

Na Perštýně

81

82

Národní třída

Spálená

Vladislavova

STARÉ MĚSTO
(Old Town)

Staroměstské nám.

24

25

23

22

19 20

21

V kolkovně

Masná

Železná

49

50

Havelská

78

Martinská

Mustek

Jungmannovo nám.

Jungmannova

NOVÉ MĚSTO
(New Town)

Haštalská

26

Dlouhá

27

Tyńská

41

42

43

Jakubská

Štupartská

39

37

Celetná

40

38

51

52

53 54

55 56

Na Příkopě

77

76

72 - 75

71

70

Václavské náměstí (Wenceslas S

69

Vodičkova

68

Puhná

where it meets Na Příkopě. You can buy handpainted eggs, wooden toys, and Easter switches (as a Czech tradition, men spank women on this holiday, an act that supposedly ensures a lady's fertility!)

The **Christmas Market** stands out as the most jubilant because of the scheduled events for children and families. Evenings feature musical performances by both adults and children. The booths strung with lights sell various stocking fillers, such as candles, ornaments, and puppets. The season starts on December 5—"Mikulas," or St. Nicholas' Day. Don't miss the chance to have some *svařené vino*, or *svařák*, mulled wine served in plastic cups—a Czech secret for surviving the long, dark winter.

SPECIALTY STORES

Antiques

Rumor has it that once the communists were out, antiques dealers from Germany and Austria came swarming in, rummaging through the country for every stick of furniture and knickknack. This could explain why the supply of interesting items seems to have leveled off, despite the rising prices in recent years. Nevertheless, there's enough here to keep any magpie interested. Just look for the word *starožitnosti* (antiques shop), which tend to be small, one-room jumbles of old glass and bric-a-brac.

Art Deco Galerie. A few steps from Old Town Square, this darling boutique has a collection of vintage treasures. You can find beaded jewelry, art deco–inspired desk lamps, and pillbox hats for the ladies who lunch. ⊠ *Michalská 21, Staré Město* ☎ *224–223–076* Ⓜ *Line A or B: Můstek.*

Art Deco Gallery Shop. This shoe-box-size shop has a great selection of art deco tea sets from the 1930s, bearing a "Made in Czechoslovakia" stamp on the bottom. The owner has English-language art books on hand so that you can read what other collectors have written about her wares. The shop is only open from 2 PM to 7 PM most days, so plan on hitting it after lunch. ⊠ *Jánský vršek 8, Malá Strana* ☎ *257–535–801* Ⓜ *Line A: Malostranská.*

Fodor'sChoice **Bric a Brac.** If you're a believer in the equation "more clutter = better,"
★ you might be inclined to think of this as the best shop in Prague. The tiny shop is really two stores next door to each other in a tiny space as big as a child's bedroom, but it's packed with antique treasures, like candle holders and tobacco tins. The owner speaks perfect English in order to answer any questions. ⊠ *Týnská 7, Staré Město* ☎ *222–326–484* Ⓜ *Line A: Staroměstská.*

Dorotheum. A local branch of the fabled 300-year-old Austrian auction house. The Dorotheum is synonymous with class when it comes to buying clocks, jewelry, porcelain knickknacks, and standing clocks. Expect prices to reflect its upscale roots. ⊠ *Ovocný trh 2, Nové Město* ☎ *224–222–001* Ⓜ *Line B: Nám. Republiky.*

JHB Starožitnosti. Near Prague's busiest shopping streets, this place specializes in 18th- and 19th-century clocks. A whirlpool of clocks crowd the store: Empire standing clocks, Bavarian cuckoo clocks, or pocket watches for the more conservative buyer. ⊠ *Panská 1, Nové Město* ☎ *222–245–836* Ⓜ *Line A: Staroměstská.*

Starožitnosti Ungelt. The house specialty here is art nouveau and art deco furniture, paintings, and glass objects that are practically museum quality. One of the best antiques dealers, this store is perfectly situated in the elaborate courtyard behind the Old Town Square's Týn church and holds some colorful goblets by Moser and wonderful Loetz vases. ⊠ *Týn 1, Staré Město* ☎ *224–895–454* Ⓜ *Line A: Staroměstská.*

Art Galleries

The best galleries in Prague are quirky and eclectic affairs, places to sift through art rather than gaze at arm's length. Many are also off the beaten track and away from the main tourist bottlenecks, which gives more incentive to seek them out.

Galerie JBK. Carefully selected Czech artists are on display at this breathable, yet intimate, gallery. The selections never disappoint. In the basement you can find a nice ensemble of antique wooden furniture. ⊠ *Betlémské nám. 8, Staré Město* ☎ *222–220–689* Ⓜ *Line B: Národní třída.*

Galerie NoD. Above the Roxy, the most popular dance club in the city, NoD consistently exhibits young and eclectic work. Funds from the club support the gallery's mission of finding the next generation of up-and-coming artists. Try to predict which Bohemian expat or local artist might be the next Picasso. ⊠ *Dlouhá 33, Staré Město* ☎ *No phone* Ⓜ *Line A: Staroměstská.*

★ **Galerie Peithner-Lichtenfels.** The crowded feel of this gallery is like a glimpse into a tormented artist's head. There are enough paintings, prints, and drawings to please even the most critical art admirer. ⊠ *Michalská 12, Staré Město* ☎ *224–227–680* Ⓜ *Line A: Staroměstská.*

Bags, Scarves & Accessories

Clothing tends to be expensive in Prague, and glamorous accessories are no exception. For lower prices, hit the chain stores like Zara, H&M, and Mango.

Accesorize. The name says it all. For every Pantone color chip, this pocket-size store probably has a hat, necklace, or scarf to match. ⊠ *Václavské nám. 1, Koruna pasáž, Nové Město* ☎ *224–219–832* Ⓜ *Line A or B: Můstek.*

Coccinelle Accessories. Trendy leather bags showcase Italian design in quality leather. ⊠ *Železná 22, Nové Město* ☎ *224–228–203* Ⓜ *Line A or B: Můstek.*

Francesco Biasia. These soft leather purses, in every shape and size imaginable, are so smooth and buttery they almost resemble a sumptuous meal. ⊠ *Pařížská 5, Staré Město* ☎ *224–812–700* Ⓜ *Line A: Staroměstská.*

Hermès. Alas, you won't find the distinguished Kelly bag at the local branch of this French institution, but it does carry a gorgeous selection of silk

Shopping, Prague-Style

LIVE LIKE THE LOCALS WHILE YOU'RE HERE: enjoy your day and don't rush it. Unlike other cities Prague has a leisurely pace. And don't forget to look up occasionally while you're shopping. Admiring the architecture is part of the experience.

Your starting point is the top of Václavské náměstí in front of the National Museum. This is the epicenter of Prague shopping.

Head down the left side of the street, facing down the square away from the museum, and check out the windows of **Marks & Spencer** while making your way toward Štěpánská ulice, where you will take a left and then turn right into the Lucerna pasáž. **Cellarius** sells bottles of Bohemian wine or sparkling wine—a good gift for the person minding your dog while you are away. This is also where you will find the boutiques of **Alice Abraham** and **Ivana Follova,** two local designers who will show you a Czech take on fashion. But while shopping, don't forget to pause and take in the lovely old arcade. It was once partly owned by former President Václav Havel, and still remains in the Havel family.

Returning to Václavské náměstí, you will find **Debenhams** across the street. Head over, then pop into H&M and other shops as you walk down the square toward the Koruna pasáž at the very bottom of the square. Here, you will see **Accesorize** to your right. Continue into the pasáž, and on the left is **Anima Tua.** At the end of the pasa'ž, take a right onto Na Příkopě. **Benetton, Mango,** and **Moser** are on your right. Walk farther up the street and **Zara** is on your left. Continue to

Bohemian Glass

the corner of Havířska, and then you have to make a choice: continue on and explore a few more stores or turn left and forge ahead.

If you want to check out **Body Basics, Yanny, H&M** (with a focus on day- and work-wear, and children's clothing), **Versace,** or **Taiza** continue straight up Na Příkopě; they are up the street on the left and beyond. If you want to hit **Mexx** and **Nautica,** which are in the **Slovanský dům** mall, then go up the street and to the right. Either way, if you explore Na Příkopě farther, you'll need to backtrack to Havířska, where you can turn right.

Back on Havířska, **Max Mara** and the toy store **Sparkys** are on your left; both are worth a stop. Walk to the end of this street, and take your first left, then your first right, and you find yourself on Železna. Walk up this street to find the dignified **Coccinelle Accessories, Marina Rinaldi,** and **Estée Lauder** on your left. Go farther and you see **Benetton** for children on your right and **Stefanel** to your left. Finally, after a few more steps, you're in Old Town Square.

Do you see Týn church to your right, and the Jan Hus monument in the middle of the square? Walk at a diagonal across the square between these landmarks. To the right of the Jan Hus monument is a walkway. Peering down, you can undoubtedly see a few vendor kiosks set up. Walk down this cobblestone path.

Once out of this walkway, notice the street on your left, Týnská, which is where you're going after you walk through the curved archway into the Týn courtyard. Here you can find adorable shops and some of the best coffee in town at **Ebel Coffee House**—just in case you need to refuel. Check out the beautiful **Botanicus** store, **Anagram Books,** and the high-end antiques store **Starožitnosti Ungelt.**

Retrace your steps out of the courtyard and turn right onto Týnská, where immediately on the left you can find **Bric a Brac.** Go ahead and rummage through old—well—bric-a-brac. Continue down this street, turn left at the first opportunity, and the second shop to your left is **Anne Fontaine.** Keep walking down the street, take a left and your first right and walk to the roundabout. Now you are on Dlouhá Street, which is the creative hub for Czech fashion designers.

Across the street and to your left is **Klára Nademlýnská.** After you check out her Bohemian styles, walk back down the street. Your first left is Dušní, where you can find **Tatiana** and **Bohème.** Go back to Dlouhá Street and turn left. Rámová Street has a quirky interior shop called **Qubus Design.** After this shop, return to Dlouhá and turn right, again backtracking. At the roundabout, look

for V kolkovně, which is in front of you if Kozí is on your right. Go down V kolkovně to find **Timoure et Group.** Take a left on Vězeňská and head to Pařížská, where you will find **Hermès, Guess,** and **Hugo Boss.** Come back down the street on the opposite side and stop by **Louis Vuitton** and **Francesco Biasia.** Of course, in true Parisian style, this street is the best place to window shop and there are plenty of cafés and restaurants.

Backtrack one block, and take a left onto Široká, then take your first left onto Maiselova, and right onto Kaprova, where you will undoubtedly smell **Lush.** Follow your nose, and you'll see it on the right. Cross the street, and take a left onto Žatecká, then take a right at the end of this street and walk about 30 feet. You're standing in front of the city library, with City Hall to your left on the square. Align yourself with the front doors of the library, and walk into the square, pass the parked cars and onto Husova Street, which is dotted with knickknack shops and galleries. At the end of this street, look up to see local artist David Černý's hanging man statue. After this, turn left onto Skořepka and stop by **Taizer Gallery,** which is on your right. Walk to the end of the street, and cross it into a brown open door that leads into a courtyard, which is the Platyž pasáž. Walk through the *pasáž,* and you will find yourself on Narodní. Turn right and walk to the corner to find **Pietro Filipi,** a Czech clothing chain. Cross the street and walk toward **Tesco,** but unless you need something—more water, deodorant, an English-language magazine, new socks—you can consider your Prague shopping blitz at an end.

6

ties and leather products. ⊠ *Pařížská 12, Staré Město* ☎ *224–818–479* Ⓜ *Line A: Staroměstská.*

Louis Vuitton. Ironically housed in a former grocery store, Louis Vuitton has added luxury to this location, making it the most fashionable address on this most fashionable of streets. Expect the classic brown and tan accessories. ⊠ *Pařížská 13, Staré Město* ☎ *224–812–774* Ⓜ *Line A: Staroměstská.*

Books & Prints

Like its antiques shops, Prague's rare-book shops, or *antikvariáts,* were once part of a massive state-owned consortium that, since the end of communism, has split up and diversified. Now, most shops cultivate their own specialties. A few feature small English-language sections with a motley blend of potboilers, academic texts, classics, and tattered paperbacks. But if you're looking for material to kill a long plane or train ride, Prague has no less than four decent English bookstores.

Anagram Books. This comfortably tiny shop in Týn Square has a wide selection of historical books about Central and Eastern Europe, an adequate fiction selection, and some beautiful art and photography books. ⊠ *Týn 4, Staré Město* ☎ *224–895–737* Ⓜ *Line B: Nám. Republiky.*

Antikvariát Karel Křenek. Dip into another era by leafing through antique lithographs, maps, and advertisements in this gorgeous antique bookstore near the Powder Tower. A very small selection of English-language books are also on sale. ⊠ *U Obceního domu 2, Nové Město* ☎ *222–314–737* Ⓜ *Line B: Nám. Republiky.*

Big Ben Bookshop. An excellent selection of new English-language fiction—both the highbrow and shiny-cover varieties—pack the shelves in this shop (only an alley and a courtyard away from Old Town Square). It's a good source for guidebooks on other cities as well as translated Czech fiction. Newspapers and magazines provide more disposable reading material. ⊠ *Malá Štupartská 5, Staré Město* ☎ *224–826–565* Ⓜ *Line B: Nám. Republiky.*

Globe Bookstore & Coffeehouse. A literary haunt for the local English-speaking community, Globe has a respectable selection if you'd just like a good read. Cozy armchairs and Internet hookups invite lingering. ⊠ *Pštrossova 6, Nové Město* ☎ *224–934–203* Ⓜ *Line B: Národní třída.*

Luxor Bookstore. This enormous Czech bookshop rivals a typical Barnes and Noble in size. Unfortunately, unless you read Czech, you won't be able to enjoy the selection. But there is a generous English-language section in the basement that even stocks audio books. ⊠ *Václavské nám. 41, Nové Město* ☎ *221–111–342* Ⓜ *Line A: Muzeum.*

Shakespeare & Sons. A bit out of the center, this shop is worth seeking out for its unbeatable selection of new and used books and special events like poetry readings. The flagship bookshop in Vršovice has a small café and an authentic literary vibe. The smaller store, near Charles Bridge, is more of a standard bookshop. ⊠ *Krymská 12, Vršovice* ☎ *271–740–839* Ⓜ *Line A: Nám. Míru, Tram 4, 22, 23.* ⊠ *U*

Lužického semináře 10, Malá Strana ☎ *257–531–894* Ⓜ *Line A: Malostranská.*

U Karlova Mostu. The preeminent Prague bookstore has a suitably book-ish location opposite the Clementinum—that elusive 15th-century man-uscript you're looking for? It's here. In addition to housing ancient books too precious to flip through, the store has a small foreign-lan-guage section, and a host of prints, maps, drawings, and paintings. ✉ *Karlova 2, Staré Město* ☎ *222-220–286* Ⓜ *Line A: Staroměstská.*

Clothing

FOR MEN & WOMEN **5 Avenue.** This discount name-brand boutique sells Ralph Lauren, DKNY, and BCBG labels. Although a plethora of dresses are in stock in different brands, styles, and sizes, there's generally only one of each. The store also provides a small selection of men's dress shirts. ✉ *Karolíny Světlé 22, Staré Město* ☎ *222-222–169* Ⓜ *Line A: Staroměstská.*

Guess by Marciano. A well-known temple to denim and sexy casual wear, this location also stocks a nice selection of watches, light summer dresses for women, and beachside linen pants for men. ✉ *Pařížská 22, Staré Město* ☎ *222–328–649* Ⓜ *Line A: Staroměstská.*

Kenvelo. An "Old Navy" for the Czech Republic, this Israeli-owned store has nearly every jean cut and style teens could want. Other streetwear is sold here but the name of the store is shouted across every stitch of clothing. ✉ *Václavské nám. 1, Nové Město* ☎ *221–111–711* Ⓜ *Line A or B: Můstek.*

Marks & Spencer. Affectionately known as "Marks and Sparks" to Brits around the world, this outpost sells everything from push-up bras to Fair Trade coffee. Styles are basic, but quality is good. ✉ *Václavské nám. 36, Nové Město* ☎ *224–237–503* Ⓜ *Line A or B: Můstek.*

Pietro Filipi. This Czech retailer has hit a niche with well-designed wardrobe basics tailored for young professionals. It's a life-saver if you need seasonal staples, like a classic black turtleneck. ✉ *Národní 31, Nové Město* ☎ *224–231–120* Ⓜ *Line B: Národní třída.*

Wilvorst. A genteel, preppy style colors the selection here, with plaid shirts for men and wool skirts for women. But with labels like Joop!, quality is the key. This store occu-pies several houses on this street, so simply meander around to browse the racks. ✉ *U Prašné brány 1, Nové Město* ☎ *222–323–573* Ⓜ *Line B: Nám. Republiky.*

FOR WOMEN The selection of women's clothing around town is improving and styles are finally breaking away from that skintight look that's more like a

V.A.T. KNOW-HOW

When making a purchase, ask for a V.A.T. refund form and find out if the merchant gives refunds (not all stores are required to do so). Have the form stamped by custom offi-cials when you leave the country and drop it off at the refund-serv-ice counter to receive 19% back on all your purchases (5% back on books or food from grocery stores). Consult Essentials at the back of the book for more information.

wetsuit than a piece of clothing. Czech women love trends, so you'll see many shops catering to the fad of the moment but serious, cutting-edge fashion is making inroads, too.

Alice Abraham. A Czech designer with a fondness for bold statements, including adding a snakeskin bodice to an evening dress. If you like to play with fashion, this is your Prague playground. ⊠ *Lucerna pasáž, Václavské nám., between Vodičkova and Štěpánská, Nové Město* 🕾 *224–214–401* Ⓜ *Line A or B: Můstek.*

Anima Tua. Women with talk-to-the-hand attitude can be found flipping through the hangers, looking at brands like Love Sex Money and Laura Biagiotti. Both evening- and daywear are sold here for equal opportunity bling-bling. ⊠ *Koruna pasáž, Václavské nám. 1, Nové Město* 🕾 *224–473–074* Ⓜ *Line A or B: Můstek.*

Anne Fontaine. Extremely specialized, the way only a Parisian boutique can be. This French designer has one obsession: the white blouse. She consistently reinvents the wheel and creates innovative, sumptuous, and expensive white button-downs. ⊠ *Masna 12, Staré Město* 🕾 *224–808–306* Ⓜ *Line A or B: Můstek.*

Bohème. The smart, high-quality knitwear here values classic over trendy. ⊠ *Dušní 8, Staré Město* 🕾 *224–813–840* Ⓜ *Line B: Nám. Republiky.*

Ivana Follová. Clothing with sharp contrasts and daring cuts are just shy of overly extravagant. ⊠ *Vodičkova 36, Nové Město* 🕾 *296–236–497* Ⓜ *Line A or B: Můstek.*

FodorśChoice ★ **Klára Nademlýnská.** The darling of the Czech fashionistas set, this designer sells both funky and conservative clothes—everything from killer pinstripe suits to floor-length halter dresses—in her Old Town boutique. Check out the accessories case for inexpensive costume jewelry. A rotating selection ensures great end-of-the-season sales. ⊠ *Dlouhá 3, Staré Město* 🕾 *224–818–769* Ⓜ *Line B: Nám. Republiky.*

Mango. Color-coordinating guesswork is already done by the displays in this Spanish chain. The cathedral-like building is packed with funky white business suits, ruffly black skirts, bow-clad kitten heels, red leather clutches, and other signature accessories. ⊠ *Na Příkopě 8, Nové Město* 🕾 *224–218–884* Ⓜ *Line A or B: Můstek.*

Marina Rinaldi. Trendy businesswomen might head to this conservative but chic shop to add a butter-yellow linen dress to their summer wardrobe or a black leather jacket to their winter wardrobe. ⊠ *Železná 22, Staré Město* 🕾 *224–234–636* Ⓜ *Line A or B: Můstek.*

Nový Svět. With the sassy careerwoman in mind, this boutique stocks sexy, beige miniskirt suits that prove business does not equal boring. There are more conservative options here, like pantsuits, along with evening wear. ⊠ *V kolkovné 5, Staré Město* 🕾 *224–813–948* Ⓜ *Line A: Staroměstská.*

Taiza. *Vogue* magazine awarded this Cuban-born, Prague-based designer with the 2002 Designers' Choice Award. Judge for yourself why his elegant evening wear fulfills red-carpet fantasies. You can find dresses covered in floral prints that explode, pinks that pop, and yellows that glow. ⊠ *V celnici 10, Nové Město* ☎ *257–315–487* Ⓜ *Line B: Nám. Republiky.*

FodorśChoice
★
Tatiana. A wink of leather trim transforms a classic into a contemporary outfit. The two Czechs behind this boutique know how to design for the modern woman who doesn't necessarily want to sacrifice sex appeal at the office or at a dinner party. ⊠ *Dušní 1, Staré Město* ☎ *224–823–723* Ⓜ *Line A: Staroměstská.*

Timoure et Group. A partnership of Czech designers who have an eye for modern but wearable clothing run this sophisticated shop. ⊠ *V kolkovné 6, Staré Město* ☎ *222–327–358* Ⓜ *Line A: Staroměstská.*

Versace. Standing apart from the other high-end labels, this small boutique near the Powder Tower offers luxurious Italian fashion in the usual Versace live-wire electric colors. ⊠ *U Prašné brány 3, Staré Město* ☎ *224–810–016* Ⓜ *Line B: Nám. Republiky.*

Yanny. With a selection of Dolce & Gabbana, Jean-Paul Gaultier, and other big-name designers, it's no surprise that this store's dresses, skirts, and tops regularly appear in magazines like *Elle* and *Dolce Vita.* ⊠ *Na Příkopě 27, Nové Město* ☎ *224–228–196* Ⓜ *Line B: Nám. Republiky.*

FOR MEN Sadly, men have fewer options in Prague when it comes to buying clothes. For the most part, fashion remains a women's pursuit (the "Queer Eye for the Straight Guy" philosophy hasn't caught on yet). Local offerings are often a season or two behind the times. The best bets are with the international designers. Don't expect low prices or a great selection of sizes.

Ermenegildo Zegna. A fashion mainstay, this Italian label has been producing some of the world's finest suits and jackets for around a century. ⊠ *U Prašné brány 3, Staré Město* ☎ *224–810–018* Ⓜ *Line B: Nám. Republiky.*

Hugo Boss. This German designer is synonymous with contemporary men's style. The shop carries both informal sportswear and some high-end suits—though the range of sizes is often limited. ⊠ *Parízská 6, Staré Město* ☎ *222–324–536* Ⓜ *Line A: Staroměstská.*

Report's. Catering to businessmen who make style their business, this Italian-owned boutique carries only the best in Italian suits and accessories. ⊠ *V kolkovné 5, Staré Město* ☎ *222–329–823* Ⓜ *Line B: Nám. Republiky.*

FOR CHILDREN Most of the quality children's clothing can be found at the mall, especially at Nový Smíchov. A stroll along Na Příkopě offers additional choices like the Slovanský dům mall, where you can also find the cheap-

> ### STRIKE A POSE
>
> Though fashion statements might be a bit different in Prague than where you are from, the go-to women's and men's magazines are not. To get a peak at what is hot in Prague, flip through the pages of the Czech versions of *Cosmopolitan, Elle, Marie Claire,* or *Esquire.*

est and trendiest clothing for tots at **Mexx** or **H&M**—half the store is devoted to children's clothing.

Benetton. Miniature tough jean vests and teeny white parachute pants are found here, where big trends are fitted for little bodies. ☒ *Železna 1, Staré Město* ☎ *224–221–910* Ⓜ *Line A or B: Můstek.*

Cosmetics & Perfume

Body Basics. A Body Shop for the Czech Republic, this ubiquitous boutique was originally founded by a Londoner. That urban ecoconscious vibe is displayed in the coolest and freshest scents for foot creams, aftershaves, and shower gels; check out the avocado scrub. Several branches are around town. ☒ *Na Příkopě 19, Nové Město* ☎ *224–231–271* Ⓜ *Line B: Nám. Republiky.*

Botanicus. If the world were a county fair, Czechs would win the blue ribbon for herbalist every year. And Botanicus is proof of their legacy. The herbs imbedded in the creams, oils, and soaps will tickle your olfactory senses. Items are tenderly wrapped in brown paper, making it an easy gift. ☒ *Týnsky Dvůr 3, Staré Město* ☎ *234–767–446* Ⓜ *Line B: Nám. Republiky.*

Clinique. Clinique-ophiles, don't fret. Occupying a corner kiosk on the first floor of the Nový Smíchov mall, the shop is here for those who forgot their foaming mousse cleanser at home. ☒ *Nový Smíchov, Plzeňská 8, Smíchov* ☎ *257–329–230* Ⓜ *Line B: Anděl.*

Lush. It looks like a cheese shop, but it's actually soap wedges getting weighed and wrapped. An import from London, this store believes in toeing a hard line on all-natural products—human beings actually *taste test* the soaps. Body creams, bath bombs, and chocolate massage bar are almost addictive. ☒ *Kaprova 13, Staré Město* ☎ *603–164–362* Ⓜ *Line A: Staroměstská.*

Sephora. This French chain is like a duty-free emporium to the 10th power and provides everything you could possibly imagine by every heavy-hitting cosmetic company. ☒ *Nový Smíchov, Plzeňská 8, Smíchov* ☎ *257–326–618* Ⓜ *Line B: Anděl.*

Food & Wine

Cellarius. This inviting shop stocks the best Moravian and Bohemian wines and spirits, as well as excellent wines from around the world. ☒ *Lucerna pasáž, Václavské nám., between Vodičkova and Štěpánská, Nové Město* ☎ *224–210–979* Ⓜ *Line A or B: Můstek.*

Fruits de France. Fresh from France, the fruits and vegetables here are some of the prettiest—and most expensive—available. A decent selection of imported French cheeses, chocolates, and wines complete the left-bank look. ⊠ *Jindřišská 9, Nové Město* ☎ *224–220–304* Ⓜ *Line A or B: Můstek* ⊠ *Bělehradská 94, Vinohrady* ☎ *222–511–261* Ⓜ *Line C: I. P. Pavlova.*

Glass

Glass has traditionally been Bohemia's biggest export and was one of the few products manufactured during Communist times that managed to retain an artistically innovative spirit. Today exquisite glasswork remains a point of national pride, and Prague has plenty of shops selling excellent Bohemian crystal. But choose carefully. Rip-offs abound in some of the flashier tourist stores.

Fodor'sChoice
★ **Artěl.** Luxury glass that's "funky" might seem like an oxymoron, but that's exactly what you'll find here. The store's U.S.-born creator, Karen Feldman, has married a modern-American style with a Czech tradition of crystal in a winning combination. Feldman is perfectly proud to say: "Everything is functional." ⊠ *Celetná 29, Staré Město* Ⓜ *Line A or B: Můstek* ⊠ *Vinohradská 164, Vinohrady* ☎ *271–732–161* Ⓜ *Line A: Jiřího z Poděbrad.*

Galerie Tesař. This shop gives you that euphoric feeling of walking into a silent room after a loud concert. After seeing the loud, vibrant colors and shapes of blown glass, this is where you will find stunning simplicity. Minimalist clear glass on silver shelves give the store a crisp modern feel. ⊠ *Skořepká 4, Staré Město* ☎ *572–695–476* Ⓜ *Line B: Národní třída.*

Galerie 'Z.' This gallery specializes in limited-edition mold-melted and blown glass. ⊠ *Michalská pasáž, Malé nám. 11, Staré Město* ☎ *224–218–248* Ⓜ *Line A or B: Můstek.*

★ **Material.** Even the door handle for this store is an artistically crafted vase, demonstrating this store's devotion to the craft. The eye-catching shop below the Charles Bridge sells glass that is crafted from the Czech company Ajeto. Rare pieces include long-stem candlesticks with glass leaves. ⊠ *U Lužického semináře 7, Malá Strana* ☎ *257–533–663* Ⓜ *Line A: Malostranská.*

Moser. An opulent flagship store of the world-famous Karlovy Vary glassmaker (started in 1857) offers the finest top-quality traditional Bohemian glass. Even if you're not in the market to buy, stop by simply to look at the elegant wood-panel display rooms on the second floor. The staff will gladly pack goods for traveling. ⊠ *Na Příkopě 12, Nové Město* ☎ *224–211–293* Ⓜ *Line B: Nám. Republiky.*

Home Design

Czech design is wonderfully rich in quality and imagination, emphasizing old-fashioned craftsmanship while often taking an offbeat, even cheeky approach.

Arzenal. You'll either love it or hate it—the eccentric work of Bořek Šípek, former President Havel's official designer back in the day, is sold in this little glass and housewares shop, not far from the Old Town Square. The glass bowls radiate head-throbbing color and contrast and some even appear to be trimmed with Medusa's hair. There's a little Thai restaurant tucked in the back. Don't ask us why. We can't figure it out either. ✉ *Valentinská 11, Staré Město* ☎ *224–814–099* Ⓜ *Line A: Staroměstská.*

FodorśChoice ★ **Modernista.** A celebration of forward-thinking design, this store expanded on Celetná into something of a 20th-century-design museum in 2006, selling cubist, modernist, and mid-century furniture and housewares. Ruby-red armchairs and cubist tea sets can give you the coolest home on the block. ✉ *Betlémské nám. 169, Staré Město* Ⓜ *Line B: Narodní Třída* ✉ *Celetná 12, Staré Město* ☎ *602–305–633* Ⓜ *Line A or B: Můstek.*

★ **Qubus Design.** An IKEA-free fun house of home design. Moose-head coat racks and galosh-shape vases prove childhood is the new black. ✉ *Rámová 3, Staré Město* ☎ *222–313–151* Ⓜ *Line B: Nám. Republiky.*

Jewelry

You won't find any jewelry steals in Prague. Garnets and amber are the Czech Republic's universal keepsake, but prices tend to be high, especially when the dollar is weak. Expect to pay the equivalent of at least $75 for a nice piece of silver jewelry with a stunning setting. Smaller pieces, amber bead bracelets or stud earrings, can be found for less than $40. Look around before making a purchase—many jewelry stores sell the same items, so you can save a few dollars by being a comparison shopper.

> **WORD OF MOUTH**
>
> "One more item to purchase . . . garnets, garnets, garnets. You'll see them everywhere, really regal, really elegant settings."   –Ginny
>
> "For garnets, be very sure you are buying 14 or 18K settings as some are set in 'pot metal.' "   –cher

Art Decoratif. The art nouveau artist Alfons Mucha lives on, not only because of the posters splashed across the city, but because his granddaughter, Jarmila Mucha Plockova, has produced designs inspired by her grandfather's work since 1992. You can even purchase a necklace in the same design that Mucha made for his wife as a wedding present. There are gorgeous vases, silk scarves, and other art nouveau tokens of the highest quality. ✉ *Široká 9, Josefov* ☎ *222–321–032* Ⓜ *Line A: Staroměstská* ✉ *Michalska 19, Staré Město* ☎ *225–777–156* Ⓜ *Line A or B: Můstek.*

Česky Garnat. Though it's flanked by kitschy tourist shops, this store is among the best in town for garnets and amber. ✉ *Celetná 4, Staré Město* ☎ *224–228–287* Ⓜ *Line A or B: Můstek.*

Halada. This shop sells sleek, Czech-designed silver jewelry; an affiliate shop at Na Příkopě 16 specializes in gold, diamonds, and pearls. ✉ *Karlova 25, Nové Město* ☎ *224–228–938* Ⓜ *Line B: Karlovo nám.* ✉ *Na Příkopě 16, Nové Město* ☎ *224–221–304* Ⓜ *Line B: Nám. Republiky.*

FodorśChoice ★ **Swarovksi Bohemia.** Nicole Kidman donned a crystal dress, while Yves Saint Laurent sported a crystal heart on a celebrated cover of *Vogue*—

and both came from this world-renowned crystal designer. Crystal jewelry with a brilliant glimmer and mid-range prices make this a must. ✉ *Celetná 11, Staré Město* ☎ *222–315–585* Ⓜ *Line A or B: Můstek.*

Marionettes

Marionettes have a long history in Bohemia, going back to the times when traveling troupes would entertain children with morality plays in town squares. The art form survives, and you won't walk long before stumbling into yet another collection of spooky puppets hanging from their strings. Most of the puppets you see in the shops are mass-produced knock-offs, but several genuine puppet-makers still carry on the craft with integrity.

Galerie Marionette. Czech and French-style marionettes dangle from the rafters as angels and devils. The local artists who peddle their creations here see marionettes as an art form, not a toy, and put detailed work into the facial features. This is where former President Bill Clinton picked up one for himself. ✉ *U Lužického semináře 7, Malá Strana* ☎ *257–535–091* Ⓜ *Line A: Malostranská.*

★ **Obchod Pod lampou.** Wall-to-wall hanging puppets can be a joy or a fright, depending on taste, with handcrafted Frankensteins or princess puppets. Prices vary for those less serious about the art and simply seeking a high-quality souvenir. ✉ *U Lužického semináře 5, Malá Strana* ☎ *No phone* Ⓜ *Line A: Malostranská.*

Marionety. The owner of this shop has a discerning collection of new and antique marionettes. Find a modern devil or, if you prefer, an antique devil from 1910, with twice the painted eeriness at twice the price. ✉ *Nerudova 51, Malá Strana* ☎ *257–533–035* Ⓜ *Line A: Malostranská.*

Pohádka. Harry Potter, devils, and angels can all be found in marionette form hanging from the ceiling or sitting on shelves. Right there among the tourist shops, this seller of marionettes offers puppets at reasonable prices. ✉ *Celetná 32, Nové Město* ☎ *No phone* Ⓜ *Line B: Nám. Republiky.*

Music & Musical Instruments

Capriccio. When you tap into your inner Mozart, this is the place to find sheet music of all kinds. ✉ *Újezd 15, Malá Strana* ☎ *257–320–165* Ⓜ *Line A: Malostranská.*

Dům Hudebnich Nastroju. Find a comprehensive selection of quality musical instruments at reasonable prices in this four-story house of music, a block up from Václavské nám. ✉ *Koruna Palace Shopping Center, Václavské nám. 1, Nové Město* ☎ *224–473–080* Ⓜ *Line A or B: Můstek.*

Bontonland Megastore. It's a mega CD shop, for sure, but Bontonland can also be mega-confusing to find. Tip: enter from the Václavské nám. entrance, rather than the metro.

> **WORD OF MOUTH**
>
> "My father always buys classical music CDs in Prague. They're cheaper than in the U.S., and there's a tremendous selection."
> –Helena

Once in, you will find more than 60 listening stands to sample the best of Czech and international artists. It has a good selection of classical music as well. ☒ *Jungmannova nám. 17, Nové Město* ☎ *224–222–501* Ⓜ *Line A or B: Můstek.*

Shoes

In the past, shoes were expensive *and* tacky. Now they're just expensive. Even the low-quality variety tend to be as pricy as electronics in Prague. But reputable local chains have improved their stock, and trendy shoe designers have added some competitive energy.

Alberto Guardiani. Displaying a good selection of classic women's shoes with a twist, this is where Prague's fashionistas buy their buckled boots and ankle-tied high heels. ☒ *Pařížská 24, Staré Město* ☎ *224–815–976* Ⓜ *Line A: Staroměstská.*

Baťa. This international shoe giant was founded on the territory of the modern-day Czech Republic in 1894. Today the *Guinness Book of World Records* claims it's the word's largest shoe retailer. Inside, find every shoe for every purpose and every age. ☒ *Václavské nám. 6, Nové Město* ☎ *224–218–133* Ⓜ *Line A or B: Můstek* ☒ *Nový Smíchov, Plzeňská 8, Smíchov* ☎ *251–512–847* Ⓜ *Line B: Anděl.*

Beltissimo. Specialties here are strappy summer sandals, high heels, and sleek loafers from the best names around, including Armani, Kenzo, and others. Check out the branch in Slovanský dům. ☒ *U Prašné brány 1, Staré Město* ☎ *222–002–320* Ⓜ *Line B: Nám. Republiky.*

Leiser. Styles are so funky they almost seem vintage, without even trying. This is a fun place where you can find anything from sneakers to pumps, for kids to adults. ☒ *U Prašné brány 1, Nové Město* ☎ *224–810–431* Ⓜ *Line B: Nám. Republiky.*

Sergio Rossi. This designer plays with stiletto shapes and leather designs to make shoes that are both wearable and memorable. ☒ *Pařížská 10, Staré Město* ☎ *224–814–779* Ⓜ *Line A: Staroměstská.*

Sporting Goods

Adidas. The staff here is helpful and genuinely athletic rather than posing as athletes for fashion's sake. Here you have a full selection of sportswear and other three-stripe Adidas swag, including—naturally—shoes. ☒ *Na Příkopě 12, Nové Město* ☎ *224–210–204* Ⓜ *Line A or B: Můstek.*

Gigasport. This is where the hardcore sport devotees shop. You can find diving fins and running shoes here, but it's best to do your own research. Unless you get lucky, the staff tends to know only the basic elements about their department. ☒ *Na Příkopě 19, Myslbek pasáž, Nové Město* ☎ *224–233–552* Ⓜ *Line B: Nám. Republiky.*

Hudy Sport. This is a good source of quality hiking and camping equipment. ☒ *Na Perštýně 14, Nové Město* ☎ *224–813–010* Ⓜ *Line B: Nám. Republiky.*

Nike. Bright lights and loud music make this spot seem more like a club than a store—make your purchase, then use those new shoes to book it out of here. Though standard sport shoes are sold here, it's more fashionable than functional. ⊠ *Václavské nám. 18, Nové Město* ☎ *224-237-921* Ⓜ *Line A or B: Můstek.*

Toys & Gifts for Children

Nearly every stationery store has beautiful watercolor or colored-chalk sets available for a pittance. The Czechs are also master illustrators, and the books they've made for young "prereaders" are beautiful. For the child with a theatrical bent, marionettes—ranging from finger-size to almost child-size—are spectacular. (see ⇨ Marionettes, *above*).

Hračky. Czech-made wooden toys and wind-up trains, cars, and animals, are on sale in this popular, delightful, and reasonably priced store. ⊠ *Pohořelec 24, Hradčany* ☎ *603-515-745* Ⓜ *Line A: Hradčanská.*

★ **Sparkys.** The best-known toy store in the city, this is a great place for huge stuffed animals and other amusements for newborns to children up to 10 years old. ⊠ *Havířská 2, Nové Město* ☎ *224-239-309* Ⓜ *Line B: Nám. Republiky.*

SHOPPING MALLS

6

Several modern shopping malls have arrived on the scene in recent years, giving Czech kids a place to go when they're skipping school. They are no different here than they are back home, but may be worth seeking out for forgotten items left at home or to catch a movie at the multiplex. The ones listed below are convenient to the center by public transportation.

Nový Smíchov. Many of the chain stores here, like H &M and Zara, can be found in the city center, leaving stores emptier during weekday afternoons and the selection a little less picked through. A video arcade here makes an ideal place to park the kids or husband while shopping. ⊠ *Plzeňská 8, Smíchov* ☎ *251-511-151* Ⓜ *Line B: Anděl.*

Palace Flora. Similar to Nový Smichov in terms of selection, Flora has the added allure of being home to Prague's IMAX cinema. An easy metro ride on Line A (green line), this was recently named the best shopping center by the Association for Real Estate Market Development. ⊠ *Vinohradská 149, Žižkov* ☎ *255-741-712* Ⓜ *Line A: Flora.*

Slovanský dům. Nautica, Tommy Hilfiger, and other quality brands give this mall enough street cred to make it selective but not so much so that it's pretentious. Be sure to stroll through to the back where the mall extends into a relaxing courtyard. It also holds the best multiplex cinemas in town. ⊠ *Na Příkopě 22, Nové Město* ☎ *257-451-400* Ⓜ *Line B: Nám. Republiky.*

DEPARTMENT STORES

Grand department stores on the order of a Harrod's or a Bloomingdale's have yet to arrive in Prague. Czech department stores tend to be relatively spartan affairs, selling ho-hum ranges of clothing, sporting goods, and kitchenware from a grouping of kiosks under one roof. Standards have risen in recent years as foreign-owned department stores have opened up local branches. But these too tend to disappoint compared with their Western branches. Still, the recent imports are usually better than their local counterparts for hard-to-find items.

Carrefour. This French chain merges department and grocery stores. Its main selling point can be summed up in three words: "open until midnight." It anchors the Nový Smíchov mall, and stocks everything from pantyhose to soy sauce. ✉ *Nový Smíchov, Plzeňská 8, Smíchov* ☎ *257–321–915* Ⓜ *Line B: Anděl.*

Debenhams. A British department store that sells quality clothing and sturdy housewares at fairly inexpensive prices, Debenhams would be comfortably at home in any suburban North American or Western European shopping mall. ✉ *Václavské nám. 21, Nové Město* ☎ *221–015–011* Ⓜ *Line A or B: Můstek.*

Kotva. The best of the Czech-run department stores is a decent place to buy small items like toiletries, pens and paper, basic clothing, electronics, and sporting goods. Although the overall mix is fairly ordinary, some rarities occasionally crop up. It's nearly the only place in Prague, for example, to buy New Balance or Saucony running shoes; the selection is small, but the prices are low. ✉ *Nám. Republiky 8, Nové Město* ☎ *224–801–111* Ⓜ *Line B: Nám. Republiky.*

Tesco. This U.K.-based department store, with a well-stocked grocery store in the basement, is a sure bet for everyday items like batteries, deodorant, electric adaptors, or even picnic supplies. A bonus is its excellent selection of English-language magazines. ✉ *Národní třída 26, Nové Město* ☎ *222–003–111* Ⓜ *Line B: Národní třída.*

Day Trips from Prague

7

WORD OF MOUTH

"We took an organized mini-bus tour from Prague one day to the church full of bones . . .it was really cool. There are strings of skulls criss-crossing the ceiling, coats of arms made from bones, pyramids of bones and best of all, a chandelier made from at least one of every bone in the body."

–Peep

By Mark Baker   **PRAGUE'S A GREAT PLACE TO HANG OUT,** but as any Czech living outside the capital can tell you, it's not the *real* Czech Republic. In the past 15 years, hundreds of millions of dollars have been pumped into Prague's economy by the many millions of visitors who have come. That's brought the Czech capital much closer to Western Europe in terms of services, infrastructure, and *attitude.*

Change outside of Prague has been much, much slower, and it would be a shame to come all this way and not see some of the rest of the country to see the contrast. One relatively easy way to glimpse life outside the capital is to take a day trip. The Prague countryside is blessed with several castle towns—all within an easy hour or two's journey by car, bus, or train, that both dazzle the eye and lend insight into life away from the capital's boutique hotels and 500 Kč dinner entrées. If castles are not your thing, the road to the northeast leads toward Germany and the ghosts of World War II in towns like Lidice and Terezín.

Karlštejn is the most popular day trip from Prague, and probably the easiest-to-reach destination. Prague residents like it, too, and on summer weekends the little village can seem almost as mobbed as the Old Town Square. Křivoklát and Český Šternberk also offer striking medieval castles but they are more remote and a little less touristy.

Konopiště has the distinction of being the home of Austrian Archduke Franz Ferdinand d'Este, whose assassination in Sarajevo in 1914 set off World War I. Some of the rooms in his castle remain pretty much as they were 100 years ago. Orlík is the most distant of the castles and therefore makes for the most remote day trip of all, but you'll be rewarded by its splendid natural setting and the dramatic castle itself.

On a different note, Terezín and Lidice are both memorials to remember the Nazi atrocities of World War II. Terezín was the most prominent concentration camp in the Czech lands, and a way station for many of Prague's Jews before their eventual transport to Auschwitz and other points east. Lidice was a Czech village razed by the Germans in retaliation for Czech patriots assassinating the Nazi wartime leader in Bohemia, Reinhard Heydrich. More educational than outright depressing, a visit to one of these places is recommended, particularly if you have not had the opportunity to visit a Holocaust site before.

Kutná Hora was a booming mining town in the Middle Ages and still displays its once immense wealth with an array of outstanding, if crumbling, buildings and the country's most impressive cathedral outside of Prague. If you visit, you can see cobbled streets beneath medieval spires, as well as a few other sites that can make your eyes widen.

With a few exceptions, most of these destinations are easy to visit on your own, either by car, train, or bus. Train and bus fares do not differ greatly, though trains are usually a bit cheaper. One advantage the train has over the bus is that it gives you a view of the countryside away from the noise and diesel fumes of the highways. Most of the destinations here are also served by guided-tour operators, though touring the countryside with them will inevitably be more expensive than going on your own.

Numbers in the margin correspond to numbers on the Day Trips from Prague and Kutná Hora maps.

About the Hotels & Restaurants

Although all the destinations in this chapter can be visited on a half- or full-day excursion from Prague, you may find yourself yearning for more peace and quiet than the capital can provide, particularly during the busiest months of the high season. There are decent options for an overnight stay near most of the day-trip excursion destinations, and happily, the prices are certainly lower than in Prague. The same is true for food. However, be prepared for less choice and fewer English-speaking staff members.

	$$$$	$$$	$$	$	¢
WHAT IT COSTS in koruna and euros					
HOTELS in koruna	over 7,000	5,000–7,000	3,500–5,000	1,500–3,500	under 1,500
HOTELS in euros	over 225	155–225	108–155	47–108	under 47
RESTAURANTS	over 500	300–500	150–300	100–150	under 100

Hotel prices are for two people in a double room with a private bath and break-fast during peak season (April through October) and generally include tax. Restaurant prices are per person for a main course at dinner and include tax.

KUTNÁ HORA

70 km (44 mi) east of Prague.

One of a dozen or so UNESCO World Heritage sites in the Czech Republic and one of the most popular day trips from Prague, Kutná Hora was once a booming silver-mining center. For a time in the late Middle Ages the town rivaled Prague for splendor and influence in Bohemia. Those days are long over and today much of the town earns its money from the tourism.

Silver was discovered here in 12th century, and for some 400 years the mines were worked with consummate efficiency. A highlight to visiting Kutná Hora is the chance to tour some of the old mine shafts and see how the silver was minted into the famed Prague groschen, one of the most widely circulated coins at the time. Much of the wealth was siphoned off to build the illustrious structures of Prague, but enough stayed in Kutná Hora to finance the construction of several imposing buildings, including what many regard as the country's most impressive Gothic cathedral outside of the capital. As the silver began to run out in the 16th and 17th centuries, Kutná Hora's importance faded. Since the early 1990s, the town has beautified itself to a degree, but modern Kutná Hora feels dwarfed by the splendors of the Middle Ages. When you arrive in Kutná Hora, head to the central square, Palackého náměstí, to get oriented. If you come into the town by bus, look for the spires and head downhill and to the left. If you come by train and get off at the Kutná Hora Město station, look at the map posted in the station and thread your way uphill and roughly to the right, through the crumbling streets until you reach Palackého náměstí. The tourist office is here; it's small, but well-organized, with a few Internet stations that you can use to check e-mail.

❶
Fodor'sChoice
★

Approaching the **Chrám svaté Barbory** (St. Barbara's Cathedral), overlooking the river, you pass through a magnificent landscape. The 10-minute stroll from the main Palackého náměstí along Barborská ulice is lined with baroque statues in front of a vast former Jesuit college as you near St. Barbara's. From a distance, the three-peak roof of the church gives the impression of a large, magnificently peaked tent more than a religious center. St. Barbara's is undoubtedly Kutná Hora's masterpiece and a high point of the Gothic style in Bohemia. Begun in the 1380s, it drew on the talents of the Peter Parler workshop as well as two luminaries of the late-Gothic of the late 15th century, Matyáš Rejsek and Benedikt Ried. The soaring roof was added as late as 1558, replaced in the 18th century, and finally restored in the late 1800s; the western facade also dates from the end of the 19th century. From here you can see the romantic view over the town, marked by the visibly tilting 260-foot-tower of St. James's Church.

St. Barbara is the patron saint of miners, and silver-mining themes dominate the interior of the church. Gothic frescoes depict angels carrying shields with mining symbols. The town's other major occupation, minting, can be seen in frescoes in the **Mintner's Chapel.** A statue of a miner,

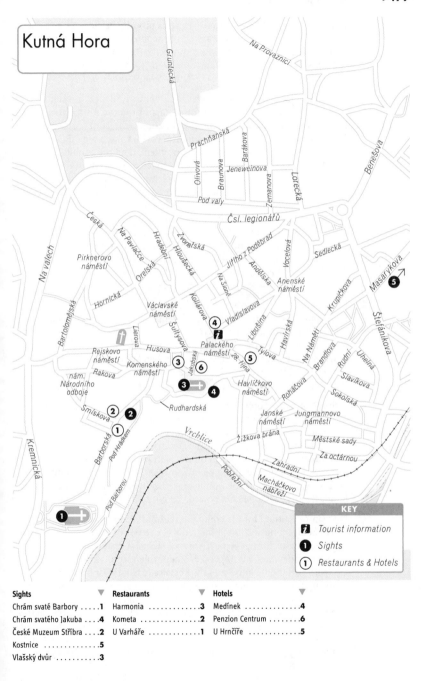

Kutná Hora

donning the characteristic smock, stands proudly in the nave and dates from 1700. But the main attraction of the interior is the vaulting itself, which carries the eye effortlessly upward. ⊠ *Barborská ul.* ☎ *No phone* 🖃 *30 Kč* ⊗ *May–Sept., Tues.–Sun. 9–6; Oct. and Apr., Tues.–Sun. 9–noon and 1–4:30; Nov.–Mar., Tues.–Sun. 9–noon and 2–4.*

❷ The **České Muzeum Stříbra** (Czech Museum of Silver), housed in the Hrádek (Little Castle) that was once part of the town's fortifications, is a museum of mining and coin production. In the 16th century, Kutná Hora boasted the deepest mines in the world, some going down as far as 500 meters. It's somewhat fitting, then, that the highlight of the Hrádek—and the focal point of the longer museum tours—is a hike down into a claustrophobic medieval mine tunnel. The small trek (you're inside for about 30 minutes) is more titillating than scary, though you may be happy you weren't a medieval miner. The cheapest tour, which doesn't include the mine, is dull, unless you're a fan of ore samples and archaeology. If it's available, go for the 1½-hour tour, which includes a portion of the displays from the museum proper, plus the mine. ⊠ *Barborská ul. 28* ☎ *327–512–159* ⊕ *www.cms-kh.cz* 🖃 *70 Kč–110 Kč* ⊗ *Apr. and Oct., Tues.–Sun. 9–5; May, June, and Sept., Tues.–Sun. 9–6; July and Aug., Tues.–Sun. 10–6.*

❸ Coins were first minted at the **Vlašský dvůr** (Italian Court) in 1300, made by Italian artisans brought in from Florence—hence the mint's odd name. It was here that the Prague groschen, one of the most widely circulated coins of the Middle Ages, was minted until 1726. There's a **coin museum**, where you can see the small, silvery groschen being struck and buy replicas. ⊠ *Havlíčkovo nám.* ☎ *327–512–873* 🖃 *50 Kč* ⊗ *Apr.–Sept., daily 9–6; Oct. and Mar., daily 10–5; Nov.–Feb., daily 10–4.*

❹ If the door to the **Chrám svatého Jakuba** (St. James's Church)—next door to the old mint—is open, peek inside. Originally a Gothic church dating from the 1300s, it was almost entirely transformed into baroque during the 17th and 18th centuries. A characteristic onion dome on the tower was added in 1737. Paintings on the wall include works from the best baroque Czech masters; the pietà is by the 17th-century painter Karel Škréta. The church is open only sporadically during the week and for Sunday mass. ⊠ *Havlíčkovo nám.* ☎ *No phone.*

❺ No trip to Kutná Hora is complete without a visit to the nearby sub-

Fodor'sChoice ★ urb of Sedlec (about 2 km [1 mi] from the center of the city), where you can find one of Europe's most chilling sights: a chapel decorated with the bones of some 40,000 people. The Kaple všech svatých (All Saints' Chapel), commonly known as the **Kostnice** (ossuary) or "Bone Church" is just up the road from the former Sedlec Monastery. The church came into being in the 16th century, when development forced the clearing of a nearby graveyard. Monks of the Cistercian order came up with the bright idea of using the bones to decorate the chapel; the most recent creations date from the end of the 19th century. The run-down **Church of the Assumption of the Virgin** at the former Sedlec monastery exemplifies the work of Giovanni Santini (1667–1723). A master of expressive line and delicate proportion, this one-of-a-kind architect fathered a bravura hybrid of Gothic and baroque. ⊠ *Zámecka 127, Sedlec* ☎ *728–125–488* ⊕ *www.kostnice.cz* 🖃 *40 Kč* ☉ *Apr.–Sept., daily 8–6; Oct., daily 9–noon and 1–5; Nov.–Mar., daily 9–noon and 1–4. Church closed Sun. and Mon.*

Where to Eat

¢–$$ ✕ **Harmonia.** A charming spot just off Komenského náměstí near St. James's, Harmonica serves good food at a good value. The small back patio is relatively secluded and the perfect place for an espresso and quiet conversation. Food, like chicken cutlets and steaks, is simple and hearty. ⊠ *Husova 104* ☎ *327–512–275* 🖃 *AE, MC, V.*

¢–$$ ✕ **Kometa.** You can't miss the big wooden patio of this Czech restaurant on the corner leading up toward St. Barbara's. Under the shade of a huge, majestic tree—and looking across to the equally majestic Jesuit College—it's one of the best places to stop for a coffee or snack on a nice day. The spacious interior is also more tolerable than many in the center of town. A predictable array of chicken and pork cutlets is included on the menu, but the waitstaff is fast and attentive. ⊠ *Barborská 29* ☎ *327–515–515* 🖃 *AE, DC, MC, V.*

¢–$$ ✕ **U Varháře.** Striking views from the terrace across the valley and over to the cathedral is the main selling point of this slightly upscale restaurant along the main walk to St. Barbara's. Though it appears at first glance to be a Czech restaurant, the menu is filled with "Czech-Mex" offerings like burritos and fajitas—served alongside standard Czech sides and salads. The food is decent, but heavy for a snack or light meal. ⊠ *Barborská 578* ☎ *327–512–769* 🖃 *AE, DC, MC, V.*

Where to Stay

$ 🏨 **Medínek.** A modern hotel situated on the main square, Medínek has clean, quiet rooms and basic services. The ground-floor restaurant serves decent Czech cooking in an atmosphere more pleasant than that found in the local beer halls. Although the hotel's 1960s architecture is a little jarring, it does offer the advantages of larger windows and more spacious rooms than those found in many older hotels. ⊠ *Palackého nám. 316, 284 01* ☎ *327–512–741* 🖷 *327–512–743* ⊕ *www.medinek. cz* ➷ *50 rooms* ⟆ *Restaurant, café, cable TV, fitness center, meeting rooms, some pets allowed (fee); no a/c* 🖃 *AE, MC, V* ⟟◉⟞ *BP.*

¢ 🏨 **Penzion Centrum.** This is by far the best value in Kutná Hora. The location is ideal—right next to St. James—and the price is outstanding. But don't expect anything more than spartan beds and a teensy bathroom. An adjoining garden has picnic tables. Bottom line: the property is clean and the staff is friendly. ⊠ *Jakubská 57, 284 01* ☎ *327–514–218* ➷ *8 rooms* ⟆ *Restaurant, some pets allowed; no a/c* 🖃 *No credit cards* ⟟◉⟞ *E.P.*

¢ 🏨 **U Hrnčíře.** Sitting next to a potter's shop this quaint inn is right next to the town center. Rooms are plain and the stairs are steep, but the friendly staff gives the hotel a decidedly homey feel. The restaurant in the back garden is strongly recommended for decent Czech food and a beautiful view overlooking St. James's Church. ⊠ *Barborská 24, 284 01* ☎ *327–512–113* ➷ *5 rooms* ⟆ *Restaurant, cable TV, some pets allowed (fee); no a/c* 🖃 *MC, V* ⟟◉⟞ *BP.*

Kutná Hora Essentials

TRANSPORTATION It's easy to get to Kutná Hora by either train or bus, and the trip in each case takes about an hour. If you take the train, be aware that attendants seldom bother telling tourists that the Kutná Hora main station is not in the town proper but in the suburb of Sedlec, about 2 km (1¼ mi) away. To continue into the town, you change to a tiny shuttle that goes the extra leg into the town center. However, since you're already in Sedlec, you also have the opportunity to take in the Bone Church, about 10 minutes away by foot from the station, before walking to the town center about 2 km (1¼ mi) away. When you're issued a ticket in Prague, it will say *město* in small print, meaning it goes to the station right in town, if the connection was available for your train time.

By car, Highway 333, the westward extension of Vinohradská třida., goes all the way to Kutná Hora. The drive takes about an hour.

VISITOR 🚩**Info-Centre Kutná Hora** ✉ Palackého nám. 377 ☎ 327-512-378 ⊕ www.kh.
INFORMATION cz or www.kutnahora.cz

KARLŠTEJN

★ ❻ *29 km (18 mi) southwest of Prague.*

If you've only got a few hours to spend outside of Prague, going to Karlštejn, an easy and delightful day trip, might make the most sense.

In spite of the ever-growing number of visitors each year—including Prague residents, who come here in droves—Karlštejn retains the spirit of a medieval village. The focal point is a stark and stunning castle perched above a road of pastel-color baroque-façaded bungalows. A classic storybook-style babbling brook parallels the main road. If that's not enough, there are plenty of pubs to keep things hopping. In September Karlštejn hosts an annual Renaissance Faire–type weekend, complete with a visit by none other than Holy Roman Emperor Charles IV, the town's founder in 1348.

The castle—which dates to the 14th century—was built to hold and guard the crown jewels. The jewels were kept in the Great Tower's **Chapel of the Holy Cross** for almost 200 years, surviving attacks from the Hussites and their catapult bombardment. (In 1619 the jewels were moved to St. Wenceslas Chapel in Prague's St. Vitus Cathedral, where they remain to this day.) Karlštejn underwent some architectural changes over the centuries. A major campaign to preserve the medieval origins of the castle was mounted in the late 1800s, and much of the form we see today is a result of this valuable work. The Chapel of the Holy Cross is still the castle's greatest treasure. Master Theodoric, Charles's court painter, covered the walls with his painting. The arched canopy above is completely gilded and set with semiprecious stones. After 19 years of closure, it reopened to the pub-

WORD OF MOUTH

"Catch a train to Karlštejn, just a short ride out, and shop for your crystal there, and also some of the best food and beer at unbelievably reasonable prices. BTW, don't forget the camera!"   –Peg

Guided Day Tours from Prague

GUIDED BUS TOURS ARE AVAILABLE from several companies for Karlštejn, Konopiště, Kutná Hora, Český Šternberk, and Terezín. The tours are more expensive than bus or train fare, but can save you the hassle of renting a car, or sorting out the often-confusing bus and train schedules. Wittmann Tours specializes in tours to Terezín.

🚌 **Martin Tour** ✉ Štěpánská 61, Nové Město ☎ 224-212-473 ⊕ www. martintour.cz. **Precious Legacy Tours** ✉ Maiselova 16, Josefov ☎ 222-320-398 ⊕ www.legacytours. cz. **Premiant City Tour** ✉ Na Příkopě 23, Nové Město ☎ 296-246-070 ⊕ www.premiant.cz. **Wittmann Tours** ✉ Mánesova 8, Vinohrady ☎ 222-252-472 ⊕ www.wittmann-tours.com.

lic in 2000, but to see it you must take a guided tour. Tours are limited in order to preserve the microclimate inside the chapel, and you should try to reserve in advance to guarantee a spot.

Climbing to the castle—along the red hiking trail that starts just beyond the upper edge of the village—takes about 20 minutes and is occasionally arduous. Once you reach the top, take time to walk the ramparts and drink in the fabulous panorama of village and countryside below. The interior tours are time-consuming—55 minutes for the first circuit and 75 minutes for the second. The Chapel of the Holy Cross, part of Tour 2, is undeniably the most compelling sight. But if you aren't a castle buff, you may want to avoid the entry fee and just enjoy the scenery. If castles are your thing, the first-circuit tour does show some interesting spaces, including Charles's bedchambers and its royal fabrics. ✉ *Karlštejn 18, Karlštejn* ☎ *311–681–617 castle information, 274–008–154 tour reservations* ⊕ *www.hradkarlstejn.cz* 🎟 *Tour 1: 220 Kč, Tour 2: 300 Kč, free admission to walk grounds* ⊗ *Apr. and Oct., Tues.–Sun. 9–4; May, June, and Sept., Tues.–Sun. 9–5; July and Aug., Tues.–Sun. 9–6; Nov.–Mar., Tues.–Sun. 9–3.*

Where to Stay & Eat

$–$$$ ✕ **Restaurace a Pension Pod dračí skálou.** This traditional hunting lodge-style restaurant is the most rustic and fun of Karlštejn's eateries. To find it follow the main road uphill out of the village about 500 meters from town. The portions of pork, chicken, beef, and game are massive. A small terrace is popular with cyclists in nice weather. ✉ *Karlštejn 130* ☎ *311–681–177* ▭ *No credit cards.*

¢ ✕▥ **U Janů.** The best out of the many touristy restaurants in the town proper, this spot is just on the upper edge of the village not far from where the castle path starts. Decent Czech-style food (¢–$$), including some game and fish options are offered on the menu. The pension can also be a comfortable place to stay if you feel like being outside of Prague for a night but close to the action at Karlštejn. ✉ *Karlštejn 28, 267 18*

🕾 *311–681–210* 🖳 *311–681–410* 📞 *4 rooms* ⚲ *Restaurant, cable TV; no a/c* ▭ *MC, V* ⦿ *EP.*

¢ ⊞ **Penzion Irena.** This quaint B&B is on a road that links to the main road up to the castle. Rooms in the stately old villa are spacious and bright; three rooms have balconies, but either way you get a pleasant view of the surrounding countryside. The owner speaks German better than English, but attempts to be accommodating. ⊠ *Karlštejn 40, 267 18* 🕾 *311–681–794* 📞 *9 rooms* ⚲ *Cable TV, some pets allowed; no a/c* ▭ *No credit cards* ⦿ *CP.*

Karlštejn Essentials

TRANSPORTATION There's no bus service to Karlštejn from Prague, but it's an easy train journey. Several trains each day leave from both Hlavní nádraží and Smíchovské nádraží—look on the schedule for trains heading to Beroun. When you arrive at the Karlštejn station, exit the station, turn right, and walk back along the small lane parallel to the railway tracks to find the town. After a few minutes, cross a bridge over the river; turn right onto the main road, which resembles a small highway (the absence of a pedestrian sidewalk doesn't bother the locals). Be wary of traffic but continue for another two or three minutes until you reach a road going up the hill to your left. This is the main road up to the village and castle.

A visit to Karlštejn can also be combined with a challenging 13-km (8-mi) hike through beautiful forests and along a small wooded waterfall from Beroun. Get off at the Beroun station, walk toward town and make a right just before an underpass. Follow the red-marked trail through the hills and dales, passing through the tiny village of Svatý Jan before arriving in Karlštejn—just above the village—about three hours later. Don't set out without water, good shoes, and, above all, a decent local hiking map.

By car from Prague, take Highway 4—on the western side of the Vltava—to the edge of the city, then go right on Highway 115, southwest through Radotín. Take the Karlštejn exit, which puts you on Highway 116, and after a few more minutes you end up beside the Berounka River. You can find a large parking lot at the bottom of the hill below Karlsßtejn. No vehicles are allowed on the road up to the castle.

VISITOR There's no tourist information center in the town of Karlštejn, but you can call the cas-
INFORMATION tle itself. Further information may be obtained from the booking office in Prague.
🚩 **National Monuments Institute for Central Bohemia** ⊠ Sabinova 5, Žižkov, Prague
🕾 274–008–154.

KŘIVOKLÁT

❼ *43 km (27 mi) west of Prague.*

If you're ready to get away from the mobs of people washing over the Charles Bridge in Prague, and you yearn for a touch of wilderness, Křivoklát is the best choice for a day trip. In dense forest (the name Křivoklát means "twisted branches"), among the rolling green hills above the

Berounka River, the castle makes for a more peaceful getaway than its more heavily touristed cousin. Once the trees begin to bloom, the area reaches the height of its beauty, and you can understand why it's often mentioned in Czech literature. Today the remote complex, with its Gothic treasures, sits high above a rather run-down village, but in the Middle Ages it was a strategically important place where political prisoners were held; it was also the scene of lavish festivities.

The roots of Křivoklát go back to the 12th century, when it was a hunting lodge for nobility. It was King Wenceslas I who commissioned the castle in the 13th century and his son, Přemysl Otakar II, who finished it. In the 14th century the future Emperor Charles IV was imprisoned here as a small boy by his father, John of Luxembourg. Charles later returned—in happier circumstances—to hunt, as did his son Wenceslas IV, who made significant alterations to the structure. The Polish King Vladislav II Jagiellon also left his mark in the 1500s (the "W" insignia of Vladislav can be seen in several places). At the end of the 16th century Křivoklát began to lose its importance. It was damaged by fire several times and fell into disrepair. After the Thirty Years' War, Křivoklát was pledged to the Schwarzenbergs and then became the property of noble families including the Fürstenbergs, who owned it from 1733 until 1929, when it passed to the Czechoslovak state.

These days, the castle draws a combination of local hikers, a few interested tourists, and film crews in search of historical authenticity. But its spirit swings back to life on the night of April 30, when many Czech villages celebrate something called *Čarodejnice*. Roughly translated as "witch-burning"—a pagan-rooted festival to ward off the winter spirit and welcome the bounty of spring—it turns Křivoklát into a gleeful scene of Slavic festivities and mock Celtic battles. Hundreds of Czechs come from Prague and the surrounding countryside to enjoy the music, merriment, and cheap wine, spiraling into the wee hours. In Prague the ceremonies to mark this event are sometimes mentioned in the entertainment sections of local papers.

One-hour tours are offered regularly in Czech language. Tours in English are available, but must be requested in advance. Look out especially for the Gothic chapel and its richly carved altarpiece (circa 1490), one of the finest still around. The tour highlight, the Great Hall, is even better. Notable for its great dimensions (28 meters long, 8 meters wide, and 8.5 meters high), it's the second-largest Gothic hall in Central Europe (after Vladislav Hall in Prague Castle). See if you can spot fragments of doodles on the walls; they were done by children in the Middle Ages and discovered only relatively recently. The tour ends at the giant round tower, which was used as a prison until the 16th century. The infamous alchemist Edward Kelley, who claimed he could turn base metals into gold, was said to have been imprisoned here.

A number of shops near the main castle entrance and in buildings around the courtyard sell crafts. Among the products for sale are traditional carved wooden items and candles. ⊠ *Křivoklát* ☎ *313–558–440 castle information, 313–558–120 tour reservations* ⊕ *www.krivoklat.*

cz 🎫 *150 Kč* 🕒 *Apr. and Oct., Tues.–Sun. 9–3; May and Sept., Tues.–Sun. 9–4; June–Aug., Tues.–Sun. 9–5; Nov., Dec., and Mar., weekends 9–3.*

/ ## Where to Stay & Eat

¢ ✕🏠 **U Jelena.** Considering hunting was a popular pastime in this village, this restaurant (¢–$$$) fits in with the theme. Game dishes are the house specialty, and relatively upscale meals are served in a genteel European setting, from the familiar *svíčková* (slices of beef loin in cream sauce) to more elaborate dishes such as venison steak with Cumberland sauce. The rooms upstairs are simply finished but have a cozy feeling thanks to wooden furnishings and pleasant lighting, and most have good views out the window to the woodsy surroundings. ⊠ *U Jelena 420, 27 023* ☎ *313–558–529* 🖨 *313–558–233* 🛏 *6 rooms* 🍴 *Restaurant, cable TV, some pets allowed; no a/c* 🖃 *AE, MC, V* 🍽 *BP.*

Křivoklát Essentials

TRANSPORTATION If you have no car, a train is the best way to reach Křivoklát. Take a local train from Hlavní nádraží or Smíchovské nádraží to Beroun (the local train from these stations to Plzeň also stops here). From here, take another local train to Rakovník, getting off at the Křivoklát stop. Plan your journey carefully—there are a only a few trains each day from Beroun to Rakovník.

If you're driving, the fastest way to Křivoklát is to follow Route 6 from Prague toward Karlovy Vary and after Jeneč turn onto Route 201 via Unhoště to Křivoklát. The trip is about an hour. For a beautifully scenic drive—and an extra 15 minutes—take the E50 Highway from Prague toward Plzeň, then exit at Křivolklát to Route 116. Follow this highway, which goes along a river before veering up into the hills, to Route 201, which winds back south toward Křivoklát. Parking is just beneath the castle.

VISITOR There's no information center in Křivoklát, but the castle can provide
INFORMATION some basic tourist information. Further information on the region is available from the tourist office in the nearby town of Rakovník.

🚩 **Rakovník Tourist Information** ⊠ Nám. Svatopluka Čecha 82, Rakovník ☎ 313–585–263

ČESKÝ ŠTERNBERK

❽ *48 km (30 mi) southeast of Prague.*

Fodor'sChoice Occupying a forested knoll over the Sázava River, the 13th-century castle here looks positively forbidding at night. In daylight, the structure, last renovated in the 18th century, is less haunting but still striking. For this castle, a guided tour is essential—but don't worry about being paraded through musty stone hallways for hours—the interiors are gorgeous and the guides are good, not only are they educational, but they're also concise, fitting the tour into 45 minutes.

The castle was founded in 1241 by Zdeslav of Divišov. Due to German influence, the coat of arms used by Zdeslav—an emblem bearing a gold, eight-pointed star—bestowed the name Šternberk on the castle, which is roughly translated as "star on the hill." After 1242 Zdeslav took on the name Zdeslav of Sternberg, and thus began the long lineage of the Sternberg family.

The structure itself was built in the early Gothic style. During the 15th and 16th centuries, following damage incurred during war, the castle underwent some architectural changes, preserving a few original details and making it stronger. The Swedes tried to conquer the castle in 1648 but failed; after the Thirty Years' War, other changes, particularly to the interiors, were made. In the first half of the 18th century the Lower Château was constructed; the French-style garden, across the river, was created in the same period.

Amazingly, the Sternberg family—one branch or another—has lived in the castle through the centuries. It gives a certain amount of authenticity to the interior, especially the gorgeous Knight's Hall, with its paintings and famous Italian stucco work. Though the castle is mostly used for tours, the Sternbergs themselves live in the upper chambers and sometimes use the lower rooms for family gatherings.

In 1948 the Sternberg family moved to a small apartment in Prague when their castle, like all Czech castles, was nationalized by the Communist government, though the father, Jiří, agreed to work as a steward and guide for the property. Through property restitution, the castle was given back to his son Zdeněk in 1992. ⊠ *Český Šternberk 1, Česky Šternberk* ☎ *317–855–101* ⊕ *www.hradceskysternberk.cz* ✍ *Guided tour 130 Kč* ☉ *Apr. and Oct., weekends 9–6; May and Sept., Tues.–Sun. 9–5; June–Aug., Tues.–Sun. 9–6; Nov.–Mar. by appointment only.*

Where to Eat

¢–$$ ✕ **Hradní Restaurace.** There's not much in the way of fine dining in Český Šternberk; one of the best options is the castle restaurant. The prices are bargain-basement, and some harder-to-find traditional Czech dishes, such as potato dumplings with smoked meat, and yeast-raised pancakes with blueberries are humble but satisfying. ⊠ *Český Šternberk 1, Česky Šternberk* ☎ *317–855–101* ▭ *No credit cards* ☉ *Closed Mon.*

Where to Stay

¢ ▥ **Parkhotel Český Šternberk.** The Parkhotel—on the opposite side of the river from the castle—doesn't have much competition; it's the only game in town for lodging. But you can find clean and cozy rooms and beautiful views of the castle. Even if you're not spending the night, the terrace is a pleasant place to stop for coffee or a bite to eat. ⊠ *Český Šternberk 46, 257 27* ☎ *317–855–168* ▤ *317–855–108* ◄ *19 rooms* ◊ *Restaurant, cable TV, meeting rooms, some pets allowed; no a/c* ▭ *No credit cards* ⌑ *EP.*

Český Šternberk Essentials

TRANSPORTATION Both trains and buses go daily to the Český Šterberk. Buses depart from Prague's southernmost bus station, Roztyly, which is about 15 minutes by metro from the city center on Line C (red line). There's no central information office there. Posted timetables are your only guide, but you can ask one of the locals to help you find the right bus. Purchase tickets directly from the driver.

Trains leave from Hlavní nádraží and stop in many small towns on the way; you will have to change trains in Čerčany, about one hour out of Prague. Though the train ride is about 20 minutes longer than the trip by bus, it's a bit more scenic. The trip takes about two hours. If you're visiting in summer you may be lucky enough to catch the old-fashioned steam train. It only runs on certain days, but seeing it pull up to the station down in the valley from the castle heights is like watching a scene from Harry Potter come to life. Ask for the *parní vlak*(steam train) at the main station.

If you're driving take the D1 Highway out of Prague (the main highway to Brno) and take the turnoff to Český Šternberk, following Route 111 to the castle, which perches over the highway. The drive takes just under an hour.

VISITOR INFORMATION   A small tourist office is below the castle near the main parking lot and can help to prebook castle tours.

🏴 **Český Šternberk Information** ✉ Český Šternberk, Český Šternberk ☎ 317–855–101 🌐 www.hradceskysternberk.cz

KONOPIŠTĚ

9 *45 km (27 mi) southeast of Prague.*

History buffs of World War I take note, Konopiště Castle could be the highlight of your trip. It was the home of none other than Franz Ferdinand d'Este, the ill-fated heir to the Austrian throne whose assassination in Sarajevo in 1914 is credited with unleashing the "Great War" that same year. Franz Ferdinand's castle and surrounding gardens, lakes, and woodland paths make for a blissfully peaceful half-day excursion from Prague. The neo-Gothic castle dates from the 14th century and was passed down through several noble families before the Hapsburg heir made it his residence in the late 19th century. Franz Ferdinand—Austrian emperor Franz Josef's oldest nephew and first in line for the Hapsburg crown—is described in history books as a bit thick, dour, and highly unpopular in Vienna. This may explain why he took up residence in what was considered at the time a remote location. He certainly spared no expense in restor-

> ## OUT OF AUSTRIA
>
> Visiting Konopiště Castle, you may find yourself wondering about Franz Ferdinand. He clearly loved travel and hunting. The numbers speak for themselves—his home is covered with almost 100,000 hunting trophies. His other great love was his wife, whom he courted in secret for two years. Against the wishes of Emperor Franz Joseph and the criticism of the court, he married his secret sweetheart. The slander that followed drove them out of Austria to Konopiště until he and his wife were assassinated on a trip to Sarajevo in 1914, triggering World War I.

ing the castle and filling its 82 rooms with outlandish paintings, statues, and curiosities.

Fodor's Choice
★
Getting to **Zámek Konopiště** (Konopiště Castle) generally involves at least a ½-km walk through the woods. At first glimpse the castle makes a strong impression; the rounded, neo-Gothic towers appear through the trees, and then you reach the formal garden with its mystical circle of classical statues. The castle dates from around 1300 and for centuries served as a bastion of the nobility in their struggle for power with the king. Franz Ferdinand's extravagant taste and lifestyle are on full display in several of the rooms, which are open to the public during the high season. A valuable collection of weapons from the 16th through 18th centuries can be seen in the Weapons Hall on the third floor. As an avid hunter, the archduke covered every surface with stuffed animals. At times the walls almost feel like a tribute to taxidermy. The interior is only open to tours; guides may not speak English, but there are English texts available. ⊠ *Zámek Konopiště, Benešov* ☎ *317–721–366* ⊕ *www.zamek-konopiste. cz* ☞ *Tours 130 Kč–260 Kč* ☉ *Apr. and Oct., Tues.–Sun. 9–3; May–Aug., Tues.–Sun. 9–5; Sept., Tues.–Sun. 9–4.*

Where to Stay & Eat

$ ✕☐ **Amber Hotel Konopiště.** A popular weekend getaway for well-heeled Prague residents who come for the fresh air and the excellent on-site tennis courts. This modern but well-maintained motel, about a 15-minute walk through the woods from the castle. Rooms are small but nicely appointed (ask for one away from the main road). Its lodgelike restaurant, Stodola ($$–$$$; open for lunch and dinner), has a fine selection of grilled meats and fish dishes. Live folk music is occasionally offered during busy weekends in season. ⊠ *Benešov, 256 01* ☎ *317–722–732* 🖷 *317–722–053* ➦ *40 rooms* ♨ *2 restaurants, cable TV, miniature golf, tennis court, pool, gym, outdoor hot tub, massage, sauna, meeting room, some pets allowed (fee); no a/c* ▤ *AE, DC, MC, V* ⏹ *BP.*

Konopiště Essentials

TRANSPORTATION   Several buses leave daily to Konopiště from Prague's Roztyly metro station, on Line C (red line), and occasionally from the main Florenc bus station. The trip takes about an hour and lets you off about ½ km from the castle. You can also take one of the frequent trains to the nearby city of Benešov, and then walk (about 30 minutes), or take a taxi or bus to the castle.

By car, take the D1 Highway southwest toward Brno, and exit following the signs to Benešov exit. Signs on this road lead you to Konopiště.

VISITOR   🛈 **Konopiště Tourist Information** ⊠ Malé nám. 1700, Benešov ☎ 317–726–004
INFORMATION

LIDICE

🔟 *18 km (11 mi) from Prague.*

No more than a speck on the map to the northwest of Prague, this tiny village was plucked out of obscurity by the Nazis during World War II to teach Czechs not to oppose German rule. In 1942 Adolf Hitler ordered

Lidice razed to the ground in retaliation for the assassination of the Nazi wartime leader in Bohemia, Reinhard Heydrich, by Czech patriots.

On the night of June 9, 1942, a Gestapo unit entered Lidice, shot the entire adult male population (192 men), and sent the 196 women to the Ravensbrück concentration camp. A handful of the 103 children in the village were sent to Germany to be "Aryanized"; the others perished in death camps. By June 10, the entire village was destroyed.

During the war and in the years immediately after, the name Lidice was known around the world as a symbol of Nazi atrocities. A group of miners from Birmingham, England, formed a committee called "Lidice Must Live" and on their initiative a new village of Lidice was rebuilt not far from the original site.

Today, however, it must be admitted that Lidice feels forgotten. For many Czechs, especially after the fall of communism, World War II feels like part of the distant past.

That's not to say a trip here is not worth the effort. The memorial and adjoining museum are deeply moving. Pair a trip here with a visit to Terezín, farther up the road, to see how World War II has etched its mark on the Czech psyche.

The **Lidice Memorial** is a haunting sight. A tall cross next to a small stream marks where the original village once stood. The monument is graphic in its depiction of the deportation and slaughter of the inhabitants. Inside a museum there's a photograph of each person and a short description of his or her fate. You can also find reproductions of the German documents ordering the village's destruction, including the Gestapo's chillingly bureaucratic reports on how the massacre was carried out and the peculiar problems encountered in Aryanizing the deported children. Exhibits highlighting the international response hold a more heartwarming message. The staff tend to speak German rather than English, but they will helpfully play a short film (about 20 minutes) in English on request, between the other showings.

Outside, you are free to wander about. The wooden cross in the field, starkly decorated with barbed wire, marks the place where the men were executed. Remains of brick walls are visible here, leftover from the Gestapo's dynamite and bulldozer rampage. There are several moving sculptures made in tribute to the horror, including a large one repre-

A MONUMENT FOR THE CHILDREN

Heartbreaking but captivating, the memorial to the child victims of Lidice is a realistic tribute to the atrocities that took place. Marie Uchytilová, a sculpture professor, was so appalled by the assassination of these children, she began a monument that would take more than two decades to complete. After her death in 1989, her husband continued to finish the sculptures. The 82 lifelike sculptures of children ranging in age from one to 15 represent the real victims. The statues are even more chilling when covered with snow.

senting the 82 children gassed by the Nazis. It's worth walking to the far end of the meadow, where the town cemetery was. Note that the Lidice museum and grounds were undergoing extensive renovation in 2006. Plans were to add more films and to expand the museum and rose garden, among other changes. ✉ *Ul. 10 června 1942* ⊕ *www.lidice-memorial.cz* 📧 *80 Kč* ☉ *Apr.–Oct., daily 9–6; Nov.–Mar., daily 9–4.*

Where to Eat

A small stand in the parking lot, typical of those in Prague's out-of-center metro stations, draws the usual small cluster of old men eating *párky* (weiners) or knocking back a shot of Fernet. The stand also sells beer, coffee, and a few other snacks. But for a real meal, it's best to get back on the bus to Prague.

Lidice Essentials

TRANSPORTATION It's a shame that an important memorial so close to Prague is so difficult to reach by public transportation. There's no train service to Lidice, leaving only regular bus service from Evropska třída near the Dejvice metro station on Line A (green line). Before getting on the bus, ask the driver if the bus stops in Lidice. (Buses heading to the larger town of Kladno pass nearby, but often do not stop at Lidice.) Tickets are purchased directly from the driver. The trip should take about 20 minutes, and when all goes well, you'll be let off at an intersection across from the memorial itself.

By car Lidice is an easy 30-minute journey. From the Dejvice area, follow Evropská třída out of Prague past the airport, then continue west on Route 551 until you see the well-marked memorial, with a parking lot, beside the highway. If you're driving, it's ideal to combine this with a trip to Terezín, about 30 km (18 mi) farther along in the same direction from Prague.

VISITOR There's no tourist information center in Lidice, but information may be
INFORMATION obtained from the memorial's museum.

TEREZÍN

⓫ *48 km (30 mi) northwest of Prague.*

Just the word Terezín (Theresienstadt in German) immediately recalls the horrors of the Jewish Holocaust for Czechs. As the main Nazi concentration camp in Bohemia, Terezín held much of Prague's large prewar Jewish population during the war. It wasn't a death camp in the way that Auschwitz was—though in the end, very few of the tens of thousands of Jews transported there survived the war.

Terezín was originally built by the Austrians in the 18th century to house soldiers guarding the Austrian frontier with Prussia. During World

War II the Germans were quick to recognize the garrison and surrounding town as a potential concentration camp.

Terezín was an exception among the many Nazi concentration camps scattered around Central Europe. The Germans, for a time, used it as a showcase camp in order to deflect international criticism of their policy toward Jews. In the early years of the war—until as late as 1944—the detainees were permitted a semblance of normal life, with limited self-government, schools, a theater, and a library. (Pictures drawn by the children at Terezín, at their drawing lessons in school, are on display in Prague's Jewish museum.) The International Red Cross was even permitted to inspect the town in 1944. Nazis prepared for the visit by sprucing it up with a fresh coat of paint.

Through 1944 and 1945, as the Nazis' war effort soured, the masquerade of their benevolence in Terezín was dropped. Train transports to Auschwitz and other death camps to the east were stepped up to a rate of several a week. In all, some 87,000 Jews from Terezín were murdered in this way, and another 35,000 died from starvation or disease. The conductor Karel Ančerl, who died in 1973, and the novelist Ivan Klíma are among the few thousand who survived imprisonment at Terezín.

The shock in visiting Terezín today is that it's pretty much remained the same. To their credit, Czechs have done very little to dress it up for visitors. You're free to walk the town's rundown streets and imagine what it must have been like to be held prisoner there. It's dark, depressing, and at the same time, profoundly engrossing.

The enormity of Terezín's role in history is difficult to grasp at first because the Czechs have put up few signs to give you guidance, but the **Památník Terezín** (Terezín Memorial) encompasses all the existing buildings that are open to the public. Buildings include the **Magdeburg Barracks,** where the Jewish Council of Elders met, and the **Jewish cemetery's crematorium** just outside the town walls.

Told in words and pictures, the town's horrific story is depicted at the **Museum of the Terezín Ghetto** (✉ Komenského ul. ☎ 416–782–577), just off the central park in town. A short documentary is also shown in many languages. Tell the staff that you speak English they'll let you roam the building and flag you down when the next English-language video is being shown.

★ The **Malá Pevnost** (Small Fortress), about 1 km (½ mi) east of Terezín, functioned as a special prison camp, holding mostly POWs or political prisoners in totally abject conditions. Around 30,000 prisoners came through here during the war. Those who did not die in detention were shipped off to other concentration camps. Above the entrance to the main courtyard stands the cruelly cynical motto ARBEIT MACHT FREI (Work Brings Freedom). Take a walk around the rooms, still holding a sad collection of rusty bed frames, sinks, and shower units. At the far end of the fortress, opposite the main entrance, is the special wing built by the Nazis when space became tight. Imagining life in the windowless cells is crushing. ✉ *Principova alej 304, Terezín* ☎ *416–782–225* ⊕ *www.pamatnik-*

terezin.cz or www.pruvodce.com/terezin ⌦ *One unit 160 Kč; all units 180 Kč* ⊘ *Ghetto Museum and Magdeburg Barracks Apr.–Oct., daily 9–6; Nov.–Mar., daily 9–5:30. Small Fortress Apr.–Oct., daily 8–6; Nov.–Mar., daily 8–4:30. Crematorium Apr.–Nov., Sun.–Fri. 10–5.*

OFF THE BEATEN PATH

STŘEKOV CASTLE – The Vltava River flows through a long, unspoiled, winding valley, packed in by surrounding hills north of Litoměřice. As you near heavily industrialized Ústí nad Labem, your vision is suddenly assaulted by the towering mass of Střekov Castle, hanging precariously on huge cliffs and rising abruptly above the right bank. The fortress was built in 1319 by King John of Luxembourg to control the rebellious nobles of northern Bohemia. During the 16th century it became the residence of Wenceslas of Lobkowicz, who rebuilt the castle in the Renaissance style. These lonely ruins have inspired many German artists and poets, including Richard Wagner, who came here on a moonlight night in the summer of 1842 and was inspired to write his romantic opera *Tannhäuser.* If you arrive on a dark night, you may be reminded of another classic—Mary Shelley's *Frankenstein.* Inside is a small historical exhibit about the Lobkowicz family and wine making. This is an interesting-looking castle, and it's probably worth a stop if you happen to be driving by, but it's not a destination unto itself. ⌧ *Na Zachazce, Ústí nad Labem* ☎ *475–530–682* ⌦ *60 Kč* ⊘ *May–Aug., Tues.–Sun. 9–5; Apr., Sept., and Oct., Tues.–Sun. 9–4.*

Where to Eat

Terezín has very little in the way of services for visitors. There are a couple of depressing haunts, serving mostly inedible pub standards from menus run off mimeograph machines. Duck out of town to nearby Litoměřice down the road about 2 km (1 mi). It's a nice river town, with a marvelous central square and several better dining options.

¢–$$ ✕ **Hotel Restaurant Salva Guarda.** Dating back to the 14th century, this stately old building is dolled up with arches and *sgraffito.* The interior is comparatively plain, but in nice weather you can relax on the patio. Czech food of the cutlet category and game dishes are served. ⌧ *Mírové nám. 12, Litoměřice* ☎ *416–732–506* ⊟ *AE, MC, V.*

Terezín Essentials

TRANSPORTATION There's no train service directly to Terezín. Several buses leave the Florenc station daily, and weekends offer a bit more choice. The trip lasts about an hour and the bus stops twice: the first stop is in town, near the Museum of the Ghetto building; the bus also stops across town closer to the Small Fortress. Both of these have ticket desks. If you're planning on hitting both, it's better to visit the museum first as it will help give perspective to the entire sight and its history.

If you're driving, take the E55 north out of Prague (this is the main highway going to Dresden and Berlin) and head toward Lovosice. You can either take Exit 35 at Doksany and follow the country road straight to Terezín or continue to Lovosice, and from there, turn right and the road leads directly into Terezín. The trip takes about 50 minutes. To visit Střekov, follow the road signs from Terezín to Litoměřice, then take Highway 261 to Ústí nad Labem.

VISITOR
INFORMATION Information on Terezín can be found by contacting the office of the memorial itself; information on the area can be obtained from the tourist office in the neighboring town of Litoměřice.

🖪 **Litoměřice Tourist Information** ✉ Mírové nám., Litoměřice ☎ 416-732-440 ⊕ www.litomerice.cz

MĚLNÍK

⑫ *About 40 km (23 mi) north of Prague.*

The town's **Zámek,** a petite castle a few blocks from the main square, grandly hovers over the confluence of the Labe (Elbe) River and two arms of the Vltava. The view here is stunning, and the sunny hillsides are covered with vineyards. Indeed, the town is known best for its special Ludmila wines made from these grapes. As the locals tell it, Emperor Charles IV was responsible for bringing wine production to the area. Having a good eye for favorable growing conditions, he encouraged vintners from Burgundy to come here and plant their vines. Every autumn, usually in late September, Mělník celebrates what is likely the region's best *Vinobraní,* an autumn festival held when barrels of young, still fermenting wine, called *burčak* are tapped. If you happen to come at this time, look for the rare red-wine version.

The courtyard's three dominant architectural styles jump out at you, reflecting alterations to the castle over the years. On the north side, note the typical arcaded Renaissance balconies, decorated with *sgraffiti.* To the west, a Gothic touch is still easy to make out. The southern wing is clearly baroque (although also decorated with arcades). Inside the castle at the back, you can find a *vinárna* (wine room) with decent food and excellent views overlooking the rivers. On the other side is a **museum** of paintings, furniture, and porcelain belonging to the old aristocratic Lobkowicz clan, which has recovered quite a few castles and estates from the state. For day-tripping oenophiles, tour the wine cellars under the castle and book a wine tasting. ✉ *Zámek Mělník* ☎ *315–622–121* 🖳 *Castle 60 Kč, wine cellar tour 25 Kč, or up to 220 Kč with wine tasting* ☉ *Castle daily 10–5. Wine cellar daily 10–6.*

Where to Eat

¢–$$$ ✕ **Zámecká Restaurace.** Right in the castle itself, you can find the best place in town to eat. It certainly has the best view. Choose the simpler and cheaper of two buffets that the castle offers. Sipping a glass of Ludmila wine and taking in the scenery is a treat at a very reasonable price. ✉ *Inside Zámek, Nám. Míru 54* ☎ *315–622–485* ▭ *No credit cards.*

Where to Stay

¢ 🏨 **Pension Hana.** Most of the better accommodations in the town are on the outskirts, but this small home with a garden is a 10-minute walk from the center. The staff don't speak English very well, but they're friendly and will work on being understood, even throwing in the odd German word. The rooms are a reasonable size, and the plaid curtains and wooden tables give them a folksy warmth. ✉ *Fügerova 714, 27 601* ☎ *315–622–485* 🖨 *315–622–485* 🖳 *10 rooms* ⚙ *Cable TV, meeting rooms; no a/c* ▭ *No credit cards* ⏹ *BP.*

Mělník Essentials

TRANSPORTATION Bus service to Mělník is better than train service—it's faster, cheaper, and more direct. The buses are run by a private company and leave throughout the day from Prague's Holešovice Station. Tickets can be purchased directly from the driver, and the ride is about 45 minutes.

If you're coming by car, take Highway 9 from Prague's northern tip, which heads all the way to Mělník. Park on the small streets just off the main square (head in the direction of the towers to find it).

VISITOR ⁊ **Mělník Tourist Information** ⊠ Nám. Míru 11, Mělník ☎ 315-627-503 ⊕ www.
INFORMATION melnik.cz

ORLÍK

⓭ *70 km (44 mi) south of Prague*

Orlík is the most remote of the usual day trips from Prague, but it's especially popular in summer when the area is a beehive of people darting around. Czech families take short vacations here, and ferry boats run up and down the river. Plan ahead and bring your swimsuit if it's a hot summer day to join in the fun. What appears as a lake is really a large reservoir held back by the Orlík dam, part of a cascade of dams on the Vltava River. Its construction in the early 1960s was epic, consuming 1,250,000 cubic meters of concrete and 50,000 tons of reinforced steel. The lake behind the dam today is about 60 meters deep.

The word *Orlík* means young eagle, and the castle **Hrad Orlík**, dating back to the 13th century, was always thought to be reminiscent of a young eagle in a nest far up on a rocky ledge. Though the builders of the original structure are not known, the current castle was built in the early Gothic style by King Wenceslas II. The castle housed important figures in Czech history such as Jan Hus, after whom the Hussites are named, and Jan Žižka, the Hussite military leader after whom Prague's Žižkov district is named. It became the property of the Schwarzenberg family in 1719. Communism nationalized the castle after World War II, then, after the Velvet Revolution, it was returned to the Schwarzenbergs in the early 1990s. The rather dramatic appearance today is mostly due to renovations in the mid-1800s in the new Gothic style. Castle tours, like those of Český Šternberk, help you appreciate the history of the castle and what you're looking at. Hour-long tours show you the portraits in the Small Empire Hall, the Napoleanic-era furnishings of the Great Empire Hall, and the incredible wooden sculpture by Jan Teska in the Teska Court. ⊠ *Hrad Orlík* ☎ *382–275–101* ⊕ *www.jiznicechy.org* ▧ *130 Kč* ☯ *Apr. and Oct., Tues.–Sun. 9–3; May and Sept., Tues.–Sun. 9–4; June–Aug., Tues.–Sun. 9–5.*

Where to Eat

¢–$$ ✕ **Restaurace a ubytovna u Cvrků.** You'd never guess it from the dusty exterior, but this is a well-run, family-owned tavern that serves excellent and cheap game dishes. A few rooms upstairs (¢) are no-frills, basic bedrooms, and the bathroom is in the hallway; they are popular among cyclers who appreciate the very cheap price. This place is in the small village as you approach the castle. ⊠ *Staré Sedlo 61, 398 07* ☎ *382–275–124* ▭ *No credit cards.*

Orlík Essentials

TRANSPORTATION   Orlík is a difficult trip to manage by public transportation; however, the hour-long drive is a snap by car. Head south out of Prague on Highway 4, which roughly follows the Vltava River, then turn right after about 45 minutes onto Highway 19. A final right turn brings you right into Orlík.

Getting to Orlík by bus is problematic—there are two or three direct connections every day leaving the Na Knízecí station, and the ride lasts a tolerable hour and 17 minutes. But returning to Prague is another story. The route back, which tours many more small villages than seems necessary and sometimes doubles back on itself, is a mildly cruel joke lasting from 2 to 3½ hours. If you decide to finish off that paperback, the Na Knízecí bus station is accessible from the south exit (the far one from the city center) of the Anděl metro station (Line B, yellow line). Make sure you ask the driver if you're on the right bus and buy the ticket from him directly. There are several buses coming back, which require a change in either Písek or Tábor; the Písek option is quicker and doesn't require a transfer from bus to train.

VISITOR   There's no tourist information center in Orlík, but information on the
INFORMATION   general area can be found by contacting the information center in Písek, about 30 km (18 mi) away.

🖪 **Písek Tourist Information** ⊠ Hejdukova 97, Písek ☎ 382-213-592 ⊕ www. icpisek.cz.

Southern Bohemia

WORD OF MOUTH

"Český Krumlov is one of the most precious, scenic towns I have ever seen in my life. And I have been to a lot of places around the globe."

—Polly Magoo

By Mark Baker   **NESTLED BETWEEN GERMANY TO THE WEST** and the former Austro-Hungarian empire to the south and east, Southern Bohemia was molded by the religious conflicts that swept through the region in the 15th century. The major fight pitted the reformists, followers of the firebrand preacher Jan Hus, against the entrenched interests of the Catholic Church and much of the nobility of the day.

Heading south out of Prague, the first large city you'll come to is Tábor, originally founded as a Hussite bastion. The word *tábor* in Czech means "camp" and that's exactly what this was: a camp of holy warriors. But the Hussite wars and the struggles afterward in the 17th century touched all of the major towns in the region. Castles, moats, and elaborate tunnels and fortifications are carved into the landscape—a testament to those turbulent times.

The Hapsburgs, in league with much of the nobility and the church, ultimately prevailed over the Hussites by the early 17th century, and the years that followed were much quieter. Large swaths of the region came under the control of the powerful noble families. From town to town, you'll see references to families like the Rosenbergs, the Schwarzenbergs, and the various who's who of "bergs" and "steins." Their largesse led to the confectionery explosion of the Renaissance, baroque, and neoclassical overlays atop the original Gothic and medieval castles you'll see nearly everywhere you go.

Today, Southern Bohemia is a peaceful place. The rolling terrain and gentle landscapes are the perfect backdrop for hiking and biking. The pace is slow, without the pressure of hitting a list of "must-see" sights. The region begins at about Tábor and runs to the Austrian border to the south. The western edge is defined by the Šumava National Forest and the highlands with Germany. In the east, Bohemia ends at an almost imperceptible border, and Moravia starts around the town of Telč. The regional capital is České Budějovice, a bustling, workaday city of 100,000 that is perhaps best known for its original—Czech—Budweiser beer, known locally as "Budvar."

The showstopper for most visitors is Český Krumlov, a town that unfolds like a children's pop-up book with its picture-perfect palace towering over a tiny warren of baroque and Renaissance houses. If you have the time, plan an overnight stay here—the standards for lodging and dining here are head and shoulders above the rest of Southern Bohemia.

The tiny fishing village of Třebon has recast itself as a bicycler's paradise, and if you have access to a bike, the rides in this area, among the lakes and ponds on the border with Austria, are stunning.

Numbers in the margin correspond to numbers on the Southern Bohemia and Český Krumlov maps.

About the Hotels & Restaurants

Outside of Prague, prices for food and hotels are lower, but service—especially functional English—sometimes lags behind. With Austria so close, you are much more likely to find German-language menus in restaurants and German-speaking staff in both restaurants and hotels.

Southern
Bohemia

		WHAT IT COSTS in koruna and euros			
	$$$$	**$$$**	**$$**	**$**	**¢**
HOTELS in Kč	over 6,500	4,000–6,500	2,200–4,000	1,200–2,200	under 1,200
HOTELS in €	over 230	140–230	80–140	40–80	under 40
RESTAURANTS	over 500	300–500	150–300	100–150	under 100

Hotel prices are for two people in a double room with a private bath and breakfast during peak season (April through October) and generally include tax. Restaurant prices are per person for a main course at dinner and include tax.

ČESKÝ KRUMLOV

48 km (29 mi) southwest of Třeboň; 186 km (112 mi) south of Prague.

It's rare that a place not only lives up to its hype but exceeds expectations.
Český Krumlov, the official residence of the Rožmberk family for some
300 years, is such a place, and the only absolute "must-see" in Southern
Bohemia. None of the surrounding towns or villages, with their main squares
and mixtures of old and new buildings, will prepare you for the beauty
of this place. Here the Vltava works its wonders as nowhere else but in

Prague itself, swirling in a nearly complete circle around the town. Across the river stands the proud Krumlov Castle, rivaling any other in size and splendor.

Český Krumlov comes alive in early summer when students from Prague and elsewhere in the country come here to hang out and work in the hotels and restaurants. Tourists from around the world—including many from Japan—mix with the day-trippers from neighboring Germany and Austria and the local residents to create a kind of carnival atmosphere. Naturally, this has its drawbacks. On summer weekends the town fills to the bursting point, making it nearly impossible to find a room or book a table at a restau-

rant. Try to time your visit here for less busy periods in spring or fall, or weekdays in summer. And always avoid arriving on a summer afternoon or evening without a room reservation in hand.

Although it's known for its castle and picturesque side streets, Český Krumlov also makes an excellent base for more active pursuits like hiking, biking, and rafting the Vltava River. Several operators in town now rent bikes and boats. Bike trails follow the road south along the Vltava and fan out across the countryside. The excellent tourist information office on the main square can provide information on equipment rentals.

Český Krumlov can be seen in a long day trip from Prague, but it's preferable to spend at least two nights here.

What to See

❶ The town's main square, **náměstí Svornosti** (Unity Square), is home base for an exploration of the Old Town. Tiny alleys fan out in all directions—there's no point in trying to plan an orderly walk. Simply choose a direction and go. Each turn seems to bring a new drop-dead gorgeous vista of the castle or a charming café or shop that begs for a stop. On the main square itself, the **town hall,** at No. 1, built in 1580, is memorable for its Renaissance friezes and Gothic arcades. You'll also find the main tourist information office here.

❷ From the main square, a street called Horní ulice leads off toward the **Městské muzeum** (City Museum). A quick visit gets you acquainted with the rise and fall of the Rožmberk dynasty. ⊠ *Horní 152* ☎ *380–711–674* 📷 *50 Kč* ☉ *May, June, and Sept., daily 10–5; July and Aug., daily 10–6; Oct.–Apr., Tues.–Fri. 9–4, weekends 1–4.*

❸ Just opposite the City Museum are the lively *sgraffiti* façades of the former Jesuitská škola (Jesuit school)—now the luxurious **Hotel Růže.**

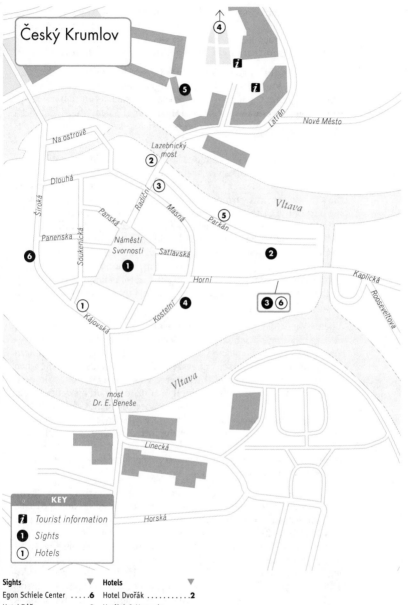

Český Krumlov

KEY

🛈 *Tourist information*
❶ *Sights*
① *Hotels*

Abundant Renaissance flourishes like these are due to the town's history as a trading route to Italy and Bavaria—making it a prime position to absorb incoming fashions. The view over the Old Town and castle is most spectacular from the hotel parking area. ⊠ *Horní 154.*

❹ The tower of the Gothic **Kostel svatého Víta** (St. Vitus's Church), built in the early 1400s, offsets the castle's larger, older tower across the river. Within the church, a marble-column baldachin shelters an elaborate baptismal font. At one time it covered the tomb of Vilém von Rozemberk (1535–92), who was one of his line's most august heads and a great patron of the town. ⊠ *Kostelní ul.*

📷 ❺ To get to **Hrad Krumlov** (Krumlov Castle), cross the Vltava on the main street, Radniční, and enter via the staircase leading up from Latrán Street, or continue a little farther up the street to the massive main gateway on the left (walking away from the main square). The oldest and most striking part of the castle is the round, 13th-century **tower,** renovated in the 16th century to look something like a minaret, with its delicately arcaded Renaissance balcony. Part of the old border fortifications, the tower guarded Bohemian frontiers from the threat of Austrian incursion. Now repainted in something like its former Renaissance finery, from various perspectives it appears pompous, absurd, astonishingly lovely—or all of these at once. From dungeon to bells, its inner secrets can be seen climbing the interior staircase.

Vilém von Rožmberk oversaw a major refurbishment of the castle, adding buildings, heightening the tower, and adding rich decorations—generally making the place suitable for one of the grandest Bohemians of the day. The castle passed out of the Rožmberks' hands, however, when Vilém's brother and last of the line, the dissolute Petr Vok, sold both castle and town to Emperor Rudolf II in 1602 to pay off his debts. Under the succeeding Eggenberg and Schwarzenberg dynasties, the castle continued to transform into an opulent palace. The Eggenbergs' prime addition was a **theater,** which was begun in the 1680s and completed in 1766 by Josef Adam of Schwarzenberg. Much of the theater and its accoutrements—sets, props, costumes, stage machinery—survive intact as a rare working display of period stagecraft.

As you enter the castle area, look into the old moats, where two playful brown bears now reside—not really much help in protecting the castle from attack. In season, the castle rooms are open to the public. Be sure to ask at the ticket office about newly accessible areas of this enormous monument, as renovations and additional openings are ongoing. One sightseeing tour focuses on the Renaissance, baroque, and rococo rooms, taking in the delightful **Maškarní Sál** (Masquerade Hall), with its richly detailed 18th-century frescoes. A second tour highlights the seigneurial apartments of the Schwarzenbergs, who owned the castle until the Gestapo seized it in 1940. (The castle became state property in 1947.)

The courtyards and passageways of the castle are open to the public year-round. After proceeding through the Renaissance-era third and fourth courtyards, you come to a wonderfully romantic elevated passageway with spectacular views of the huddled houses of the Old Town. The Austrian Expressionist painter Egon Schiele often stayed in Český Krumlov in the early 1900s and liked to paint this particular view over the river; he titled his Krumlov series *Dead City*. From the river below, the elevated passageway is revealed as the middle level of **most Na plášti** (Cloaked Bridge), a massive construction spanning a deep ravine. Below the passageway are three levels of high arches, looking like a particularly elaborate Roman viaduct. On top runs a narrow three-story block of enclosed passages dressed in light blue and white. At the end of the passageway you come to the theater, then to the nicely appointed **castle garden,** rather formal at the near end, leafy and contemplative on the other. In the middle is an 18th-century summer house with a modern, revolving open-air stage in front. Performances are held here in summer. ✉ *Český Krumlov* ☎ *380–711–687* ✉ *Garden free, castle tours 150 Kč, tower 30 Kč, theater tours 180 Kč* ⊘ *Garden Apr.–Oct., daily. Castle interior Apr. and Oct., Tues.–Sun. 9–4; May and Sept., Tues.–Sun. 9–5; June–Aug., Tues.–Sun. 9–6. Tower May and Sept., daily 9–5; June–Aug., Tues.–Sun. 9–4. Theater May–Sept., daily 10–4; Oct., daily 10–3.*

❻ The **Egon Schiele Center** exhibits the work of Schiele and other 20th-century and contemporary European and Czech artists in a rambling Renaissance building near the river. The museum closes occasionally during the winter season. ✉ *Široká 70–72* ☎ *380–704–011* ⊕ *www.schieleartcentrum.cz* ✉ *180 Kč* ⊘ *Daily 10–6.*

Where to Eat

¢–$
Fodor's Choice
★

✕ **Na Louži.** Lovingly preserved wood furniture and paneling lends a traditional touch to this warm, inviting, family-run pub. The food is unfussy and satisfying; look for the *pstruh* (trout) with potatoes. Finish off with *ovocný knedlíky,* delicious, traditional Czech fruit dumplings that are frustratingly hard to find on menus around the country. The five country-style rooms upstairs (¢) are small but comfortable enough for an overnight stay; breakfast is included. ✉ *Kájovská 66* ☎☎ *380–711–280* ▭ *No credit cards.*

Where to Stay

Český Krumlov is crammed with pensions and private rooms for rent. Prices have risen in recent years, but a good double room in a pension can still be found for around 800 Kč a person per night. The best place to look is along the tiny Parkán ulice, which parallels the river just off the main street. A safe bet is the house at **Parkán No. 107** (☎ 380–716–396), containing several nice rooms and friendly management to boot.

$$$–$$$$
Fodor's Choice
★

▦ **Hotel Růže.** Converted from a Renaissance monastery, this excellent hotel is only a two-minute walk from the main square. The decor is Ye Olde Bohemian but tastefully done, even extending to the bathroom "thrones." The rooms are spacious, and a few have drop-dead views of the castle, so ask to see several before choosing. Note that some double rooms have two narrow single beds, while some singles have beds large enough for two. The restaurant offers top-knotch dining in a setting that's formal but not stuffy. ✉ *Horní 154, 381 01* ☎ *380–772–100* ▦ *380–713–146* ⊕ *www.hotelruze.cz* ▭ *71 rooms* ⌂ *2 restaurants,*

8

café, cable TV, indoor pool, gym, hair salon, massage, sauna, bicycles, dry cleaning, laundry service, business services, meeting room, some pets allowed; no a/c ⊟ *AE, MC, V* ⫶◯⫶ *BP.*

$$ ⊞ **Hotel Dvořák.** Eminently comfortable and completely modernized, this small hotel has three things going for it: location, location, location. It's situated smack in the center of the historic district, right by the old Barber's Bridge. ⊠ *Radniční 101, 381 01* ☎ *380–711–020* 🖷 *380–711–024* ⊕ *www.dvorakck.genea2000.cz* 🔊 *17 rooms, 3 suites* ⚫ *Restaurant, in-room safes, cable TV, sauna, bar, dry cleaning, laundry service, business services; no a/c* ⊟ *AE, DC, MC, V* ⫶◯⫶ *BP.*

$$ ⊞ **Hotel U města Vídně.** The "Hotel at the City of Vienna" is a tastefully restored town house, situated near the town gates, a short stroll from the center. The rooms—with antique furnishings and modern conveniences—are all different, so ask to see a few before choosing one. The manager is often willing to negotiate down on rack rates if it's a slow night. One of the rooms is barrier-free, an extra comfort for disabled guests. ⊠ *Latrán 77, 381 01* ☎ *380–720–111* 🖷 *380–720–119* ⊕ *www. hmv.cz* 🔊 *66 rooms* ⚫ *Restaurant, café, cable TV, gym, sauna, laundry service, Internet, some free parking* ⊟ *AE, MC, V* ⫶◯⫶ *CP.*

★ $ ⊞ **Hotýlek & Hospoda u malého Vítka.** Just a couple of doors up from the Dvořák Hotel toward the central square, this charming hotel has been thoughtfully renovated with a tasteful touch. The rooms are minimal with traditional wooden furniture and fittings. The most highly decorative feature must be the names of the rooms themselves. They are all based on titles of Czech fairy tales. The eye for traditional details extends to the hotel restaurant, complete with a "wine room." ⊠ *Radniční 27, 381 01* ☎ *380–711–925* 🖷 *380–711–937* ⊕ *www.vitekhotel.cz* 🔊 *45 rooms* ⚫ *Restaurant, bicycles, bar, wine bar, some pets allowed (fee); no a/c* ⊟ *AE, MC, V* ⫶◯⫶ *BP.*

Nightlife & the Arts

Český Krumlov hosts numerous summertime cultural events, including Renaissance faires, a chamber-music festival (in June and July), organ and piano festivals (July), and the top-notch International Music Festival in the castle (August), with performances by leading Czech and foreign classical ensembles. Theater and opera companies from České Budějovice perform in the castle garden in the summer.

Český Krumlov Essentials

TRANSPORTATION A direct bus to Český Krumlov leaves Prague from both the Florenc and the Na Knížecí stations. The trip lasts three hours and costs 140 Kč. There's no direct train; with a change at České Budějovice, a train trip clocks in at more than four hours and costs 220 Kč. Note that the train station is a 20-minute hike to the main square. The bus station is much closer.

Car travel from Prague is fairly straightforward and takes three hours. Simply follow the directions to České Budějovice, and once there follow the signs to Český Krumlov. When you arrive in Český Krumlov, you'll be confronted by a confusing array of public parking areas, with no indication of how close the parking lot is to the Old Town. One safe bet is to use Parking Lot No. 2, which if you follow the tiny lanes as far as they go, will bring you to just behind the town brewery, and an easy 10-minute walk from the main square.

VISITOR
INFORMATION The tourist information office in the main square is one of the most resourceful in the Czech Republic. Not only does the staff dispense the standard "what to see and do" type of information, they will help you book accommodations, arrange bus and train travel (domestic and international), or even rent a bike or boat. They have a few computers available for checking e-mail, and the adjoining gift shop sells useful items like hiking and biking maps, and even postage stamps for postcards. Make this your first stop on arrival.

The Vltava travel agency is an authority on boating and biking possibilities. It also has an in-house pension and can help book accommodation.

🏛 **Český Krumlov Tourist Information** ✉ Nám. Svornosti 2 ☎ 380‒704‒621 ⊕ www.ckrumlov.cz

🏛 **Vltava** ✉ Kájovska 62 ☎ 380‒711‒978 ⊕ www.ckvltava.cz

OFF THE
BEATEN
PATH

HRAD ROŽMBERK (Rosenberg Castle) – This darkened castle keeps a lonely vigil atop the hill overlooking the Vltava River, about 30 km (18 mi) south of Český Krumlov. During the Cold War, this area was a virtual no-man's land, straddling the Czech-Austrian border. Today the town is slowly putting itself back on the map and merits a few hours exploration. If you've got a nice full day, rent bikes in Česky Krumlov and follow the lightly traveled road about 90 minutes. ✉ *Rožmberk nad Vltavou* ☎ *380‒749‒838* ⊕ *www.hrad-rozmberk.cz* 🎟 *150 Kč* ☉ *May and Sept., Tues.–Sun. 9–4; June–Aug., Tues.–Sun. 9–5; Apr. and Oct., weekends 9–4.*

TÁBOR

❼ *90 km (54 mi) south of Prague.*

Looking at Tábor now, it's hard to believe that this was once a counterculture utopia and fortress. In the 15th century the town began as an encampment for religious reformers centered around the teachings of the anti-Catholic firebrand preacher, Jan Hus. After Hus was burned at the stake at Lake Constanz, his followers came here by the thousands to build a society opposed to the excesses of Rome and modeled on the primitive communities of the early Christians. Tábor quickly evolved into the symbolic and spiritual center of the Hussites and, along with Prague, served as the bulwark of the religious reform movement.

The 1420s in Tábor were heady days for the reformers. Private property was denounced, and the many poor who made the pilgrimage to Tábor were required to leave their possessions at the town gates. Some sects rejected the doctrine of transubstantiation (the belief that the Eucharistic elements become the body and blood of Christ), turning Holy Communion into a bawdy, secular feast of bread and wine. Other reformers considered themselves superior to Christ—who by dying had shown himself to be merely mortal.

War fever in Tábor ran high, and the town became one of the focal points of the Hussite Wars (1419–34), which pitted reformers against an array of foreign crusaders, Catholics, and noblemen. Under the brilliant military leadership of the one-eyed general, Jan Žižka, the Taborites enjoyed early successes, but the forces of the established church and the nobility

> **MOM WAS RIGHT**
>
> Echoing the advice of mom's everywhere, be sure to bring a sweater when you walk through the tunnels. Even on hot summer days, the temperature never exceeds 50 degrees Fahrenheit.

proved too mighty in the end. Žižka died in 1424, and the Hussite uprising ended 10 years later. Still, many of the town's citizens resisted recatholicization. Fittingly, following the Battle of White Mountain in 1620 (the final defeat for the Czech Protestants), Tábor was the last city to succumb to the conquering Hapsburgs.

Many of Tabor's original fortifications can still be seen today, including parts of the town walls and the elaborate system of underground tunnels running below the main square. The original purpose of the tunnels is disputed. Some sources say the townspeople used the tunnels for hiding in and storing ammunition during the religious wars; others say they were used only as cellars for storing food. Nevertheless, their scope is amazing. The tunnels run to some 10 mi in length. Tábor is also blessed with several nice places to stay. If you're in the neighborhood and it's getting late, consider a stopover.

Žižkovo náměstí (Žižka Square) is dominated by a large, 19th-century bronze statue of the gifted—and partly blind—Hussite military leader Jan Žižka. The stone tables in front of the Gothic town hall and the house at No. 6 date from the 15th century and were used by the Hussites to give daily communion to the faithful. Many fine houses that line the square bear plaques describing their architectural style and original purpose. Be sure to stroll the tiny streets around the square, as they curve around, branch off, and then stop; few lead back to the main square. This bemusing layout, created in the 15th century, was done purposely to thwart incoming invasions.

The **Husitské muzeum** (Hussite Museum), just behind the town hall, documents the history of the religious reformers. This is also where you can also enter part of the extensive labyrinth of tunnels below the Old Town. The tour of the tunnels takes about 20 minutes. ⊠ *Žižkovo nám. 2* ☎ *381–252–242* ⊕ *www.husmuzeum.cz* ☜ *Museum and tunnel tours 40 Kč–60 Kč* ☉ *Apr.–Oct., daily 8:30–5; Nov.–Mar., weekdays 8:30–5.*

Pražská ulice is a main route to the newer part of town, delightfully lined with beautiful Renaissance façades. If you turn right at Divadelní and head to the Lužnice river, you can see the remaining walls and fortifications of the 15th century, evidence of the town's vital function as a stronghold.

Hrad Kotnov (Kotnov Castle), rising above the river in the distance, dates from the 13th century and was part of Tábor's earliest fortifications. The large pond to the northeast of the Old Town was created as a reservoir in 1492. ⊠ *Klokotská* ☎ *381–252–242* ⊕ *www.husmuzeum. cz* ⊡ *Castle 40 Kč, tower 20 Kč* ⊙ *May–Sept. 8:30–5; other times by appointment.*

Where to Stay

$$ ▥ **Dvořák.** Upbeat—even slick—modern furnishings decorate this shiny new hotel, occupying a historic building that was once the city's brewery. The rooms are a nice change of pace from the puritan, standard-issue bed and nightstands of typical Czech hotels, and the "let's get down" attitude extends to the main lobby and café bar. It's clean, well-run, and a great choice. ⊠ *Hradební 3037, 390 01* ☎ *381–251–290* 🖷 *381–251–299* ⊕ *www.orea.cz* 🖙 *72 rooms* ⌂ *Restaurant, café, wine bar, minibars, cable TV, Internet* ▱ *AE, DC, MC, V* ¶❢¶ *BP.*

$$ ▥ **Nautilus.** A real find. This tiny boutique hotel, right on the edge of
FodorśChoice Tabor's charming central square, exhibits touches of Bohemian crafts-
★ manship in the architecture, beautiful antiques in the rooms, and elegant, original art on the walls. The hotel's restaurant—"Goldie"—is, bar none, the best place to eat in the city. Very few central squares in the Czech Republic are blessed with such an elegant and comfortable place to stay. Don't pass this up. ⊠ *Žižkovo nám. 20, 390 01* ☎ *380–900–900* 🖷 *380–900–999* ⊕ *www.hotelnautilus.cz* 🖙 *22 rooms* ⌂ *Restaurant, wine bar, cable TV* ▱ *AE, DC, MC, V* ¶❢¶ *BP.*

★ **$** ▥ **Pension 189 Karel Bican.** The service couldn't be nicer at this lovely family-run pension, nor could the soothing view of the river from some rooms. The building dates from the 14th century, and the Bicans will gladly show you the house's own catacombs, which once linked up to the medieval tunnel network. When it's hot outside, you can chill out in the cool basement lounge. Some rooms have cooking facilities. The level of comfort exceeds that found in many a Czech "luxury" hotel. ⊠ *Hradební 189, 390 01* ☎🖷 *381–252–109* ⊕ *www.globalnet.cz/ bican* 🖙 *6 rooms* ⌂ *Some kitchenettes, minibars, cable TV, sauna, bicycles, some pets allowed; no a/c* ▱ *AE, MC, V* ¶❢¶ *BP.*

Tábor Essentials

TRANSPORTATION Direct buses to Tábor leave Prague from the Na Knížecí station; the trip typically takes 90 minutes and costs about 80 Kč. The train fare is nearly twice as much, and the journey can last for two hours, starting at the Hlavní nádraží (Main station). By car, the distance is about 90 km (56 mi) and should take a little more than an hour.

VISITOR ▤ **Tábor Tourist Information** ⊠ Žižkovo nám. 2 ☎ 381–486–230 ⊕ www.
INFORMATION tabor.cz

PÍSEK

❽ *44 km (28 mi) west of Tábor; 103 km (62 mi) south of Prague.*

If it weren't for Písek's 700-year-old **Gothic bridge,** peopled with baroque statues, you could easily skip this town. Compared with the adorably picturesque Český Krumlov or even Třeboň, Písek's main square, Velké náměstí, seems dull, despite its many handsome Renaissance and baroque houses. However, the bridge, a five-minute walk from the main square along Karlova ulice, was built in the 1260s—making it the oldest bridge in the Czech Republic, surpassing Prague's Charles Bridge by 90 years. Přemysl Otakar II commissioned it, seeking a secure crossing for his salt shipments over the difficult Otava River. As early as the 9th century, Písek stood at the center of one of the most important trade routes to the west, linking Prague to Passau and the rest of Bavaria, and in the 15th century it became one of five major Hussite strongholds. The statues of saints weren't added to the bridge until the 18th century. One of the statues was damaged and all the paving stones washed away during the devastating floods of 2002, but the bridge itself survived and has now been nicely restored.

Just off the main square, look for the 240-foot tower of the early-Gothic **Mariánský chrám** (Church of Mary). Construction began at about the time the bridge was built. The lone surviving tower was completed in 1487. On the inside, look for the *Madonna of Písek,* a 14th-century Gothic altar painting. On a middle pillar is a rare series of early-Gothic wall paintings dating from the end of the 13th century. ✉ *Bakaláře at Leoše Janáčka.*

Located inside a 13th-century castle's frescoed medieval halls, the **Prácheňské Museum** documents the history of Písek and its surroundings, including the Czech fishing industry (with the additional original touch of live fish in large aquarium). ✉ *Velké nám. 114* ☎ *382–201–111* 💰 *30 Kč* ✆ *Mar.–Sept., Tues.–Sun. 9–6; Oct.–Dec., Tues.–Sun. 9–5.*

OFF THE
BEATEN
PATH
ZVÍKOV – Need another castle fix? Head for Zvíkov Castle, about 18 km (11 mi) north of Písek. The castle, at the confluence of the Otava and Vltava rivers, is impressive for its authenticity. Unlike many other castles in Bohemia, Zvíkov survived the 18th and 19th centuries unrenovated and still looks exactly as it did 500 years ago. ✉ *Rte. 138, 18 km (11 mi) north of Písek* ☎ *382–285–676* 💰 *90 Kč* ✆ *May and Sept., Tues.–Sun. 9:30–4; June–Aug., Tues.–Sun. 9–5; Apr. and Oct., weekends 9:30–3:30.*

Where to Stay

$ 🏨 **U Kaplicky.** A cute family-run hotel built in 1993, U Kaplicky serves a loyal clientele of mostly weekenders from Austria and Germany. The modern furnishings are nondescript, but clean and comfortable. It's closer to town and more intimate than the other modern hotels in this area. ✉ *Budějevovická 2404, 397 01* ☎ *382–216–269* 🖨 *382–215–300* ⊕ *www.hotelukaplicky.cz* 📞 *25 rooms* ⟡ *Restaurant, cable TV, tennis courts, minibars, parking* ▭ *AE, DC, MC, V* 🍴 *CP.*

Pisek Essentials

TRANSPORTATION There's no direct train from Prague to Písek. Buses leave from the Na Knížecí station and will take you there for 80 Kč–90 Kč in approximately two hours. If you drive, the trip should take no more than 90 minutes.

VISITOR
INFORMATION 🚩 **Pisek Tourist Information** ✉ Heydukova 97 ☎ 382-213-592 ⊕ www.icpisek.cz

TŘEBOŇ

⑨ *48 km (28 mi) south of Tábor; 138 km (83 mi) south of Prague.*

Třeboň and carp are almost synonymous in the Czech Republic. If you're in the area in late autumn, you may be lucky enough to witness the great carp harvests, when tens of thousands of the glittering fish are netted from ponds in the surrounding area. Traditionally, they are served breaded and fried as the centerpiece of Christmas Eve dinner. But regardless of the season, you'll find carp on every menu in town. Don't be afraid to order it; the carp here are not the notorious bottom-feeders they are elsewhere, but are raised in clean ponds and served as a fresh catch.

Třeboň itself is a miniature jewel of town. It was settled during the 12th century by the Wittkowitzes (later called the Rožmberks, or Rosenbergs), once Bohemia's noblest family. From the 14th to the end of the 16th century, the dynasty dominated southern Bohemia; they amassed their wealth through silver, real estate, and fish farming. You can see their emblem, a five-petal rose, on castles, doorways, and coats of arms all over the region. Their official residence was 40 km (25 mi) to the southwest, in Český Krumlov, but Třeboň was an important second residence and repository of the family archives, which still reside in the town's château.

It was thanks to the Rožmberk family that this landlocked town became the center of the Czech Republic's fishing industry. During the 15th and 16th centuries, the Rožmberks peppered the countryside with hundreds of enormous ponds, partly to drain the land and partly to breed fish. Carp-breeding remains big business here. The closest pond, **Rybník Svět** (Svět Pond), is on the southern edge of town; try to fit in a stroll along its banks. You can even swim here in summer (the pond has pleasant, sandy beaches), but it can get crowded.

Třeboň has also recently developed into a mecca for cyclists, and an elaborate chain of cycling and hiking trails snake through the area's ponds and peat bogs. Several places in town now rent cycles in season. There's also a nascent spa industry underway and some places even offer elaborate "peat" treatments.

The partially intact town defenses, made up of walls, 16th-century

FOR PEAT'S SAKE

Like a mud mask to the tenth power, peat baths are another Třeboň specialty. Unlike most Czech spas that developed from a mineral spring, spa culture here arose out of the soil. The peat here is rich in iron, supposedly helpful for a variety of bone and joint disorders, along with giving a glow to your skin. For some, the treatments are a deliciously squishy sensation; for others, it's like taking a dip in a smelly bog. The **Bertiny Lázně** (384-754-111) and the **Lázně Aurora** (384-750-111) spas offer peat treatments along with more standard massages and sauna fare.

gates, and three bastions, are among the best-preserved in the Czech Republic. Near the **Svinenská Gate,** there's an 18th-century brewery, still producing outstanding beer. The main square, Masarykovo náměstí (Masaryk Square), is adorned with a collection of arcaded Renaissance and baroque houses. Look for the **Bílý Koníček** (Little White Horse), the best-preserved Renaissance house on the square, dating from 1544. It's now a modest hotel and restaurant—the perfect spot to enjoy some excellent local beer. ⊠ *Masarykovo nám. 97* ☎ *384–721–213* ⊕ *www. hotelbilykonicek.cz.*

The entrance to **Zámek Třeboň** (Třeboň Château) lies at the southwest corner of the square. From the outside it looks plain and sober, with its stark white walls, but the walls of the inner courtyard are covered with*graffito.* Several different tours of the interior feature sumptuous re-creations of the Renaissance lifestyle enjoyed by the Rožmberks and apartments furnished in late-19th-century splendor. The last of the Rožmberks died in 1611, and the castle eventually became the property of the Schwarzenberg family, who built their family tomb in a grand park on the other side of Svět Pond. It's now a monumental neo-Gothic destination for Sunday-afternoon picnickers. ⊠ *Masarykovo nám.* ☎ *384–721–193* 🎫 *Tour of family tomb 20 Kč, tour of apartments 130 Kč* ☉ *Apr., May, Sept., and Oct., Tues.–Sun. 9–4; June–Aug., Tues.–Sun. 9–5.*

The **Kostel svatého Jiljí** (Church of St. Giles), adjoining the former Augustine monastery just north of the main square, once held a set of altar paintings by the Master of the Wittingau Altar (Wittingau is the German name for Třeboň). The church, with its row of slender columns dividing a double nave, exemplifies the Gothic style of southern Bohemia. ⊠ *Husova.*

Where to Eat

★ ¢–$ ✕ **Na Rožmberské Baště.** This informal, family-run place is the perfect little nook to try the locally harvested *kapr* (carp), usually served fried with a side of french fries and tartar sauce. Other fresh-water fish are here in abundance, including river trout and eel. No-smoking tables are available. ⊠ *Rožmberská 59* ☎☎ *380–711–280* 🚫 *No credit cards.*

Where to Stay

Several new privately owned pensions have opened their doors in the past couple of years. Most are located along tiny Rožmberská ulice or Husova ulice—both of which flank central Masarykovo námněstí. Stroll along the street and stop in if one appeals, or you can ask at the tourist information center on the square; they can help book rooms.

★ $$ 🏨 **Zlatá Hvězda.** Hotel Bílý Koníček at the other end of the square may get all the attention for its cute, castlelike exterior, but the "Golden Star" hotel is better appointed and more comfortable. The hotel was thoroughly upgraded a few years back, when the plain rooms got a much-needed facelift and the addition of new facilities—like a fitness room. ⊠ *Masarykovo nám. 107, 379 01* ☎ *384–757–111* 📠 *384–757–300* ⊕ *www.zhvezda.cz* 🛏 *48 rooms* ⟁ *Restaurant, cable TV, gym, bowling, pub, Internet, meeting room, parking (fee); no a/c* 🚫 *AE, DC, MC, V* 🍴 *BP.*

Třeboň Essentials

TRANSPORTATION A direct bus from the Florenc station goes to Třeboň in 2½ hours for about 110 Kč. Although a train trip requires to change at Veselí, it takes the same amount of time but it's more expensive.

VISITOR 🔲 **Třeboň Tourist Information** ✉ Masarykovo nám. 103 ☎ 384-721-169 ⊕ www.
INFORMATION trebon-mesto.cz.

JINDŘICHŮV HRADEC

❿ *28 km (17 mi) southwest of Třeboň; 158 km (95 mi) south of Prague.*

The ancient, picturesque town of Jindřichův Hradec, which dates to the end of the 12th century, is mirrored in the reflective waters of the Vajgar Pond right in the town's center. Originally a market colony near the border between Bohemia and Moravia, the town acquired a castle to protect it. Under the castle's guard, the town grew in size and importance, and these days it's a regional administrative center.

The modern town admittedly looks a little scruffy in spots. But the good news is that pockets of the town are exhibiting little signs of renewed cultural life in and around the crumbling façades and seemingly forgotten alleyways. A number of cultural events are held here each year, including Concertino Praga (an international radio competition for young musicians), a folk music festival called "Folkloric Rose," the South Bohemian Music Festival, and occasional classical music concerts in castle Rondel.

The surrounding countryside has earned the nickname "Czech Canada" for its unspoiled beauty with more ponds, forests, hills, and numerous scattered granite outcrops. It's popular among Czechs for cycling, hiking, and boating possibilities.

Imposing Renaissance houses surround the **náměstí Míru** (Main Square). The open space in front of the late baroque town hall is dominated by a decorated column of the Holy Trinity. This fine example of local sculpture was paid for by the local postmaster in 1764, a rare gift from an individual with such a modest profession.

★ A short walk from the town square leads to the gates of the **castle.** Behind the courtyard and its lovely Italian arcades, the core of the castle is pure Gothic splendor, reflected not only in its thick defensive walls and round tower but also in the **murals** covering interior corridors. Colorful examples of medieval coats of arms and a panorama depicting the legend of St. George on the murals date from 1338. In the course of centuries, buildings of an adjoining Renaissance-era château were added to the early Gothic castle, together forming a large complex, the Czech Republic's third-largest in size. There are three different marked routes through the castle for visitors to follow.

The most singular attraction within the Renaissance chateau must be the **rondel,** a circular, domed building like a tiered birthday cake decorated in the mannerist style of the late 16th century. It was designed by Italian architect Baldassare Maggio as a ballroom, and the delicate

8

Guided Day Tours to Southern Bohemia

GUIDED BUS TOURS ARE AVAILABLE from several companies covering several of the destinations in Southern Bohemia. Most need to be booked at least a day in advance. These are only two of many organizers.

Martin Tours (☎ 224–212–473 ⊕ www.martintour.cz) departs from Staroměstské náměstí (Old Town Square) and náměstí Republiky (Republic Square). All itineraries in Southern Bohemia are about 10 hours and include lunch.

Čedok (☎ 224–197–242) offers the same trips as Martin Tours, but also does longer itineraries. One three-day Čedok trip includes the highlights of Southern Bohemia with lodging at České Budějovice and Český Krumlov, or at Třeboň, Jindřichův Hradec, and Telč. The main Prague departure point is náměstí Republiky (Republic Square) in central Prague, opposite the Prašná brána (Powder Tower). Čedok also offers spa and reconditioning programs at the Třeboň Spa for a week or two.

---

pink-and-white decorations summon up a confectionery image of aristocratic dancers and musicians. The unique underground music chamber was connected to the main hall by a circular aperture in the center of the dance floor. A large decorative vase standing over this hole not only acted as a sound amplifier but also prevented the lordly dancers from falling in. Even without this peculiar feature, the acoustics of the rondel remain especially good, and it's often still used for classical concerts in summer. The castle is said to be haunted by the White Lady, who appears clad in diaphanous white but wearing long black gloves on her ghostly arms; when she is seen, it is said a member of the ruling Černín family is about to die. ⊠ *Dobrovského 1* ☎ *384–321–279* 🎫 *160 Kč* 🕐 *June–Aug., Tues.–Sun. 9–5.30; Apr. and Oct., Tues.–Sun. 10–4; May and Sept., Tues.–Sun. 10–5.*

In the 13th century, a Franciscan monastery was built adjacent to the **Kostel svatého Jana** (Church of St. John). The extensive murals in the clerestory of the church date from the first half of the 14th century and portray scenes from the lives of Christ, the Apostles, and various Czech saints. They also demonstrate the medieval necessity for pictorial stories to educate the illiterate population. On the south side of the sanctuary you can see the chapel of St. Nicholas, which was built in 1369. The vaulted ceiling is supported by a single central pillar and this is one of the earliest buildings using this construction in Bohemia. Although the church is open to the public only in high summer season, there are occasional evening concerts in other months. ⊠ *Štítného* 🎫 *20 Kč* 🕐 *July and Aug., daily 9–noon and 12:30–4:30.*

Overlooking Jindřichuv Hradec is the tall **Proboštský Kostel** (Church of the Assumption), which dates from the beginning of the 15th century. By coincidence, the church's location intersects with the earth's 15th meridian. A viewing gallery can be visited near the top of the church tower, and it provides extensive views across the surrounding area. However, those views demand the sacrifice of climbing 157 steps. ⊠ *Za kostelem* 🎫 *Tower 20 Kč* ⊙ *June–Aug., daily 10–noon and 1–4; Apr., May, and Sept.–Jan., weekends 10–noon and 1–4.*

Founded in 1882, the **Muzeum Jindřichohradecka** holds an extraordinary Christmas nativity scene that's become its principal attraction. This huge, mechanical creche was built by one committed craftsman, Mr. Krýza, who dedicated more than 60 years to its creation in the latter part of the 19th century. The old mechanism has now been replaced with an electrical system, but the primitive charm of the moving figures remains. Amazingly, the scene contains 1,398 figures. Another unusual exhibit is the re-creation of a parlor from the home of the Czech opera star Emmy Destinnova, who was famous in the early 20th century. Destinnova's taste favored the eccentric, and it's remarkable that the diva should have reposed on a sofa made from so many antlers. ⊠ *Balbínovo nám. 19* ☎ *384–363–660* ⊕ *www.muzeum.esnet.cz* 🎫 *60 Kč* ⊙ *June–Sept., daily 8:30–noon and 12:30–5; Apr., May, and Oct.–Jan., Tues.–Sun. 8:30–noon and 12:30–5.*

Where to Stay

$$ 🏨 **Hotel Concertino.** Safely removed from the castle and its supposed hauntings, this hotel overlooks the town square. The façade suggests a charming period conversion, but once inside, modernity is the keynote. The hotel provides a series of up-to-date business services. ⊠ *Míru nám. 141, 377 01* ☎ *384–362–320* 🖷 *384–362–323* ⊕ *www.concertino.cz* 📞 *33 rooms* ☖ *Restaurant, in-room safes, minibars, cable TV, hair salon, billiards, paddle tennis, bar, pub, laundry service, meeting rooms, parking (fee); no a/c* ⊟ *AE, DC, MC, V* |◯| *EP.*

★ ¢ 🏨 **Hotel Bílá paní.** This charming, cheaper alternative to the Concertino has the added benefit of being right next to the castle. The "White Lady" hotel takes its name from the famous ghost who is reputed to haunt the castle itself. The rooms may not be on the level for a *graund dame,* but they are presentable and clean, and some offer a view of the castle tower. ⊠ *Dobrovského 54, 377 01* ☎ *384–363–329* 🖷 *384–362–660* 📞 *9 rooms* ☖ *Restaurant, cable TV, some pets allowed; no a/c* ⊟ *MC, V* |◯| *BP.*

Jindřichův Hradec Essentials

TRANSPORTATION Jindřichův Hradec is about three hours from Prague by bus; a bus from the Florenc station costs about 120 Kč. The train from Hlavní nádraží (Main station) will require a change at Veselí and takes 15 minutes more than the bus. It also costs more, at a fare of about 200 Kč.

VISITOR INFORMATION 🇫 **Jindřichův Hradec Tourist Information** ⊠ Panská 136 ☎ 384-363-546 ⊕ www.jh.cz.

HLUBOKÁ NAD VLTAVOU

⑪ *17 km (10½ mi) southwest of Trébon; 155 km (93½ mi) south of Prague.*

Fodor'sChoice
★

With a cluster of white rooks flanking its walls, this is one of the Czech Republic's most curious châteaux. Although the structure dates from the 13th century, what you see is pure 19th-century excess, perpetrated by the wealthy Schwarzenberg family attempting to prove their good taste. If you think you've seen this castle somewhere before, you're probably thinking of Windsor Castle, near London, which served as the template. Take a tour; the pompous interior reflects the no-holds-barred tastes of the time, and many individual pieces are interesting. The wooden Renaissance ceiling in the large dining room was removed by the Schwarzenbergs from the castle at Český Krumlov and brought here. Also look for the beautiful late-baroque bookshelves in the library.

If your curiosity in Czech painting wasn't satisfied in Prague, have a look at the **Galerie Mikolaše Alše** (Aleš Art Gallery; ☎ 387–967–041) in the Riding Hall, which displays a major collection of Gothic art and an exhibition of modern Czech works. The gallery is also a popular spot for chamber concerts. ⊠ *Zamék 142, off Rte. 105 or 146, Hluboká nad Vltavou* ☎ *387–967–045* ⊕ *www.zamekhluboka.cz* 🖾 *180 Kč castle, 40 Kč Aleš Art Gallery* ⊙ *Castle: Apr.–June, Sept., and Oct., Tues.–Sun. 9–4:30; July and Aug., daily 9–5. Aleš Art Gallery: May–Sept., daily 9–5; Oct.–Apr., Tues.–Sun. 9–3:30.*

Care for a brisk walk? Follow the yellow trail signs 2 km (1 mi) to the **Lovecká chata Ohrada** (Ohrada Hunting Lodge), which houses a museum of hunting and fishing and also has a small zoo for children. ⊠ *Zamék Ohrada 1, off Rte. 105, Hluboká nad Vltavou* ☎ *387–965–340* 🖾 *40 Kč* ⊙ *June–Aug., daily 9–5:30; May and Sept., Tues.–Sun. 9–5:30; Apr. and Oct., Tues.–Fri. 9–3; Nov.–Mar. by appointment.*

Hluboká nad Vltavou Essentials

TRANSPORTATION　The journey from Prague to Hluboká—either by train from the Hlavní nádraží (Main station) or by bus from the Florenc coach—station is 2½ hours unless you get one of the local connections that stops in every small town (in which case the trip takes 3½ hours). The train ticket costs about 200 Kč, the bus ticket 120 Kč. You may find it more convenient to stay overnight in České Budějovice and see the castle in the morning after a 20-minute trip either by local bus or train.

ČESKÉ BUDĚJOVICE

⑫ *26 km (16 mi) southwest of Trébon; 164 km (99 mi) south of Prague.*

České Budějovice is the largest city in Southern Bohemia and the community's center and transportation hub. Not nearly as charming as its smaller neighbors, the town still merits a few hours of exploration if you happen to have a stopover. The major attraction is the enormously proportioned main square named after King Přemysl Otakar II and lined with arcaded houses. The well-preserved Gothic Dominican monastery and Church of the Virgin on Piaristické náměstí make for interesting sightseeing. But the town's real claim to fame is its beer—the slightly sweetish *Budvar,* which can be found across the country and around the world. Unfortunately, you can't tour the Budvar brewery itself, but the beer easily found at pubs around town—simply look for the "Budvar" sign.

To get a good view over the city, climb the 360 steps up to the Renaissance gallery of the **Černá věž** (Black Tower), at the northeast corner of the square next to St. Nicholas's Cathedral. ⊠ *Nám. Přemysla Otakara II* ☐ *25 Kč* ☉ *Apr.–June, Sept., and Oct., Tues.–Sun. 10–6; July and Aug., daily 10–6.*

A source of pride for České Budějovice, **Koněspřežka** is the oldest railway station on the continent. Designed to transport salt to Bohemia from Linz in Austria, a horse-driven railway was built between 1825 and 1832. One of the first major industrial developments in Europe, it reduced the journey between Linz and České Budějovice from two weeks to four days. Public transport was introduced soon afterward. The station is now a part of the city museum. ⊠ *Mánesova 10* ☎ *386–354–820* ⊕ *www.jiznicechy.org* ☐ *25 Kč* ☉ *May–Sept., Tues.–Sun. 9–12:30 and 1–5.*

Founded in 1877 the **Jihočeské Museum** started with a couple of hundred donated items in three rooms in the town hall on the main square. Nowadays, the large collections are held and displayed in the main building and at four other locations outside the town. The major exhibits include theme collections portraying the history of the town and the region through an extensive variety of artifacts that include metalwork, ceramics, glass, and furniture. A fascinating large-scale model shows the Old Town and its picturesque medieval walls and towers. A regular series of temporary exhibitions also runs alongside the permanent ones. ⊠ *Dukelská 1* ☎ *386–356–447* ☐ *80 Kč* ☉ *Tues.–Sun. 9–12:30 and 1–5.*

OFF THE BEATEN PATH

HOLAŠOVICE – Peppered with small country homes and farmsteads, this traditional Czech village is so well preserved, it's been designated a UNESCO cultural heritage site. Some of the houses date back to the town's founding in the 13th century. Others bear "rural baroque" ornamentation or custard yellow façades. A small exhibition at no. 60 offers an insight into village life. For one weekend each summer the Selské slavnosti (Peasant Festival) unites the inhabitants and visitors with a whole range of musical entertainments and craft demonstrations.

You can see the village easily in an hour, at which time the hungry traveler may be delighted to find genuine South Bohemian cooking in the village pub, or *hospoda*. Holašovice is a short 18-km (11-mi) drive to the west of České Budějovice, but don't set out without excellent directions and a good map. The small highway that leads to the village is almost impossible to find in hectic daytime traffic. Inquire at the tourist information office about local bus service. ☎ *387–982–145* ⊕ *www.holasovice.cz* ☉ *Apr.–Oct., Tues.–Sun. 9–5.*

Where to Stay

★ **$$–$$$**   ☐ **Grand Hotel Zvon.** Old-fashioned, well-kept, and comfortable, this historic hotel has a winning list of attributes including an ideal location right on the main square. A room with a view, however, costs extra, but these rooms are considerably larger and brighter and include large period bathtubs. ⊠ *Nám. Přemysla Otakara II 28, 307 01* ☎ *387–311–384* 🖷 *387–311–385* ⊕ *www.hotel-zvon.cz* ⤳ *75 rooms* ⚭ *2 restaurants,* *café, some minibars, cable TV, pub, parking (fee), some pets allowed (fee); no a/c* ▭ *AE, DC, MC, V* ⧁ *BP.*

$ ⊡ **Hotel Bohemia.** The combination of two old burgher houses formed

Fodor'sChoice this hotel. The building, listed as a monument, has been modernized but

★ still retains its centuries-old ceilings. Refurbishment resulted in a pleasant design in a quiet part of the old town. The adjoining wine-bar restaurant serves excellent local dishes. ⊠ *Hradební 20, 370 01* ☎ *386–360–691* 🖷 *386–360–691* ⊕ *www.bohemiacb.cz* ⇆ *18 rooms* ☖ *Restaurant, minibars, cable TV, laundry service, free parking, some pets allowed; no a/c* ▭ *AE, MC, V* ⧁ *BP.*

Nightlife & the Arts

As a regional capital, **České Budějovice** keeps its own theater, ballet, orchestra, and opera companies. Unlike theater, music knows no language barriers, and the local opera company is regularly praised for the quality of its productions. Summer performances are held in Český Krumlov Castle park. It's worth noting that these tickets are very popular and are often sold out a month in advance. They can be obtained from the theater box office in České Budějovice. ⊠ *Dr. Stejskala 23* ☎ *386–356–925* ⊕ *www.jihoceskedivadlo.cz.*

České Budějovice Essentials

TRANSPORTATION The trip to České Budějovice from Prague takes about 2½ hours by either bus or train. Be careful to choose a *rychlík* not a *osobní* train (express, as opposed to passenger train), which would make your journey four hours. Trains go from the Hlavní nádraží (Main station) and cost about 220 Kč; buses leave from both Florenc and Na Knížecí and cost 130 Kč. Car travel affords the greatest ease and flexibility. České Budějovice lies on the main artery through the region, the two-lane E55 south from Prague, which, though often crowded, is in relatively good shape. The journey by car should take no more than about 2½ hours.

VISITOR 🖪 **České Budějovice Tourist Center** ⊠ Přemysla Otakára II nám. 2 ☎ 386-801-414
INFORMATION ⊕ www.c-budejovice.cz.

Western Bohemia

WORD OF MOUTH

"If you go to Karlovy Vary, be sure to have a flavored spa wafer (or two!) I kind of regretted not buying a box to take home. I know at the time it seemed like a touristy thing to do, but the wafers were not a bad deal."

—MelissaHI

By Mark Baker **WESTERN BOHEMIA WAS KNOWN AS THE PLAYGROUND** of Central Europe's rich and famous. Its three well-known spas, Karlovy Vary, Mariánské Lázně, and Františkovy Lázně (also known by their German names, Karlsbad, Marienbad, and Franzensbad, respectively), were the annual haunts of everybody who was anybody: Johann Wolfgang von Goethe, Ludwig van Beethoven, Karl Marx, and England's King Edward VII, to name but a few.

The spas suffered dramatically in the decades after World War II. The concept of a luxurious health spa was anathema to the ruling Communist government; many of the spa facilities were transformed into sterile hospitals, and some of the nicest properties were transformed into recuperation center for workers.

The years since 1989 have been kinder to the spa resorts. Although progress has been slow, all three are gradually recapturing their magic. Karlovy Vary is the jewel in the crown. Helped by its annual international film festival and a heavy infusion of mainly Russian private capital, Karlovy Vary flaunts the look of an international spa destination. Františkovy Lázně, too, is on the comeback trail. The city officials have used bucket loads of Kaiser-yellow paint to spruce up those aging Empire façades and the parks have gotten a much-needed makeover. Only Mariánské Lázně feels stuck in the past, though work is underway there, and it may only be a couple of years away from returning to the spotlight.

The local concept of a "spa" may differ from what you are used to back home. In the Czech Republic, spas are seen as serious health treatments, complete with physical examinations, blood tests, and various infusions to complement the waters, relaxation, and massage. The modern concept of a spa resort—with its New Age aromatherapy, hot stones, and crystals—is beginning to spread its influence, but a "spa" in this part of the world still mostly means doctors, nurses, and lab coats. That said, many hotels and resorts do offer walk-in massages and other services for casual visitors. The best place to inquire is at your hotel or the tourist information center.

Aside from the spas, the area is full of historic features stemming from the wealth it accrued as the district's important trade route into Germany and Italy. A strong Germanic influence can still be seen, particularly in towns like Cheb. Everywhere in the region you'll see German day-trippers, mostly pensioners on coach tours dropping by for a walk around town and a slice of apple strudel before hitting the trail back to Germany.

Numbers in the margins refer to the Western Bohemia and Karlovy Vary maps.

About the Hotels & Restaurants

The quality of hotels in Western Bohemia is on par with those in Prague, (something that can't be said about some other parts of the country) and most establishments have standard amenities, including satellite

TV, room phones, and private bathrooms. One difference from the hotels in Prague: the peak season is shorter, running from May through September. Another difference: the staff tends to speak a very limited amount of English—German and Russian are much more common, in keeping with the majority of visitors. Prices have risen dramatically in recent years, making private accommodation a more attractive offer. The local tourist offices usually keep lists of pensions and private rooms.

WHAT IT COSTS in koruna and euros					
	$$$$	$$$	$$	$	¢
HOTELS in Kč	over 6,500	4,000–6,500	2,200–4,000	1,200–2,200	under 1,200
HOTELS in €	over 230	140–230	80–140	40–80	under 40
RESTAURANTS	over 500	300–500	150–300	100–150	under 100

Hotel prices are for two people in a double room with a private bath and breakfast during peak season (May through September). Restaurant prices are per person for a main course at dinner and include 19% V.A.T.

KARLOVY VARY

132 km (79 mi) west of Prague on Rte. 6 (E48).

Karlovy Vary—often known outside the Czech Republic by its German name, Karlsbad—is the most famous Bohemian spa. It's named for Emperor Charles IV, who allegedly happened upon the springs in 1358 while on a hunting expedition. As the story goes, the emperor's hound fell into a boiling spring and was scalded. Charles had the water tested and, familiar with spas in Italy, ordered the village of Vary to be transformed into a haven for baths. The spa reached its golden age in the 19th century, when aristocrats from all over Europe came for treatments. The long list of those who "took the cure" includes Peter the Great, Goethe, Schiller, Beethoven, and Chopin. Even Karl Marx, when he wasn't decrying wealth and privilege, spent time at the wealthy and privileged resort; he wrote some of *Das Kapital* here between 1874 and 1876.

Pulling off an extraordinary comeback, Karlovy Vary has emerged after decades of Communist neglect that left many buildings crumbling into dust behind beautiful façades. Much of the reconstruction has been led not by Czechs, but by Russians. Since the days of Peter the Great, Karlovy Vary has held a deep fascination for Russians, and many of them have poured their newly gained wealth into properties here. Don't be surprised to hear Russian spoken widely in the streets or see it used as the second language, after Czech, on restaurant menus.

Karlovy Vary's other vehicle in luring attention and investment has been its international film festival. Every year during the first week of July, international stars and film fans flock to this spot. Some recent attendees include Sharon Stone, Morgan Freeman, and even an aging Gregory Peck. If you're planning on visiting at this time, line up your hotel room well in advance.

Whether you're arriving by bus, train, or car, your first view of the town approaching from Prague will be of the run-down section on the banks of the Ohře River. Don't despair: continue along the main road—following the signs to the Grandhotel Pupp—until you are rewarded with a glimpse at the lovely main street in the older spa area, situated gently astride the banks of the little Teplá ("Warm") River. (Drivers, note that driving through or parking in the main spa area is allowed only with a permit obtained at your hotel.) The walk from the new town to the spa area is about 20 minutes.

The Historická čtvrt (Historic District) is still largely intact. Tall 19th-century houses, with decorative and

> **TO YOUR HEALTH**
>
> Becherovka, herbal alcoholic liqueur, is often referred to as the "The Thirteenth Spring" in Karlovy Vary. Many Czechs believe this locally produced drink does indeed have medicinal properties, such as aiding in digestion. The recommended dosage is three small cups a day: one before lunch, one before dinner, and one before bedtime.

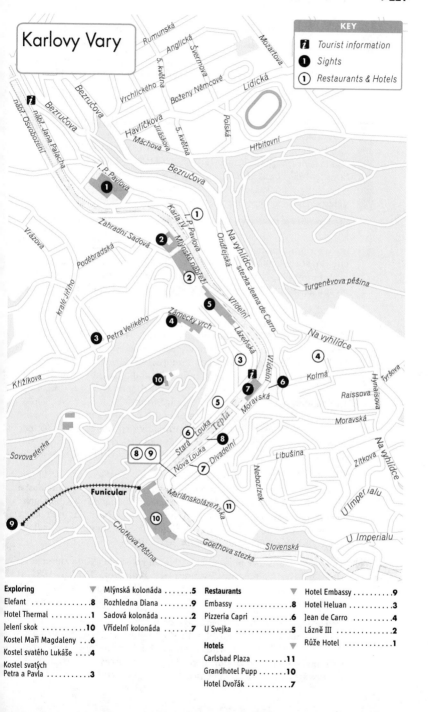

Karlovy Vary

KEY

ℹ️ *Tourist information*

❶ *Sights*

① *Restaurants & Hotels*

Guided Day Tours to Western Bohemia

GUIDED ONE-DAY BUS TOURS FROM PRAGUE ARE AVAILABLE from several companies to the larger spa towns of Karlovy Vary and Mariánské Lázně.

Martin Tours (☎ 224–212–473 ⊕ www.martintour.cz) offers regular trips to Karlovy Vary and Mariánské Lázně for 1,350 Kč and 1,600 Kč respectively, which includes sightseeing and lunch. Tour time is about 10 hours. Martin Tours is one of the larger tour operators in the country, so expect a large group along with you.

Tip Top Travel (☎ 267–914–576 ⊕ www.tiptoptravel.cz) offers a combined Karlovy Vary–Mariánské Lázně tour for 2,100 Kč. The tour lasts about nine hours and the price includes a pickup at your hotel.

often eccentric façades, line the spa's proud riverside streets. Throughout, you can see colonnades full of people sipping the spa's hot sulfuric water from funny, pipe-shape drinking cups. At night the streets fill with steam escaping from cracks in the earth, giving the town a slightly macabre feel.

What to See

❼ Shooting its scalding water to a height of some 40 feet, the Vřídlo is indeed the Karlovy Vary's hottest and most dramatic gusher, and built around it is the jarringly modern **Vřídelní kolonáda** (Vřídlo Colonnade). Walk inside the arcade to watch hundreds of patients take the famed Karlsbad drinking cure. They shuffle somnambulistically up and down, eyes glazed, clutching drinking glasses filled periodically at one of the five "sources." The waters, which range from 30°F to 72°F, are said to be especially effective against diseases of the digestive and urinary tracts. They're also good for gout (which probably explains the spa's former popularity with royals). If you want to join the crowds and take a sip, you can buy your own spouted cup from vendors within the colonnade. ✉ *Vřídelní ul., near Kosterní nám.*

★ ❻ To the right of the Vřídlo Colonnade, steps lead up to the white **Kostel Maří Magdaleny** (Church of Mary Magdalene). Designed by Kilian Ignaz Dientzenhofer (architect of the two churches of St. Nicholas in Prague), this is the best of the few baroque buildings still standing in Karlovy Vary. ✉ *Moravská ul.* ☎ *No phone* ☉ *Daily 9–6.*

❺ The neo-Renaissance pillared hall **Mlýnská kolonáda** (Mill Colonnade), along the river, is the town's centerpiece. Built from 1871 to 1881, it has four springs: Rusalka, Libussa, Prince Wenceslas, and Millpond. ✉ *Mlýnské nábřeží.*

❷ Delicately elegant, the **Sadová kolonáda** (Park Colonnade) is laced with white wrought iron. It was built in 1882 by the Viennese architectural duo Fellner and Helmer, who sprinkled the Austro-Hungarian Empire with many such edifices during the late 19th century. He also designed the town's theater, the quaint wooden Tržní kolonáda (Market Colonnade) next to the Vřídlo Colonnade, and one of the old bathhouses. ✉ *Zahradní.*

❶ The 20th century raises its head in the form of the huge, bunkerlike **Hotel Thermal,** across the river from the historic district. Built in the late 1960s as the Communist idea of luxury, the building is jarring to the eye. But a visit to the rooftop pool is nothing short of spectacular. Even if you don't feel like a swim, it's worth taking the winding road up to the baths for the view. ✉ *I. P. Pavlova 11* ☎ *359–001–111* 💳 *50 Kč per hour* ⊙ *Pool daily 8–8; café Tues.–Sun. 10–6.*

❹ A five-minute walk up the steep Zámecký vrch from the Market Colonnade brings you to the redbrick Victorian **Kostel svatého Lukáše** (St. Luke's Church), once a gathering point for the local English community. ✉ *Zámecký vrch at Petra Velikého.*

❿ From Kostel svatého Lukáše, take a sharp right uphill on a redbrick road, then turn left onto a footpath through the woods, following signs to **Jelení skok** (Stag's Leap). After a while steps lead up to a bronze statue of a deer looking over the cliffs, the symbol of Karlovy Vary. From here a winding path threads toward a little red gazebo opening onto a mythical panorama. ✉ *Sovava trail in Petrova Výšina park.*

Fodor'sChoice ★

NEED A BREAK?

After reaching the summit of Stag's Leap, reward yourself with a light meal at the nearby restaurant **Jelení skok.** There may be an entrance fee if a live band is playing (but you'll also get the opportunity to polka). If you don't want to walk up, you can drive up a signposted road from the Victorian church.

---

❸ The splendid Russian Orthodox **Kostel svatých Petra a Pavla** (Church of Sts. Peter and Paul) has six domes. It dates from the end of the 19th century and is decorated with paintings and icons donated by wealthy Russian visitors. ✉ *Třída Krále Jiřího.*

❾ Give your feet a rest. You won't need to walk to one of the best views of the town. Even higher than Stag's Leap sits an observation tower, **rozhledna Diana,** accessible by funicular from behind the Grandhotel Pupp. There's an elevator to the top of the tower. ✉ *Výšina přátelství* 💳 *Funicular 30 Kč one-way, 50 Kč round-trip; tower 10 Kč* ⊙ *June–Sept., Mon.–Thurs. and Sun. 11–9, Fri. and Sat. 11–11; May and Oct., Tues., Wed., and Sun. 11–6, Fri. and Sat. 11–7; Mar., Apr., Nov. and Dec., Wed.–Sun. 11–5.*

❽ On one of the town's best shopping streets you can find **Elefant,** carrying the torch for a dying breed of sophisticated coffeehouses. This is the spot for that mandatory apple strudel and coffee. ✉ *Stará louka 30* ☎ *353–222–544.*

Where to Eat

Unfortunately, the culinary scene in Prague has yet to spark off in Karlovy Vary. The variety and quality of the food generally still lags well behind the quality of the hotels and the demands of the visitors. The riverbank is lined with nondescript Czech restaurants on both sides. These are fine for a plate of pork or a schnitzel, but are unlikely to leave a lasting positive impression. Hotel food tends to be better.

9

$$–$$$　✕ **Embassy.** Cozy and sophisticated, this wine restaurant, conveniently
Fodor'sChoice　near the Grandhotel Pupp, serves an innovative menu by local standards.
　　★　Tagliatelle with smoked salmon in cream sauce makes an excellent main
course, as does roast duck with cabbage and dumplings. The wine list
features Czech varieties like the dry whites Rulandské bílé and Ryzlink
Rýnský (the latter being the domestic version of the Riesling grape) and
some pricey imports. For a romantic evening, request one of the tables
on the bridge over the river. ⊠ *Nová louka 21* ☎ *353–221–161* ▤ *AE,
DC, MC, V.*

$$–$$$　✕ **Pizzeria Capri.** This riverfront pizzeria has become an institution dur-
ing the annual film festival. The walls are decked out with photos of
the owner smiling next to Hollywood stars. The pizza and fresh-fish dishes
range from good to very good. On a warm evening in summer sit out
along the sidewalk. ⊠ *Stará Louka 42* ☎ *353–236–090* ▤ *MC, V.*

$–$$　✕ **U Švejka.** Usually when a restaurant has the name "Schweik" in it—
from the novel "Good Soldier Schweik"—it means one thing: tourist
trap. But this local Schweik incarnation is a cut above its brethren. If
you're looking for a simple, decent Czech pub, with good local cooking and excellent beer, you've found it. ⊠ *Stará Louka 10* ☎ *353–232–276*
▤ *No credit cards.*

Where to Stay

★ **$$$–$$$$**　▥ **Carlsbad Plaza.** An eye-popping new luxury hotel, not far from the
Grandhotel Pupp, Carlsbad Plaza is aimed at attracting Karlovy Vary's
wealthiest visitors. Everything here speaks refinement, down to the
lunchtime dress code: "jacket and tie" for men. Reserve the "Moser"
suite if you've just cashed out your 401K. The staff tries hard to main-
tain the highest standards, but the overall effect is a little chilly. The rooms
are tastefully furnished, with all modern conveniences. The "wellness
center" (a small pool and sauna complex), spa, and fitness centers offer
every comfort and treatment yet invented. ⊠ *Mariánskolázeňská 23,
360 01* ☎ *352–441–111* 🖷 *353–236–392* ⊕ *www.carlsbadplaza.cz*
⤳ *146 rooms, 14 suites* ⌕ *4 restaurants, nightclub, minibars, cable TV,
health club, spa, hair salon, some pets allowed (fee)* ▤ *AE, MC, V* ❍| *BP.*

$$$　▥ **Hotel Dvořák.** This hotel set local standards when it first opened in
1990 and has continued to keep pace with the competition. It's a well-
run, comfortable, and costly place with an excellent in-house restaurant
and full spa facilities. The hotel occupies three renovated town houses
along the main spa avenue; request a room with a bay-window view of
the town. Weeklong spa packages here begin at around €750 per person in high season. The staff can help book last-minute spa activities,
like massages. ⊠ *Nová louka 11, 360 21* ☎ *353–224–145*
🖷 *353–222–814* ⊕ *www.hotel-dvorak.cz* ⤳ *96 rooms, 10 suites*
⌕ *Restaurant, café, cable TV with movies, pool, gym, hair salon, spa,
casino, Internet, parking (fee) some pets allowed (fee); no a/c in some
rooms* ▤ *AE, DC, MC, V* ❍| *BP.*

$$–$$$　▥ **Grandhotel Pupp.** The granddaddy of them all, this is one of Central
Fodor'sChoice　Europe's most famous resorts, going back some 200 years. Standards and
　　★　service slipped under the Communists, when the hotel was called "Moskva-
Pupp," but the highly professional management has more than made up
for the decades of neglect. The vast public rooms exude the very best taste,

circa 1913, when the building was completed. Every July, the Pupp houses international movie stars in town for the Karlovy Vary International Film Festival. (The adjacent Parkhotel Pupp, under the same management, is a more affordable alternative.) ⊠ *Mírové nám. 2, 360 91* ☎*353–109–630* 🖷*353–226–638* ⊕*www.pupp.cz* ⚓*75 rooms, 34 suites* ⌂ *4 restaurants, in-room safes, minibars, cable TV with movies, health club, sauna, spa, lounge, casino, 2 nightclubs, Internet, some pets allowed (fee); no a/c in some rooms* ▭ *AE, DC, MC, V* ⎟⊙⎟ *BP.*

$$ 🏨 **Hotel Embassy.** On a peaceful bend of the river, this family-run hotel's spacious, well-appointed rooms usually include a sitting table and chairs or a couch with accompanying coffee table. The Embassy is more intimate and personal than the Carlsbad Plaza or Grandhotel Pupp, with the same high level of excellence in its restaurant, rooms, and staff. It also offers greens-fee discounts and starting times at four local courses for the golf-obsessed, and massages and spa treatments for those who are not. ⊠ *Nová Louka 21, 360 01* ☎ *353–221–161* 🖷 *353–223–146* ⊕ *www. embassy.cz* ⚓ *18 rooms, 2 suites* ⌂ *Restaurant, minibars, cable TV, billiards, bar, Internet, some pets allowed (fee); no a/c* ▭ *AE, MC, V* ⎟⊙⎟ *BP.*

Fodor'sChoice
★

$$ 🏨 **Jean de Carro.** Three buildings comprise the Jean de Carro framed on a hilltop on a side street above the spa—giving it a panoramic view. Grab a seat at one of the outdoor umbrella-covered tables to while away the hours picking out Karlovy Vary's landmarks and enjoying its lush, green surroundings. Best of all, every room in this hotel offers views of the town. ⊠ *Stezka Jeana de Carro 4–6, 360 01* ☎ *353–505–111* 🖷*353–505–151* ⊕*www.premium-hotels.com* ⚓ *25 rooms, 7 suites* ⌂ *Restaurant, cable TV, bar, parking (fee), some pets allowed (fee); no a/c* ▭ *AE, MC, V* ⎟⊙⎟ *BP.*

$$ 🏨 **Lázně III.** Neo-Gothic in style, this spa hotel serves the general public as well as patients of the facility. The rooms are spartan, but classical-music lovers may find it charming, as the Karlovy Vary Symphony Orchestra plays in a concert hall located in the same building.

> **CAUTION** ⚠
>
> The waters from natural springs are loaded with minerals, which means they often have a sulfuric smell and taste—not necessarily the most appetizing thing. You may want to sip it at first as you get used to the flavor.

⊠ *Mlýnské nábřeží 5, 360 01* ☎ *353–223–473* 🖷 *353–225–641* ⊕ *www.lazneiii.cz* ⚓ *16 rooms, 2 suites* ⌂ *Restaurant, café, cable TV, hair salon, bar* ▭ *AE, MC, V* ⎟⊙⎟ *BP.*

$ 🏨 **Hotel Heluan.** A clean, safe bet if you've arrived in town without reservations and don't want to spend your savings on a room. Rooms are starkly furnished—and not nearly as exciting as the stately exterior and public areas. But no matter. The location, right at the center of the main spa area, couldn't be better. ⊠ *Tržíště 41, 360 01* ☎ *353–321–111* 🖷 *353–321–111* ⊕ *www.travelguide.cz/heluan* ⚓ *25 rooms* ⌂ *Restaurant, minibars, cable TV, bar, some pets allowed (fee); no a/c* ▭ *AE, MC, V* ⎟⊙⎟ *BP.*

$ 🏨 **Růže Hotel.** More than adequately comfortable and well-priced given its location smack in the center of the spa district, this is a relatively inexpensive choice if you prefer a full hotel to a pension or private room. ☒ *I. P. Pavlova 1, 360 01* ☎ *353–221–846 or 353–221–853* ☕ *20 rooms* ☖ *Restaurant, cable TV; no a/c* ▭ *AE, V* ℣ *BP.*

Nightlife & the Arts

California Club. There's enough space for you and 249 of your closest friends in this West Coast–theme club. DJs spin "oldies" (which usually means music from the 1970s on up) or disco, depending on the night. The kitchen is open late (until 3:30 AM, except for Sunday, when it closes at 12:30) for hungry night owls. There's no cover, and it's open from 1 PM until 5 AM. ☒ *Tyršova 1753/2* ☎ *353–222–087.*

Calypso. Black leather, marble, and chrome mix with the mirrors set the scene for this disco. Oldies are the house special on Friday from 8 PM until 4 AM; Saturday features pop and disco during similar hours. Snacks are available until midnight. ☒ *Staromlýnská 31* ☎ *608–070–072.*

Club Propaganda. The center of Karlovy Vary's underground music scene, this club is in a former ballroom. It showcases DJs spinning nightly as well as the occasional live rock act. ☒ *Jaltská 7* ☎ *353–233–792.*

Grandhotel Pupp. This upscale funhouse consists of the two nightclubs and the casino of the biggest hotel in town. Gamble the night away within the mirrored walls and under the glass ceiling of the Pupp Casino Club, or settle into a cocktail and some cheesy live crooning at the English-theme Becher's Bar. ☒ *Mírové nám. 2* ☎ *353–109–111.*

Lázně III. If you're looking to get your high-culture fix, the Karlovy Vary Symphony Orchestra plays regularly at this hotel, a spa facility that doubles as an important cultural center for the town. Head to the Antonín Dvořák Music Hall on the first floor of the building to catch the concerts. ☒ *Mlýnské nábř. 5* ☎ *353–225–641.*

Sports & the Outdoors

Nature-lovers and exercise addicts rejoice. Karlovy Vary is a town made for staying active in the outdoors. For example, marked hiking trails snake across the beech-and-pine-covered hills that surround the town on three sides. If you walk past the Grand Hotel Pupp, away from the center, and follow the paved walkway that runs alongside the river for about 10 minutes, you will discover a Japanese garden. A multiday canoeing competition, the Mattoni Canoe Race, is held in the Teplá river in front of the Thermal Hotel every May; it's the largest contest of its kind in the country.

Karlovy Vary's warm, open-air public pool on top of the **Thermal Hotel** (☒ I. P. Pavlova) offers the experience of swimming at a cozy bathtub temperature even in the coolest weather; the view over the town is outstanding. Even if you are not staying at the hotel, you can still take a dip in the waters for 50 Kč per hour. The **Karlovy Vary Golf Club** (☒ Pražská 125 ☎ 353–331–001 ⊕ www.golfresort.cz) is just out of town on the road to Prague; greens fees are 1,650 Kč for 18 holes.

Shopping

A cluster of exclusive stores huddle around the Grandhotel Pupp and back toward town along the river on Stará Louka. Lesser-known, high-quality makers of glass and porcelain can also be found on this street. If you're looking for an inexpensive but nonetheless singular gift from Karlovy Vary, consider a bottle of the bittersweet (and potent) Becherovka, a liqueur produced by the town's own Jan Becher distillery. Another thoughtful gift would be one of the pipe-shape ceramic drinking cups used to take the drinking cure at spas; you can find them at the colonnades. Boxes of tasty *oplatky* (wafers), sometimes covered with chocolate, can be found at shops in all of the spa towns. The challenge is stopping yourself from dipping into the box if you intend to give it as a gift.

For traditional-style porcelain and glass, try **Karlovarský porcelán** (⊠ Tržiště 27 ☎ 353–225–660). **Kolonáda** (⊠ I. P. Pavlova 15) sells boxes of heavenly spa wafers. Looking a bit like flattened-out manhole covers, the hazelnut- or chocolate-filled treats are the perfect confection on a sunny day. The store is generally closed from 12:30 to 1 PM for lunch. To glass enthusiasts, Karlovy Vary is best known as the home of **Moser** (⊠ Tržíště 7 ☎ 353–235–303 ⊕ www.moser.cz), one of the world's leading producers of crystal and decorative glassware. For one-of-a-kind works of glass or porcelain, stop by **Galerie U Dvou Čápú** (⊠ Stará Louka 26 ☎ 353–223–641)

Karlovy Vary Essentials

TRANSPORTATION Frequent bus service between Prague and Karlovy Vary makes the journey only about two hours each way, and the ticket costs about 120 Kč. Avoid the train. The Prague–Karlovy Vary run takes far longer than it should—more than three hours by the shortest route—and costs more than double the price of a bus ticket. If you're driving, you can take the E48 directly from Prague to Karlovy Vary, a drive of about 1 1/2 hours in light traffic.

VISITOR
INFORMATION 🏢 **Karlovy Vary Tourist Information** ⊠ Lázeňská 1 Karlovy Vary ☎ 353–224–097 ⊕ www.karlovyvary.cz.

CHEB

⑪ *42 km (26 mi) southwest of Karlovy Vary; 174 km (105 mi) southwest of Prague.*

Known for centuries by its German name of Eger, the old town of Cheb tickles the German boarder in the far west of the Czech Republic. The town has been a fixture of Bohemia since 1322 (when it was handed over to King Jan, as thanks for his support of a Bavarian prince), but as you walk around the beautiful medieval square, it's hard to remember you're not in Germany. The tall merchants' houses surrounding the main square, with their long, red-tile, sloping roofs dotted with windows like droopy eyelids, are more Germanic in style than anything else in Bohemia. You will also hear a lot of German on the streets from the many day-trippers coming here from across the border.

Germany took possession of the town in 1938 under the terms of the notorious Munich Pact. But following World War II, virtually the entire German population was expelled, and the Czech name of Cheb was officially adopted. During the Cold War, Cheb suffered as a Communist outpost along the heavily fortified border with West Germany.

Now tensions have melted and Cheb is making an obvious economic comeback. The town center merits a few hours of strolling.

The **"Roland" statue** in the middle of the central square, náměstí Krále Jiřího z Poděbrad, is similar to other Roland statues seen throughout Bohemia, attesting to the town's royal privileges. This one represents the town hero, Wastel of Eger. Look carefully at his right foot, and you can see a small man holding a sword and a head—this shows the town had its own judge and executioner.

In the lower part of náměstí Krále Jiřího z Poděbrad stand two rickety-looking groups of timbered medieval buildings, 11 houses in all, divided by a narrow alley. The houses, forming the area known as **Špalíček,** date from the 13th century and were once home to many Jewish merchants. **Židovská ulice** (Jews' Street), running uphill to the left of the Špalíček, served as the actual center of the ghetto. The small unmarked alley running to the left off Židovská—called ulička Zavražděných (Lane of the Murdered) though not signposted—was the scene of an outrageous act of violence in 1350. Pressures had been building for some time between Jews and Christians. Incited by an anti-Semitic bishop, the townspeople finally chased the Jews into the street, closed off both ends, and massacred them. Now only the name attests to the slaughter. ⊠ *Nám. Krále Jiřího z Poděbrad.*

The **Chebské muzeum** (Cheb Museum) in the Pachelbel House was the setting for a Macbeth-like murder during Thirty Years' War. It was in this house that the great general Albrecht von Wallenstein, was murdered in 1634 on the orders of his own emperor, the Hapsburg emperor Ferdinand II, who was provoked by Wallenstein's increasing power and rumors of treason. According to legend, Wallenstein was on his way to the Saxon border to enlist support to fight the Swedes when his own officers barged into his room and stabbed him through the heart with a stave. In his memory, Wallenstein's stark bedroom has been left as it was with its four-poster bed and dark red velvet curtains. (The story also inspired playwright Friedrich Schiller to write the *Wallenstein* trilogy; he planned the work while living at the top of the square at No. 2.) Aside from preserving this scene, the museum is interesting in its own right, with a Wallenstein family picture gallery, a section on the history of Cheb, and a collection of minerals (including one discovered by Goethe). There's also the stuffed remains of Wallenstein's horse, who died in battle. ⊠ *Nám. Krále Jiřího z Poděbrad 4* ☎ *354–400–620* ⊕ *www. muzeumcheb.cz* ✎ *50 Kč* ☯ *Mar.–Dec., Tues.–Sun. 9–noon and 1–5.*

The plain but imposing **Kostel svatého Mikuláše** (Church of St. Nicholas) was begun in 1230, when the church belonged to the Order of the Teutonic Knights. You can still see Romanesque windows on the towers; tinkering throughout the centuries added an impressive Gothic portal and a baroque interior. Just inside the Gothic entrance is a wonderfully faded plaque commemorating the diamond jubilee of Hapsburg emperor Franz Joseph in 1908. ⊠ *Kostelní nám.* ☎ *354–422–458.*

Built with blocks of lava taken from the nearby Komorní Hůrka volcano, **Chebský hrad** (Cheb Castle), stands on a cliff overlooking the Ohře

River up Křižovnická, behind the Church of St. Nicholas. The castle—now a ruin—was built in the late 12th century for Holy Roman Emperor Frederick Barbarossa. Red-brick walls are 17th-century additions. Inside the castle grounds is the carefully restored double-decker **Romanesque chapel**, notable for the many lovely columns with heads carved into their capitals. The rather dark ground floor was used by commoners. A bright, ornate top floor was reserved for the emperor and his family, who entered via a wooden bridge leading to the royal palace. ⊠ *Dobrovského 21* ☎ *354–422–942* ⊕ *www.muzeumcheb.cz* ⊡ *30 Kč* ☽ *Apr. and Oct., Tues.–Sun. 9–4; May and Sept., Tues.–Sun. 9–5; June–Aug., Tues.–Sun. 9–6.*

Where to Eat

¢–$$ ✕ **Kavárna Špalíček.** This is the best choice out of an indistinguishable group of restaurants on and along the square that have sprung up to cater to visiting Germans. It has a nice selection of standard pork and chicken dishes, with the added charm of being in the ancient Špalíček complex. ⊠ *Nám. Krále Jiřího z Poděbrad* ☎ *736–759–409* ▤ *No credit cards.*

Where to Stay

$ ⊡ **Barbarossa.** One block from the main square, this charming family-run hotel is a favorite among visiting Germans, so book ahead, especially on weekends. The clean rooms are simply furnished in modern style. The bathrooms are new. ⊠ *Jateční 7, 350 02* ☎ *354–423–446* ⊕ *www.hotel-barbarossa.cz* ⤳ *15 rooms with bath* ♨ *Restaurant, cable TV, parking (fee), some pets allowed (fee); no a/c* ▤ *AE, MC, V* ❑❘ *BP.*

Cheb Essentials

TRANSPORTATION The journey from Prague to Cheb is about 3½ hours each way, whether you are taking the bus or the train; expect to pay almost twice as much to ride the train. The price for the bus trip is 150 Kč, the price for the train ride 280 Kč. If you're driving, you can take the E50 and then the 21 from Prague to Cheb, a drive of about 2½ hours, though traffic can sometimes be heavy.

VISITOR INFORMATION 🚩 **Tourist Info Cheb** ⊠ Nám. Krále Jiřího z Poděbrad 33, Cheb ☎ 354–440–302 or 354–422–705 ⊕ www.mestocheb.cz.

FRANTIŠKOVY LÁZNĚ

⑫ *6 km (4 mi) north of Cheb; 180 km (109 mi) southwest of Prague.*

Františkovy Lázně, or Franzensbad, is the smallest of the three main Bohemian spas, and truth be told it isn't really in the same league as Karlovy Vary. The main spa area is only a few blocks and aside from a dozen or so cafés to enjoy an apple strudel or ice cream, there isn't much to see or do. That said, the uniform, Kaiser-yellow Empire architecture is adorable. And the gardens surrounding the main spa area—both the manicured "French" gardens and the wilder "English"-style parks—are really lovely and perfect for a simple stroll. Summer is particularly pleasant, when a small orchestra occupies the gazebo in the Městkské sady (city park) and everyone sits in lawn chairs listening.

The healing properties of the waters here were recognized as early as the 15th century, but Františkovy Lázně only came into its own at the start of the 19th century. Like Bohemia's other spas, Františkovy Lázně drew some of the cream of crop of European society, including one Ludwig Van Beethoven, who came here in 1812. But it remained in Cheb's shadow and the spa stayed relatively small. In the years following World War II, the spa declined; most of the buildings were given over to factories and organizations to use as convalescent centers. Františkovy Lázně also developed a reputation for helping women with fertility problems and Milan Kundera used it as the humorous, small-town backdrop for his novel, "The Farewell Party." Since 1989 the town has worked hard to restore the yellow façades to their former glory.

The best way to approach Františkovy Lázně is simply to find **Národní ulice,** the main street, and walk.

Red markers indicate a path from Cheb's main square westward along the river and then north past **Komorní Hůrka.** The extinct volcano is now a tree-covered hill, but excavations on one side have laid bare the rock, and one tunnel remains open. Goethe instigated and took part in the excavations, and you can still—barely—make out a relief of the poet carved into the rock face.

A fascinating peek into spa culture is housed in the small **Lázeňský muzeum** (Spa Museum), just off Národní ulice. There's a wonderful collection of spa-related antiques, including copper bathtubs and a turn-of-the-20th-century exercise bike called a Velotrab. The guest books provide insight into the cosmopolitan world of pre–World War I Central Europe. The book for 1812 contains the entry "Ludwig van Beethoven, composer from Vienna." ⊠ *Ul. Doktora Pohoreckého 8* ☎ *354–542–344* ⊠ *20 Kč* ☉ *Tues.–Fri. 10–5, weekends 10–4; usually closed mid-Dec.–mid-Jan.*

The main spring, **Františkův pramen,** is under a little gazebo filled with brass pipes. The colonnade to the left once displayed a bust of Lenin that was replaced in 1990 by a memorial to the American liberation of the town in April 1945. To the right, in the garden, you'll see a statue of a small cherub, holding a fish. In keeping with the fertility theme, women are encouraged to touch the fish (or whatever other part of the cherub that might help!) to ensure their own fertility. The oval neoclassical temple just beyond the spring (amazingly, *not* painted yellow and white) is the **Glauberova dvorana** (Glauber Pavilion), where several springs bubble up into glass cases. ⊠ *Národní ul.*

Where to Stay & Eat

Most of the establishments in town depend on spa patients, who generally stay for several weeks. Spa treatments usually require a medical check and cost substantially more than the normal room charge. Walk-in treatment can be arranged at some hotels or at the information center. Signs around town advertise massage therapy and other treatments for casual visitors.

$ ✕🖼 **Slovan Hogast.** A cheaper but comfortable alternative to the Tři Lilie hotel, Slovan Hogast has an eccentric, original turn-of-the-20th-century design that survived a renovation in the 1970s. The airy rooms are clean and comfortable, and some have a balcony overlooking the main street. The main-floor restaurant (¢–$$) serves above-average Czech dishes such as *svíčková* (beef sirloin in a citrusy cream sauce) and roast duck. ☒ *Národní 5, 351 01* 🕾 *354–542–841* 🖶 *354–542–843* ⬦ *25 rooms, 19 with bath* ⟐ *Restaurant, café, refrigerators, cable TV, bar, Internet, meeting room, some pets allowed (fee); no a/c* ⊟ *AE, MC, V* ⭘ *BP.*

$$ 🖼 **Tři Lilie.** "Three Lilies," which once accommodated the likes of Goethe

Fodor'sChoice and Metternich, immediately reestablished itself as the most comfort-

★ able spa hotel in town after an expensive renovation in 1995. In the center of the spa quarter, the yellow, three-story building has what many others lack—air-conditioning. Some of the rooms have balconies with French doors. It is thoroughly elegant, from guest rooms to brasserie. ☒ *Národní 3, 351 01* 🕾 *354–208–900* ⬦ *31 rooms* ⟐ *Restaurant, café, cable TV, some pets allowed (fee)* ⊟ *AE, MC, V* ⭘ *BP.*

Františkovy Lázně Essentials

TRANSPORTATION Expect to spend about four hours each way traveling between Prague and Františkovy Lázně via bus or train. As with other destinations, you'll pay almost double for riding the rails. Costs are about 170 Kč one-way for the bus, 300 Kč for the train. Frequent buses run to and from Cheb. If you're driving, you can take the E50 and then the 21 from Prague to Františkovy Lázně, a drive of about three hours.

VISITOR ℹ **Františkovy Lázně Tourist Information** ☒ Tři Lilie Travel Agency, Národní 3,

INFORMATION Františkovy Lázně 🕾 354–201-111 ⊕ www.franzensbad.cz.

MARIÁNSKÉ LÁZNĚ

9

⑬ *30 km (18 mi) southeast of Cheb; 47 km (29 mi) south of Karlovy Vary.*

Once Bohemia's star spa town, Mariánské Lázně now plays second fiddle to Karlovy Vary. While the latter, with its glitzy international film festival and wealthy "New Russian" residents, has succeeded in luring investors, Mariánské Lázně seems to survive largely on the apple-strudel, day-tripping crowd coming over from Germany. Busloads of German retirees arrive daily, discharging their passengers to walk the promenades and repair over ice cream and cake before boarding the coach back home. This trade keeps the properties in business but hardly brings the capital influx needed to overhaul the spa facilities.

The grounds have remained lush and lovely, especially the upper part of the spa area near the Grandhotel Pacifik. Here you'll find the colonnades and fountains and river walks you expect from a once-world-famous spa. And the woods surrounding the town are magnificent. But parts of the spa, especially the lower part of the park grounds, still look scruffy, a legacy of the Communist era, when spas were transformed into sterile hospitals.

It wasn't always this way. A hundred years ago, Mariánské Lázně, or Marienbad as it was known, was one of Europe's finest resorts. It was a favorite of Britain's King Edward VII. Goethe and Chopin also came. Mark Twain, on a visit in 1892, couldn't get over how new everything looked. Twain—who had a natural aversion to anything too healthy— labeled the town a "health factory."

The best way to experience the spa—short of signing up for a week- long treatment—is simply to buy a spouted drinking cup (available at the colonnades) and join the rest of the sippers taking the drinking cure. Be forewarned, though: the waters from the Rudolph, Ambrose, and Caroline springs, though harmless, all have a noticeable diuretic effect. For this reason they're used extensively in treating disorders of the kid- ney and bladder.

Walking trails of varied difficulty levels surround the resort in all direc- tions, and one of the country's best golf courses lies about 3 km (2 mi) to the east of town. Hotel staff can also help arrange activities such as tennis and horseback riding. For the less intrepid, a simple stroll around the gardens, with a few deep inhalations of the town's clean air, is enough to restore a healthy sense of perspective.

For information on spa treatments, inquire at the main **spa offices** (⊠ Masarykova 22 ☎ 354–623–061 ⊕ www.marienbad.cz). Walk-in treatments can be arranged at the **Nové Lázně** (New Spa; ⊠ Reitenberg- erova 53 ☎ 354–644–111).

OFF THE BEATEN PATH

CHODOVÁ PLANÁ – Need a break from the rigorous healthiness of spa life? The Pivovarská restaurace a muzeum ve skále (Brewery Restaurant & Museum in the Rock) is a few miles south of Mariánské Lázně in an underground complex of granite tunnels that have been used to age beer since the 1400s. Generous servings of Czech dishes—including a whole roast suckling pig—can be ordered to accompany the strong, fresh Chodovar beer tapped directly from granite storage vaults. Giant tanks of aging beer and brewing memorabilia can be seen through glass win- dows on the way in. You can tour the brewery, but tours are conducted in German only. The brewery also offer "beer spas," starting at around 550 Kč. A beer-lover's fantasy, clients dip into a 20-minute soak in warm dark "bathing beer," followed by a 20-minute relaxation period. The brewery promises it will cause a mild and gradual rise in heart activity and "scour away any unhealthy substances that may have accumu- lated." ⊠ Pivovarská 107, Chodová Planá ☎ 374–798–122 ⊕ www. chodovar.cz ⊠ Museum free, tour 50 Kč ⊗ Daily 11–11; brewery tours daily at 2.

Where to Eat

$$–$$$ ✗ **Churchill's.** Dark-wood paneling, a serpentine bar, and a mixture of tables and booths give this restaurant a comfy British pub vibe. It's in the same building as the Excelsior hotel but with a separate entrance. Decent steaks, fish, and salads are all available, as are some limited veg- etarian options. ⊠ Hlavní 121 ☎ 354–697–235 ⊟ AE, MC, V.

★ **$$–$$$** ✗ **Koliba.** An excellent alternative to the hotel restaurants in town, Koliba serves grilled meats and shish kebabs, plus tankards of Moravian wine (try the dry, cherry-red Rulandské červené), with traditional gusto. Occasionally fiddlers play rousing Moravian folks tunes. Exposed wooden ceiling beams add to the rustic charm to the inn's 15 rooms that face the surrounding nature preserve. ⊠ *Dusíkova 592* ☎ *354–625–169* ▭ *MC, V.*

¢–$$ ✕ **Filip.** This bustling wine bar is where locals come to find relief from the hordes of tourists. There's a nice selection of traditional Czech dishes—mainly pork, grilled meats, and steaks. ⊠ *Poštovní 96* ☎ *354–626–161* ▭ *No credit cards.*

¢–$$ ✕ **Paradiso.** Fast pasta and pizza dishes are all served with a welcome smile. Keep your pizza simple—ham or just cheese are recommended—or you can end up with a soggy pie. ⊠ *Hlavní 166* ☎ *603–742–292* ▭ *No credit cards.*

Where to Stay

Hotel prices have risen in recent years and many properties are terribly overpriced for what is offered. Bear in mind too that the glorious Empire and neoclassical façades of many of the hotels and spas are rarely reflected in the disappointingly sterile rooms. Read the price list carefully—some of the spas now calculate the price of a room on a per person basis. You can get better deals by booking packages, including spa treatments, in advance from the hotel. Check the hotel's Web site for current offers. Private accommodation can also offer a real savings. The best place to look for a private room is along Paleckého ulice and Hlavní třída, south of the main spa area, or look in the neighboring villages of Zádub and Závišín.

★ $$$ ⊞ **Hotel Nové Lázně.** This neo-Renaissance, multitower hotel and spa—opened in 1896—lines a large part of one side of the park. In the center of the building, a cast-iron sculpture of the donor of health, Hygiea, is carried by the sea god Triton, the son of Neptune, who stands on top, stressing the importance of water in spa treatments. Inside, the complex of Roman baths is decorated with marble, and houses period frescoes. This is a serious spa, aimed at spa package devotees rather than overnight visitors. ⊠ *Reitenbergerova 53, 353 01* ☎ *354–644–111* 🖷 *354–644–044* ⊕ *www.marienbad.cz* ⊃ *97 rooms, 1 suite* ⌂ *Restaurant, café, minibars, cable TV, gym, spa, bar; no a/c in some rooms* ▭ *AE, MC, V* ⊚| *BP.*

$$$ ⊞ **Grandhotel Pacifik.** This regal hotel, at the top of Hlavní street with commanding views of the main spa area, has been thoroughly renovated and now may be the best of the bunch. It has a full range of spa and wellness facilities. The rooms are toned down and tastefully mod-

> ### WORD OF MOUTH
>
> "Here are a couple of examples to give you some some idea of how inexpensive Mariánské Lázně was. We went on a 25-minute horse-drawn carriage ride for less than $15. My wife was in heaven, buying a purse for $60 that she felt would easily have been twice to three times that much back home. Even parking fines were cheap. We got a "boot" locked onto our rental car and were forced to pay the paltry sum of $15 to get it unlocked. $15? I almost laughed at the policeman when he told me how much it was."   –turnip

9

ern in contrast to the over-exuberant balcony-studded, yellow façade. Rooms with a view over the park are worth the extra money. ⊠ *Mírové nám. 84, 353 48* ☎ *354–651–111* 🖷 *354–651–200* ⊕ *www.marienbad. cz* ↘ *95 rooms, 7 suites* ⟋ *Restaurant, coffee shop, minibars, Internet, cable TV, spa* ═ *AE, MC, V* ℠ *BP.*

$$ 🏨 **Centrální Lázně.** Near the colonnade and Ambrose Spring, this eggshell-white spa hotel offers unusual treatments such as magnetotherapy and peat packs. The wooden pavilion of the Mary Spring, used in special "gaseous" therapy, stands opposite the entrance to the courtyard. Patients enter the pavilion and stand in the carbon-dioxide-laden vapors while being supervised by health-care specialists. Judging by the number of seniors sitting around the lobby, it's a favorite with the over-70 set. ⊠ *Goethovo nám. 1, 353 43* ☎ *354–634–111* 🖷 *354–634–200* ⊕ *www. marienbad.cz* ↘ *98 rooms, 1 suite* ⟋ *Restaurant, café, refrigerators, cable TV, hair salon, spa; no a/c in some rooms* ═ *AE, MC, V* ℠ *BP.*

$$ 🏨 **Hotel Bohemia.** As a slightly cheaper alternative to some of the posher places in town, this late-19th-century hotel feels like a throwback. The crystal chandeliers in the lobby and the graciously proportioned rooms— some with a balcony off the front—feel like stepping into the days of Goethe. The plain furnishings, however, recall the days before 1989 when the spas were used as recuperation centers for factory workers. The helpful staff can arrange spa treatments and horseback riding. An annex, Dependence, has added 12 additional suites. ⊠ *Hlavní třída 100, 353 01* ☎ *354–610–111* 🖷 *354–610–555* ⊕ *www.orea.cz/bohemia* ↘ *72 rooms, 4 suites, 12 additional suites in Dependence* ⟋ *Restaurant, café, cable TV, lounge, some pets allowed (fee); no a/c* ═ *AE, MC, V* ℠ *BP.*

$$ 🏨 **Parkhotel Golf.** A room at this stately villa, 3½ km (2 mi) out of town on the road to Karlovy Vary, requires some advanced booking. The large open rooms are cheery and modern. The restaurant on the main floor is excellent, but the main draw is the 18-hole golf course on the premises, one of the best in the Czech Republic, opened in 1905 by King Edward VII. ⊠ *Zádub 580, 350 01* ☎ *354–622–651* 🖷 *354–622–655* ↘ *28 rooms* ⟋ *Restaurants, minibars, cable TV, 18-hole golf course, tennis court, pool, spa, nightclub, Internet, meeting room, parking (fee), some pets allowed (fee); no a/c* ═ *AE, DC, MC, V* ℠ *BP.*

$$ 🏨 **Villa Butterfly.** Decorated with the works of some of the country's top artists, the interior and exterior of this modern, angular art nouveau–style hotel could almost double as a gallery. Female figurines stand on the roof, arms outspread like a butterfly's wings, seemingly about to take flight. Ask for a room in the front, as the view of the forested hills is outstanding. ⊠ *Hlavní třída 655, 353 01* ☎ *354–654–111* 🖷 *354–654–200* ⊕ *www.marienbad.cz* ↘ *88 rooms, 8 suites* ⟋ *2 restaurants, room service, some in-room hot tubs, minibars, cable TV, spa, bar, library, Internet* ═ *AE, MC, V* ℠ *BP.*

$ 🏨 **Koliba.** This is a perfect choice if you're just here for a day or two, puttering around town without an interest in lavish spa treatments. This hunting-style lodge is situated above and behind the main spa area, about a 15-minute walk from town. What makes this place so special are the exceptionally cute, clean, rustic rooms and the over-the-top friendliness of the staff. Some of the best grilled dishes in town are served in the highly

Fodor'sChoice
★

stylized romantic restaurant. ⊠ *Dusíkova 592* ☎ *354–625–169* 📠 *354–626–310* ⊕ *koliba.xercom.cz* ➯ *12 rooms* ♢ *Restaurant, café, minibars, cable TV, some pets allowed (fee); no a/c* ⊟ *AE, DC, MC, V* ⊺◎⌐*BP.*

Nightlife & the Arts

The West Bohemian Symphony Orchestra performs regularly in the New Spa (Nové Lázně). The town's annual Chopin festival each August brings in pianists from around Europe to perform the Polish composer's works.

Casino Lil (⊠ Anglická 336 ☎ 354–623–293) is open daily from 2 PM to 7 AM. For late-night drinks, try the **Parkhotel Golf** (⊠ Zádub 580 ☎ 354–622–651), which has a good nightclub.

Mariánské Lázně Essentials

TRANSPORTATION Regular bus and train service between Prague and Mariánské Lázně makes the journey about three hours each way. Although similar in travel time, the train costs practically twice as much as the bus. Expect to pay 150 Kč one-way for the bus, 250 Kč for the train. If you're driving, you can take the E50 and then the 21 from Prague to Mariánské Lázně, a drive of about two hours.

VISITOR 🚩 **Mariánské Lázně Tourist Information** (Cultural and Information Center) ⊠ Hlavní
INFORMATION 47, Mariánské Lázně ☎ 354–625–892 or 354–622–474 ⊕ www.marianskelazne.cz.

PLZEŇ

⑭ *92 km (55 mi) southwest of Prague.*

Plzeň—or Pilsen in German, as it's better known abroad—is the industrial heart of Western Bohemia and the region's biggest city. But for visitors, the city is known as a beer mecca. Anyone who loves the stuff must pay homage to the enormous Pilsener Urquell brewery, where modern "Pils"-style beer was first developed more than 150 years ago. Brewery tours are available and highly recommended. There's even a brewing museum here for intellectual beer aficionados.

Another item of interest—particularly for Americans—is historical. While most of the Czech Republic was liberated by Soviet troops at the end of World War II, Plzeň was liberated by the U.S. Army, led by General George S. Patton. Under the Communists, this fact was not widely acknowledged. But since 1989 the liberation week celebrations held in May have gotten bigger and bigger each passing year. If you're traveling in the area at this time, it's worth stopping by to take part in the festivities. To this day Plzeň retains a certain "pro-American" feeling that other towns in the Czech Republic lack, and there's even a big statue here emblazoned with an enthusiastic: "Thank You, America!," written in both English and Czech. You'll find it, naturally, at the top of Americká Street near the intersection with Klatovská. You can learn all about the liberation at the new Patton Memorial.

Fodor'sChoice The **Pilsner Urquell Brewery** is a must-see for any beer lover. The first Pil-
★ sner beer was created in 1842 using the excellent Plzeň water, a special malt fermented on the premises, and hops grown in the region around

Žatec. Guided tours of the brewery, complete with a visit to the brewhouse and some beer tastings, are offered daily at 12:30 and 2. The brewery is east of the city near the railway station. ✉ *U Prazdroje 7* ☎ *377–062–888* ⊕ *www.prazdroj.cz* 🖾 *120 Kč* ⊙ *Tours daily at 12:30 and 2.*

NEED A BREAK? If you visit the Pilsner Urquell Brewery, carry on drinking and find some cheap traditional grub at the large **Na Spilce** (✉ U Prazdroje 7) beer hall just inside the brewery gates. The pub is open weekdays and Saturday from 11 AM to 10 PM, Friday from 11 AM to 11 PM, and Sunday from 11 AM to 7 PM.

The **Pivovarské muzeum** (Brewery Museum) is in a late-Gothic malt house, one block northeast of náměstí Republiky. All kinds of fascinating paraphernalia trace the region's brewing history, including the horse-drawn carts used to haul the kegs. ✉ *Veleslavínova 6* ☎ *377–235–574* ⊕ *www.prazdroj.cz* 🖾 *100 Kč* ⊙ *Daily 10–6.*

★ The **Plzeň Historical Underground,** dating from the 13th century, is a web of multilevel tunnels that were used for storing food and producing beer and wine. Many of the labyrinthine passageways are dotted with wells and their accompanying wooden water-pipe systems. Tours last about 40 minutes. ✉ *Perlová 4* ☎ *377–225–214* 🖾 *45 Kč* ⊙ *Apr.–Nov., Wed.–Sun. 9–4; June–Sept., Tues.–Sun. 9–4.*

The **U.S. General George S. Patton Memorial** tells the story, with exhibits and photos, of the liberation of Plzeň from the Nazis by U.S. soldiers on May 6, 1945. As the story goes, Patton wanted to press on from Plzeň to liberate Prague, but was prevented from doing so by an agreement between the U.S. and the Soviet Union that stated Czechoslovakia was to remain under Soviet influence. The museum was dedicated in 2005 on the 60th anniversary of Plzeň's liberation. ✉ *Pobřežní 10* ☎ *377–320–414* ⊕ *www. pattonmemorial.cz* 🖾 *45 Kč* ⊙ *Tues.–Sun. 10–6.*

> **WORD OF MOUTH**
>
> "There are hundreds of shops in Prague selling all kinds of crystal from chandeliers to sherry glasses. We bought some stuff in Prague last year and it was 40% cheaper in Plzeň for exactly the same thing." —Mucky

The city's architectural attractions center on the main **náměstí Republiky** (Republic Square). Dominated by the enormous Gothic **Chrám svatého Bartoloměje** (Church of St. Bartholomew), the square commands an impressive presence being one of the largest in Bohemia. And the church, at 335 feet, is among the tallest in the Czech Republic. Around the square, mixed in with its good selection of stores, are a variety of other architectural jewels, including the town hall, adorned with *sgraffiti* and built in the Renaissance style by Italian architects during the town's heyday in the 16th century. The **Great Synagogue,** which claims to be the second-biggest in Europe, is a few blocks west of the square, just outside the green strip that circles the old town.

Where to Eat

$–$$ ✕ **Dominik Café.** Blue lights, stained-glass cubes, and columns etched with Keith Haring–esque figures make this funky upstairs café an attractive spot to park yourself for pizzas, salads, and some meaty dishes. ✉ *Dominikánská 3* ☎ *377–323–226* ☾ *Closed Sun.*

$–$$ ✕ **Maxim Cafe.** A wraparound bar forms the center of this restaurant with iron candleholders and copies of French artwork on the walls. Italian food and many varieties of chicken are available. If it's cool outside, ask for a table in the heated and covered patio, which is comfortably set in between the café and an adjacent building. ✉ *Martinská 8* ☎ *377–323–076* ⊟ *AE, MC, V.*

$–$$ ✕ **U Mansfeldu.** Fresh Pilsner Urquell and variations on classic Czech dishes draw diners to this Pilsner Urquell–sponsored restaurant. A gleaming copper hood floats above the taps in traditional pub style, and the patio invites visitors to spend the evening sipping cold beer and enjoying treats such as turkey escalope in a potato pastry or roasted goose livers in red wine and almonds. ✉ *Dřevěná 9* ☎ *377–333–844* ⊟ *AE, MC, V* ☾ *Closed Mon.*

¢–$$ ✕ **Continental.** Five minutes on foot from the main square, this late-19th-century restaurant remains a good choice. In its glory days, movie stars like Ingrid Bergman and Marlene Dietrich stayed in this hotel, and the owners are working to recapture that glamour. The restaurant serves dependably satisfying traditional Czech dishes such as onion soup and *svíčková* (beef sirloin in a citrusy cream sauce). ✉ *Zbojnická 8, 305 31* ☎ *377–235–292* ⊟ *AE, DC, MC, V.*

¢–$$ ✕ **El Cid.** Strawberry-infused *mojitos* wash down excellent tapas dishes at this Spanish-style restaurant along the old town walls, just across from the Continental Hotel. Pictures of bullfighters line the yellow walls, while a patio overlooks the sprawling Křižíkovy park. ✉ *Křižíkovy sady 1* ☎ *377–224–595* ⊟ *AE, MC, V.*

¢–$ ✕ **Cafe Bar Praga.** Lots of chrome and black mixed with wood accents create a modern setting for this sleek café. The menu lists some Czech specialities, but judging from the orders coming from the kitchen, the emphasis is on sweets, including rich slices of cake. A lengthy list of juices keeps things light and fresh. ✉ *Rooseveltova 9* ☎ *777–199–142* ⊟ *AE, MC, V.*

¢–$ ✕ **Caffe Fellini.** Right across from St. Bartholomew Church, this dessert spot, with its outdoor patio overlooking the square, is a great place to cool down. Order some ice cream or a piece of cake and take in the front-row views. ✉ *Nám. Republiky* ☎ *377–423–965* ⊟ *No credit cards.*

¢ ✕ **Slunečnice.** The sunny interior here echoes its name, which means sunflower. This vegetarian café is a good place to grab a ready-made sandwich or a cheap buffet meal of rice and fresh vegetables. Vegan products and "bio juices" are also available. ✉ *Jungmannova 4* ☎ *377–236–093* ☾ *Closed weekends.*

Where to Stay

$$ ⌂ **Hotel Central.** Czar Alexander of Russia once stayed here when the hotel was a charming inn known as the Golden Eagle. Now an angular 1960s structure, this hotel is recommendable for its sunny rooms,

9

friendly staff, and great location, right on the main square. Breakfast costs a few koruna extra. ⊠ *Nám. Republiky 33, 301 00* ☎ *377–226–757* 🖷 *377–226–064* ⊕ *www.central-hotel.cz* ⤴ *77 rooms* ⌂ *Restaurant, café, cable TV, bar, Internet, some pets allowed (fee); no a/c* ⊟ *AE, DC, MC, V* ¶⊙¶ *EP.*

\$\$ ⊡ **Hotel Continental.** Large rooms with space for all your bags and double doors that block out sound are features that help this hotel stand out. In addition, the furnishings, which include antique mirrors and armoires, make for historic but comfortable surroundings. A slow but steady renovation is ongoing. ⊠ *Zbrojnická 8, 305 34* ☎ *377–235–292* 🖷 *377–221–746* ⤴ *44 rooms, 3 suites* ⌂ *Restaurant, café, cable TV, bar; no a/c* ⊟ *AE, MC, V* ¶⊙¶ *BP.*

★ **\$\$** ⊡ **Hotel Gondola.** A superb choice, the Gondola is clean and quiet, with superior modern facilities, including air-conditioning—all just a few steps away from the central square. The owners have gone out of their way to make it cozy—the rooms have separate baths and showers and high-speed Internet access. Outside it seems inconspicuous but inside it's a real gem. ⊠ *Pallova 12, 301 37* ☎ *377–994–211* ⊕ *www.hotelgondola. cz* ⤴ *12 rooms* ⌂ *Restaurant, cable TV, in-room broadband, free parking* ⊟ *AE, DC, MC, V* ¶⊙¶ *BP.*

\$ ⊡ **Pension K.** A great choice for the lower-budget traveler, this pension, inside a charming 18th century town house, is in a quiet spot just off the city center. The rooms are basic, but the staff is friendly. ⊠ *Bezručova 13* ☎🖷 *377–329–683* ⤴ *15 rooms* ⌂ *Cable TV; no a/c* ⊟ *AE, MC, V* ¶⊙¶ *BP.*

Nightlife

House of Blues (⊠ Černická 10 ☎ 377–224–294), related to the American chain in name only, showcases live blues and rock acts. Ignore the mirrored disco ball on the ceiling—ashtrays on every table let you know you're in a real joint. **Jazz Rock Cafe** (⊠ Sedláčkova 18 ☎ No phone) gives you a license to party. Drop by on Wednesday to catch some live blues or jazz music.

Klec (⊠ Dřevěná 6 ☎ 602–457–288), with its mottled blue and orange walls and a metal balcony, is a hangout for the teen-to-twentysomething set, with music to match. **Maxim Music Club** (⊠ Martinská 8 ☎ 377–323–076) features different music every night of the week. Call first to check if that evening's performance will be jazz, rock, blues, dance music, or some other genre. Doors open at 6; closing time is around 5 AM. **Zach's pub** (⊠ Palackého nám. ☎ 377–223–176) highlights various live acts, including Latin and blues, outdoors on its summer patio.

Plzeň Essentials

TRANSPORTATION Frequent bus and train service between Prague and Plzeň makes the journey about 1½ hours each way. Bus fares are significantly less than train fares. Expect to pay about 100 Kč for the bus, 150 Kč for the train. If you're driving, you can take the E50 directly to Plzeň, a drive of about one hour.

VISITOR   🚩 **Plzeň City Information Centre** ⊠ Nám. Republiky 41, Plzeň ☎ 378–035–330
INFORMATION   ⊕ www.plzen-city.cz.

Moravia

WORD OF MOUTH

"I always found the district of Moravia to be a really nice area, lots of castles in the hills, and untouched medieval villages and towns."

–philstravels

By Mark Baker
THE CZECH REPUBLIC'S OTHER HALF, Moravia, is frequently overlooked by visitors. No cities here can compare with the noble beauty of Prague, and Moravia's gentle mountains suffer in comparison to the more rugged Tatras in Slovakia just to the east. Yet Moravia's colorful villages and rolling hills do merit a few days of exploration. Come here for the good wine, good folk music, friendly faces, and languid pace.

Despite sharing a common political union for more than 1,000 years with Bohemians, Moravians still consider themselves distinct from "Czechs." (Though it must be said those differences are not always apparent to visitors.) The Moravian dialect of Czech is softer and—as Moravians insist—purer than that spoken in Bohemia. It's hard to generalize, but in a word the Moravians are "earthier" than their Bohemian cousins. They tend to prefer a glass of wine—or even better fiery *slivovice* (plum brandy)—to beer. Folk music, all but gone in Bohemia, is still very much alive in Moravia. And Catholicism is still a part of life here—particularly in cities like Olomouc—in a way that died out long ago in much of Bohemia.

Historically, the three most important Moravian towns have been Brno, Olomouc, and Znojmo, and those three are still impressive today. Brno—a bustling industrial center of about half a million people—has some of the country's best theater, and an impressive stock of Bauhaus and constructivist buildings from the early 20th century. Olomouc—long a bastion of the Austro-Hungarian empire—boasts two enormous central squares, a clock tower, and the country's largest trinity column. Znojmo is one of the chief wine-making centers, and makes for romantic exploration through the region's vineyards.

If your time is limited or you're just passing through, be sure at least to plan a stopover in the town of Telč in the south. Its enormous central square is like the backdrop of a film set.

Numbers in the margin correspond to numbers on the Moravia and Brno maps.

About the Hotels & Restaurants

Compared to Prague, change has been slow to arrive in Moravia after 1990, especially beyond Brno. The good news: food and hotels are priced lower. The bad news: service—particularly finding staff that speak any level of functional English—truly lags behind. You're much more likely to find German-language menus in restaurants and German-speaking staff in both

---

MARK'S TOP 5 MORAVIA PICKS

1. Telč: In a country of town squares this is far and away the most impressive.
2. Villa Tugendhat (Brno): I'm a big fan of early modern architecture, and Brno was far ahead of its time.
3. Olomouc: A trinity column that's so amazing it's under UNESCO protection.
4. Lednice Chateau: A delightful castle, with huge gardens and even a minaret out back!
5. Mikulov's Jewish Quarter: It's exciting to watch the city start to embrace its recent past.

And after that you can always repair to a wine cellar in the hills.

restaurants and hotels. On the plus side, hotel and restaurant workers tend to be friendlier in Moravia and a bit more attentive than they are in Prague.

Don't expect gastronomic delights in Moravia. Choices are limited to ho-hum pork and chicken dishes. In mountainous areas, inquire locally about the possibility of staying in a *chata* (cabin). These are abundant, and they often carry a bit more of the Moravia spirit than the faceless modern hotels. Many lack modern amenities, though, so be prepared to rough it a bit.

	$$$$	$$$	$$	$	¢
WHAT IT COSTS in koruna and euros					
HOTELS in Kč	over 6,500	4,000–6,500	2,200–4,000	1,200–2,200	under 1,200
HOTELS in €	over 230	140–230	80–140	40–80	under 40
RESTAURANTS	over 500	350–500	150–350	100–150	under 100

Hotel prices are for two people in a double room with a private bath and breakfast during peak season (March through October, excluding July and August) and generally include 5% V.A.T. Restaurant prices are per person for a main course at dinner and include 19% V.A.T.

JIHLAVA

❶ *124 km (75 mi) southeast of Prague.*

Rolling highlands mark the border between Bohemia and Moravia, and just off the main highway from Prague to Brno lies the old mining town of Jihlava, a good place to begin an exploration of Moravia. If the silver mines here had just held out a few more years, the townspeople claim, Jihlava could have become a great European city. Still, there are several interesting churches clustered on or around the town's main square.

Rivaled in size only by those in Cologne and Kraków, the town's enormous main square, **Masarykovo náměstí** (Masaryk Square), was one of the largest in Europe during the 13th century. But unfortunately for Jihlava, the mines went bust during the 17th century, and today the square bears witness to the town's formerly oversized ambitions. A few of the town walls and gates are still in place. Occasionally, the old tunnels under the main square are open to the public. At the north end of the square, a column, built in 1690, gives thanks because a plague epidemic bypassed the town. For many years a pillory stood here, and it was the site for executions. Lower down in the square, two elaborate stone fountains, both dedicated to Roman gods, were built in 1797. On the eastern side of the square is the Municipal Hall, which was built in 1425 and renovated in 2004. Some garish buildings from the 1980s that don't fit in with the rest of the historical structures line the square's outer rim.

Up in the northwest corner of the town square, the **Kostel svatého Ignáce** (St. Ignatius Church) holds a rare Gothic crucifix, created during the 13th century for the early Bohemian king Přemysl Otakar II. The church is relatively young for Jihlava. It was built at the end of the 17th century displaying ceiling frescoes, altar, stucco work, and pulpit that are all fine examples of baroque craftsmanship. The church courtyard has an entrance to the town's underground tunnel system, which are open April through December. ⊠ *Masarykovo nám.*

The town's most striking building is the Gothic **Kostel svatého Jakuba** (St. James the Greater Church), east of the main square. With its uneven Gothic towers, its Gothic, baroque interior, and a font dating from 1599—a masterpiece of the Renaissance style—the church offers ornamentation through the ages. Note the baroque Chapel of the Holy Virgin, sandwiched between two late-Gothic chapels, with an oversize 14th-century pietà. The tower, which offers a good view, is occasionally open to the public. ⊠ *Farní ul.* 🎫 *20 Kč* ⊗ *Tower: June and Sept., weekends, 10–1 and 2–6; July and Aug., Tues.–Sun., 10–1 and 2–6.*

Where to Stay & Eat

¢–$ ✕🏨 **Zlatá Hvězda.** A beautiful Renaissance house provides the framework for this reconstructed old hotel centrally located on the main square. In keeping with the building, rooms are comfortable and surprisingly elegant, with wood ceilings and down comforters. You're a short walk from Jihlava's restaurants and shops, though the on-site café (¢–$$$) and wine bar are among the best in town. ⊠ *Masarykovo* *nám. 32, 586 01* ☎ *567–320–782* 🖨 *567–309–496* ⊕ *www.zlatahvezda. cz* ⇆ *17 rooms, 1 apartment* ⟁ *Restaurant, café, cable TV, bar, meeting room, some pets allowed; no a/c* ⊟ *AE, MC, V* ⦿❙ *EP.*

Jihlava Essentials

TRANSPORTATION Visiting Jihlava from Prague is easiest if you drive. By car, take Highway E65, and change to E59 at Exit 112. Jihlava is on the main road. With good traffic, the trip is about an hour.

A bus is usually your next best option to Jihlava. Direct buses to Jihlava leave from the Florenc bus station in Prague and cost around 100 Kč; if you take a direct bus, your travel time to Jihlava will be around 1½ to 2 hours.

Train service fron Prague's main train station, Hlavní nádraži, requires at least one change. Depending on your connection, the trip can take from just under two hours to well over three hours. The price for the trip varies, but it's generally double the amount of bus fare, around 200 Kč.

VISITOR 🖪 **Jihlava Tourist Information** ✉ Masarykovo nám. 19 ☎ 567-167-120 ⊕ www.
INFORMATION jihlava.cz

TŘEBÍČ

➋ *27 km (16 mi) southeast of Jihlava; 35 km (21 mi) east of Telč; 151 km (91 mi) southeast of Prague.*

UNESCO declared the looping streets in the Jewish Quarter and an ornate basilica in Třebíč World Heritage Sites in 2003. The town is first mentioned in 1101, but it was almost completely destroyed in a war in 1468 and then rebuilt. Though known for its historic buildings, Třebíč also has a few modern ones in the art nouveau, cubist, and functionalist styles. Guided tours of the town are available in English from the information center on Karlovo náměstí 53.

★ A spiraling maze of winding streets, the **Židovská čtvrť** (Jewish Quarter) has two synagogues and other buildings formerly used by the town's Jewish community. The **Front Synagogue** on Tiché náměstí is now used for Protestant services. The **Rear Synagogue** (✉ Subakova 44 ☎ 568–823–005) sometimes has concerts or exhibitions, which sometimes cost a small admission. The **Jewish Cemetery** (✉ Hrádek 14 ☎ 568–827–111) has 3,000 tombstones dating from the Renaissance up to the 20th century. It's free to enter. Several houses in the district are intriguing, including a pink Renaissance house with an overhanging second floor at Pokorný 5. A trail of signs in English point out the remarkable spots. Remember your manners—most houses in this area are not museums and people actually live in them. ⊞ *Rear Synagogue 40 Kč, Jewish Cemetery free* ⊙ *Rear Synagogue: June–Sept., weekdays 9–noon and 1–5, weekends 1–5; Oct.–May, weekends 1–5. Jewish Cemetery: May–Sept., daily 8–8; Oct., Mar., and Apr., daily 8–6; Nov. and Feb., daily 9–4.*

The late Romanesque and early Gothic **Bazilika sv. Prokupa** (St. Procopius Basilica) remains true to its original layout from when it was begun in

10

1260. New sections were added up to the 1950s, but the oldest parts are easy to spot. Look for a very heavy style, with lots of stone and few windows. Two baroque towers at the front were added in the early 1700s by architect F. M. Kaňka. One of the oldest sections is the crypt, with Romanesque pillars and arches. The adjoining château displays a collection of Nativity scenes, 250 tobacco pipes, folk art items, and even some mineral samples. ⊠ *Zámek 1* ☎ *777–746–982* 🖃 *Basilica 40 Kč* 🕙 *Apr.–Sept., Tues.–Fri. 8–11:30 and 1–5, weekends 1–5.*

Třebíč Essentials

TRANSPORTATION Ideally, you should combine Třebíč with a visit to Jihlava or Telč. Direct train travel to Třebíč from Jihlava takes around 45 minutes to over an hour and costs around 65 Kč; there's no direct train service to Jihlava from Telč. A direct bus from Jihlava to Třebíč takes about the same amount of time but costs around 40 Kč; from Telč, the bus trip takes less than 45 minutes and costs less than 30 Kč.

Car travel from Telč is direct on Route 23 and takes about 20 minutes. From Jihalva, it's fastest to get back on Highway E50 and go east to Velké Meziříčí. Then go south on Route 360; the trip should take about 30 minutes.

VISITOR   🚺 **Třebíč Tourist information** ⊠ Karlovo nám. 53 ☎ 568-847-070 ⊕ www.
INFORMATION kviztrebic.cz.

TELČ

❸ *30 km (19 mi) south of Jihlava; 154 km (94 mi) southeast of Prague, via Rte. 406*

Don't be fooled by the dusty approach to the little town of Telč or the unpromising, unkempt countryside surrounding the place. Telč is a knockout. It has an even more impressive main square than that of Jihlava, but what strikes the eye most here is not just its size but the unified style of the buildings. On the lowest levels are beautifully vaulted Gothic halls, just above are Renaissance floors and façades, and all the buildings are crowned with rich Renaissance and baroque gables.

Fodor'sChoice **Náměstí Zachariáše z Hradce,** the main square, is so perfect you feel like
★ you've stepped into a painting, not a living town. Zacharias of Neuhaus, the town's namesake, allegedly created the architectural unity. During the 16th century, so the story goes, the wealthy Zacharias had the castle—originally a small fort—rebuilt into a Renaissance château. But the town's dull buildings clashed so badly, Zacharias had the square rebuilt to match the castle's splendor. Luckily for architecture fans, the Neuhaus dynasty died out shortly thereafter, and succeeding nobles had no desire to outfit the town in the latest architectural fashions.

If you've come by car, park outside the main walls on the side south of town and walk through the **Great Gate,** part of the original fortifications dating to the 13th century. As you approach on Palackého ulice, the square unfolds in front of you, laced with the château at the northern end and beautiful houses, bathed in pastel, ice-cream shades. Fans of Renaissance reliefs, note the *sgraffito* corner house at No. 15, etched like fine porcelain. The house at No. 61, across from the Černý Orel Hotel, also bears intricate details.

Credit the Italians for transforming **Statní zámek Telč** (Telč château) from a Gothic castle into a refined Renaissance château. The château, grouped in a complex with the former **Jesuit college** and **Kostel svatého Jakuba** (Church of St. James), was built during the 14th century, perhaps by King John of Luxembourg, the father of Charles IV. Renovation, overseen by Italian masters, took place between 1553 and 1568. In season you can tour the castle and admire the rich Renaissance interiors. Given the reputation of nobles for lively, lengthy banquets, the chastising *sgraffito* relief in the dining room depicting gluttony (in addition to the six other deadly sins) seems odd indeed. Other interesting rooms with *sgraffiti* include the Treasury, the Armory, and the Blue and Gold chambers. A curious counterpoint to all this Renaissance splendor is the castle's permanent exhibit of paintings by leading Czech modernist Jan Zrzavý. There are two tours: the first goes through the Renaissance chambers; the second displays the rooms that were used as recently as 1945. ⊠ *Statní zámek Telč, nám. J. Kypty* ☎ *567-243-943* 🎫 *Tours 140 Kč each, with English printed text; gallery 30 Kč* ☯ *Apr. and Oct., Tues.–Sun. 9–noon and 1–4; May–Sept., Tues.–Sun. 9–noon and 1–5.*

NEED A BREAK? Obey your sweet tooth and indulge in good freshly made cakes or an ice-cream cone at **Cukrárna u Matěje,** a little café and pastry shop at Na baště 2, on the street leading past the château to a small lake.

A tiny street leading off the main square takes you to the 160-foot Romanesque tower of the **Kostel svatého Ducha** (Church of the Holy Spirit), a solid tower finished off in conical gray peaks. This is the oldest standing structure in Telč, dating from the first quarter of the 13th century. The interior, however, is a confused hodgepodge, as the style was fiddled with repeatedly, first in a late-Gothic makeover and then refashioned again because of fire damage. ⊠ *Palackého ul.*

10

Where to Stay & Eat

$ ✕🏨 **Černý Orel.** In a lemon-yellow baroque house on the square, this is a decent older hotel that nevertheless has maintained suitably high standards. The public areas mix architectural details, such as vaulted ceilings with plush, contemporary armchairs, but the basic rooms are inviting and well-balanced. Ask for a room overlooking the square. Even if you don't stay here, take a meal at the very good hotel restaurant ($–$$$$), arguably the best place in town for straightforward beef and pork dishes. ⊠ *Nám. Zachariáše z Hradce 7, 588 56* ☎ *567-243-220* 🖷 *567-243-221* ⊕ *www.hotelcernyorel.cz* ⇆ *30 rooms, 25 with bath* ♤ *Restaurant, cable TV, bar, meeting room, some pets allowed (fee); no a/c* ⊟ *AE, MC, V* ⦿I *BP.*

$ 🏨 **Celerin.** Occupying a tiny corner of the square on the opposite side from the castle, this is the nicest hotel in town. Room No. 5 features some bright, 19th-century period furnishings and a pretty view of the square. The attic rooms are larger, with modern furnishings. ⊠ *Nám.*

Zachariáše z Hradce 1/43, 588 56 ☎ *567–213–580* 🖷 *567–213–581*
🖅 *10 rooms* ⊕ *www.hotelcelerin.cz* ♨ *Restaurant, cable TV, some
pets allowed (fee); no a/c* ⊟ *AE, DC, MC, V* ⊠ *BP.*

Telč Essentials

TRANSPORTATION A car is your best option, and makes it easy to combine a trip to Telč
with a stop en route in Jihlava. From Prague, take Highway E50 and
E59 through Jihlava south to Route 23 and then east. The trip takes
less than two hours without stops.

Direct bus service leaves from Prague's Florenc bus station and takes
just under three hours; the fare is approximately 110 Kč. From Jihlava,
a direct bus can take from 40 to 90 minutes and costs around 40 Kč.

Train service from Prague requires several changes and takes more than
four hours, so it isn't a practical option. It's recommended only for those
who want the scenic route. Train service from Jihlava also requires a
change and takes more than an hour. The cost from Jihlava is less than
60 Kč.

VISITOR
INFORMATION
🖅 **Telč Tourist Information** ⊠ Nám. Zachariáše z Hradce 10 ☎ 567-112-407 ⊕ www.
telc-etc.cz.

ZNOJMO

❺ *229 km (140 mi) southeast of Prague.*

As a border town, Znojmo is enjoying something of a renaissance since
the fall of the Iron Curtain, relishing a renewed day-to-day contact
with Austrians just over the border.

Traditionally, Znojmo has been one of the most important Moravian
towns—alongside Brno and Olomouc. The Přemyslid prince Břetislav
I built a fortress here in the 11th century, and in 1226 Znojmo became
the first Moravian town (ahead of Brno) to receive town rights from
the king.

But when the Iron Curtain sealed off Znojmo from its hinterland to the
south after World War II, it weathered years of deterioration. The beautiful Old Town Hall was destroyed at the end of the war and rebuilt in
a Socialist Realist style that jars with the rest of the square. Factory and
high-rise housing complexes were built around the center and much of
the old-world charm that lingered was spoiled.

Still, things in Znojmo are now on the upswing. The town's riverside
neighborhood is positively funky, with little pensions, pubs, and coffee
shops springing up. Be sure to take a walk through some of the old streets
around the Mikulášské náměstí and toward the river. These new pensions mean Znojmo is now suitable—even recommendable—for an
overnight stay.

Znojmo—along with Mikulov and Valtice—form the center of the country's wine industry. The annual wine harvest festival in September brings
thousands here every year. Be sure to book ahead if you plan to arrive
mid-month. And it may sound odd, but Znojmo is doubly blessed with

excellent beer. The town brewery—Hostan—turns out beer that regularly bests Bohemian brews in competitions. The city is also evolving into an activity center, thanks to Znojmo lying on the main Prague–Vienna bicycle trail. Several bike trails converge on the city and fan out in all directions.

Ideally a small tour of the town would begin with **Masarykovo náměstí** (Masaryk's Square), Znojmo's main square. The square and the adjoining 14th-century town hall are attractive but certainly not what they used to be. The town hall was destroyed in 1945, just before the end of the war, and all that remains of the original structure is the 250-foot Gothic tower you see at the top of the square. From here, follow Zelinářská ulice, which trails from behind the town hall's tower to the southwest in the direction of the river.

The grand, Gothic **Kostel svatého Mikuláše** (Church of St. Nicholas; ⊠ Nám. Mikulášské) dates from 1338, but it's topped off with a 19th-century neo-Gothic tower. If you can get into the church, look for the impressive sacraments house, which was built around 1500 in late-Gothic style. Just behind the Kostel svatého Mikulášle is the curious, tiny, two-story **Kostel svatého Václava** (Church of St. Wenceslas; ⊠ Nám. Mikulášské), built at the end of the 15th century. The upper level of this diminutive white church is dedicated to St. Anne, the lower level to St. Martin. Along the medieval ramparts that separate the town from the river stands the original 11th-century **Rotunda svaté Kateřiny** (St. Catherine's Rotunda; ⊠ Hradní), surprisingly still in good condition. Step inside to see a rare cycle of restored frescoes from 1134 depicting various members of the early Přemyslid dynasty. The path to visit the rotunda starts just beside the Hostan brewery.

Where to Stay & Eat

Two claims to fame have endeared Znjmo to the hearts (and palates) of Czechs and Moravians everywhere. The first is the Znojmo gherkin, first cultivated in the 16th century. You can find this tasty stuff in restaurants all over the country. Just look for the *Znojmo* prefix—as in *Znojemský guláš*, a tasty stew spiced with pickles. Znojmo's other culinary contribution is wine. As the center of the Moravian wine industry, this is the perfect spot to pick up a few bottles of your favorite grape. The best designations to look for, in addition to Znojmo, are Mikulov and Valtice. Some of the best varieties of grapes are Rulandské and Vavřinecké (for red) and Ryzlink and Müller Thurgau (for white).

★ $ ✕⊞ **Pension Jesuitská.** Leading a new breed of pensions in town with modern, tastefully furnished rooms tucked away in traditional burghers' houses, this hotel is one of the best. Placed along a pedestrian street just off the main Horní náměstí, the hotel also holds a restaurant (¢–$$) with excellent Moravian cooking and a good selection of local wines. ⊠ *Jesuitská 5, 669 02* ☎ *515–221–440* 🖷 *515–224–496* ⊕ *www.jesuitska. cz* ↩ *8 rooms* ⌂ *Restaurant, wine bar, free parking; no a/c* 🖃 *AE, MC, V* ⏐◯⏐ *BP.*

$ ⊞ **Penzion Kaplanka.** A child-friendly, family-run pension tucked away in a historic 15-century house, Kaplanka has an excellent view of the river valley and beyond. Kids will adore the little swimming pool in the backyard surrounded by a garden. There's a picnic and barbecue area in the back to relax around on a warm summer evening. The rooms themselves are plain, but clean and comfortable for a short stay. ⊠ *U Branky 485, 669 02* ☏ *775–552–212* ⊕ *www.kaplanka.cz* ⟲ *10 rooms* ⌂ *Cable TV, some pets allowed, pool, picnic area* ⊟ *No credit cards* �� *BP.*

OFF THE BEATEN PATH

❹

A profoundly striking and colorful castle in Moravia lies just a half-hour's drive or bus ride to the west of Znojmo. For nearly 1,000 years **CHÂTEAU VRANOV NAD DYJÍ** (Vranov Château) – marked out the border between Bohemia and Austria. But staring up at the enormous structure from the road below, you can't help but think it's a motley collection of architectural styles. In the foreground, the solemn Renaissance tower rises over some Gothic fortifications. On the left is a golden baroque church, and there's a beautiful pink-and-white dome to the back. Peel your eyes off the castle's mongrel exterior and tour its mostly baroque (and more harmonious) interior. The most impressive room is certainly the 43-foot-high elliptical Hall of Ancestors, the work of the Viennese master Johann Bernhard Fischer von Erlach (builder of the Clam-Gallas Palace in Prague and the Hofburg in Vienna). ⊠ *Zámecka ul. 93, Vranov* ☏ *515–296–215* ⯇ *Château 65 Kč, château with English-language text 150 Kč, church 30 Kč* ⊘ *Castle Apr. and Oct., weekends 9–4; May, June, and Sept., Tues.–Sun. 9–5; July and Aug., Tues.–Sun. 9–6. Church June, weekends 9–5; July and Aug., Sun.–Tues. 9–6; other times by arrangement.*

Znojmo Essentials

TRANSPORTATION Znojmo, along the main route to Vienna, is easily reached by car from Prague or Brno. Take Highway E50 southeast from Prague, then turn south on Highway E59 near Jihlava. The trip is just under 200 km (120 mi) and takes about two hours. From Brno, the trip is about 70 km on Highway E461 and Highway 53 and takes under an hour.

Direct buses leave from Prague's Florenc bus station for the 210-km (126-mi) trip, which takes at least three hours; the cost is about 150 Kč. From Brno, the 67-km (40-mi) trip by direct bus takes 1 hour and 15 minutes and costs around 60 Kč.

Train travel requires a change in Brno and at least one more change. From Brno, the trip takes about two hours and costs around 120 Kč.

VISITOR INFORMATION 🖪 **Znojmo Tourist information** ⊠ Obroková 10 ☏ 515–222–552 ⊕ www.znojmocity.cz.

MIKULOV

❻ *54 km (34 mi) east of Znojmo; 283 km (174 mi) southeast of Prague.*

In many ways, Mikulov is the quintessential Moravian town, with pastel pink-and-yellow buildings and green rolling hills. For centuries it was one of the most important towns in the region—the seat of the Lichtenstein family in the late Middle Ages and then later the home to the powerful Dietrichstein family. The castle's size and splendor demonstrate

Mikulov's onetime crucial position astride the traditional border between Moravia and Austria.

But Mikulov began an extended decline in the 19th century when the main railroad line from Vienna bypassed the town in favor of Břeclav. Historically, Mikulov was the center of Moravia's Jewish community, growing to a population of several thousand at one point, but many Jews left to seek their fortunes in bigger cities. The 20th century was especially cruel to Mikulov. The Nazis Aryanized many of the industries and deported remaining Jews. After the war, many local industries—including the all-important wineries— were nationalized. Mikulov stagnated as a lonely outpost at the edge of the Iron Curtain.

Recent years have seen a slow revival. Much of the wine industry is back in private hands and standards are rising. Day-trippers from Austria have spurred development of a nascent tourist industry. And after many decades of decline, the old Jewish Quarter is getting overdue attention. Although the Jewish community is still tiny—numbering just a handful of people—work is underway to try to preserve some of the remaining houses in the quarter. You can tour the quarter; where many of the houses are now marked with plaques explaining their significance. The Jewish cemetery is one of the largest in Central Europe and a must-see if you're passing through.

Grape-harvesting time in October provides an ideal moment to visit and enjoy the local pastoral delights. Head for one of the many private *sklípeks* (wine cellars) built into the hills surrounding the town. The tradition in these parts is simply to knock on the door; more often than not, you'll be invited in by the owner to taste a recent vintage. If you visit in early September, try to hit Mikulov's renowned wine-harvest festival, which is celebrated with traditional music, folk dancing, and much guzzling of local Riesling.

10

The arresting **Mikulov zámek** (Mikulov Château) looms over the tiny main square and surrounding area. Built as the Gothic-era residence of the noble Liechtenstein family in the 13th century, the château later served as the residence of the powerful Dietrichsteins. Napoléon Bonaparte also stayed here in 1805 while negotiating peace terms with the Austrians after winning the Battle of Austerlitz (Austerlitz is now known as Slavkov, near Brno). Sixty-one years later, Bismarck used the castle to sign a peace treaty with Austria. The castle's darkest days came at the end of World War II, when retreating Nazi SS units set fire to it. Much of what you see today—though it looks deceptively ancient—is relatively new, having been rebuilt after World War II. The château holds the **Regionální Muzeum** (Regional Museum), exhibiting period furniture and local wine-making items, including a remarkable wine cask made in 1643, with a capacity of more than 22,000 gallons. ⊠ *Zámek 5* ☎ *519–510–255* ▦ *60 Kč* ☉ *May–Sept., Tues.–Sun. 8–6; Apr., weekends 9–4.*

Little of Mikulov's once-thriving Jewish Quarter, *Židovská čtvrt'*, has survived. The community once numbered several thousand people, and the town was the seat of the chief rabbi of Moravia from the 17th to the 19th centuries. Several respected Talmudic scholars, including Rabbis Jehuda Loew and David Oppenheimer, lived and taught here. What's left can be seen on a stroll down Husova ulice, which was once the center of the quarter. An information board near the corner with Brněnská ulice explains the significance of the community and what happened to it. The most important building still standing is the 16th-century **Altschul** (Upper Synagogue). ⊠ *Husova 11* ☉ *May–Sept., Tues.–Sun. 1–5.*

Fodor's Choice
★
Mikulov's massive and moving **Jewish Cemetery** is not far from Husova ulice, just off Brněnská. The cemetery gate is usually locked, but the key may be borrowed from the Efram Gallery at Husova 4. Out of respect for Jewish customs, the key is not given out on Saturday. ⊠ *Off Brněnská ul.*

Where to Stay & Eat

★ ¢–$ ✕▦ **Rohatý Krokodýl.** Prim and nicely renovated, this hotel sits in the middle of the former Jewish quarter, on Husova ulice. The doubles are on the small side, but the suites, which cost just a little more, are quite roomy. Facilities are the best in Mikulov, particularly the ground-floor restaurant ($–$$), which serves a typical but delicately prepared selection of traditional Moravian dishes. ⊠ *Husova ul. 8, 692 01* ☎ *519–510–692* 🖷 *519–511–695* ⊕ *www.rohatykrokodyl.cz* ⇆ *14 rooms* ⚭ *Restaurant, cable TV, pub, some pets allowed (fee); no a/c* ➡ *AE, MC, V* ◯*| BP.*

Mikulov Essentials

TRANSPORTATION
Mikulov is best combined with a trip to Brno. Direct bus service from Brno's Zvonařka bus station to Mikulov, a 50-km (30-mi) trip, takes under an hour and costs less than 50 Kč.

Train service from Brno requires a change, usually at Břeclav. It takes a little more than an hour and costs quite a bit more than bus fare at 170 Kč.

By car, the trip is south of Brno on Highway E65 to Břeclav and then east on Route 40. The trip takes a little over 30 minutes.

VISITOR
INFORMATION
🚹 **Mikulov Tourist Information** ⊠ Nám. 1, Mikulov ☎ 625–510–855 ⊕ www. mikulov.cz.

VALTICE

❼ *13 km (8 mi) east of Mikulov mi) southeast of Prague.*

Palaces, obelisks, colonnades, and other exotic structures are dotted throughout Valtice and the nearby town of Lednice that collectively form a UNESCO World Heritage Site Bestowed on the region by the Liechtenstein family in the 18th and 19th centuries, they transformed the entire area into a massive manmade park. Admittedly, it looks a little forlorn these days. The communists did not take kindly to the whimsical fantasies of the nobility, and filled the empty spaces with now-dilapidated public housing and collective farms. Since 1989, though, the region's fortunes have improved. The palaces are getting cleaned up, new pensions and restaurants have opened, and the towns are vigorously promoting their position at the center of the Moravian wine industry. The local tourist offices can advise on the best places to sample wines, or trek out for hiking and biking. The main Prague–Vienna bike trail crosses through the area, and excellent trails lead in all directions. Valtice is a compact little town wholly dominated by the captivating **Valtice zámek** (Valtice Château), just off the main street. The palais was built for the Liechtenstein family by a group of leading baroque architects, among them Fischer von Erlach. Painted ceilings, ornate woodwork, and some 365 windows provide flair for the opulent home. You can tour more than a dozen rooms, the chapel, and a picture gallery. The massive gardens out back are open to the public without having to pay a fee. ⊠ *Zámek 1* ☎ *519–352–423* 💷 *70 Kč, guided tour in German (occasionally in English) 140 Kč* ☉ *Apr., Sept., and Oct., Tues.–Sun. 9–4; May–Aug., Tues.–Sun. 8–5.*

Fodor'sChoice
★

Just 7 km (4 mi) northeast of Valnice is the **Château Lednice na Moravé,** a must-see if you happen to be in the area. The dining room alone, with resplendent blue-and-green silk wall coverings embossed with the Moravian eagle, makes the visit memorable. The grounds, not to be outdone by the sumptuous interior, has a 200-foot-tall minaret and a massive greenhouse filled with exotic flora. The absolute splendor of the palais and gardens contrasts sharply with the workaday reality of Lednice. ⊠ *Lednice* ☎ *519–340–128* 💷 *Tours 80 Kč–100 Kč, minaret 15 Kč* ☉ *Apr. and Oct., Tues.–Sun. 9–4; May–Sept., Tues.–Sun. 9–6.*

Where to Stay & Eat

★ **$–$$** ✕ **Keltkská Restaurace Avalon.** A lovely neighborhood spot on a small street that runs off the right-hand side of the main square. Keltkská means "Celtic," but don't ask us why. Most of the main courses run to the usual steaks, pork, and chicken dishes, albeit done with more care and flavor than the usual joint. The real draws here are the tiny garden on a warm night and the in-house tearoom on a chilly evening. ⊠ *Příční 46* ☎ *519–352–252* 🍴 *No credit cards.*

¢ 🏨 **Hotel Hubertus.** A rare treat for the Czech Republic—you can actually spend the night in a wing of the Valtice palace. Room rates are inexpensive for the location, so don't expect palatial interiors that match the setting—but that said, the proprietors have tried to make the rooms inviting, with high ceilings and fresh flowers. ⊠ *Zámek 1, 691 42* ☎ *519–352–537* 🖷 *519–352–538* ⊕ *www.hotelhubertus.cz* 🛏 *29 rooms, 22 with bath* ⚒ *Restaurant, bar, meeting room, some pets allowed; no a/c, no TV in some rooms* 🍴 *AE, MC, V* ❑ *BP.*

Valtice Essentials

TRANSPORTATION   Lednice and Valtice are less than 10 km (6 mi) apart. You'll find frequent bus service between the main square of Lednice and the Besední dům of Valtice, a 17-minute ride, for around 12 Kč.

By car, Valtice is 12 km (7 mi) southeast of Mikulov via Route 40. The trip takes around 15 minutes. Valtice is also reachable by car from Brno

10

via Highway E65 southeast to Břeclav, which you switch to Route 40 and continue west for about 15 km (9 mi). The trip is about an hour.

Direct bus service from Brno's Zvonařka bus station to Lednice is a 77-km (46-mi) trip that takes 90 minutes and costs about 65 Kč; from there, you take the local bus to Valtice.

VISITOR
INFORMATION 🏠 **Valtice Tourist Information** ⊠ Nám. Svobody 4, Valtice ☎ 519-352-978 ⊕ www. radnice-valtice.cz.

Lednice Tourist Information ⊠ Zámecké nám. 68, Lednice ☎ 517-340-986.

BRNO

202 km (122 mi) southeast of Prague via Hwy. E65

Nicknamed the "Manchester of Moravia," Brno (pronounced *burr*-no) has a different feel from other Czech or Moravian cities. Beginning with a textile industry imported from Germany, Holland, and Belgium, Brno became a leading industrial center of the Austro-Hungarian empire during the 18th and 19th centuries. Some visitors search in vain for an extensive old town, pining for the traditional arcaded storefronts that typify other historic Czech towns. But instead you'll see fine examples of the Empire and neo-Renaissance styles, their formal, geometric façades more in keeping with the conservative tastes of the 19th-century middle class.

In the 1920s and '30s, the city became home to some of the best young architects working in the early-modern, Bauhaus, and "international" styles. Experimentation wasn't restricted to architecture. Leoš Janáček, an important composer of the early-modern period, lived and worked in Brno, as did Austrian novelist Robert Musil. That artistic support continues today, and the city is considered to have some of the best theater and performing arts in the country, as well as a small but thriving café scene.

Avoid Brno at trade-fair time (the biggest are in early spring and early autumn), when hotel and restaurant facilities are strained. If the hotels are booked, the tourist information center at the town hall will help you find a room.

Numbers in the text correspond to numbers in the margin and on the Brno map.

Exploring Brno

▌ A GOOD
WALK

Begin the walking tour at the triangular **náměstí Svobody** ⑧ in the heart of the commercial district, which lends itself an Austrian vibe. Then walk up Masarykova ulice toward the train station and make a right through the small arcade at No. 6 to see the animated Gothic portal of the **Stará radnice** ⑨. Return to Masarykova ulice and walk a little farther until you see the large open-air cabbage market, **Zelný trh** ⑩, down a small side street to your right. On the far side of the market, dominating the square, stands the severe Renaissance Dietrichsteinský palác at No. 8—

now home to the Moravian Regional Museum. Enter a little gate to the left of the palace and walk into the garden, where stairs lead down to the baroque church **Kostel Nalezení svatého Kříže** ⑪.

Towering above the church and market is the **Chrám svatých Petra a Pavla** ⑫, the Cathedral of Saints Peter and Paul, a fixture of the Brno skyline. The best way to get to it is to return to Zelný trh (via the little street off Kapucínské náměstí), make a left, and walk up narrow Petrská ulice, which begins just to the right of the Dietrichsteinský palác. Before leaving the church area, stroll around the pretty park and grounds.

Return to the juncture of Petrská and Biskupská and follow Biskupská to Starobrněnská ulice. Turn left until you reach the busy Husova třída. Continue the tour by turning right along Husova and then left down the calmer residential street of Pellicova. Brno's unique beauty is captured in neighborhoods such as this one, with its attractive houses, each in a different architectural style. Many houses incorporate stark, geometric elements of the early-modern period (1920s and 1930s).

Begin the ascent to the **Hrad Špilberk** ⑬ from here. There's no direct path to the castle; just follow your instincts (or a detailed map) upward, and you can get there. After taking in the view from the top, and possibly a stop at the castle museum, stroll back down one of the windy paths to Husova třída and have a look in two of the Czech Republic's finest museums: the **Uměleckoprůmyslové muzeum** ⑭ and, a block farther down Husova, Brno's modern-art museum, the **Pražákův palác** ⑮. For old art culled from Moravian churches and estates, make sure to pay a visit to the **Místodržitelský palác** ⑯. It's also worth it to find a way to Ludwig Mies van der Rohe's **Villa Tugendhat** ⑰, one of the city's best-known works of modern architecture. The house is a bit off the beaten track, so you will need to travel there by car, taxi, or tram. **Muzeum Romské kultury** ⑱ is about halfway between the historical sights of the city center and Villa Tugendhat, accessible by the same tram lines as Villa Tugendhat.

TIMING A walking tour of Brno takes two to three hours strolling at a leisurely pace. Allow a couple of hours to fully explore the Špilberk Castle. Museum enthusiasts could easily spend a half-day or more browsing through the city's many collections. Brno is relatively busy on weekdays, surprisingly slow on weekends.

WORD OF MOUTH

"Here's a quick thought or two about driving in the Czech Republic. The roads are NARROW! The Czech drivers are both very courteous and absolute maniacs. They have an arrangement that if you want to pass on a two-lane road, the person in front of you slides over to the right as much as they can and oncoming traffic slides to their right. . . . [But] the roads themselves were in good condition and there was plenty of well-marked signage to help you find your way around. If you can drive in the US of A you shouldn't have any real problems driving in the Czech Republic."   –turnip

10

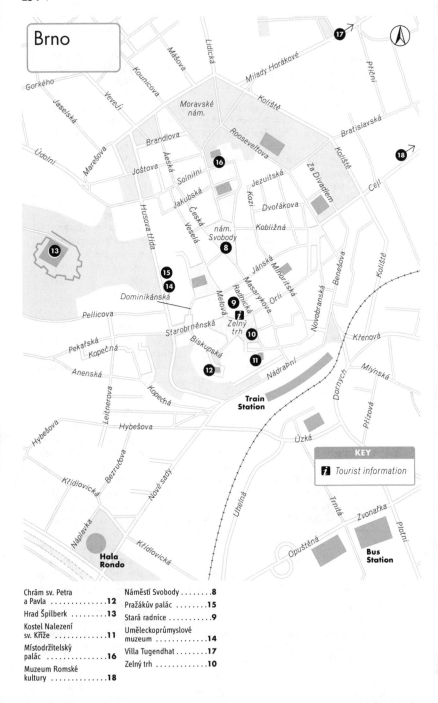

Brno

KEY

🛈 *Tourist information*

Train Station

Bus Station

Hala Rondo

What to See

⑫ Chrám svatých Petra a Pavla (Cathedral of Saints Peter and Paul). Best admired from a distance, the silhouette of slim neo-Gothic twin spires—added in the 20th century—give the cathedral a touch of Gothic dignity. Up close, the interior is light and tasteful but hardly mind-blowing. This is the church pictured on the face of the 10-Kč coin. ☒ *Petrov, at Petrská ul.* 🖼 *Free* ☉ *Daily dawn–dusk; closed during services.*

★ **⑪ Kostel Nalezení svatého Kříže** (Church of the Holy Cross). If you've ever wondered what a mummy looks like without its bandages, this church will hold the answer. Formerly part of the Capuchin Monastery, the Church of the Holy

---

SAVED BY THE BELL

During the Thirty Years' War, Brno faced a fierce attack by Swedish troops. Brno's resistance had been determined, and the Swedish commander decided if the town couldn't be taken by noon the next day, they would give up the fight. Word of this reached the cathedral's bell ringer, and just as the Swedish troops were preparing their final assault, they rang the noon bells—an hour early. The ruse worked, and the Swedes decamped. The cathedral bells proved to be the final defensive strategy that saved the town from being taken.

Cross combines a baroque form with a rather stark façade. Enter the *krypta* (crypt) in the basement and the mummified remains of some 200 nobles and monks from the late 17th and 18th centuries are displayed, ingeniously preserved by a natural system of air circulating through vents and chimneys. The best-known mummy is Colonel František Trenck, commander of the brutal Pandour regiment of the Austrian army, who, at least in legend, spent several years in the dungeons of Špilberk Castle before finding his final rest here in 1749. Experts have concluded that his head is real, contrary to stories of its removal by a thief. A note of caution about the crypt: the graphic displays can be frightening to children (and even some adults), so ask at the admission desk for a small brochure (20 Kč) with pictures that preview what's to come. ☒ *Kapucínské nám. 5* 🖼 *542–213–232* ⊕ *www.volny.cz/kapucini.brno* 🖼 *40 Kč* ☉ *May–Sept., Mon.–Sat. 9–11:45 and 2–4:30, Sun. 11–11:45 and 2–4:30; Oct.–mid-Dec. and mid-Jan.–Apr., Tues.–Sat. 9–11:45 and 2–4:30, Sun. 11–11:45 and 2–4:30.*

⑯ Místodržitelský palác (Governor's Palace). Moravia's strong artistic ties to Austria can be seen in the impressive collection of Gothic, baroque, and 19th-century painting and sculpture found in this splendid palace. Particularly interesting are Austrian painter Franz Anton Maulbertsch's ethereal rococo pageants. ☒ *Moravské nám. 1A* 🖼 *542–321–100* ⊕ *www.moravska-galerie.cz* 🖼 *40 Kč* ☉ *Apr.–Sept., Wed. and Fri.–Sun. 10–6, Thurs. 10–7; Oct.–Mar., Wed. and Fri.–Sun. 10–5, Thurs. 10–6.*

⑱ Muzeum Romské kultury (Museum of Romani Culture). A small but singular museum devoted to the culture of the Roma, as Gypsies prefer to be called, is halfway from Brno's historical center to the Villa Tugendhat. To bridge crosscultural understanding, as Roma people are often the victims of discrimination, this museum was dedicated to their culture and history. Exhibits deal with traditional occupations, dress, and

10

lifestyles. A study room has documents and photographs. ✉ *Bratislavská 67* ☎ *545–571–798* ⊕ *www.rommuz.cz* 🎫 *40 Kč* 🕐 *Tues.–Fri. 10–6.*

❽ Náměstí Svobody (Freedom Square). The best place to start any walking tour, this is the focal point of the city and a centerpiece for the massive effort to modernize the area. The square underwent extensive renovation in 2006 and adjoining streets feature some of the city's best shopping. Anyone who has been to Vienna might experience déjà vu here, as many of the buildings were designed by 19th-century Austrian architects. Especially noteworthy is the stolid Klein Palace at No. 15, built by Theophil Hansen and Ludwig Foerster, both prominent for their work on Vienna's Ringstrasse.

⑮ Pražákův palác (Pražák Palace). The largest collection of modern and contemporary Czech art outside of Prague lines the walls of this handsome, 19th-century neo-Renaissance building. If you've already seen these same artists represented in Prague's major galleries, you may be tempted to adopt a been-there-done-that attitude. But the emphasis here is on Moravian artists, who tended to prefer rural themes—their avant-garde concoctions have a certain folksy flavor. ✉ *Husova 18* ☎ *542–215–758* ⊕ *www.moravska-galerie.cz* 🎫 *40 Kč* 🕐 *Apr.–Sept., Wed. and Fri.–Sun. 10–6, Thurs. 10–7; Oct.–Mar., Wed. and Fri.–Sun. 10–5, Thurs. 10–6.*

★ ⑬ Hrad Špilberk (Spielberg Castle). Once among the most feared places in the Hapsburg Empire, this fortress-cum-prison still broods over Brno behind menacing walls. The castle's advantageous location brought the early lords of the city, who moved here during the 13th century from neighboring Petrov Hill. Successive rulers gradually converted the old castle into a virtually impregnable fortress. Indeed, it successfully withstood the onslaughts of Hussites, Swedes, and Prussians over the centuries; only Napoléon, in 1809, succeeded in occupying the fortress. But the castle's fame comes from its gruesome history as a prison for enemies of the Austro-Hungarian monarchy and, later for the Nazis' prisoners during World War II. Although tales of torture during the Austrian period are probably untrue (judicial torture had been prohibited prior to the first prisoners' arrival in 1784), conditions for the hardest offenders were hellish: they were shackled day and night in dank, dark catacombs and fed only bread and water. The castle complex is large, and the various parts generally require separate admissions. The **casemates** (passages within the walls of the castle) have been turned into an exhibition of the late-18th-century prison and their Nazi-era use as an air-raid shelter. You can see the entire castle grounds as well as the surrounding area from the **observation tower.** Above ground, a **museum** in the fortress starts off with more displays on the prison era with detailed English texts. Included in the tour of the museum is an exhibition on the history of Brno, including several panoramic paintings showing the city in the 17th century, and photos showing then-and-now views of 19th- and 20th-century redevelopment in the Old Town. One of the best of the permanent exhibitions, in room No. 5, focuses on the city's modern architectural heritage. You'll find room after room of sketches, drawings, and photographs of the most important buildings built in the

1920s and '30s. Unfortunately, most of the descriptions are in Czech, but if you speak the language, you'll be in heaven. ⊠ *Špilberk 1* ☎ *542–123–611* 🖂 *Casemates 30 Kč, museum 100 Kč; Casemates, tower, and exhibitions, 120 Kč* ☉ *Casemates and tower May, June, and Sept., Tues.–Sun. 9–6; July and Aug., daily 9–6; Oct.–Apr., Tues.–Sun. 9–5. Museum Apr.–Sept., Tues.–Sun. 9–6; Oct.–Mar., Wed.–Sun. 10–5.*

NEED A BREAK? After climbing to the Špilberk Castle and touring several museums, what could be better than a nice cold beer? The **Stopkova pivnice** (⊠ Česká 5) will set you up with one. If you're hungry, try the house goulash, a tangy mixture of sausage, beef, rice, egg, and dumpling.

❾ Stará radnice (Old Town Hall). The oldest secular building in Brno exhibits an important Gothic portal. This door is the work of Anton Pilgram, architect of Vienna's St. Stephen's Cathedral. It was completed in 1510, but the building itself is about 200 years older. Look above the door to see a badly bent pinnacle that looks as if it wilted in the afternoon sun. This isn't the work of vandals but was apparently done by Pilgram himself out of revenge against the town. According to legend, Pilgram had been promised an excellent commission for his portal, but when he finished, the mayor and city councillors reneged on their offer. Pilgram was so angered by the duplicity that he purposely bent the pinnacle and left it poised, fittingly, over the statue of justice.

Just inside the door are the remains of two other famous Brno legends, the **Brno Dragon** and the **wagon wheel.** The dragon—actually an alligator—apparently turned up at the town walls one day in the 17th century and began eating children and livestock. As the story goes, a gatekeeper came up with the idea of stuffing a freshly slaughtered goat with limestone. The dragon devoured the goat, swallowing the limestone as well, and when it drank at a nearby river, the water mixed with the limestone and burst the dragon's stomach (the scars on the preserved dragon's stomach are still clearly visible). The story of the wagon wheel, on the other hand, concerns a bet placed some 400 years ago that a young wheelwright, Jiří Birek, couldn't chop down a tree, form the wood into a wheel, and roll it from his home at Lednice (53 km [33 mi] away) to the town walls of Brno—all between sunup and sundown. The wheel stands as a lasting tribute to his achievement. (The townspeople, however, became convinced that Jiří had enlisted the help of the devil to win the bet, so they stopped frequenting his workshop; poor Jiří died penniless.)

No longer the seat of the town government, the Old Town Hall holds exhibitions and performances, and the town's tourist information office. To find out what's on, ask in the information center just inside Pilgram's portal. The view from the top of the tower is one of the best in Brno, but the climb (five flights) is strenuous. ⊠ *Radnická 8* ⊕ *www.kultura-brno.cz* 🖂 *Tower 20 Kč* ☉ *Apr.–Sept., daily 9–5.*

★ ⑭ Uměleckoprůmyslové muzeum (Museum of Applied Arts). Arts and crafts shine in this museum, which is without a doubt the Czech Republic's best.

It has an assemblage of artifacts far more extensive than the truncated collection in Prague's museum of the same name. The collection includes Gothic, art nouveau, and Secessionist pieces, as well as an excellent, comprehensive overview of Bohemian and Moravian glass. Keep an eye out for the elegant furniture from Josef Hoffmann's Wiener Werkstätte (Vienna Workshop). Milan Knížák's jagged, candy-color table provides a striking example of contemporary work. ⊠ *Husova 14* ☎ *532–169–111* ⊕ *www.moravska-galerie.cz* ✉ *40 Kč* ☺ *Tues.–Sun. 9–5.*

⑰ Villa Tugendhat. Designed by Ludwig Mies van der Rohe and completed
Fodor'sChoice in 1930, this austere, white Bauhaus villa counts among the most im-
★ portant works of the modern period and is now a UNESCO World Heritage Site. Function and the use of geometric forms are emphasized. The Tugendhat family fled before the Nazis, and their original furnishings vanished. Replicas of Mies's cool, functional designs have been installed in the downstairs living area. Some of the original exotic wood paneling and an eye-stopping onyx screen remain in place. The best way to get there is to take a taxi or Tram 3, 5, or 11 to the Dětská nemocnice stop and then walk up unmarked Černopolní ulice for 10 minutes or so; you'll be able to see the modernist structure up on the hill. Advance reservations for tours are highly recommended. The building is undergoing a long-term renovation, and is occasionally closed to the public. ⊠ *Černopolní 45* ☎ *545–212–118* ⊕ *www.tugendhat-villa.cz* ✉ *120 Kč* ☺ *Wed.–Sun. 10–6; last tour starts at 5.*

⑩ Zelný trh (Cabbage Market). Only in this Cabbage Market could Brno begin to look like a typical Czech town—not just for the many stands from which farmers still sell vegetables but also for the flamboyant **Parnassus Fountain** that adorns its center. This baroque outburst (inspiring a love-it-or-hate-it reaction) couldn't be more out of place amid the formal elegance of most of the buildings on the square. But when Johann Bernhard Fischer von Erlach created the fountain in the late 17th century, it was important for a striving town like Brno to display its understanding of the classics and of ancient Greece. Therefore Hercules slays a three-headed dragon, while Amphitrite awaits the arrival of her lover—all incongruously surrounded by farmers hawking turnips and onions. What could be more Czech?

OFF THE
BEATEN
PATH

MORAVSKÝ KRUMLOV – Admirers of art nouveau master Alfons Mucha may find themselves drawn 50 km (30 mi) off the main highway linking Mikulov and Brno. This town château is the unlikely home of one of Mucha's most celebrated works, his 20-canvas *Slav Epic*, which tells the story of the emergence of the Slav nation. The enormous work was not well received when it was completed in 1928; painters at the time were more interested in imitating modern movements and considered Mucha's representational art to be old-fashioned. The city of Prague owns the paintings and has from time to time said it was going to relocate them, but so far no concrete action has been taken. A music festival takes place here in June. ⊠ *Zámecká 1* ☎ *515–322–789* ☺ *Apr.–June, Sept., and Oct., Tues.–Sun. 9–4; July and Aug., Tues.–Sun. 9–5* ✉ *50 Kč.*

Where to Stay & Eat

$$–$$$$ ✕ **U Královny Elišky.** With rooms named "The Musketeer" and "The Napoléon" and a menu full of wild game and fish, this 14th-century wine cellar turned restaurant remains true to its historic roots. In summer the historic ambience gets kicked up a notch as the garden becomes an arena for fencers in historical dress crossing swords, while spectators enjoy roast suckling pig or lamb. The adjacent pension (¢) offers eight reasonably comfortable rooms at a good price (rates double during major trade fairs, however). ⊠ *Mendlovo nám. 1A, 603 00* ☎ *543–212–578 restaurant, 543–216–898 pension* ⊟ *No credit cards* ⊙ *Restaurant closed Sun. and Mon. No lunch.*

$–$$ ✕ **Restaurace Špalíček.** This homey pub with a terrific central location right on the edge of the Zelný trh (Cabbage Market). The menu features the standard roast pork and dumplings kind of thing, but in a comfortable and merry setting. On a warm evening in summer sit outside and bask in the view on the square. ⊠ *Zelný trh 12* ☎ *542–211–5526* ⊟ *No credit cards.*

$–$$ ✕ **Taj.** Ethnic food in Brno is rarely attempted. This Indian eatery hidden upstairs in a Victorian house creates a nice atmosphere and delicious samosas. Once you cross the tiny bridge over a man-made indoor stream, you can sit in the Indian-theme main room and choose from the vegetarian or meat dishes. Some dishes can be prepared on a lava grill, which is brought out to your table. Lunch specials are a real value. ⊠ *Běhounská 12/14* ☎ *542–214–372* ⊟ *AE, DC, MC, V.*

¢–$ ✕ **Zemanova kavárna.** A contemporary re-creation of a landmark 1920s coffeehouse (the original was razed by the Communists to make way for a theater), this spot is high on flapper style. Everything from the light fixtures to the furniture was faithfully copied from the original interior. The lofty ceilings provide pleasant, lilting acoustics, and the food isn't bad either: the few main courses are Czech with a dash of French, such as pepper steak with fries. ⊠ *Jezuitská 6, between Za Divadlem and Koliště* ☎ *542–217–509* ⊟ *DC, MC, V.*

$$–$$$ ▨ **Grandhotel Brno.** If you are traveling to Brno by train, this hotel makes a fine choice, being just across the street from the station. The hotel dates from 1870, but got a thorough facelift in the late 1980s making it both comfortable and convenient. High standards are maintained through the hotel's association with an Austrian chain. Service is attentive; the rooms, though small, are well-appointed, with coffered ceilings and leather sofas. Ask for a room at the back, facing the town and away from the station. ⊠ *Benešova 18/20, 657 83* ☎ *542–518–138* 🖷 *542–210–345* ⊕ *www.grandhotelbrno.cz* ⤺ *116 rooms* ᗧ *3 restaurants, minibars, cable TV with movies, gym, sauna, casino, nightclub, Internet, meeting rooms, some pets allowed (fee); no a/c* ⊟ *AE, DC, MC, V* ⎔ *BP.*

$$–$$$ ▨ **Royal Ricc.** Lovingly restored from a baroque town house, this boutique hotel retains period details, like exposed-beam ceilings. Some of the rooms even have functional stoves made with tiles. The location is central, just a short stroll up from the Zelný trh (Cabbage Market). ⊠ *Starobrněnská 10, 602 00* ☎ *542–219–262* 🖷 *542–219–265* ⊕ *www.*

FodorsChoice
★

10

romantichotels.cz 🖈 *30 rooms* ⚭ *Restaurant, in-room safes, minibars, cable TV, Internet* 🖃 *AE, DC, MC, V* ⎮O⎮ *BP.*

$$ 🖭 **Slavia.** The century-old Slavia, just off the main Česká ulice, feels a little dated, but the prices here are lower than at the comparable Grand Hotel and the location is excellent. The rooms are spacious and clean. Ask to see a few before choosing since they are not uniform. The café, with adjacent terrace, is a good place to enjoy a cool drink on a warm afternoon. 🖂 *Solniční 15/17, 622 16* ☏ *542–321–249* 🖷 *542–211–769* ⊕ *www.slaviabrno.cz* 🖈 *81 rooms* ⚭ *Restaurant, café, in-room safes, minibars, cable TV, some pets allowed, no-smoking rooms; no a/c* 🖃 *AE, DC, MC, V* ⎮O⎮ *BP.*

★ **$** 🖭 **Hotel Pegas.** A little inn with a reasonable price and central location, Pegas has plain rooms that are snug and clean, with wood paneling and down comforters. The staff is helpful, friendly, and even speaks English. An in-house microbrewery and restaurant will have beer-lovers doing their sightseeing at the bottom of a tasty mug of lager. 🖂 *Jakubská 4, 602 00* ☏ *542–210–104* 🖷 *542–211–232* ⊕ *www.hotelpegas.cz* 🖈 *14 rooms* ⚭ *Restaurant, minibars, pub, some pets allowed; no a/c* 🖃 *DC, MC, V* ⎮O⎮ *BP.*

Nightlife & the Arts

Brno is renowned throughout the Czech Republic for its theater and performing arts. Jacket-and-tie cultural events take place at a few main venues, both slightly northwest of the center of town, a five-minute walk from náměstí Svobody. Check the schedules at the theaters or pick up a copy of *Do města/Downtown,* Brno's free fortnightly bulletin of cultural events.

In Brno you can buy tickets for performing arts productions at individual theater box offices or at the central **Předprodej vstupenek** (Ticket office 🖂 Běhounská 17).

One of the country's best-known fringe theater companies, **Divadlo Husa na provázku** (Goose on a String Theater; 🖂 Zelný třída 9, at Petrská ulice ☏ 542–211–630), has its home in Brno. Opera and ballet productions are held at the modern **Janáček Theater** (🖂 Rooseveltova 7 ☏ 542–158–252). The **Mahen Theater** (🖂 Rooseveltova 1 ☏ 542–158–252) is the city's principal venue for dramatic theater.

A few blocks north of the city center, **Klub Alterna** (🖂 Kounicova 48 ☏ 541–212–091) hosts good Czech jazz and folk performers.

Shopping

Bright red, orange, and yellow flower patterns are the signature folk pottery look in Moravia. You can find these products in stores and hotel gift shops throughout the region. For sophisticated artwork, including paintings and photography, stop by **Ambrosiana** (🖂 Jezuitská 11 ☏ 542–214–439). For rare books, art monographs, old prints, and a great selection of avant-garde 1920s periodicals, stop by **Antikvariát Alfa** (🖂 Jánská 11, in arcade ☏ 542–211–947). English-language paperbacks and art books are sold at **Knihkupectví Jiří Šedivý** (🖂 Masarykova

6 ☎ 542–215–456). **S: Lukas** (✉ Kapucínské nám. 5 ☎ 542–221–358) stocks handmade textiles, ceramics, and glass.

Brno Essentials

If you've arrived at Brno's main train station and are stuck for a room, try the accommodations service on the far left of the main hall, nominally open around the clock.

TRANSPORTATION TO BRNO — Bus connections from Prague's Florenc terminal to Brno are frequent, and the trip is a half-hour shorter than the train route. Most buses arrive at the main bus station, a 10-minute walk from the train station. Some buses stop next to the train station. Buses also run between Brno and Vienna's Wien-Mitte station, stopping at Mikulov. Departures leave Brno for Vienna at 7:30 AM daily and at 5:30 PM every day except Tuesday.

Brno—within easy driving distance of Prague, Bratislava, and Vienna—is 196 km (122 mi) from Prague and 121 km (75 mi) from Bratislava. The E65 highway links all three cities.

Comfortable EuroCity or InterCity trains run six times daily, making the three-hour run from Prague to Brno's station. They depart either from Prague's main station, Hlavní nádraží, or the suburban nádraží Holešovice. Trains leaving Prague for Bratislava, Budapest, and Vienna normally stop in Brno (check timetables to be sure).
🚆 **Hlavní nádraží** ✉ Nádraží 1 ☎ 542–214–803 ⊕ www.idos.cz. **Main bus station** (ÚAN Zvonařka) ✉ Zvonařka 1 ☎ 543–217–733.

TRANSPORTATION AROUND BRNO — Trams are the best way to get around the city. Tickets cost 8 Kč–24 Kč, depending on the time and zones traveled, and are available at newsstands, yellow ticket machines, or from the driver. Single-day, three-day, and other long-term tickets are available. Most trams stop in front of the main station (Hlavní nádraží). Buses to the city periphery and nearby sights such as Moravský Kras in northern Moravia congregate at the main bus station, a 10-minute walk behind the train station. To find it, simply go to the train station and follow the signs to ČSAD.

The nominal taxi fare is about 22 Kč per km (½ mi). There are taxi stands at the main train station, Výstaviště exhibition grounds, and on Joštova Street at the north end of the Old Town. Brush up on your Czech—dispatchers usually don't understand English.

TRAVEL AGENCIES — 🚆 **Čedok** ✉ Nádraží 10/12 ☎ 542–321–267.

VISITOR INFORMATION — 🚆 **Brno Tourist Information** ✉ Radnická 8, Old Town Hall ☎ 542–423–960 ⊕ www.ticbrno.cz ✉ Nádraží 8, across from train station ☎ 542–211–090.

SLAVKOV U BRNA

⑲ *20 km (12 mi) east of Brno; 216 km (134 mi) southeast of Prague.*

One of the great battles of European history unfolded here, where the armies of Napoléon met and defeated the combined forces of Austrian emperor Franz II and Czar Alexander I in 1805. If the name doesn't ring a bell, that's because Slavkov is better known as Austerlitz. Dig out your copy of *War and Peace.* You'll find no better account. Scattered about the rolling agricultural landscapes between Slavkov and Brno are a number of battle monuments linked by walking paths. Napoléon directed his army from Žuráň Hill, above a small town called Šlapanice (which can be reached from Brno by train or bus). Several miles southeast of Šlapanice an impressive memorial to the fallen of all three nations, the Mohyla míru (Cairn of Peace), crowns a hill above the village of Prace. Alongside the cairn is a small museum devoted to the battle. Several days of events commemorate the battle every year around December 2.

★ Memorabilia about the battle of Austerlitz is exhibited in the **Historické muzeum** (History Museum); it's well worth visiting, particularly if you're interested in European history. The building itself is rather plain as a baroque château and is less impressive than the displays on the Three Emperors, the gardens, or the battlefield itself. ⊠ *Palackého nám. 126* ☎ *544–221–685* ⊕ *www.zamek-slavkov.cz* ✉ *60 Kč* ⊙ *Apr., Oct., and Nov., Tues.–Sun. 9–4; May and Sept., Tues.–Sun. 9–5; June, daily 9–5; July and Aug., daily 9–6; Dec.–Feb. by appointment.*

Slavkov u Brna Essentials

TRANSPORTATION Slavkov u Brna is best visited as a side trip from Brno. By car, the trip is 22 km (13 mi) via Highway E50 and takes about 15 minutes.

Direct trains leave from Brno several times a day for the 27-km (16-mi) trip that takes 25 minutes and costs around 40 Kč.

Direct bus service leaves from Brno's Zvonařka bus station for a 22-km (13 mi) trip, which takes 30 minutes and costs around 25 Kč.

KROMĚŘÍŽ

⑳ *70 km (42 mi) east of Brno, 40 km (24 mi) south of Olomouc; 296 km (182 mi) southeast of Prague.*

Kroměříž Château. The former summer palace of archbishops of Olomoucone, this is one of Moravia's UNESCO World Heritage Sites. Although the building dates back to 1260, the current romantic and neoclassical look comes from a 1752 renovation. In keeping with its use as a summer palace, weapons and hunting trophies make up part of the objects on display. Most of the objects come from one hunt when Russian Czar Alexander III came in 1885 and met with Austrian Emperor Franz Josef. The library hall has thousands of rare books plus a lovely allegorical ceiling fresco. But even more opulent is the Assembly Hall, which housed Austria's parliament in 1848, and has another ceiling fresco and several chandeliers. A masterpiece by Titian in the painting gallery is the cherry on top of this decorative confection. The château is also renowned for its two gardens. The Podzámecká Garden is a fairly wild park with a river flowing through it. The Libosad, the more famous of the two, is about a kilometer from the château; it's a mathematically plotted flower garden with rotunda in the middle and statue-filled colonnade on the side. ⊠ *Směnovní nám. 1* ☎ *573–502–011* ⊕ *www. azz.cz* ✉ *Tours: Historical halls 90 Kč, 180 with English explanation;*

art gallery 50 Kč; sala terrena 20 Kč. Tower: 40 Kč. Podzámecká Garden free ☉ *Apr. and Oct., weekends 9–5; May, June, Sept., Tues.–Sun. 9–5; July and Aug., Tues.–Sun. 9–6.*

Kroměříž Essentials

TRANSPORTATION It's best to combine a trip to Kroměříž with Brno or Olomouc; it's somewhat closer to Olomouc.

By car from Brno follow the signs in the direction of Olomouc. Kroměříž is east on Highway E462 to Vyškov, where you turn onto Route 41. The trip is about 70 km (45 mi) and takes about an hour.

Direct bus service from Brno's Zvonařka bus station takes 1¼ hours and costs around 55 Kč. Direct bus service from Olomouc's main bus station takes between 60 and 90 minutes and costs around 40 Kč.

Train service from Brno is inconvenient and expensive, requiring at least one change, usually at Kojetín; the trip takes almost two hours and costs around 100 Kč. Train service from Olomouc's main station requires at least one change, usually at Hulín, and takes at least 1¼ hours; the 45-km (27-mi) trip costs around 65 Kč.

MORAVSKÝ KRAS

☾ **21** *30 km (19 mi) north of Brno; 226 km (141 mi) southeast of Prague.*

If all these regimented baroque palaces leave you feeling out of touch with nature, take a short trip north from Brno up the Svitava Valley and into the Moravský Kras (Moravian Karst), an area of limestone formations, underground stalactite caves, rivers, and tunnels. The most interesting part of the karst is in the vicinity of Blansko and includes several caves. You can arrange tours 8 km (5 mi) from the outskirts of Blansko at the Skalní Mlýn Hotel or the Moravian Karst information office.

Kateřinská jeskyně (Catherine Cave; Skalní mlýn) is set amid thickly forested ravines. Visitors taking the half-hour tour are serenaded by recorded opera tunes. ⊠ *Skalní mlýn* ☎ *516–413–575* ⊕ *www.cavemk. cz* ⊠ *40 Kč* ☉ *Apr.–Sept., daily 8–4; Mar. and Oct., daily 8–2; hrs vary depending on number of visitors.*

Fodor'sChoice The most interesting of the Moravian caves is **Punkevní jeskyně** (Punkva
★ Cave), reminiscent of the mythical River Styx. A tour includes a boat trip along an underground river to the watery bottom of **Macocha Abyss,** the deepest drop of the karst (more than 400 feet). On this tour, a little motorized "train" links the Skalní Mlýn Hotel to the Punkva Cave, from where a funicular climbs to the lip of Macocha Abyss. Punkva Cave is normally open year-round, but check with the information service for up-to-date information. Remember to arrive at least an hour before scheduled closing time in order to be sure to catch the day's last tour. ⊠ *Skalní mlýn* ☎ *516–413–575* ⊕ *www.cavemk.cz* ⊠ *Cave 100 Kč, funicular 50 Kč* ☉ *Punkva Cave Apr.–Sept., daily 8–3:30; Oct.–Mar., daily 8–2. Funicular Apr.–Sept., daily 8–5; Oct.–Mar., hrs vary depending on number of visitors.*

Moravský Kras Essentials

TRANSPORTATION   The caves are accessible from Blansko, which is just north of Brno. Direct train service from Brno's main train station leaves several times a day for the 22-km (13-mi) trip that takes 30 minutes and costs around 35 Kč.

Bus service requires a change at Lipůvka and takes 1 hour and 10 minutes for a 32-km (19-mi) trip that costs 22 Kč. The caves are a 5-km (3-mi) hike outside of Blansko.

By car, take Highway E461 north of Brno to Route 379, and then go east, just past Blansko. The trip is about 25 km (15 mi) and takes less than a half hour.

Under or above ground, the walking is excellent in the karst, and if you miss one of the few buses running between the town of Blansko and the cave region, you may have to hoof it. Try to obtain a map in Brno or from the Moravian Karst information office in the settlement of Skalní Mlýn. Look for Čertův most (Devil's Bridge), a natural bridge high over the road just past the entrance to Catherine Cave. You can follow the path, indicated with yellow markers, from the cave for another couple of miles to the Macocha Abyss. Before setting out, check with the information office or at the bus station for current bus schedules; for much of the year the last bus from Skalní Mlýn back to Blansko leaves at around 3 PM.

OLOMOUC

★ *77 km (48 mi) northeast of Brno; 275 km (165 mi) east of Prague.*

Olomouc (pronounced OH-LOH-MOATS) is a handsome district capital, with some beautifully restored baroque houses along its broad central squares and the country's largest trinity column—another UNESCO World Heritage Site. Its laid-back, small-town feel, compared with bustling Brno, and the presence of a charming, inexpensive pension right in town make it an easy choice for an overnight stay.

Olomouc owes its relative prosperity to its loyalty to the Austro-Hungarian empire. In the revolutionary days of the mid-19th century, when the rising middle classes throughout the empire were asserting their independence from the nobility, the residents of Olomouc remained true to the ruling Hapsburgs. During the revolutions of 1848, the royal family even fled here from Vienna for protection. Mozart, Mahler, and other famous composers stopped by on occasion, leaving behind a musical heritage that is still alive today with an active classical music scene.

The most prominent open space in Olomouc is the triangular Horní náměstí (Upper Square). Four of the city's half-dozen renowned **baroque fountains,** depicting Hercules (1687), Caesar (1724), Neptune (1695), and Jupiter (1707), dot the square and the adjacent other large square, Dolní náměstí (Lower Square) to the south.

A discount card called the **Olomouc card** is valid for most tourist sites in and around the city and is available for 160 Kč for 48 hours. Admission to the Town Hall tower, botanical gardens, zoo, Hrad Bouzov, Hrad

Šternberk, and other sites is included. The card also provides discounts at some restaurants, pools, fitness centers, and hotels. You can buy the card—and get more information on discounts and deals—at the main tourist information center at Horní náměstí 1.

Fodor'sChoice
★
The eccentric **Morový sloup** (Trinity Column), in the northwest corner of Horní náměstí, is one of the best surviving examples of the Olomouc baroque style, which was prevalent in this region of Moravia after the Thirty Years' War in the 17th century. At 35 meters, it's the tallest column devoted to victims of the plague in the Czech Republic. The column alone (not the rest of the square) is a UNESCO World Heritage Site. Its construction began in 1717, but it was not completed until 1754, long after the death of its principal designer, Václav Render, who left all his wealth to the city of Olomouc so that the column could be finished. Inside is a small chapel that, unfortunately, is never open. ⊠ *Horní nám.*

Olomouc's central square is marked by the bright, spire-bedecked Renaissance **Radnice** (Town Hall) with its 220-foot tower. The tower was constructed in the late 14th century. The Astronomical Clock on the outside was built in 1422 and once rivaled the one in Prague. It was mostly destroyed by an artillery shell on the last two days of World War II. The modern Socialist-Realist mosaic decorations of the current clock date from 1955. Be sure to look inside the town hall at the beautiful stairway. You can also visit a large Gothic banquet room in the main building, with scenes from the city's history, and a late-Gothic chapel. Tours of the tower and chapel are given several times daily; contact the tourist office in the town hall. ⊠ *Horní nám.* ☎ *585–513–385 tourist office* 🎫 *Tours 20 Kč* ☉ *Mar.–Oct., daily 9–7; Nov.–Feb., daily 9–5.*

NEED A BREAK?
Wooden paneling and floral upholstery in the **Café Mahler** (⊠ Horní nám. 11) recall the taste of the 1880s, when Gustav Mahler briefly lived around the corner while working as a conductor at the theater on the other side of the Upper Square. It's a good spot for ice cream, cake, or coffee, or simply to sit back and take in the lovely square.

10

The original **Chrám svatého Mořice** (Church of St. Maurice) stood just north of the Horní náměstí in 1257, but nothing is left of that structure. A new church was started in 1412 on the same site and remodelled many times. Its current fierce, gray exterior dates from the middle of the 16th century. A sculpture of Christ on the Mount of Olives dates to the 15th century. The baroque organ inside, the largest in the Czech Republic, originally contained 2,311 pipes until it was expanded in the 1960s to more than 10,000 pipes. An international organ festival takes place in the church every September. ⊠ *Jana Opletalova ul.* ☉ *Hrs are sporadic, but church is often open during day.*

The interior of triple-dome **Kostel svatého Michala** (St. Michael's Church) casts a dramatic spell. The frescoes, the high and airy central dome, and the shades of rose, beige, and gray trompe-l'oeil marble on walls and arches work in concert to present a harmonious whole. The decoration followed a fire in 1709, only 30 years after the original construction.

The architect and builder are not known, but it's surmised they are the same team that put up the Church of the Annunciation on Svatý Kopeček (Holy Hill), a popular Catholic pilgrimage site just outside Olomouc. ⊠ *Žerotínovo nám., one block uphill from Horní nám., along Školní ul.* ⊙ *Hrs are sporadic, but church is often open during day.*

Between the main square and the **Dóm svatého Václava** (Cathedral of St. Wenceslas) lies a peaceful neighborhood given over to huge buildings, mostly belonging either to the university or the archbishop. The church itself is impressive, but its Gothic appearance comes only from a 19th-century makeover. ⊠ *Václavské nám.* ⊙ *Daily 9–6.*

★ Next to the Cathedral of St. Wenceslas is the small entrance to the **Palác Přemyslovců** (Přemyslid Palace), which houses a museum where you can see early-16th-century wall paintings decorating the Gothic cloisters and, upstairs, a wonderful series of two- and three-arch Romanesque windows. This part of the building was used as a schoolroom some 700 years ago, and you can still make out drawings of animals engraved on the walls by young vandals. ⊠ *Václavské nám.* 🎫 *40 Kč* ⊙ *Apr.–Oct., Tues.–Sun. 9–12:30 and 1–5.*

At the **Děkanství** (Deacon's House) in 1767, the young musical prodigy Wolfgang Amadeus Mozart, age 11, spent six weeks recovering from a mild attack of chicken pox. The 16-year-old King Wenceslas III suffered a much worse fate here in 1306, when he was murdered, putting an end to the Přemyslid dynasty. These two unusual claims to fame, build the mystery of this house, but sadly, it isn't open to the public. ⊠ *Václavské nám.*

OFF THE BEATEN PATH

★ **HRAD BOUZOV** (Bouzov Castle) – One of Moravia's most impressive castles—30 km (18 mi) west of Olomouc—has been featured in several fairy-tale films. Its present romanticized exterior comes from a remodeling at the turn of the 20th century, but the basic structure dates back to the 1300s. Owned by the Order of Teutonic Knights from the late 1600s up to the end of World War II, it was later confiscated by the state. Inside, the knights' hall has extensive carved-wood decorations and wall paintings that look old, even if many are reconstructions. Other rooms have collections of period furniture. The castle kitchen, which was used up to 1945, is one of the best preserved examples. Four tours are available, with the grand tour offering most of the highlights. The supplementary tour (doplňková trasa) includes a secret passage. You can easily arrange a tour from the tourist information office in Olomouc; the castle is included in the Olomouc card. ⊠ *Bouzov 8, Bouzov* 🕿 *585–346–201* 🎫 *Classic tour 100 Kč, grand tour 140 Kč* ⊙ *Apr. and Oct., weekends 9–3; May–Sept., Tues.–Sun. 9–4.*

Where to Stay & Eat

$–$$$ ✕ **Moravská restaurace a vinarná.** Traditional Moravian dishes like roast duck with cabbage, chicken breast stuffed with almond butter, or roast piglet are served in a rustic interior. The wine cellar, open weekdays, is a bit homier than the street-level restaurant. The staff wears folk costumes, and live musicians sometimes perform folk music of the region. International wines are available alongside a large selection of Moravian wine. ⊠ *Horní nám. 23* ☎ *585–222–868* ⊟ *AE, MC, V.*

$–$$ ✗ **Hanácká Hospoda.** Offering a lower-key, cheaper dining alternative to the Moravská, this popular local pub serves staples like pork, chicken, and duck, but nicely turned out. A quieter, no-smoking room is available at the back. According to an inscription on the outside of the house Mozart stayed here as a young boy on a trip with his parents. ⊠ *Dolní nám. 38* ☎ *585–237–186* ⊟ *No credit cards.*

$ ▦ **Flora.** The words "traditional Communist-era hotel" don't evoke comfort, but this one was made much more inviting by a thorough makeover of the lobby and public areas. The rooms are small but clean, and the price is reasonable. It's a 15-minute walk from the main square. ⊠ *Krapkova 34, 779 00* ☎ *585–422–200* 🖷 *585–421–211* ⊕ *www.hotel-flora.cz* 🛏 *140 rooms, 4 suites* 🍴 *Restaurant, cable TV, some pets allowed (fee); no a/c* ⊟ *AE, DC, MC, V* ¶⊙¶ *BP.*

★ $ ▦ **U Dómu.** Each of the rooms in this quiet, family-run pension just off Vaclavské náměstí sleeps up to four and has a small kitchenette. Modern furnishings are somewhat dull, but the cleanliness of the rooms and the friendliness of the staff makes up for it. It's an excellent value. ⊠ *Dómská 4, 772 00* ☎ *585–220–502* 🖷 *585–220–501* 🛏 *6 rooms* 🍴 *Kitchenettes, cable TV; no a/c* ⊟ *AE, MC, V* ¶⊙¶ *BP.*

Olomouc Essentials

TRANSPORTATION Olomouc lies about an hour by car or train from Brno. The drive is quick and comfortable mostly along a four-lane highway. Follow the signs to Olomouc on the D1 highway.

Traveling from Prague, in addition to driving, you can take either a train or a bus. By car, follow the D1 motorway south to Brno and then follow the signs and turnoffs to Olomouc from Brno. The trip will take about three hours in moderate traffic.

Direct train travel from Prague takes at least 3¼ hours and costs around 300 Kč for the 250-km (150-mi) trip.

Direct bus service from Prague's Florenc bus station takes between four and five hours and costs around 170 Kč for the 262-km (157-mi) trip. Bus service with a change in Brno can be faster, however, at 3½ hours; the 300-km (180-mi) trip costs about 280 Kč.

VISITOR 🚩 **Olomouc Tourist Information** ⊠ Radnice, Horní nám., Olomouc ☎ 585–513–385
INFORMATION ⊕ www.olomouc-tourism.cz.

10

UNDERSTANDING PRAGUE

PRAGUE AT A GLANCE

Fast Facts

Nicknames: City of a Hundred Spires, the Golden City, Paris of the Twenties in the Nineties, the Heart of Europe
Type of government: Democratic self-governed municipality with 57 districts, each with elected bodies and administrative offices and a municipal assembly, with 70 members elected according to a system of proportional representation. Members of the Assembly elect the mayor of the city and 11 members of the City Council.
Population: 1.2 million

Population Density: 2,419 people per square km (6,250 people per square mi)
Median age: 38.6
Ethnic groups: Czech 93%; other (Moravian, Slovak, Polish, German, Ukrainian, Vietnamese) 7%
Religion: Unaffiliated 67%; Roman Catholic 18%; other 8%; Hussite 2%; Evangelical 1%

If not us, who? If not now, when?
–Slogan by Czech university students
in Prague, November 1989

Geography & Environment

Latitude: 50° N (same as Amiens, France; Krakow, Poland; Vancouver, Canada)
Longitude: 14° E (same as Valletta, Malta; Tripoli, Libya)
Elevation: 245 meters (803 feet)
Land area: 496 square km (192 square mi)
Terrain: Straddles the Vltava River
Natural hazards: Floods

Environmental issues: General air quality has improved since the 1989 Velvet Revolution, but pollutants from vehicle traffic are increasing. The city estimates that about a third of the population lives with excessive noise, mostly road traffic.

Prague is like a vertical
Venice . . . steps everywhere.
–Penelope Gilliatt

Did You Know?

• Since 1995 several services have driven drunk drivers home in Prague. The companies send two men in a car to wherever an inebriated driver is, using one of the employees to get the driver home, while the other follows in a car. One of the largest companies makes 200 trips per night. The Czech Republic has a zero-tolerance policy for drunk driving.

• Prague's U Fleku brewery is one of the world's oldest, operating since

1499. The city's ties to beer include the world's first beer museum, printing of first brewing textbook, and the world's first president, Prague native Václav Havel, to have written a play based on his experiences working in a brewery.

• The Vltava River reaches its widest point of 330 meters (1,080 feet) in Prague. Many of the city's bridges were put in over ancient fords.

TIME'S MAGPIE

FORGET THE LONG DAYS. When the days are long, bands of Germans and Italians and Japanese and British mob the narrow streets of Old Town, and herds of American college students in velvet jester hats and PRAGUE DRINKING TEAM T-shirts stampede across the Charles Bridge singing Pearl Jam songs. But in March or April, the worst of the winter is over and tourist hoards have yet to descend; by early September the summer crowds have dispersed. On the edge of a season it is still possible to duck onto a narrow, cobbled side street to find it deserted and to feel time straddling centuries the way Prague straddles its river. So many of Europe's cities have been bombed and burnt and torn down and rebuilt again that their physical history survives in stray fragments or not at all, but Prague is time's magpie, hoarding beautiful, eclectic bits from each successive era. In Prague, Gothic towers neighbor eleventh-century courtyards, which lead to Baroque and Renaissance houses with twentieth-century bullets embedded in their walls. Art Nouveau hotels abut formerly socialist department stores that now sell French perfume and American sneakers. Through a combination of luck, circumstance, and obstinance, Prague has stockpiled ten centuries of history.

The city's unrelenting profusion of stimuli forces the brain to screen things out, until one day a new sort of detail will ambush an unconscious filter and then appear everywhere, remaking once-familiar streets. Almost every city block displays a plaque commemorating Prague's countless martyrs from across the centuries—resistance fighters and outspoken nationalists, religious heroes and fallen soldiers. Usually these plaques are placed over doorways, or just above eye level on a building's edge. Small and made of dark, weathered metal, they are easily over-looked but upon noticing one the rest appear, Prague's long, sad memory emerging with each additional step. It becomes impossible to go anywhere without noticing more names; Prague becomes a city overrun by death. Then, the eye will be diverted from the funereal by an ornamental frog decorating a doorway or a marble frieze of a violinist fronting an apartment building that was a music school a century before. It becomes apparent that almost every building is charmingly adorned—even in the shabbier neighborhoods lion heads roar above doorways or cherubs recline below windows. The memorial plaques fade into the background.

The nemesis of ornament, Prague's graffiti also exists at first as visual static, soft and persistent and easily glossed over. Spray paint crawls across delicate art nouveau facades; black tags mar eighteenth-century marble; names are keyed into granite landings and wooded window sills. In the wake of the Velvet Revolution, graffiti has spread like mold along the city's edifices, leaving practically no surface untouched. Here, where old beautiful buildings are the default rather than the treasured exceptions to time's entropic rule—and where rich architecture belies an impoverished budget—it's impossible to safeguard everything. Freed from Communism's straitjacket, the entire city is now wrapped in scrawl.

But the beauty of Prague's youth almost excuses their penchant for vandalism. Preternaturally appealing creatures with sculptural faces, creamy skin, and long, supple limbs, they lean against buildings, cigarettes dangling from their lips. They sip slow drinks in cafes; they spill onto the streets in acid-washed jeans. They cultivate looks of boredom that highlight their full lips and Slavic cheekbones. Their attractiveness is alarming in its universality and in its disappearance at the earliest intimation of middle age. Prague's denizens breathe coal-laced air, drink polluted water, and live on boiled dumplings and pork cutlets, beer and cigarettes—a diet that generally allots a person only three good decades. Faces become haggard and loose-skinned; bellies grow and arms become flaccid; spines curve; strange lumps and moles appear.

In Prague there is no culture of continuing care facilities or retirement communities. The old are not shunted away, nor do they move to sunny locales with more golfing opportunities. Prague is home to stooped old ladies with necks crooked like canes, and old ladies with perfect posture. There are old ladies in sensible, square-toed shoes and old ladies with sagging pantyhose stuffed inside bright red Mary Janes, old ladies with large handbags and fuzzy wool caps they knit themselves, and old ladies in ratty fur coats. In Prague the blue-haired old lady is no less common than the violet-haired old lady or the scarlet-haired old lady—punk rock dye-jobs hallucinatory in their vibrancy, and which are still commonplace a decade after the arrival of Western cosmetics might have been expected to impose a certain refinement of hue. Sometimes old ladies are in the company of old men but mostly old ladies are alone, or with old lady friends, or with small, unfriendly dogs. Husbands die, and perhaps there is a small pension, but old ladies still carry baskets filled with groceries. They still make their painstaking way down sidewalks and hold their breath as they risk the first stair of a speeding escalator.

The velocity and intensity with which Prague's inhabitants age merely mirrors time's unlikely acrobatics from one city block to the next. A street frequently occupies two centuries at once. In the city center, a TGI Friday's inhabits an eighteenth-century mansion; signs posted on elegant, antique streetlamps display the word CASINO in Czech, English, Japanese, and Hebrew; a fourteenth-century boulevard contains a McDonald's, a Pizza Hut, and numerous discos, its sidewalk hucksters proclaiming the virtues of nearby strip clubs.

Prague's magpie instincts are not strictly temporal. The mad rush toward Westernization has resulted in a spectacular street mélange of consumer culture, international tourism, and incipient capitalism. In Old Town, a restaurant tout sports an oversized sombrero and a Mexican poncho on which are emblazoned the words PIZZA and FELAFEL, while a restaurant named Chicago advertises Mexican cuisine. A gaggle of schoolgirls squawks, in accented English, "We're from Belgium, mighty mighty Belgium," their voices echoing through the streets. A flock of Japanese tourists photographs the clock tower from the opposite side of Old Town Square, their flashes impotent against the deepening night. Kerchiefed, thick-fingered snack-stand proprietors vend—in addition to the traditional sausages and fried cheese—a frozen treat called "Rentgen!" a fluorescent yellow Popsicle on a black skeleton-shaped stick, bearing a radioactive symbol on its wrapper. On a pedestrian plaza, a street vendor waves a crumpled piece of paper at a cop in desperation, blocking his briefcase of fake Soviet artifacts with his body. From a loudspeaker fronting a downtown bingo hall, a voice drones each successive number in a robotic monotone that suggests imminent death from boredom. At a tram stop, a stray mutt trots back and forth before a woman eating a roll until she feeds him some crumbs. Prague's human beggars opt for complete prostration, face down on their elbows and knees, hands proffered in supplication, a square of newspaper tucked under their legs for cushioning, but the dogs have better luck.

In the years since Communism's demise, gambling has become as common as graffiti. Along neighborhood streets, twenty-four-hour *hernas* advertise the day's accumulated jackpot on digital street displays, while inside the door, catatonic men feed coins into slot machines. Off-track betting parlors inhabit every major subway station. It's easy to become disheartened. Hopefully, discouragement will cast the gaze downward to Prague's sidewalks. They are not concrete or slate, but marble mosaics that stretch from the city's touristed center to its most ordinary neighborhoods; they are part of the city's fabric, nearly daring to be overlooked. There are never more than two colors of stone to a sidewalk, but those colors change. Sometimes the stones are gray and white, sometimes roseate and white, marble cubes the size of children's blocks forming patterns that shift from block to block— sometimes diamonds, sometimes a checkerboard, sometimes squares of varying shape. Who decides the pattern? Is there a plan in a municipal building somewhere mandating which city block receives nesting squares and which lines of diamonds? Occasionally small piles of marble cubes rest beside a patchy sidewalk, waiting to be set in place by a sidewalk fixer in blue overalls. Oblivious to the street traffic, he will patiently tap each stone into place with a metal mallet and a bricklayer's hammer, his methods no different from the pavers of 1763. In the intervening years, empire has been replaced by Communism, which has been supplanted by capitalism, each passing era leaving its mark but not obscuring what came before. The sidewalks persist in their mosaic geometrics. Whether ruled by emperor or dictator or venture capitalist, Prague is simply too old and its habits too engrained not to remain faithful to itself.

–Myla Goldberg

From TIME'S MAGPIE: A Walk in Prague by Myla Goldberg. Copyright © 2004 Myla Goldberg.

A SHORT HISTORY OF THE CZECH REPUBLIC

VISITING THE CZECH REPUBLIC TODAY, you'll find a thriving member of the European Union and the NATO military alliance. The past decade and a half—since the peaceful overthrow of communism in 1989—has brought a steady stream of foreign investment into the economy and a cultural revival on par with the glory days of the First Republic, when Czechoslovakia first emerged as an independent nation after World War I. A big part of that cultural revival has been a renewed interest in the country by foreign visitors. Today, Prague is one of the top five urban destinations in Europe—strong evidence of the city's wide appeal beyond its borders.

To Czechs with long memories this all seems too good to be true. The country's geographic position in the heart of Europe meant that for centuries turmoil and subjugation were far more frequent than peace and prosperity. In the 15th century, the country was riven by religious conflicts between Protestants and Catholics. In the stormy 17th century, the territory of the Czech Republic fell firmly under Austrian Hapsburg domination—remained so for the next 300 years. The 20th century brought with it the first taste of independence and prosperity, only to have that brutally crushed by the Nazis and then by the Soviet Union. If Czechs these days seem a little lackadaisical about their membership in the European Union and their relatively bright prospects, it's only because they can't believe the good times are here to stay.

Beginnings

The first record of modern human activity in this part of the world comes from the Romans, who in the early centuries of the first millennium wrote that Celtic tribes had settled here—though the Romans themselves had not settled this far north. One of these Celtic tribes was known as

the "Bojj." The modern word "Bohemia" (land of the Bojj) comes from this.

History is still a little muddy at this point, but from around the year 500 onward a great migration took place throughout Central and Eastern Europe. These early migrants to the territory of present-day Bohemia and Moravia were mostly from Central Asia and points east. Around the year 700 and after the area fell largely under the control of the early Slavic peoples.

The record becomes clearer around the year 800 with the formation of the Great Moravian Empire. This was the high point of Moravian history, and the empire once embraced large parts of present-day Bohemia, Moravia, Slovakia, and Poland. The empire was in turn conquered by the Magyars (Hungarians) in the year 896, with the easternmost points of the empire, including Slovakia, pledging allegiance to Hungarian rulers; the "Czech lands"—Bohemia and Moravia—fell under the Western powers and allegiance to Rome. Until the modern Czechoslovak state was formed in 1918, this was the last time the Czechs and Slovaks shared a common kingdom, and this 1,000-year separation accounts for much of the lingering cultural differences between the two.

It's about this time in history that references to Prague start appearing. The origins of Prague begin with the legend of the beautiful Queen Libuše. It is said she stood on Vyšehrad hill one day in the 9th century and predicted that a great city would someday be there. Today, you can still scramble up that rock and look out onto the city that Libuše foretold.

The first Bohemian dynasty, based in Prague, began around the 10th century. The Přemyslids—as they were known—were a bloodthirsty bunch, and early accounts of the dynasty are filled with tales of deception and murder. One of the early benevolent Přemyslid rulers was St. Wenceslas. He is the patron saint of Bohemia and the man for whom Wenceslas Square in Prague—and countless other squares and streets around the country—is named. He had the misfortune of being murdered on the orders of his brother Boleslav in the town of Stará Boleslav in 935.

A Kingdom Grows in Power

If St. Wenceslas was one early hero, a second great man was Emperor Charles IV—the man whose name graces not only the most famous bridge in Prague, but also a very famous street (Karlova ulice), a square (Karlovo náměstí), and Charles University. Charles was born in 1316 and assumed the throne of the Bohemian king—and by election Holy Roman Emperor—in 1346. During Charles's 30-year reign Prague became one of the most important cities in Europe. It was Charles who layed out the bridge that would later bear his name, as well as laying the plans for St. Vitus Cathedral and many other great buildings in Prague. Charles University was the first seat of higher learning in Central Europe. Historians say it was Charles's vision that laid out the New Town (Nové Město) stretching beyond the walls and fortifications of the Old Town. Without Charles IV it's safe to say Prague would be nothing like it is today.

Darkness falls

The 1400s were turbulent years for Bohemia and much of Central Europe. The principal issue was religion, pitting a battle between the Protestant reformers and the Catholic Church. Prague was fertile ground for the reformers, particularly the teachings of the priest Jan Hus, who preached in the Czech language (instead of Latin) at Betlémská kaple in the Old Town. Hus railed against Rome and what he perceived as the excesses and unholy lives of the popes. He was excommunicated in 1412 and burned at the stake in Constance (in present-day Germany) three years later.

Hus's teachings spoke directly to the poor, disaffected Czechs of his day, and his death served only to radicalize his followers. Many of these "Hussites"—as they were known—gathered in the southern Bohemian city of Tábor and launched a series of attacks against the mainly Catholic nobility and the pope's armies were sent to quash the rebellion. The Hussites—led by their one-eyed general Jan Žižka—prevailed in the early fighting, but were ultimately defeated at the Battle of Lipany in 1434. Today, Hus continues to widely be admired—and there's an enormous, if overly romanticized statue, of him on Old Town Square—but the Czech Republic these days is a country of agnostics and a religious fervor of the Hussite variety is almost unknown.

Enter the Hapsburgs

The 16th century saw a slow and steady revival of the Czech lands that culminated toward the end of the century with the rule of Hapsburg Emperor Rudolf II. By all accounts, Rudolf was a highly eccentric royal who much preferred the mysticism of Prague to the finery of Vienna. He formally moved the Hapsburg court from Vienna to Prague and opened it up to some of the most brilliant and wackiest painters, astronomers, architects, and alchemists of his day. If you can speak of a second golden age for the city, this was certainly it. Rudolf's rule from 1576 to 1611 saw the city prosper.

But as with the first golden age, it didn't last long. The festering tensions between Protestants and Catholics exploded once again after the Hapsburgs rescinded religious freedoms granted to the Protestants. The Protestants retaliated in 1618 by tossing out two Catholic governors from a window—which among other things gave us the word "defenestration." That sparked a series of wars that would engulf much of Europe. In 1620, the Catholic Hapsburgs routed the Czechs at the battle of Bílá Hora (White Mountain) just outside of Prague—and would rule the country until 1918. The Austrians sealed their victory by executing 27 Bohemian nobleman on Old Town Square. You can still see the 27 white crosses on the ground where the men were hanged or put to the sword.

Prague largely stagnated in the years after 1620, as the Hapsburg capital shifted back to Vienna and Bohemia became part of the Austrian hinterland. German became the language of everyday life and Czech was on the verge of extinction.

Industrialization in the 19th century, however, proved a great boon to Bohemia and Moravia. Cities like Prague, České Budějovice, Plzeň, and Brno became powerful industrial centers. The new wealth helped to fund what became known as the Czech National Revival that championed the use of Czech language over German and the development of uniquely "Czech" music, arts, and architecture. In a real sense, Czech culture was reborn and reinvented at this time. The great buildings of this period include the Národní muzeum (National Museum) and the Národní divadlo. (National Theater).

Liberation & a New Dictator

World War I dealt a death blow to the Austro-Hungarian empire, which included Bohemia and Moravia, but proved a blessing in disguise for the Czechs. Czech patriots saw the war as an opportunity to gain independence and spent the war years lobbying the Allied powers—above all the United States—to form an independent nation together with Slovakia. The union with Slovakia was odd in that Czechs and Slovaks had not formed a common state for 1,000 years—but they did share more or less a common language and a desire to unite. In 1918 U.S. President Woodrow Wilson gave his blessing to "Czecho-Slovakia" and in October 1918 the new nation was born.

An earnest, bespectacled philosophy professor, Tomáš Masaryk, became the first elected president of the new Czechoslovakia in 1920. The 1920s and part of the '30s—now fondly remembered as the "First Republic"—were excellent years, and saw an explosion in economic prosperity, the arts, and architecture. Czechoslovakia became one of the most prosperous countries in the world and boasted one of the few genuine democracies in Europe.

Sadly, this too didn't last long. Following Adolph Hitler's rise to power in Germany, many ethnic Germans in Czechoslovakia—particularly those living in the border region, the "Sudetenland"—began to agitate against the Czechs to join the Reich. The word "Munich" in the Czech Republic will forever by synonymous with "appeasement." It was there in 1938 the British Prime Minister Neville Chamberlain agreed to allow Hitler to annex the Sudentenland in a bid to secure, as Chamberlain said, "peace in our time." Within less than a year, Hitler had occupied all of the Czech lands.

Throughout World War II, the Czech lands were occupied by the Nazis; Slovakia, meanwhile, became an "independent" Nazi puppet state. Czechoslovak President Edvard Beneš (1884–1948) fled to England in 1940, where he faced an uphill battle with the Western leaders who continued for some time to advocate Hitler's appeasement.

The Czech resistance movement was small but dedicated. Their greatest success was the assassination of the vicious *Reichsprotektor* Reinhard Heidrich just outside of Prague in 1942. The Czechs suffered terrible retributions for this act, especially the obliteration of Lidice and Ležáky, two small central-Bohemian villages.

The end of the war brought a brief period of hope to the country. The western part of Czechoslovakia, including the city of Plzeň, was liberated by the U.S. Army under the command of General George S. Patton. He was prevented, however, from going on to Prague under an agreement with the Russians reached earlier at the

Yalta Conference. Prague instead was liberated by the Russian Red Army. Czechoslovakia, like all of the smaller countries to the east of Germany, was given over to the Soviet sphere of influence.

Communists Take Hold

In the first postwar vote in 1946, the exhausted electorate turned to the Communist Party more out of desperation than conviction. A third of the vote went to the communists, and they formed the first government under their leader Klement Gottwald. Two years later, the communists staged the so-called "February Coup," taking full control and banning opposition parties. Gottwald (1896–1953) became the first "working class President" of Czechoslovakia. Industry and agriculture were nationalized, and a series of purges and show trials, under the auspices of Soviet "advisers," began.

The 1950s were hard years, but by the next decade, the Soviet repression had begun to ease. As was the case so often in the Czech Republic, it was the intellectual community—writers, musicians, and filmmakers—who were at the forefront of the liberalization. Meeting the intellectuals halfway was the recently appointed First Secretary of the Communist Party: Alexander Dubček (1921–92), whose program to create what he called "Socialism With a Human Face" became synonymous with the "Prague Spring" of 1968.

The end came relatively quickly. In the eyes of Moscow, this cultural renaissance had begun to break away from good communist behavior. On the night of August 20, 1968, forces from all Warsaw Pact nations (except Romania) entered Czechoslovakia to put an end to the Prague Spring. As Russian tanks roamed the streets, the Czechoslovak leaders were taken to Moscow, where they were forced to sign a memorandum "requesting" the extended presence of Soviet troops to protect against further insurgency. Protesting against the invasion of his country, student Jan Palach

(1948–69), immolated himself in Wenceslas Square in January 1969.

For the next two decades Czechoslovakia was to experience some of the most repressive conditions in the Eastern Bloc. "Normalization" did not depend on show trials and executions, as in the 1950s, but steadily ground the population down through economic and bureaucratic oppression. Once again it was the scholarly types, among them future President Václav Havel, who led what resistance there was.

Velvet Revolution

Not with a bang but with a whimper, the communist regime ended suddenly at the end of 1989. With Mikhail Gorbachev in power in the Soviet Union, the fear of a Soviet-led invasion had receded throughout Eastern Europe. Communist regimes tottered one by one that year in Poland, Hungary, East Germany, and finally Czechoslovakia.

In Prague the beginning of the end started on November 17, 1989—now recognized as a national holiday. Students had staged a relatively small protest strike and were walking along the river and then toward Wenceslas Square along Národní třída, when they were stopped by police and forcibly prevented from going farther. The official news carried little information on the action, yet word spread quickly throughout the population. Protests on subsequent days brought out more and more people until thousands, and then hundreds of thousands, were massing on Wenceslas Square, jangling their keys, and telling the communist authorities it was time to leave.

So often in the past, it seems the Czechs have been blessed with the right man at the right time. And in 1989 that man was Václav Havel (b. 1936), a playwright and essayist with a long history of resistance to the communist government and no taint of collaboration. He quickly emerged as the face of the Velvet Revolution; one of the leading slogans on protests signs that November was *"Havel na hrad!"* (Havel to the castle!). By the end of that year, Havel was in charge, and the communists were effectively gone. Because the revolution had transpired without major bloodshed, it became known as the "Velvet" Revolution.

The years immediately after 1989 brought one possibly unanticipated result: the split-up of Czechoslovakia. The forces that broke up this relatively successful union were complicated and probably ultimately irresistible. Many Czechs feared that a relatively poor Slovakia would drain away the state budget. For many Slovaks, the promise of an independent state was simply too tempting. On January 1, 1993, the two countries amicably agreed to go their separate ways in a parting local wags quickly dubbed the "Velvet Divorce."

–Mark Baker

THE CZECHS & THEIR BEER

IN SOME PRAGUE PUBS, the minute you sit down a waiter comes and puts a beer (*pivo*) in front of you, making a little stroke-mark on a long, thin piece of paper. What else would anybody want but a beer? And why would anybody leave before the paper is filled with stroke marks? After all, Czech beer is, arguably, some of the best in all of Europe, and the Czechs are devoted consumers. Local consumption per capita is the highest of any country, with each person drinking about 43 gallons per year. Beer is much more popular in Bohemia than in Moravia, which means some thirsty Bohemians are picking up the slack for their vinophilic Moravian co-citizens.

Beer has been an integral part of Czech culture since the Dark Ages. Hops were an important crop as early as AD 900. In 1088 there's mention of a tax on hops in the foundation charter of Vyšehrad signed by Czech ruler Vratislav II. Laws originally only allowed home brewing, but by 1118, a communal brewery was established in Cerhenice, halfway between Prague and Kutná Hora. Special permission was needed to establish breweries for a long time after.

Holy Roman Emperor Rudolf II, who emptied Prague's royal coffers trying to turn lead into gold, made at least one sensible investment during his reign. In 1583 he sank some money into the already existing Krušovice brewery, which is still running as a "royal brewery" and uses his name and likeness in their ad campaigns. His physician maintained that beer was good for health, a notion that is still widely held among the local population.

Other breweries have equally historical roots. Regent beer, for example, has been made in Třeboň since 1379; the brewery was founded by Augustinian monks and expanded in 1482 by the noble Rožmberk—or Rosenberg—family, which explains the five-petal rose on the label.

Other beers claim an even older heritage but are seldom seen outside the small area where they are produced. In Prague the brewpub U Fleků has been making dark beer since 1499, although the current recipe dates from the turn of the 20th century.

One legend has it that a *vodník,* a kind of water sprite from fairy tales, went into a pub on Prague's Kampa Island. He declared the beer to be little more than the river water he was used to drinking and put a curse on the place. The exact location of the cursed pub is unknown. But the importance of the breweries is much less in question. In most beer-making towns (including Prague), special messengers were always ready at the main water towers to notify the breweries first in case a fire or other catastrophe was going to disrupt the water supply.

Almost all of the beer currently made in the Czech Republic is Pilsner-style beer, a light, golden-hue variety that was developed in 1842 in Plzeň, also known as Pilsen, in the west of Bohemia. Even if a beer label claims that the brewery has been around for centuries—and it very well may have been—the flavor of its beer is probably of more recent vintage. Before the 1840s, wheat beers were popular, especially dark brews in the Prague area. Dark beers (*černé* or *tmavé*) now make up only a few percentage points of the country's beer production and consumption. What gives Czech beer its distinctive bitter flavor are said to be the special hops from the Žatec region.

One step toward standardizing beer quality was the development of the Balling Scale, by Czech chemist Karl Josef Napoleon Balling in the mid-19th century, to designate the amount of malt sugar at the start of fermentation. Most Czech pubs still designate beer as 10, 12, or more "degrees" (the word degree here referring not to the temperature but to the sugar content and thus the strength of the beer). A 10-degree beer has between 3% and 4% alcohol, with a 12-degree beer somewhat more. When you order a beer in a pub, you may be asked if you want a 10-degree beer, a *desítka*, or a 12-degree beer, a *dvanáctka*.

The country's largest and most famous beer producer, Pilsner Urquell, is still based in Plzeň. It has swallowed up a lot of its competition, though it still keeps the formerly independent brand names of Radegast and Kozel alive. The international conglomerate SABMiller now owns Pilsner Urquell, and the company has started to produce some Pilsner Urquell in Poland. Aggressive marketing has made the 12-degree Pilsner Urquell and its 10-degree sister brew Gambrinus the most common beers in Czech pubs.

Staropramen, brewed in Prague, is served in many central Bohemian pubs and has a large following. Staropramen is now owned by Belgian-based Interbrew. Pubs that carry Staropramen have recently started to carry imported Belgian beer on tap as well, but the reception for milder-flavor imports has been a bit slow. Budvar, or Budweiser, is based in the southern Bohemian city of České Budějovice, and is one of the best-known names in beer-making. The company is involved in a long-running international legal dispute with Anheuser-Busch of the U.S. over the use of the name Budweiser. In German, České Budějovice was called Budweis. The Czech brand has won the rights to the name Budweiser in several important European markets. Budvar tastes sweeter than its main rivals.

A recent trend in Czech pubs has been a return to unpasteurized beer. Pasteurizing beer helps beer to last longer, but heating the beer also damages its flavor. Several pubs with a high turnover have installed special tanks. Most carry Pilsner Urquell, but other brands are getting in on the trend as well. The unpasteurized beer is slightly cloudy and has a more pronounced hops flavor. Look for a sign near the door proclaiming the pub a *tankovná* if you'd like to try some unpasteurized beer.

If you had any doubts about the importance of beer in Czech culture, you can easily see its influence in popular literature and movies. Playwright and former President Václav Havel set one of his most famous plays, *Audience,* in a small-town brewery. Havel, who eschewed most pomp, also liked to take visiting dignitaries to local pubs. Jaroslav Hašek's main character in *The Good Soldier Švejk* spends most of his free time either in pubs or looking for pubs around the time of World War I. Švejk tells another soldier to meet him at a certain pub at 6 o'clock after the war, since he basically intends on being in the pub every night once his service is over. The pub he mentions, U Kalicha, is still around, and like several others it capitalizes on the image of the carefree, beer-guzzling, harmless soldier. The book also warned that any government that altered the price of beer would not last long. Jan Neruda's characters also typically frequented pubs in his *Malá Strana Stories*. He tried to paint fairly sympathetic pictures of the common man.

Much of Bohumil Hrabal's fiction also addresses pub culture. *The Snowdrop Festival,* based on his stories, was filmed in 1983 by Jiří Menzel. Menzel's Oscar-nominated *My Sweet Little Village,* bas an early script by *Kolya* writer Svěrák, has a famous bit aᵇ beer on the proper step or musical romantic com ers (*Starci na chmeᶦ* most popular C was released into a mᵛ

BOOKS & MOVIES

Books

English readers have an excellent range of both fiction and nonfiction about the Czech Republic at their disposal. The most widely read Czech author of fiction in English is probably Milan Kundera, whose well-crafted tales illuminate both the foibles of human nature and the unique tribulations of life in Communist Czechoslovakia. *The Unbearable Lightness of Being* takes a look at the 1968 invasion and its aftermath through the eyes of a strained young couple. *The Book of Laughter and Forgetting* deals in part with the importance of memory and the cruel irony of how it fades over time; Kundera was no doubt coming to terms with his own forgetting as he wrote the book from his Paris exile. *The Joke,* Kundera's earliest work available in English, takes a serious look at the dire consequences of humorlessness among Communists.

Born and raised in the German-Jewish enclave of Prague, Franz Kafka scarcely left the city his entire life. *The Trial* and *The Castle* strongly convey the dread and mystery he detected beneath the 1,000 golden spires of Prague. Kafka worked as a bureaucrat for 14 years, in a job he detested; his books are, at least in part, an indictment of the bizarre bureaucracy of the Austro-Hungarian Empire, though they now seem eerily prophetic of the even crueler and more arbitrary Communist system that was to come.

In contrast, Jaroslav Hašek wandered far and wide, from childhood to his early death. Often described as an anarchist, Hašek was big and bawdy, often drunk, and fond of practical jokes. His unfinished novel *The Good Soldier Švejk* (often with the extended title *The Good Soldier Švejk and His Fortunes in the War*) stars an idiot savant, who, by following orders to the letter, undermines the the Austro-Hungarian army in War I. Švejk has commonly been heralded as typical of the Czech character by surviving absurd situations through his subversive wit and by thumbing his nose behind authority's back.

The most popular Czech authors at the close of the 20th century were those banned by the Communists after the Soviet invasion of 1968. Václav Havel and members of the Charter 77 group illegally distributed self-published manuscripts, or *samizdat* as they were called, of these banned authors—among them, Bohumil Hrabal, Josef Škvorecký, and Ivan Klíma. Many claim to have shared a table with Hrabal, perhaps the most beloved of all Czech writers, at his favorite pub in Prague, U Zlatéyho tygra. Hrabal's books include *I Served the King of England* and the lyrical *Too Loud a Solitude,* which is narrated by a lonely man who spends his days in the basement compacting the world's greatest works of literature along with bloodied butcher paper into neat bundles before they get carted off for recycling and disposal. Škvorecký sought refuge and literary freedom in Toronto in the early 1970s; his book *The Engineer of Human Souls* reveals the double censorship of the writer in exile—censored in the country of his birth and unread in his adopted home. Still, Škvorecký did gain a following thanks to his translator, Paul Wilson—who lived in Prague in the 1960s and '70s until he was ousted for his assistance in dissident activities. Wilson also set up 68 Publishers, which is responsible for the bulk of Czech literature from that period that is translated into English. Novelist, short story writer, and playwright Ivan Klíma is now one of the most widely read Czech writers in English; his books include the novels *Judge on Trial* and *Love and Garbage,* and *The Spirit of Prague,* a collection of essays about life in the post-Communist Czech Republic.

Václav Havel, onetime dissident playwright turned president of the Czech Republic, is essential nonfiction reading. The best place to start is probably *Living in Truth,* which provides an absorbing overview of his own political philosophy and of Czechoslovak politics and history since 1968. Other recommended books by Havel include *Disturbing the Peace* (a collection of interviews with him) and *Letters to Olga.* Havel's plays explore the absurdities and pressures of life under the former Communist regime; the best example of his absurdist dramas is *The Memorandum,* which depicts a Communist bureaucracy more twisted than the streets of Prague's Old Town.

Among the most prominent of the younger Czech writers is Jáchym Topol, whose *A Visit to the Train Station* documents the creation of a new Prague with a sharp wit that cuts through the false pretenses of American youth occupying the city.

Prague figures in the work not only of Czech authors but also American and British writers, who have flocked to Prague to lead the expat life since 1990. Novelist Myla Goldberg revisits Prague in her collection of essays *Time's Magpie.* The characters of *Prague,* a novel by Arthur Phillips, have settled for Budapest, but it's Prague where they wish they lived. Writer John Banville collects his musings on Prague in *Prague Pictures.* Or you can visit Prague in the 1970s in Philip Roth's *The Prague Orgy.*

Movies

Since the end of World War II, the Czech film industry has experienced two vastly differing conditions that have influenced its output. Until the fall of Communism the industry was state-run, which meant no box-office issues but strong censorship. Hand-in-hand with such freedom from commercial concerns, the famous FAMU school in Prague produced many cerebral filmmakers. The best-known period of Czech film came in the 1960s, when the Czech New Wave was at the forefront of the movement for liberalization. In addition, Czech animation has long been widely respected for its formal invention and haunting mix of fantasy and black humor, as seen in Jan Švankmajer's *Little Otik,* an adaptation of a Czech fairy tale starring a tree stump that comes to life as a ravenous baby.

Miloš Forman is perhaps the best known Czech director. He emigrated to the United States in 1968, returning to Prague briefly in the early 1980s to film *Amadeus.* His "New Wave" films tend to involve everyday characters that are neither hero nor villain and include the satirical farce *Fireman's Ball* and the somewhat more sober *Loves of a Blonde.*

The tragicomic themes that many films of the New Wave investigate are exemplified in *The Shop On Main Street* (which received an Academy Award for best foreign-language film in 1966). Jan Kadar's and Elmar Klos's film concerns the predicament of a simple man who is caught between his conscience and his ability to ensure his personal safety from totalitarian authorities, in this case the occupying Nazis.

Jiří Menzel joined Forman in his exploration of a magnified realism, dallying on ostensibly mundane details. Menzel was another Oscar winner in 1968 with *Closely Observed Trains.* Adapted from Hrabal's novel by Menzel and the author himself, the tale follows a young railway dispatcher who is far more concerned with losing his virginity than resisting the Nazi occupation.

At the other end of the style spectrum were formal experimenters. Věra Chytilová's *Daises* features the crazed and destructive antics of two young girls, and it's either a bold expression of the director's flair for groundbreaking structure or a jumble of haphazard images. Possibly both. Meanwhile Jan Němec made his biggest impression, both on audiences and the censors, with the menacing and highly stylized *The Party and the Guests,* a condemnation of surrender to dominant ideology. Jaromil Jireš's starkly political version of Kundera's novel *The Joke* contrasts with his surreal vampire story: *Valerie and Her Week of Wonders.*

In 1990 Czech filmmakers were freed from the state censors but also suddenly cast into the free-market jungle. The older generation has struggled under these conditions, but younger directors have managed to produce a healthy number of thoughtful yet commercially viable films. The most successful of these has been Jan Svěrák, thanks in part to his saccharine tooth. *Kolya* (winner of the Academy Award for best foreign-language film in 1996), set in the final days of Communism, follows the transition of an aging bachelor when he inherits a young Russian "son." A more recent film, *Dark Blue World,* is an awkward yet somehow satisfying concoction of numerous story lines spanning fractured time lines and two languages.

In contrast, Petr Zelenka offers a darkly ironic sense of humor. *Year of The Devil* is a mock documentary following a local folk-rock band; the six disparate stories in *Buttoners* are only cobbled together at the finale. Jan Hřebejk is apparently working his way through contemporary history in chronological order, his films grounded in the gentle self-depreciation and humanism inherent in Czech humor. *Divided We Fall* is set in World War II; *Cozy Dens* deals with the period leading up to the 1968 invasion, and in *Pupendo* we are plunged back into "normalization" in the 1980s.

Recently, historic locations in Prague have become the darlings of Hollywood, and films as disparate as *Van Helsing* and *Everything Is Illuminated* have been shot in the city. Keep yourself amused during your visit by spotting stars, and later amaze your friends by pointing out which Prague street the particular action hero or bewigged dandy is pacing in each scene. Spot your favorite pub in *Mission Impossible, XXX,* or Terry Gilliam's *The Brothers Grimm* to name but three. In 2006, Karlovy Vary had its moment to shine in the Queen Latifah vehicle *Last Holiday.*

CZECH VOCABULARY

Czech is considered a difficult language, but it is pronounced phonetically.

Consonants

c = a "ts" sound, as in *its*
č = a "ch" sound, as in *chair*
ch = a hard "ch" sound, as in *loch*
j = a "y" sound, as in *yes*
ň = an "ny" sound, as in *canyon*

r̆ = a combination of "r" and "z," as in *Dvorak*
š = an "sh" sound, as in *shine*
z = a "z" sound, as in *zero*
ž = a "zh" sound, as in *pleasure*

Vowels

a = a short sound, as in *lamb*
e = a short sound, as in *best*
ě = a short "ye," as in *yes*
i, y = a short sound, as "i" in *city*
o = a short sond, as in *book*
u = pronounced as "oo" in *book*

á = a long sound, as in *father*
é = pronounced as "ai" in *air*
í, ý = as a long "e" sound, as in *meet*
ó = pronounced as "o" in *more*
ú, ů = prounced as "oo" in *boom*

Basics

English	Czech	Pronunciation
Yes/no	Ano/ne	**ah**-no/neh
Please	Prosím	**pro**-seem
Thank you (kindly)	Děkuji	**dyek**-oo-yee
Excuse me	Pardon	**par**-don
Sorry [for doing something]	Promiňte	**proh**-meen-yteh
I'm sorry [about something]	Lituji	**liht**-oo-yee
Hello [during the day]	Dobrý den	**dohb**-ree den
Good evening	Dobrý vecer	**dohb**-ree veh-chehr
Goodbye [formal]	Na shledanou	**nas**-khleh-dah-noh-oo
Goodbye [informal]	Ahoj	**ah**-hoy
Today/During the day	Dnes	dnes
Tonight	Dnes večer	**dnes** veh-chehr
Tomorrow	Zítra	**zee**-trah
Do you speak English?	Mluvíte anglicky?	**mloo**-vit-eh ahng-**glit**-ski?
I don't speak Czech.	Nemluvím česky.	**neh**-mluv-eem **ches**-ky
I don't understand.	Nerozumím	**neh**-rohz-oom-eem
Please speak slowly.	Prosím, mluvte pomalu.	**pro**-seem, **mloov**-teh **poh**-mah-lo
Please write it down.	Prosím napište to.	**pro**-seem nah-**peesh**-teh toh
Please show me.	Ukažte mně	oo-**kazh**-te mnye

I am American (m/f).	Jsem Američan/ Američanka	sem ah-**mer**-i-chan/ ah-**mer**-i-chan-ka
I am English (m/f).	Jsem Angličan/ Angličanka	sem **ahn**-gli-chan/ **ahn**-gli-chan-ka
I am Australian (m/f).	Jsem Australan/ Australanka	sem **aus**-trah-lahn/ **aus**-trah-lahn-ka
I am Canadian (m/f).	Jsem Kanad'an/ Kanad'anka	sem **Kah**-nahd-yan/ **Kah**-nahd-yank-a
Right/left	Vlevo/ vpravo	**vleh**-voh/ **vprah**-voh
Open/closed	Otevřeno/ Zavřeno	**Oh**-tev-rzh-ehn-oh/ **zav**-rzh-ehn-oh
Arrival/departure	Příjezd/ Odjezd	**przhee**-yeezhd/ **oh**-dy eezhd
Where is . . . ?	Kde je . . .?	g-deh yeh
. . . the train station?	. . . Nádraži?	nah-**drah**-zee
. . . the bus station?	. . . Autobus?	**au**-toh-boos
. . . the bus stop?	. . . Autobus?	**au**-toh-boos
. . . the airport?	. . . Letiště?	**leh**-tish-tyeh
. . . a post office?	. . . Pošta?	**po**-shta
. . . a bank?	. . . Banka?	**bahn**-ka
. . . a hotel?	. . . Hotel?	**hoh**-tel
. . . an internet café?	. . . Internetová kavárna?	in-ter-net-oh-vah kah-**ver**-na
. . . a restroom?	. . . Toaleta?	**toha**-leh-tah
Stop here.	Zastavte tady.	**zah**-stahv-teh **tah**-dee
I would like . . .	Chtěl bych . . .	kh-tyel bihk
How much does it cost?	Kolik to stojí?	ko-**lik** toh **stoy**-ee
Letter/postcard	Dopis/pohlednice	doh-**pis**-ee/**poh**-hled-nit-seh
By airmail	Letecky	**leh**-tet-skee
Help!	Pomoc!	**po**-motz

Meeting people

My name is . . .	Jmenuji se . . .	ymen **weh**-seh
What is your name?	Jak se jmenujete?	yahk seh ymeh-**noo**-yeh-teh
Where do you live?	Odkud jste?	**od**-kood ysteh
What do you study?	Co studujete?	tsoh **stud**-yeh-teh
What is your major?	Jaký obor?	ya-**kee** oh-bor
What is your occupation?	Kde pracujete?	kdeh **prats**-oo-yet-eh
What music do you like?	Jakou hudbu posloucháte?	ya-koo hood-boo **pos**-loots-hat-eh

Let's have a coffee.	Půjdeme na kávu?	**pood**-yuh-deh-meh nah **kah**-voo
You are beautiful.	Jste krásná/ krásný (f/m)	yes-teh **krahs**-nah **krahs**-nee
You have lovely eyes.	Máte krásné oči.	**mah**-teh **krahs**-neh oats-ee
I like you.	Líbíte se mi.	**lee**-bee-teh seh mee
I love you.	Miluji Vás.	**mee**-lu-yee vahs
Stop harassing me!	Neobtěžujte mne!	**neh**-ohb-tyeh-zhyuy-teh muh-neh
I've got to go.	Musím jít	**moo**-seem yeet

Numbers

One	Jeden	ye-**den**
Two	Dva	dvah
Three	Tři	tshree
Four	Čryři	ch'**ti**-zhee
Five	Pět	pyet
Six	Šest	shest
Seven	Sedm	**sed**-oom
Eight	Osm	**oh**-soom
Nine	Devět	**deh**-vyet
Ten	Deset	**deh**-set
Eleven	Jedenáct	yeh-**deh**-nahtst
Twelve	Dvanáct	**dvah**-nahtst
Thirteen	Třináct	trzhee-**nahtst**
Fourteen	Čtrnáct	chtihr-**nahtst**
Fifteen	Patnáct	pat-**nahtst**
Sixteen	Šestnáct	shest-**nahtst**
Seventeen	Sedmnáct	sedm-**nahtst**
Eighteen	Osmnáct	ohsm-**nahtst**
Nineteen	Devatenáct	**deh**-vah-teh-**nahtst**
Twenty	Dvacet	**dvah**-tset
Thirty	Třicet	**trzhee**-tset
Fourty	Čtyřicet	**chtee**-rzhee-tset
Fifty	Padesát	**pah**-deh-saht
Sixty	Šedesát	**sheh**-deh-saht
Seventy	Sedmdesát	**sedm**-deh-saht
Eighty	Osmdesát	**ohsm**-deh-saht
Ninety	Devadesát	**deh**-vah-deh-saht
One hundred	Sto	stoh
One thousand	Tisíc	**tee**-seets

Days of the Week

Sunday	Neděle	**neh**-dyeh-leh
Monday	Pondělí	**pon**-dye-lee
Tuesday	Úterý	**oo**-teh-ree
Wednesday	Středa	**stshreh**-da
Thursday	Čtvrek	**ch't'v'r**-tek
Friday	Pátek	**pah**-tek
Saturday	Sobota	**so**-boh-ta

Where to Sleep

A room	Pokoj	**poh**-koy
The key	Klíč	kleech
With a bath/a shower	S koupelnou/sprchou	s'**ko**-pel-noh/**sp'r**-khoh

Food

A restaurant	Restaurace	**reh**-stau-rah-tseh
The menu	Jídelní lístek	**yee**-dell-nee **lis**-tek
The check, please.	Účet, prosím.	**oo**-chet **pro**-seem
I'd like to order this.	Chtěl bych tohle	khteel bikh **toh**-leh
Breakfast	Snídaně	**snyee**-dan-ye
Lunch	Oběd	**ob**-yed
Dinner	Večeře	**ve**-cher-zhe
Bread	Chléb	khleb
Butter	Máslo	**mah**-slo
Salt/pepper	Sůl/pepř	sool/pepsh
Bottle	Láhev	**lah**-hev
Red/white wine	Cervené/bílé víno	**cher**-ven-eh/**bee**-leh **vee**-no
Beer	Pivo	**piv**-oh
(Tap) water	Voda	**vo**-da
Sparkling water	Sodovka	**soh**-dohv-ka
Mineral water	Minerálka	min-eh-**rahl**-ka **vo**-da
Milk	Mléko	**mleh**-koh
Coffee	Káva	**kah**-va
Tea (with lemon)	Čaj (s citrónem)	tchai (se tsi-**tro**-nem)
Chocolate	Čokoláda	cho-koh-**lah**-da

Prague
Essentials

There are planners, and there are those who fly by the seat of their pants. We happily place ourselves among the planners. Our writers and editors try to anticipate all the issues you may face before and during any journey, and then they do their research. This section is the product of their efforts. Use it to get excited about your trip to Prague, to inform your travel planning, or to guide you on the road should the seat of your pants start to feel threadbare.

GETTING STARTED

We're really proud of our Web site: Fodors.com is a great place to begin any journey. Scan Travel Wire for suggested itineraries, travel deals, restaurant and hotel openings, and other up-to-the-minute info. Check out Booking to research prices and book plane tickets, hotel rooms, rental cars, and vacation packages. Head to Talk for on-the-ground pointers from travelers who frequent our message boards. You can also link to loads of other travel-related resources.

■ RESOURCES

ONLINE TRAVEL TOOLS

All About Prague **Czech Tourist Authority** ⊕ www.czechtourism.com.
Currency Conversion **Google** ⊕ www.google.com does currency conversion. Just type in the amount you want to convert and an explanation of how you want it converted (e.g., "14 Swiss francs in dollars"), and then voilà. **Oanda.com** ⊕ www.oanda.com also allows you to print out a handy table with the current day's conversion rates. **XE.com** ⊕ www.xe.com is a good currency conversion Web site.
Safety **Transportation Security Administration** (TSA) ⊕ www.tsa.gov.
Time Zones **Timeanddate.com** ⊕ www.timeanddate.com/worldclock can help you figure out the correct time anywhere in the world.
Weather **Accuweather.com** ⊕ www.accuweather.com is an independent weather-forecasting service. **Weather.com** ⊕ www.weather.com is the Web site for the Weather Channel.
Other Resources **CIA World Factbook** ⊕ www.odci.gov/cia/publications/factbook/index.html has profiles of every country in the world. It's a good source if you need some quick facts and figures.

VISITOR INFORMATION

The Prague Information Service maintains three helpful information offices—the most useful, and most overcrowded, is in the former Town Hall building (just to the left of the clock tower) on Old Town Square. The office can advise on walking tours, as well answer basic questions and arrange accommodation.
Before You Leave **Czech Tourist Authority** ⊕ www.czechtourism.com.
In Prague **Prague Information Service** (PIS) ⊠ Staroměstská radnice (Old Town Hall), Staré Město ☏ No phone ⊕ www.pis.cz ⊠ Hlavní nádraží, lower hall, Staré Město ☏ No phone ⊠ Malostranská mostecká věž, Malá Strana ☏ No phone.

■ THINGS TO CONSIDER

GOVERNMENT ADVISORIES

As different countries have different world views, look at travel advisories from a range of governments to get more of a sense of what's going on out there. And be sure to parse the language carefully. For example, a warning to "avoid all travel" carries more weight than one urging you to "avoid nonessential travel," and both are much stronger than a plea to "exercise caution." A U.S. government travel warning is more permanent (though not necessarily more serious) than a so-called public announcement, which carries an expiration date.

The U.S. Department of State's Web site has more than just travel warnings and advisories. The consular information sheets issued for every country have general safety tips, entry requirements (though be sure to verify these with the country's embassy), and other useful details.

■ TIP→ Consider registering online with the State Department (https://travelregistration.state.gov/ibrs/), so the government will know to look for you should a crisis occur in the country you're visiting.
General Information & Warnings **U.S. Department of State** ⊕ www.travel.state.gov.

GEAR

Prague's climate is Continental, so in summer plan on relatively warm days and cool nights. Spring tends to be wet and cool; fall is drier but also on the chilly side. In winter, pack plenty of warm clothes and plan to use them. An umbrella is a good idea any time of year. Note that areas in higher elevations tend to stay very cool even in mid-summer.

In general, pack for comfort rather than for style. Casual dress is the norm for everyday wear, including at most restaurants. Men will need a sport coat for an evening out at a concert or the opera. Shorts for men are not as common in Prague as they are in North America. In the evening, long pants are the norm, even in summer.

Many areas are best seen on foot, so take a pair of sturdy walking shoes and be prepared to use them. High heels will present considerable problems on the cobblestone streets of Prague.

Some items that you take for granted at home are occasionally unavailable or of questionable quality in Eastern and Central Europe, though the situation has been steadily improving. Toiletries and personal-hygiene products have become relatively easy to find, but it's always a good idea to bring necessities when traveling in outlying areas.

PASSPORTS & VISAS

Citizens of the U.S. need only a valid passport to enter the Czech Republic and can stay for as long as 90 days without a visa. It's a good idea to make sure your passport is valid for at least six months on entry. If you plan on living or working in the Czech Republic, be advised that long-term and work visas must be obtained outside the country. Contact the Czech embassy or consulate in their home country well in advance of their trip.

PASSPORTS

We're always surprised at how few Americans have passports—only 25% at this writing. This number is expected to grow in coming years, when it becomes impossible to reenter the United States from trips to neighboring Canada or Mexico without one. Remember this: a passport verifies both your identity and nationality—a great reason to have one.

U.S. passports are valid for 10 years. You must apply in person if you're getting a passport for the first time; if your previous passport was lost, stolen, or damaged; or if your previous passport has expired and was issued more than 15 years ago or when you were under 16. All children under 18 must appear in person to apply for or renew a passport. Both parents must accompany any child under 14 (or send a notarized statement with their permission) and provide proof of their relationship to the child.

There are 13 regional passport offices, as well as 7,000 passport acceptance facilities in post offices, public libraries, and other governmental offices. If you're renewing a passport, you can do so by mail. Forms are available at passport acceptance facilities and online.

The cost to apply for a new passport is $97 for adults, $82 for children under 16; renewals are $67. Allow six weeks for processing, both for first-time passports and renewals. For an expediting fee of $60 you can reduce this time to about two weeks. If your trip is less than two weeks away, you can get a passport even more rapidly by going to a passport office with the necessary documentation. Private expediters can get things done in as little as 48 hours, but charge hefty fees for their services.

■ TIP→ Before your trip, make two copies of your passport's data page (one for someone at home and another for you to carry separately). Or scan the page and e-mail it to someone at home and/or yourself.

VISAS

A visa is essentially formal permission to enter a country. Visas allow countries to keep track of you and other visitors—and generate revenue (from application fees). You *always* need a visa to enter a foreign country; however, many countries routinely issue tourist visas on arrival, particularly to U.S. citizens. When your passport is stamped or scanned in the immigration line, you're actually being issued a visa. Sometimes you have to stand in a separate line and pay a small fee to get your stamp before going through immigration, but you can still do this at the airport on arrival. Getting a visa isn't always that easy. Some countries require that you arrange for one in advance of your trip. There's usually—but not always—a fee involved, and it may be nominal ($10 or less) or substantial ($100 or more).

If you must apply for a visa in advance, you can usually do it in person or by mail. When you apply by mail, you send your passport to a designated consulate, where your passport will be examined and the visa issued. Expediters—usually the same ones who handle expedited passport applications—can do all the work of obtaining your visa for you; however, there's always an additional cost (often more than $50 per visa).

Most visas limit you to a single trip—basically during the actual dates of your planned vacation. Other visas allow you to visit as many times as you wish for a specific period of time. Remember that requirements change, sometimes at the drop of a hat, and the burden is on you to make sure that you have the appropriate visas. Otherwise, you'll be turned away at the airport or, worse, deported after you arrive in the country. No company or travel insurer gives refunds if your travel plans are disrupted because you didn't have the correct visa.

U.S. Passport Information **U.S. Department of State** ☎ 877/487-2778 ⊕ http://travel.state.gov/passport.

U.S. Passport & Visa Expeditors **A. Briggs Passport & Visa Expeditors** ☎ 800/806-0581 or 202/464-3000 ⊕ www.abriggs.com. **American Passport Express** ☎ 800/455-5166 or 603/559-9888 ⊕ www.americanpassport.com. **Passport Express** ☎ 800/362-8196 or 401/272-4612 ⊕ www.passportexpress.com. **Travel Document Systems** ☎ 800/874-5100 or 202/638-3800 ⊕ www.traveldocs.com. **Travel the World Visas** ☎ 866/886-8472 or 301/495-7700 ⊕ www.world-visa.com.

SHOTS & MEDICATIONS

If you plan on doing a lot of hiking or camping, note that tick-borne Lyme disease is a serious risk in the woodlands of the Czech Republic. Schedule vaccinations well in advance of departure because some require several doses, and others may cause uncomfortable side effects.

■ TIP→ If you travel a lot internationally—particularly to developing nations—refer to the CDC's *Health Information for International Travel* (aka Traveler's Health Yellow Book). Info from it is posted on the CDC Web site (www.cdc.gov/travel/yb), or you can buy a copy from your local bookstore for $24.95.

To avoid problems clearing customs, diabetic travelers carrying needles and syringes should have on hand a letter from their physician confirming their need for insulin injections.

For more information *see* Health *under* On the Ground in Prague, *below.*

Health Warnings **National Centers for Disease Control & Prevention** (CDC) ☎ 877/394-8747 international travelers' health line ⊕ www.cdc.gov/travel. **World Health Organization** (WHO) ⊕ www.who.int.

TRIP INSURANCE

What kind of coverage do you honestly need? Do you even need trip insurance at all? Take a deep breath and read on.

We believe that comprehensive trip in-

PACKING 101

Why do some people travel with a convoy of huge suitcases yet never have a thing to wear? How do others pack a duffle with a week's worth of outfits *and* supplies for every contingency? We realize that packing is a matter of style, but there's a lot to be said for traveling light. These tips help fight the battle of the bulging bag.

Make a list. In a recent Fodor's survey, 29% of respondents said they make lists (and often pack) a week before a trip. You can use your list to pack and to repack at the end of your trip. It can also serve as record of the contents of your suitcase—in case it disappears in transit.

Think it through. What's the weather like? Is this a business trip? A cruise? Going abroad? In some places dress may be more or less conservative than you're used to. As you create your itinerary, note outfits next to each activity (don't forget accessories).

Edit your wardrobe. Plan to wear everything twice (better yet, thrice) and to do laundry along the way. Stick to one basic look—urban chic, sporty casual, etc. Build around one or two neutrals and an accent (e.g., black, white, and olive green). Women can freshen up looks by changing scarves or jewelry. For a week's trip, you can look smashing with three bottoms, four or five tops, a sweater, and a jacket.

Be practical. Put comfortable shoes at the top of your list. (Did we need to say this?) Pack lightweight, wrinkle-resistent, compact, washable items. (Or this?) Stack and roll clothes, so they'll wrinkle less. Unless you're on a guided tour or a cruise, select luggage you can readily carry. Porters, like good butlers, are hard to find these days.

Check weight and size limitations. In the United States you may be charged extra for checked bags weighing more than 50 pounds. Abroad some airlines don't allow you to check bags over 60 to 70 pounds, or they charge outrageous fees for every excess pound—or bag. Carry-on size limitations can be stringent, too.

Check carry-on restrictions. Research restrictions with the TSA. Rules vary abroad, so check them with your airline if you're traveling overseas on a foreign carrier. Consider packing all but essentials (travel documents, prescription meds, wallet) in checked luggage. This leads to a "pack only what you can afford to lose" approach that might help you streamline.

Rethink valuables. On U.S. flights, airlines are liable for only about $2,800 per person for bags. On international flights, the liability limit is around $635 per bag. But items like computers, cameras, and jewelry aren't covered, and as gadgetry regularly goes on and off the list of carry-on no-no's, you can't count on keeping things safe by keeping them close. Although comprehensive travel policies may cover luggage, the liability limit is often a pittance. A home-owner insurance policy may cover you sufficiently when you travel—or not.

Lock it up. If you must pack valuables, use TSA-approved locks (about $10) that can be unlocked by all U.S. security personnel.

Tag it. Always tag your luggage; use your business address if you don't want people to know your home address. Put the same information (and a copy of your itinerary) inside your luggage, too.

Report problems immediately. If your bags—or things in them—are damaged or go astray, file a written claim with your airline *before leaving the airport*. If the airline is at fault, it may give you money for essentials until your luggage arrives. Most lost bags are found within 48 hours, so alert the airline to your whereabouts for two or three days. If your bag was opened for security reasons in the States and something is missing, file a claim with the TSA.

surance is especially valuable if you're booking a very expensive or complicated trip (particularly to an isolated region) or if you're booking far in advance. Who knows what could happen six months down the road? But whether you get insurance has more to do with how comfortable you are assuming all that risk yourself.

Comprehensive travel policies typically cover trip-cancellation and interruption, letting you cancel or cut your trip short because of a personal emergency, illness, or, in some cases, acts of terrorism in your destination. Such policies also cover evacuation and medical care. Some also cover you for trip delays because of bad weather or mechanical problems as well as for lost or delayed baggage. Another type of coverage to look for is financial default— that is, when your trip is disrupted because a tour operator, airline, or cruise line goes out of business. Generally you must buy this when you book your trip or shortly thereafter, and it's only available to you if your operator isn't on a list of excluded companies.

If you're going abroad, consider buying medical-only coverage at the very least.

Neither Medicare nor some private insurers cover medical expenses anywhere outside of the United States besides Mexico and Canada (including time aboard a cruise ship, even if it leaves from a U.S. port). Medical-only policies typically reimburse you for medical care (excluding that related to preexisting conditions) and hospitalization abroad, and provide for evacuation. You still have to pay the bills and await reimbursement from the insurer, though.

Expect comprehensive travel insurance policies to cost about 4% to 7% of the total price of your trip (it's more like 12% if you're over age 70). A medical-only policy may or may not be cheaper than a comprehensive policy. Always read the fine print of your policy to make sure that you are covered for the risks that are of most concern to you. Compare several policies to make sure you're getting the best price and range of coverage available.

Trip Insurance Resources

INSURANCE COMPARISON SITES		
Insure My Trip.com		www.insuremytrip.com.
Square Mouth.com		www.quotetravelinsurance.com.
COMPREHENSIVE TRAVEL INSURERS		
Access America	866/807-3982	www.accessamerica.com.
CSA Travel Protection	800/873-9855	www.csatravelprotection.com.
HTH Worldwide	610/254-8700 or 888/243-2358	www.hthworldwide.com.
Travelex Insurance	888/457-4602	www.travelex-insurance.com.
Travel Guard International	715/345-0505 or 800/826-4919	www.travelguard.com.
Travel Insured International	800/243-3174	www.travelinsured.com.
MEDICAL-ONLY INSURERS		
International Medical Group	800/628-4664	www.imglobal.com.
International SOS	215/942-8000 or 713/521-7611	www.internationalsos.com.
Wallach & Company	800/237-6615 or 504/687-3166	www.wallach.com.

BOOKING YOUR TRIP

Unless your cousin is a travel agent, you're probably among the millions of people who make most of their travel arrangements online. But have you ever wondered just what the differences are between an online travel agent (a Web site through which you make reservations instead of going directly to the airline, hotel, or car-rental company), a discounter (a firm that does a high volume of business with a hotel chain or airline and accordingly gets good prices), a wholesaler (one that makes cheap reservations in bulk and then resells them to people like you), and an aggregator (one that compares all the offerings so you don't have to)? Is it truly better to book directly on an airline or hotel Web site? And when does a real live travel agent come in handy?

ONLINE

You really have to shop around. A travel wholesaler such as Hotels.com or Hotel-Club.net can be a source of good rates, as can discounters such as Hotwire or Price-line, particularly if you can bid for your hotel room or airfare. Indeed, such sites sometimes have deals that are unavailable elsewhere. They do, however, tend to work only with hotel chains (which makes them just plain useless for getting hotel reservations outside of major cities) or big airlines (so that often leaves out upstarts like JetBlue and some foreign carriers like Air India). Also, with discounters and wholesalers you must generally prepay, and everything is nonrefundable. And before you fork over the dough, be sure to check the terms and conditions, so you know what a given company will do for you if there's a problem and what you'll have to deal with on your own.

■ TIP→ **To be absolutely sure everything was processed correctly, confirm reservations made through online travel agents, discounters, and wholesalers directly with your hotel before leaving home.**

Booking engines like Expedia, Traveloc-ity, and Orbitz are actually travel agents, albeit high-volume, online ones. And airline travel packagers like American Airlines Vacations and Virgin Vacations—well, they're travel agents, too. But they may still not work with all the world's hotels.

An aggregator site will search many sites and pull the best prices for airfares, hotels, and rental cars from them. Most aggregators compare the major travel-booking sites such as Expedia, Travelocity, and Orbitz; some also look at airline Web sites, though rarely the sites of smaller budget airlines. Some aggregators also compare other travel products, including complex packages—a good thing, as you can sometimes get the best overall deal by booking an air-and-hotel package.

WITH A TRAVEL AGENT

If you use an agent—brick-and-mortar or virtual—you'll pay a fee for the service. And know that the service you get from some online agents isn't comprehensive. For example Expedia and Travelocity don't search for prices on budget airlines like JetBlue, Southwest, or small foreign carriers. That said, some agents (online or not) do have access to fares that are difficult to find otherwise, and the savings can more than make up for any surcharge.

A knowledgeable brick-and-mortar travel agent can be a godsend if you're booking a cruise, a package trip that's not available to you directly, an air pass, or a complicated itinerary including several overseas flights. What's more, travel agents that specialize in a destination may have exclusive access to certain deals and insider information on things such as charter flights. Agents who specialize in types of travelers (senior citizens, gays and lesbians, naturists) or types of trips (cruises, luxury travel, safaris) can also be invaluable.

A top-notch agent planning a trip to Russia will make sure you get the correct visa

Online Booking Resources

AGGREGATORS		
Kayak	www.kayak.com	looks at cruises and vacation packages.
Mobissimo	www.mobissimo.com.	
Qixo	www.qixo.com	compares cruises, vacation packages, and even travel insurance.
Sidestep	www.sidestep.com	compares vacation packages and lists travel deals.
Travelgrove	www.travelgrove.com	compares cruises and packages.
BOOKING ENGINES		
Cheap Tickets	www.cheaptickets.com	discounter.
Expedia	www.expedia.com	large online agency that charges a booking fee for airline tickets.
Hotwire	www.hotwire.com	discounter.
lastminute.com	www.lastminute.com	specializes in last-minute travel; the main site is for the U.K., but it has a link to a U.S. site.
Luxury Link	www.luxurylink.com	auctions (surprisingly good deals) as well as offers on the high-end side of travel.
Onetravel.com	www.onetravel.com	discounter for hotels, car rentals, airfares, and packages.
Orbitz	www.orbitz.com	charges a booking fee for airline tickets, but gives a clear breakdown of fees and taxes before you book.
Priceline.com	www.priceline.com	discounter that also allows bidding.
Travel.com	www.travel.com	allows you to compare its rates with those of other booking engines.
Travelocity	www.travelocity.com	charges a booking fee for airline tickets, but promises good problem resolution.
ONLINE ACCOMMODATIONS		
Hotelbook.com	www.hotelbook.com	focuses on independent hotels worldwide.
Hotel Club	www.hotelclub.net	good for major cities worldwide.
Hotels.com	www.hotels.com	big Expedia-owned wholesaler that offers rooms in hotels all over the world.
Quikbook	www.quikbook.com	"pay when you stay" reservations that let you settle your bill at check out, not when you book.
OTHER RESOURCES		
Bidding For Travel	www.biddingfortravel.com	good place to figure out what you can get and for how much before bidding on, say, Priceline.

application and complete it on time; the one booking your cruise may get you a cabin upgrade or arrange to have bottle of champagne chilling in your cabin when you embark. And complain about the surcharges all you like, but when things don't work out the way you'd hoped, it's nice to have an agent to put things right.

■ TIP→ Remember that Expedia, Travelocity, and Orbitz are travel agents, not just booking engines. To resolve any problems with a reservation made through these companies, contact them first.

Travel agencies can be useful for visitors to Prague; they can provide you with information and then book your tickets. Čedok, the ubiquitous Czech travel agency, provides general tourist information and city maps. Čedok will also exchange money, book accommodations, arrange guided tours, and book passage on airlines, buses, and trains. You can pay for Čedok services, including booking rail tickets, with any major credit card. The main office is open weekdays from 8:30 to 6 and Saturday from 9 to 1. Note there are limited weekend hours.

In the U.S., an agency like Tatra Travel, which specializes in Eastern and Central Europe, can save you money booking non-stop flights to the Czech Republic; the agency also can book Czech Airlines travel packages.

Agent Resources American Society of Travel Agents ☏ 703/739-2782 ⊕ www. travelsense.org.

Prague Travel Agents American Express ✉ Václavské nám. 56, Nové Město ☏ 224-219-992. **Čedok** ✉ Na Příkopě 18, Staré Město ☏ 224-197-111 ⊕ www.cedok.cz. **Prague International** ✉ Senovážné nám. 23, Nové Město ☏ 224-142-431 ⊕ www. pragueinternational.cz.

U.S. Travel Agent Tatra Travel ✉ 212 E. 51 St., New York, NY ☏ 212/486-0533 ⊕ www. tatratravel.com.

10 WAYS TO SAVE

1. Join "frequent guest" programs. You may get preferential treatment in room choice and/or upgrades in your favorite chains.

2. Call direct. You can sometimes get a better price if you call a hotel's local toll-free number (if available) rather than a central reservations number.

3. Check online. Check hotel Web sites, as not all chains are represented on all travel sites.

4. Look for specials. Always inquire about packages and corporate rates.

5. Look for price guarantees. For overseas trips, look for guaranteed rates. With your rate locked in you won't pay more, even if the price goes up in the local currency.

6. Look for weekend deals at business hotels. High-end chains catering to business travelers are often busy only on weekdays; to fill rooms they often drop rates dramatically on weekends.

7. Ask about taxes. Verify whether local hotel taxes are included in quoted rates. In some places taxes can add 20% or more to your bill.

8. Read the fine print. Watch for add-ons, including resort fees, energy surcharges, and "convenience" fees for such things as unlimited local phone service you won't use or a free newspaper in a language you can't read.

9. Know when to go. If your destination's high season is December through April and you're trying to book, say, in late April, you might save money by changing your dates by a week or two. Ask when rates go down, though: if your dates straddle peak and non-peak seasons, a property may still charge peak-season rates for the entire stay.

10. Weigh your options (we can't say this enough). Weigh transportation times and costs against the savings of staying in a hotel that's cheaper because it's out of the way.

APARTMENT & HOUSE RENTALS
HOME EXCHANGES

With a direct home exchange you stay in someone else's home while they stay in yours. Some outfits also deal with vacation homes, so you're not actually staying in someone's full-time residence, just their vacant weekend place.

Exchange Clubs Home Exchange.com ☎ 800/877-8723 ⊕ www.homeexchange. com; $59.95 for a 1-year online listing. **HomeLink International** ☎ 800/638-3841 ⊕ www. homelink.org; $80 yearly for Web-only membership; $125 includes Web access and 2 catalogs. **Intervac U.S.** ☎ 800/756-4663 ⊕ www.intervacus.com; $78.88 for Web-only membership; $126 includes Web access and a catalog.

HOSTELS

Hostels offer bare-bones lodging at low, low prices—often in shared dorm rooms with shared baths—to people of all ages, though the primary market is young travelers, especially students. Most hostels serve breakfast; dinner and/or shared cooking facilities may also be available. In some hostels you aren't allowed to be in your room during the day, and there may be a curfew at night. Nevertheless, hostels provide a sense of community, with public rooms where travelers often gather to share stories. Many hostels are affiliated with Hostelling International (HI), an umbrella group of hostel associations with some 4,500 member properties in more than 70 countries. Other hostels are completely independent and may be nothing more than a really cheap hotel.

Membership in any HI association, open to travelers of all ages, allows you to stay in HI-affiliated hostels at member rates. One-year membership is about $28 for adults; hostels charge about $10–$30 per night. Members have priority if the hostel is full; they're also eligible for discounts around the world, even on rail and bus travel in some countries.

Hostelling International–USA ☎ 301/495-1240 ⊕ www.hiusa.org.

▌AIRLINE TICKETS

Most domestic airline tickets are electronic; international tickets may be either electronic or paper. With an e-ticket the

Online Booking Resources

CONTACTS		
At Home Abroad	212/421-9165	www.athomeabroadinc.com.
Barclay International Group	516/364-0064 or 800/845-6636	www.barclayweb.com.
Drawbridge to Europe	541/482-7778 or 888/268-1148	www.drawbridgetoeurope.com.
Homes Away	416/920-1873 or 800/374-6637	www.homesaway.com.
Hometours International	865/690-8484	thor.he.net/~hometour.
Interhome	954/791-8282 or 800/882-6864	www.interhome.us.
Suzanne B. Cohen & Associates	207/622-0743	www.villaeurope.com.
Vacation Home Rentals Worldwide	201/767-9393 or 800/633-3284	www.vhrww.com.
Villanet	206/417-3444 or 800/964-1891	www.rentavilla.com.
Villas & Apartments Abroad	212/213-6435 or 800/433-3020	www.vaanyc.com.
Villas International	415/499-9490 or 800/221-2260	www.villasintl.com.
Villas of Distinction	707/778-1800 or 800/289-0900	www.villasofdistinction.com.
Wimco	800/449-1553	www.wimco.com.

only thing you receive is an e-mailed receipt citing your itinerary and reservation and ticket numbers. The greatest advantage of an e-ticket is that if you lose your receipt, you can simply print out another copy or ask the airline to do it for you at check-in. You usually pay a surcharge (up to $50) to get a paper ticket, if you can get one at all. The sole advantage of a paper ticket is that it may be easier to endorse over to another airline if your flight is canceled and the airline with which you booked can't accommodate you on another flight.

■ TIP→ Discount air passes that let you travel economically in a country or region must often be purchased before you leave home. In some cases you can only get them through a travel agent.

Prague is served by a growing number of budget carriers, which connect the Czech capital to several cities in the U.K. and across the European continent. These airlines are a great and cheap way to travel within Europe—though since the flights are popular be sure to book well in advance. Budget carriers, however, are usually not much help in cutting costs when traveling from North America. Most of these carriers operate out of secondary airports (for example, Stansted in London instead of Heathrow, where most trans-Atlantic flights land; Orly in Paris instead of the larger Charles de Gaulle airport). This means travelers must not only change airlines but also airports, which can add frustration and expense. Also consider limits on both carry-on and checked baggage, which are often more stringent on budget carriers than on large international carriers.

■ RENTAL CARS

When you reserve a car, ask about cancellation penalties, taxes, drop-off charges (if you're planning to pick up the car in one city and leave it in another), and surcharges (for being under or over a certain age, for additional drivers, or for driving

10 WAYS TO SAVE

1. Nonrefundable is best. If saving money is more important than flexibility, then non-refundable tickets work. Just remember that you'll pay dearly (as much as $100) if you change your plans.

2. Comparison shop. Web sites and travel agents can have different arrangements with airlines and offer different prices for exactly the same flights.

3. Beware those prices. Many airline Web sites—and most ads—show prices *without* taxes and surcharges.

4. Stay loyal. Stick with one or two frequent-flier programs. You'll rack up free trips faster and you'll accumulate more quickly the perks that make trips easier. On some airlines these include a special reservations number, early boarding, access to upgrades, and roomier economy-class seating.

5. Watch those ticketing fees. Surcharges are usually added when you buy your ticket anywhere but on an airline Web site. (That includes by phone—even if you call the airline directly—and paper tickets regardless of how you book.)

6. Check early and often. Start looking for cheap fares up to a year in advance. Keep looking till you find a price you like.

7. Don't work alone. Some Web sites have tracking features that will e-mail you immediately when good deals are posted.

8. Jump on the good deals. Waiting even a few minutes might mean paying more.

9. Be flexible. Look for departures on Tuesday, Wednesday, and Thursday, typically the cheapest days to travel. And check on prices for departures from alternative airports.

10. Weigh your options. What you get can be as important as what you save. A cheaper flight might have a long layover rather than being nonstop, or it might land at a secondary airport, where your ground transportation costs might be higher.

across state or country borders or beyond a specific distance from your point of rental). All these things can add substantially to your costs. Request car seats and extras such as GPS when you book.

Rates are sometimes—but not always—better if you book in advance or reserve through a rental agency's Web site. There are other reasons to book ahead, though: for popular destinations, during busy times of the year, or to ensure that you get certain types of cars (vans, SUVs, exotic sports cars).

■ TIP→ Make sure that a confirmed reservation guarantees you a car. Agencies sometimes overbook, particularly for busy weekends and holiday periods.

Several major agencies have offices at the airport and also in the city. Prices can differ greatly, so be sure to shop around. Major firms like Avis and Hertz offer Western makes starting at around $45 per day or $300 per week, which includes insurance, damage waiver, and V.A.T. (value-added tax); cars equipped with automatic transmission and air-conditioning are available, but are generally more expensive.

Car Rental Resources

AUTOMOBILE ASSOCIATIONS		
U.S.: American Automobile	315/797-5000 most contact Association (AAA) with the organization is through state and regional members.	www.aaa.com;
National Automobile Club	650/294-7000 membership for CA residents only.	www.thenac.com;
LOCAL AGENCIES		
Agile	777-272-766	www.agile.cz.
Alimex	233-350-001	www.alimexcr.cz.
Avis	221-851-229	www.avis.cz.
Budget	224-889-995 or 220-113-253	www.budget.cz.
Europcar	235-364-531 or 224-811-290	www.europcar.cz.
Hertz	233-326-714, 222-231-010, or 224-394-174	www.hertz.cz.
Nationa	224-923-719	www.nationalcar.cz.
MAJOR AGENCIES		
Alamo	800/522-9696	www.alamo.com.
Avis	800/331-1084	www.avis.com.
Budget	800/472-3325	www.budget.com.
Hertz	800/654-3001	www.hertz.com.
National Car Rental	800/227-7368	www.nationalcar.com.
WHOLESALERS		
Auto Europe	888/223-5555	www.autoeurope.com.
Europe by Car	212/581-3040 in New York, 800/223-1516	www.europebycar.com.
Eurovacations	877/471-3876	www.eurovacations.com.
Kemwel	877/820-0668	www.kemwel.com.

It's best to reserve your rental car before you leave home, and it may be less expensive as well. Smaller local companies, on the other hand, can rent Czech cars for significantly less, but the service and insurance coverage may be inferior.

Drivers from the U.S. need no international driving permit to rent a car in the Czech Republic, only a valid domestic license, along with the vehicle registration. If you intend to drive across a border, ask about restrictions on driving into other countries. The minimum age required for renting is usually 21 or older, and some companies also have maximum ages; be sure to inquire when making your arrangements. The Czech Republic requires that you will have held your driver's license for at least a year before you can rent a car.

CAR-RENTAL INSURANCE

Everyone who rents a car wonders whether the insurance that the rental companies offer is worth the expense. No one—including us—has a simple answer. It all depends on how much regular insurance you have, how comfortable you are with risk, and whether or not money is an issue.

If you own a car, your personal auto insurance may cover a rental to some degree, though not all policies protect you abroad; always read your policy's fine print. If you don't have auto insurance, then seriously consider buying the collision- or loss-damage waiver (CDW or LDW) from the car-rental company, which eliminates your liability for damage to the car. Some credit cards offer CDW coverage, but it's usually supplemental to your own insurance and rarely covers SUVs, minivans, luxury models, and the like. If your coverage is secondary, you may still be liable for loss-of-use costs from the car-rental company. But no credit-card insurance is valid unless you use that card for *all* transactions, from reserving to paying the final bill. All companies exclude car rental in some countries, so be sure to find out about the destination to which you are traveling.

10 WAYS TO SAVE

1. Beware of cheap rates. Those great rates aren't so great when you add in taxes, surcharges, and insurance. Such extras can double or triple the initial quote.

2. Rent weekly. Weekly rates are usually better than daily ones. Even if you only want to rent for five or six days, ask for the weekly rate; it may very well be cheaper than the daily rate for that period of time.

3. Don't forget the locals. Price local car-rental companies as well as the majors.

4. Airport rentals can cost more. Airports often add surcharges, which you can sometimes avoid by renting from an agency whose office is just off airport property.

5. Wholesalers can help. Investigate wholesalers, which don't own fleets but rent in bulk from firms that do, and which frequently offer better rates (note that you must usually pay for such rentals before leaving home).

6. Look for rate guarantees. With your rate locked in, you won't pay more, even if the price goes up in the local currency.

7. Fill up farther away. Avoid hefty refueling fees by filling the tank at a station well away from where you plan to turn in the car.

8. Pump it yourself. Don't buy the tank of gas that's in the car when you rent it unless you plan to do a lot of driving.

9. Get all your discounts. Find out whether a credit card you carry or organization or frequent-renter program to which you belong has a discount program. And confirm that such discounts really are a deal. You can often do better with special weekend or weekly rates offered by a rental agency.

10. Check out package rates. Adding a car rental onto your air/hotel vacation package may be cheaper than renting a car separately on your own.

■ TIP→ Diners Club offers primary CDW coverage on all rentals reserved and paid for with the card. This means that Diners Club's company—not your own car insurance—pays in case of an accident. It *doesn't* mean your car-insurance company won't raise your rates once it discovers you had an accident.

Some countries require you to purchase CDW coverage or require car-rental companies to include it in quoted rates. Ask your rental company about issues like these in your destination. In most cases it's cheaper to add a supplemental CDW plan to your comprehensive travel-insurance policy (⇨ Trip Insurance *under* Things to Consider *in* Getting Started, *above*) than to purchase it from a rental company. That said, you don't want to pay for a supplement if you're required to buy insurance from the rental company.

■ TIP→ You can decline the insurance from the rental company and purchase it through a third-party provider such as Travel Guard (www.travelguard.com)—$9 per day for $35,000 of coverage. That's sometimes just under half the price of the CDW offered by some car-rental companies.

TRAIN TICKETS

The Eurail Pass and the Eurail Youthpass are not valid for travel within the Czech Republic, and most rail passes, such as the Czech Flexipass, will wind up costing more than what you'd spend buying tickets on the spot, particularly if you intend to travel mainly in the Czech Republic, since international tickets normally are more expensive. However, the European East Pass, is good for first-class travel on the national railroads of the Czech Republic, Austria, Hungary, Poland, and Slovakia. The pass allows five days of unlimited travel within a one-month period for $220, and it must be purchased from Rail Europe before your departure. The many Czech rail passes available are useful chiefly to regular travelers. A discount applies to any group of 2 to 15 people traveling second class (*sleva pro skupiny*). It's always cheaper to buy a return ticket.

Foreign visitors will find it easiest to inquire at the international booking offices of major stations for the latest discounts and passes that will apply to them.

Rail Europe ✉ 226–230 Westchester Ave., White Plains, NY 10604 ☎ 877/257-2887 ⊕ www.raileurope.com.

▐ GUIDED TOURS

Guided tours are a good option when you don't want to do it all yourself. You travel along with a group (sometimes large, sometimes small), stay in prebooked hotels, eat with your fellow travelers (the cost of meals sometimes included in the price of your tour, sometimes not), and follow a schedule. But not all guided tours are an if-it's-Tuesday-this-must-be-Prague experience. A knowledgeable guide can take you places that you might never discover on your own, and you may be pushed to see more than you would have otherwise. Tours aren't for everyone, but they can be just the thing for trips to places where making travel arrangements is difficult or time-consuming (particularly when you don't speak the language). Whenever you book a guided tour, find out what's included and what isn't. A "land-only" tour includes all your travel (by bus, in most cases) in the destination, but not necessarily your flights to and from or even within it. Also, in most cases prices in tour brochures don't include fees and taxes. And remember that you'll be expected to tip your guide (in cash) at the end of the tour.

Major U.S. agencies often plan trips covering Prague and the Czech Republic. Abercrombie & Kent, Inc. is one agency that offers package tours to the area. The largest Czech agency, Čedok, also offers package tours.

SPECIAL-INTEREST TOURS

One reason visitors come to the Czech Republic is to connect with their Jewish Heritage. Wittmann Tours provides not only coverage of the main sights in Prague, but excursions to smaller Czech towns and Trebic.

Recommended Companies Abercrombue & Kent ☎ 800–554–7016 ⊕ www. abercrombiekent.com. **Čedok** ☎ 800–554–7016 ⊕ www.cedok.com. **Wittmann Tours** ☎ 222–252–472 ⊕ www. wittmann-tours.com.

∎ VACATION PACKAGES

Packages *are not* guided excursions. Packages combine airfare, accommodations, and perhaps a rental car or other extras (theater tickets, guided excursions, boat trips, reserved entry to popular museums, transit passes), but they let you do your own thing. During busy periods packages may be your only option, as flights and rooms may be sold out otherwise. Packages will definitely save you time. They can also save you money, particularly in peak seasons, but—and this is a really big "but"—you should price each part of the package separately to be sure. And be aware that prices advertised on Web sites

and in newspapers rarely include service charges or taxes, which can up your costs by hundreds of dollars.

∎ TIP➔ Some packages and cruises are sold only through travel agents. Don't always assume that you can get the best deal by booking everything yourself.

Each year consumers are stranded or lose their money when packagers—even large ones with excellent reputations—go out of business. How can you protect yourself? First, always pay with a credit card; if you have a problem, your credit-card company may help you resolve it. Second, buy trip insurance that covers default. Third, choose a company that belongs to the United States Tour Operators Association, whose members must set aside funds to cover defaults. Finally, choose a company that also participates in the Tour Operator Program of the American Society of Travel Agents (ASTA), which will act as mediator in any disputes. You can also check on the tour operator's reputation among travelers by posting an inquiry on one of the Fodors.com forums.

Both Czech Airlines and Austrian Airlines offer good-value hotel-and-air packages to Prague, particularly in the off-season. The online discounter Go-Today.com usually has discounted travel packages to Prague, though flights often require a transfer in Europe and hotels are usually not in the city center.

Austrian Air Vacations ☎ 800/790–4682 or 404/240–0949 ⊕ www.austrianairlines.com. **ČSA Airtours** ☎ 800/224–2365 or 212/765–6588 ⊕ usa.csa.cz. **Go-Today.com** ☎ 425/487–9632 ⊕ www.go-today.com.

Organizations American Society of Travel Agents (ASTA) ☎ 703/739–2782 or 800/965–2782 ⊕ www.astanet.com. **United States Tour Operators Association** (USTOA) ☎ 212/599–6599 ⊕ www.ustoa.com.

∎ TIP➔ Local tourism boards can provide information about lesser-known and small-niche operators that sell packages to only a few destinations.

NAVIGATING PRAGUE

Basic navigating vocabulary: *ulice* (street, abbreviated to ul.); *náměstí* (square, abbreviated to nám.); and *třída* (avenue). In Prague, the blue signs mark the tradtional street address, while the red signs are used to denote the number of the building for administrative purposes.

TRANSPORTATION

Prague is divided into 10 administrative districts. "Prague 1" encompasses the Old Town, Malá Strana, part of the New Town, and the Castle district, and is the area where visitors tend to spend most of their time. Residents in conversation will often refer to the districts by number to orient themselves geographically ("x is in Prague 1" or "y is in Prague 7"). These district numbers correspond roughly to the city's traditional neighborhoods. The neighborhood of Vinohrady, which lies just to the east of Wenceslas Square, for example, is mostly in Prague 2. Other common neighborhoods and district numbers include: Žižkov, Prague 3; Smíchov, Prague 5; and Holešovice, Prague 7. These names—along with the district numbers—appear on street signs.

■ TIP➜ **Ask the local tourist board about hotel and local transportation packages that include tickets to major museum exhibits or other special events.**

■ BY AIR

The nonstop flight from New York to Prague takes about 8 hours, but the entire journey will take longer (12 to 15 hours) if you have to change planes at a European hub. If you have a stopover, be sure to leave at least 90 minutes (two hours is ideal) between connections to allow both you and your luggage to make the next flight. The flight from London to Prague takes about 2 hours; the flight from Vienna to Prague takes less than an hour.

Airlines & Airports **Airline and Airport Links.com** ⊕ www.airlineandairportlinks.com has links to many of the world's airlines and airports.

Airline Security Issues **Transportation Security Administration** ⊕ www.tsa.gov has answers for almost every question that might come up.

Air Travel Resources in

AIRPORTS

Prague's Ruzyně Airport is the country's main international airport and lies about 15 km (10 mi) northwest of the city center. The airport has two terminals—*Sever 1* (North 1, or N1) and *Sever 2* (North 2, or N2)—so make sure to read your ticket carefully to see where you are arriving at and departing from. The trip from the airport to the downtown area by car or taxi will take about 30 minutes—add another 20 minutes during rush hour (7 AM to 9 AM and 4 PM to 6 PM).

Airport Information **Ruzyně Airport** ☎ 220-113-314 ⊕ www.csl.cz.

GROUND TRANSPORTATION

There are several options for getting into town from the airport, depending on the amount of time you have, your budget, and the amount of luggage.

The cheapest option is Prague's municipal bus service, Bus 119, which leaves from just outside the arrivals area and makes the run to the Dejvická metro station (on the green line, A) every 15 minutes or so during weekdays and less frequently on weekends and evenings. The 20 Kč ticket—plus an extra 10 Kč ticket if you have a large bag—can be purchased at the yellow vending machine at the bus stop and includes a transfer to the metro. To reach Wenceslas Square, get off at Můstek station.

The Čedaz minibus shuttle links the airport with the central náměstí Republiky (Republic Square), which is not far from the Old Town Square. It runs regularly between 5:30 AM and 9:30 PM daily and makes an intermediate stop at the Dejvická metro station. The one-way fare is 90 Kč. You can also take a Čedaz minibus directly to your hotel for 370 Kč—650 Kč, which is often less than the taxi fare.

A taxi ride to the center will set you back about 600 Kč–700 Kč; the fare will be higher for destinations outside of the center and away from the airport. Be sure to

FLYING 101

Flying may not be as carefree as it once was, but there are some things you can do to make your trip smoother.

MINIMIZE THE TIME SPENT STANDING IN LINE. Buy an e-ticket, check in at an electronic kiosk, or—even better—check in on your airline's Web site before leaving home. Pack light, and limit carry-on items to only the essentials.

ARRIVE WHEN YOU NEED TO. Research your airline's policy. It's usually at least an hour before domestic flights and two to three hours before international flights. But airlines at some busy airports have more stringent requirements. Check the TSA Web site for estimated security waiting times at major airports.

GET TO THE GATE. If you aren't at the gate at least 10 minutes before your flight is scheduled to take off (sometimes earlier), you won't be allowed to board.

DOUBLE-CHECK YOUR FLIGHT TIMES. Do this especially if you reserved far in advance. Schedules change, and alerts may not reach you.

DON'T GO HUNGRY. Ask whether your airline offers anything to eat; even when it does, be prepared to pay.

GET THE SEAT YOU WANT. Often you can pick a seat when you buy your ticket on an airline Web site. But it's not guaranteed; the airline could change the plane after you book, so double-check. You can also select a seat if you check in electronically. Avoid seats on the aisle directly across from the lavatories. Frequent fliers say those are even worse than back-row seats that don't recline.

GOT KIDS? GET INFO. Ask the airline about its children's menus, activities, and fares. Sometimes infants and toddlers fly free if they sit on a parent's lap, and older children fly for half price in their own seats. Also inquire about policies involving car seats; having one may limit seating options. Also ask about seat-belt ex-tenders for car seats. And note that you can't count on a flight attendant to produce an extender; you may have to ask for one when you board.

CHECK YOUR SCHEDULING. Don't buy a ticket if there's less than an hour between connecting flights. Although schedules are padded, if anything goes wrong you might miss your connection. If you're traveling to an important function, depart a day early.

BRING PAPER. Even when using an e-ticket, always carry a hard copy of your receipt; you may need it to get your boarding pass, which most airports require to get past security.

COMPLAIN AT THE AIRPORT. If your baggage goes astray or your flight goes awry, complain before leaving the airport. Most carriers require this.

BEWARE OF OVERBOOKED FLIGHTS. If a flight is oversold, the gate agent will usually ask for volunteers and offer some sort of compensation for taking a different flight. If you're bumped from a flight *involuntarily*, the airline must give you some kind of compensation if an alternate flight can't be found within one hour.

KNOW YOUR RIGHTS. If your flight is delayed because of something within the airline's control (bad weather doesn't count), the airline must get you to your destination on the same day, even if they have to book you on another airline and in an upgraded class. Read the Contract of Carriage, which is usually buried on the airline's Web site.

BE PREPARED. The Boy Scout motto is especially important if you're traveling during a stormy season. To quickly adjust your plans, program a few numbers into your cell: your airline, an airport hotel or two, your destination hotel, your car service, and/or your travel agent.

agree on the fare with the driver before leaving the airport to avoid any unpleasant surprises at the end of the ride. If you have access to a telephone, you can order a taxi from private companies like AAA Taxi. Their fare to the center is about 500 Kč.

Prague Airport Shuttle offers transport to your hotel for a fixed price between 650 Kč and 1,200 Kč, depending on the number of passengers (1–8). The company promises to wait up to an hour from your originally scheduled arrival if your flight is delayed or if customs and immigration are slow. Reservations must be made in advance via e-mail.

AAA Radiotaxi ☎ 222-333-222 ⊕ www.aaa. radiotaxi.cz. **Čedaz** ☎ 220-114-286. **Prague Airport Shuttle** ☎ 602-395-421 ⊕ www. prague-airport-shuttle.com.

FLIGHTS

ČSA (Czech Airlines), the Czech national carrier, at the time of this writing was the only airline to offer nonstop flights from the United States (from New York's Newark airport) to Prague (daily flights during the busiest season). Most major U.S.-based airlines fly to Prague through codeshare arrangements with their European counterparts. However, nearly all the major European airlines fly there, so it's usually easy to connect through a major European airport (such as London–Heathrow, Paris, Amsterdam, or Vienna) and continue to Prague; indeed, flights between the U.K. and Prague are numerous and frequent, including some on cheap discount airlines, though in London most of these leave from Gatwick or Stansted airports rather than Heathrow, making them less attractive options for Americans. Fares from the U.S. tend to rise dramatically during the busy summer season, particularly from June through August or September. There are many discounts during the slow winter months.

Airline Contacts American Airlines ☎ 800/ 433-7300, 224-234-985 in Prague ⊕ www. aa.com. **Continental Airlines** ☎ 800/523-3273 for U.S. reservations, 800/231-0856 for international reservations, 221-665-133 in Prague ⊕ www.continental.com. **Czech Airlines (ČSA)** ☎ 239-007-007 in Prague, 800/ 223-2365 in U.S. ⊕ www.csa.cz. **Delta Airlines** ☎ 800/221-1212 for U.S. reservations, 800/241-4141 for international reservations, 224-946-733 in Prague ⊕ www.delta.com. **Northwest Airlines** ☎ 800/225-2525 ⊕ www.nwa.com. **United Airlines** ☎ 800/ 864-8331 for U.S. reservations, 800/538-2929 for international reservations ⊕ www.united. com.

Budget Airlines in Europe EasyJet ⊕ www.easyjet.com. **Germanwings** ☎ 800-142-287 in Prague, 800-142-287 ⊕ www.germanwings.com. **Sky Europe** ☎ 900-141-516 in Prague (toll number) ⊕ www.skyeurope.com. **Smart Wings** ☎ 255-700-827 ⊕ www.smartwings.net.

▌BY BUS

The Czech complex of regional bus lines known collectively as ČSAD operates its dense network from the sprawling Florenc station. For information about routes and schedules, consult the confusingly displayed timetables posted at the station or visit the information window in the lower-level lobby, which is open daily from 6 AM to 9 PM. The company's Web site will give you bus and train information in English (click on the British flag).

Most, but not all, buses use the Florenc station. Some buses—primarily those heading to smaller destinations in the south of the country—depart from above Roztyly metro station (red line, C). You won't know beforehand which buses leave from Roztyly, so you will have to ask first at Florenc. There's no central information center at Roztyly; you simply have to sort out the timetables at the bus stops or ask someone.

Buses offer an easier and quicker alternative to trains for many destinations. The western Bohemian spa town of Karlovy Vary, for example, is an easy two-hour bus ride away. The same journey by train—because of the circuitous rail route through the north of the country—often takes five or six hours.

Nearly any town or city in the Czech Republic, at least in theory, is reachable by bus, but bear in mind that the lines primarily serve the needs of commuters and run most frequently on work days. Bus service falls off sharply on nights, weekends, and holidays.

Bus Information ČSAD Florenc station ✉ Křižíkova 4, Karlín ☎ 900-119-041 ⊕ www.idos.cz Ⓜ Line B and C: Florenc

▌ BY CAR

Traveling by car has some obvious advantages: it offers much more flexibility and is often quicker than a bus or train. But these advantages can be outweighed by the costs of the rental and gasoline, as well as the general hassles of driving in the Czech Republic. Most of the roads in the country are of the two-lane variety, and are often jammed with trucks. Frequent detours and road construction can add hours to a trip. And then there's parking. It's impossible in Prague and often difficult in the larger cities and towns outside of the capital. If you do decide to rent a car and drive, don't set out without a large, up-to-date Český Autoatlas, available at gas stations and bookstores.

If you intend to visit only Prague, you can—and should—do without a car. The city center is congested and difficult to navigate, and you can save yourself a lot of frustration by sticking to public transportation.

A special permit is required to drive on expressways and other four-lane highways. Rental cars should already have a permit affixed to the windshield. Temporary permits—for 15 days (200 Kč) or two months (300 Kč)—are available at border crossings, post offices, and some large service stations.

GASOLINE

Gas stations are frequent on major thoroughfares and near large cities. Many are open around the clock. At least two grades of unleaded gasoline are sold, usually 91–93 octane (regular) and 94–98 octane (super), as well as diesel. The average cost of a gallon of gasoline is at least twice that in the U.S. The Czech word for gasoline is "benzin," and at the station you pump it yourself.

■ TIP→ Occasionally an attendant might come out and wash your windshield. A tip of 5Kč to 10 Kč is sufficient for this.

PARKING

Finding a parking spot in Prague can be next to impossible. Most of the spaces in the city center, Prague 1, are reserved for residents; so you'll have to look for public lots with machines that issue temporary permits (look for the big blue "P" on machines). To use the machines, insert the required amount of change—usually 10 Kč to 20 Kč an hour—then place the ticket in a visible spot on the dashboard. Violators will find their cars towed away or immobilized by a "boot" on the tire. Some hotels offer parking—and this is a real advantage—though you may have to pay extra.

Parking is generally unrestricted outside of the immediate downtown area, Prague 1, though vacant spots can still be hard to find. If you have a car and you need to get rid of it, try parking it along one of the side streets in Vinohrady above and behind the National Museum, or on one of the streets in Prague 6 or Prague 7 across the river and north of the Old Town. There's an underground lot at náměstí Jana Palacha, near Old Town Square. There are also park-and-ride (P+R) lots at distant suburban metro stations, including Skalka (Line A), Zličín and Český Most (Line B), and Nádraží Holešovice and Opatov (Line C).

ROAD CONDITIONS

The Prague city center is mostly a snarl of traffic, one-way cobblestone streets, and tram lines. Driving outside of the capital is less hectic, but still often crowded. The Czech Republic has few four-lane highways, and even busy stretches are served by relatively narrow two-lane roads. As the country tries to upgrade its roads, expect frequent construction delays and detours.

RULES OF THE ROAD

The Czech Republic follows the usual Continental rules of the road. A right turn on red is permitted *only* when indicated by a green arrow. Signposts with yellow diamonds indicate a main road where drivers have the right of way. The speed limit is 130 kph (78 mph) on four-lane highways, 90 kph (56 mph) on open roads, and 50 kph (30 mph) in built-up areas and villages. Speed checks in villages are common. Seat belts are compulsory, and drinking before driving is absolutely prohibited. Passengers under 12 years of age, or less than 150 cm (5 feet) in height, must ride in the back seat.

▌BY PUBLIC TRANSIT

Prague has an excellent public transit system, which includes a clean and reliable underground subway system—called the metro—as well as an extensive tram and bus network. Metro stations are marked with an inconspicuous M sign. A refurbished old tram, No. 91, travels through the Old Town and Lesser Quarter on summer weekends. Beware of pickpockets, who often operate in large groups on crowded trams and metro cars.

The basic, transferrable metro and tram ticket costs 20 Kč. It permits one hour's travel throughout the metro, tram, and bus network between 5 AM and 8 PM on weekdays, or 90 minutes' travel at other times. Single-ride tickets cost 14 Kč and allow one 15-minute ride on a tram or bus, without transfer, or a metro journey of up to four stations lasting less than 30 minutes (transfer between lines is allowed). If you're carrying a big bag, you need to buy an additional 10 Kč ticket.

Tickets (*jízdenky*) can be bought at dispensing machines in the metro stations and at some newsstands.

You can also buy a one-day pass allowing unlimited use of the system for 80 Kč, a 3-day pass for 220 Kč, a 7-day pass for 280 Kč, or a 15-day pass for 320 Kč. The passes can be purchased at the main metro stations, from ticket machines, and at some newsstands in the center. A pass is not valid until stamped in the orange machines in metro stations or aboard trams *and* the required information is entered on the back (there are instructions in English).

The trams and metros shut down around midnight, but special night trams, numbered 50 to 59, and some buses run all night. Night trams run at 30-minute intervals, and all routes intersect at the corner of Lazarská and Spálená streets in the New Town, near the Národní třída metro station. Schedules and regulations in English are on the transportation department's official Web site. Travel Information Centers provide all substantial information about public transport operation, routes, timetables, etc. They are at major metro stations and at both terminals at the airport.

Validate your metro ticket at an orange stamping machine before descending the escalator. Trains are patrolled often; the fine for riding without a valid ticket is 800 Kč, but the fine is reduced if you pay on the spot. Tickets for buses are the same as those used for the metro, although you validate them at machines inside the bus or tram.

Transit Information Web Sites **Dopravní Podnik** ⊕ www.dpp.cz.

Transit Information Centers **Anděl** ☏ 296–191–817. **Mustek** ☏ 296–191–817. **Muzeum** ☏ 296–191–817. **Nádraží Holešovice** ☏ 296–191–817. **Ruzyně Airport** ☏ 296–191–817.

Lost & Found **Lost & Found** ✉ Karoliny Světlé 5, Staré Město ☏ 224–235–085.

▌BY TAXI

Taxis are a convenient way of getting around town, particularly in the evening, when the number of trams and metro trains starts to thin out. But be on the lookout for dishonest drivers, especially if you hail a taxi on the street or from one of the taxi stands at heavily touristed areas like Wenceslas

Square. Typical scams include drivers doctoring the meter or failing to turn the meter on and then demanding an exorbitant sum at the end of the ride. In an honest cab, the meter starts at about 30 Kč and increases by 25 Kč per km (½ mi) or 4 Kč per minute at rest. Most rides within town should cost no more than 150 Kč to 200 Kč. The best way to avoid getting ripped off is to ask your hotel or restaurant to call a cab for you. If you have to hail a taxi on the street, agree with the driver on a fare before getting in. (If the driver says he can't tell you what the approximate fare will be, that's almost a sure sign he's giving you a line.) If you have access to a phone, a better bet is to call one of the many radio-operated companies, like AAA Taxi. The drivers are honest and the dispatchers speak English.

Taxi Companies **AAA Radiotaxi**
☎ 222-333-222 ⊕ www.aaa.radiotaxi.cz.
City Taxi ☎ 257-257-257 ⊕ www.citytaxi.cz.

▌ BY TRAIN

Prague is serviced by two international train stations, so always make certain you know which station your train is using. The main station, Hlavní nádraží, is about 500 yards east of Wenceslas Square via Washingtonova ulice. The other international station is Nádraží Holešovice, in a suburban area about 2 km (1 mi) north of the city center along the metro Line C (red line). Nádraží Holešovice is frequently the point of departure for trains heading to Berlin, Vienna, and Budapest. Two other large stations in Prague service mostly local destinations. Smíchovské Nádraží—southwest of the city center across the Vltava (on metro Line B, yellow line)—services destinations to the west, including trains to Karlštejn. Masarykovo Nádraží, near náměstí Republiky in the center of the city, services mostly suburban destinations.

For train times consult the timetables posted at the stations. On timetables, departures (*odjezd*) appear on a yellow background; arrivals (*příjezd*) are on white. There are two information desks at the main station,

Hlavní nádraží, though service is often surly. The main Čedok office downtown can advise on train times and schedules.

■ TIP→ Remember to always compare the price and travel times of buses and trains when planning sidetrips from Prague. Many times, bus tickets cost about half the price and get you to your destination in half the time.

On arriving at Hlavní nádraží the best way to get to the center of town is by metro. The station lies on metro Line C (red line), and is just one stop from the top of Wenceslas Square (station: Muzeum)—travel in the direction of Haje station. You can also walk the 500 yards or so to the square, though the area around Hlavní nádraží is depressing, and the walk is not advisable late at night. A taxi ride from the main station to the center should cost about 100 Kč. To reach the city center from Nádraží Holešovice, take the metro Line C (red line) four stops to Muzeum; a taxi ride should cost roughly 200 Kč to 250 Kč.

The state-run rail system is called České dráhy (ČD). On longer runs, it's not really worth taking anything less than an express (*rychlík*) train, marked in red on the timetable. Tickets are still inexpensive: a second-class ticket from Prague to Brno—a distance of 200 km—cost about 300 Kč. A 40 Kč to 60 Kč supplement is charged for the excellent international expresses, EuroCity (EC) and InterCity (IC), and for domestic SuperCity (SC) schedules. A 20 Kč supplement applies to reserved seats on domestic journeys. If you haven't bought a ticket in advance at the station (mandatory for seat reservations), you can buy one aboard the train from the conductor. It's possible to book sleepers (*lůžkový*) or the less-roomy couchettes (*lehátkový*) on most overnight trains. You do not need to validate your train ticket before boarding. The main Čedok office downtown can also book domestic and international tickets and advise on sleeper options.

Čedok ✉ Na Příkopě 18, Nové Město
☎ 224-197-111 ⊕ www.cedok.cz.

ON THE GROUND

■ COMMUNICATIONS

INTERNET

Internet is widely available at hotels and many provide Wi-Fi. Cafés with Internet stations are also all over Prague and you'll find you can check your e-mail everywhere from the local bookstore to the Laundromat.

Cybercafes ⊕ www.cybercafes.com lists more than 4,000 Internet cafés worldwide.

PHONES

The good news is that you can now make a direct-dial telephone call from virtually any point on earth. The bad news? You can't always do so cheaply. Calling from a hotel is almost always the most expensive option; hotels usually add huge surcharges to all calls, particularly international ones. In some countries you can phone from call centers or even the post office. Calling cards usually keep costs to a minimum, but only if you purchase them locally. And then there are mobile phones (⇨ *below*), which are sometimes more prevalent—particularly in the developing world—than land lines; as expensive as mobile phone calls can be, they are still usually a much cheaper option than calling from your hotel.

The country code for the Czech Republic is 420. To call the Czech Republic from outside the country, dial the international access prefix, then "420," and then the nine-digit Czech number. To call from the U.S., for example, dial "011-420-xxx-xxx-xxx."

CALLING WITHIN THE CZECH REPUBLIC

Now that most people in Prague have mobile phones, working phone booths are harder to find. If you can't find a working booth on the street, the telephone office of the main post office is the best place to try. Once inside, follow signs for TELEGRAF/TELEFAX.

Coin-operated pay phones are rare. Most newer public phones operate only with a special telephone card, available from post offices and some newsstands in denominations of 150 Kč and up. Since the boom in mobile phone use, both the cards and working pay phones are becoming scarce. A short call within Prague costs a minimum of 4 Kč from a coin-operated phone or the equivalent of 3.5 Kč (1 unit) from a card-operated phone. The dial tone is a series of alternating short and long buzzes.

You can reach an English-speaking operator from one of the major long-distance services on a toll-free number. The operator will connect your collect or credit-card call at the carrier's standard rates. In Prague, many phone booths allow direct international dialing.

There are no regional or area codes in the Czech Republic. Numbers that start with the first three digits running from 601 to 777, however, are mobile phones and the charge may be correspondingly higher. When calling a Czech number from within the Czech Republic, do not use the country code or any prefixes; simply dial the nine-digit number.

CALLING OUTSIDE THE CZECH REPUBLIC

When dialing out of the country, the country code is 1 for the United States and Canada. To dial overseas directly, first dial 00 and then the country code of the country you are calling. A call to the United States or Canada, for example, would begin 00-1, followed by the U.S. or Canadian area code and number.

The post office telephone operator can place your international call, or simply ask the receptionist at your hotel to put the call through for you. In the latter instance, the surcharges and rates will probably be very high.

Access Codes AT&T ☎ 0/042-000-101. **BT Direct** ☎ 0/042-004-401. **CanadaDirect**

☎ 0/042-000-151. **MCI** ☎ 0/042-000-112. **Sprint** ☎ 0/042-087-187.
Other Contacts International Operator ☎ 133004. **International Directory Assistance** ☎ 1181.

CALLING CARDS

With the prepaid Karta X (300 Kč to 1,000 Kč), rates to the U.S. are roughly 13 Kč per minute; a call to the U.K. costs about 12 Kč per minute. The cards are available at many money-changing stands and can work with any phone once you enter a 14-digit code. You do not need to find a booth with a card slot to use the cards.

MOBILE PHONES

If you have a multiband phone (some countries use different frequencies than what's used in the United States) and your service provider uses the world-standard GSM network (as do T-Mobile, Cingular, and Verizon), you can probably use your phone abroad. Roaming fees can be steep, however: 99¢ a minute is considered reasonable. And overseas you normally pay the toll charges for incoming calls. It's almost always cheaper to send a text message than to make a call, since text messages have a very low set fee (often less than 5¢).

If you just want to make local calls, consider buying a new SIM card (note that your provider may have to unlock your phone for you to use a different SIM card) and a prepaid service plan in the destination. You'll then have a local number and can make local calls at local rates. If your trip is extensive, you could also simply buy a new cell phone in your destination, as the initial cost will be offset over time.

■ TIP → **If you travel internationally frequently, save one of your old mobile phones or buy a cheap one on the Internet; ask your cell phone company to unlock it for you, and take it with you as a travel phone, buying a new SIM card with pay-as-you-go service in each destination. Cellular Abroad** ☎ 800/287-5072 ⊕ www.cellularabroad.com rents and sells GSM

LOCAL DO'S & TABOOS

GREETINGS

Day-to-day interaction with Czechs is not much different than it is with North Americans or other Europeans. In general, Czechs are more reserved in their dealings with foreigners than, say, Greeks or Italians might be, but are nevertheless cordial and polite. On being introduced, it's common to shake hands; kissing on the cheeks is reserved for family members and close friends. On entering a shop it's usual to say "hello" (*Dobrý den*) to the shopkeeper, and to say "good bye" (*na shledanou*) on leaving. It's considered rude to speak too loudly in public, though this "rule" is often suspended in pubs.

DOING BUSINESS

There are no special rules of business etiquette that would be seen as outside the norm in Europe or in North America. Punctuality is valued and seen as a sign of reliability. Meetings will usually begin and end with a firm handshake. Your Czech counterpart is likely to say his or her surname as he shakes your hand for the first time. You can do the same. It's customary during or after a meeting to exchange business cards. Resist the temptation to address someone by their first name in the initial meetings. This might be seen as too familiar. At business lunches, feel free to order an alcoholic beverage if you want. There's no stigma attached to having a wine or beer "on the job."

LANGUAGE

One of the best ways to avoid being an Ugly American is to learn a little of the local language. You need not strive for fluency; even just mastering a few basic words and terms is bound to make chatting with the locals more rewarding. Czech, the official language of the Czech Republic, is a western Slavic language that is nearly identical to Slovak and closely related to Polish. Czechs learn English in schools. Outside of Prague, English comprehension is slightly less common.

CON OR CONCIERGE?

Good hotel concierges are invaluable—for arranging transportation, getting reservations at the hottest restaurant, and scoring tickets for a sold-out show or entrée to an exclusive nightclub. They're in the know and well connected. That said, sometimes you have to take their advice with a grain of salt.

It's not uncommon for restaurants to ply concierges with free food and drink in exchange for steering diners their way. Indeed, European concierges often receive referral *fees*. Hotel chains usually have guidelines about what their concierges can accept. The best concierges, however, are above reproach. This is particularly true of those who belong to the prestigious international society of Les Clefs d'Or.

What can you expect of a concierge? At a typical tourist-class hotel you can expect him or her to give you the basics: to show you something on a map, make a standard restaurant reservation (particularly if you don't speak the language), or help you book a tour or airport transportation.

Savvy concierges at the finest hotels and resorts, can arrange for just about any good or service imaginable—and do so quickly. You should compensate them appropriately. A $10 tip is enough to show appreciation for a table at a hot restaurant. But the reward should really be much greater for tickets to that opera that's been sold out for months.

phones and sells SIM cards that work in many countries. **Mobal** ☎ 888/888-9162 ⊕ www.mobalrental.com rents mobiles and sells GSM phones (starting at $49) that will operate in 140 countries. Per-call rates vary throughout the world. **Planet Fone** ☎ 888/988-4777 ⊕ www.planetfone.com rents cell phones, but the per-minute rates are expensive.

▌ CUSTOMS & DUTIES

You're always allowed to bring goods of a certain value back home without having to pay any duty or import tax. But there's a limit on the amount of tobacco and liquor you can bring back duty-free, and some countries have separate limits for perfumes; for exact figures, check with your customs department. The values of so-called "duty-free" goods are included in these amounts. When you shop abroad, save all your receipts, as customs inspectors may ask to see them as well as the items you purchased. If the total value of your goods is more than the duty-free limit, you'll have to pay a tax (most often a flat percentage) on the value of everything beyond that limit.

There are few restrictions on what you can take out of the Czech Republic. The main exception is items with special historical or cultural value. To be exported, an antique or work of art must have an export certificate. Reputable shops should be willing to advise customers on how to comply with the regulations. If a shop can't provide proof of the item's suitability for export, be wary.

Under certain circumstances, you can receive a refund of the 19% value-added tax payable on purchases over 2,500 Kč, provided the goods are taken out of the country soon after purchase. Ask about "Tax Free Shopping" at the store when you purchase the goods and make sure to collect all of the necessary stamps and receipts. You can get a cash refund at the airport. **U.S. Information** **U.S. Customs and Border Protection** ⊕ www.cbp.gov.

▌ DAY TOURS & GUIDES

BOAT TOURS

You can take a 30- to 60-minute boat trip along the Vltava year-round from several boat companies that are based on the quays near the Malá Strana side of the Charles Bridge. It's not really necessary to buy tickets in advance, though you can;

boats leave as they fill up. One of the cruise companies stands out, and it's on the Old Town side of the bridge. Prague-Venice Cruises operates restored, classic canal boats from late 19th century; the company operates one larger boat that holds 35 passengers and 8 smaller boats that hold 12 passengers.

■ TIP→ **Take one of the smaller boats—particularly one of the uncovered ones—if you can, for a more intimate narrated cruise of about 45 minutes along the Vltava and nearby canals.**

Refreshments are included in all cruises. You actually set sail from beneath the last remaining span of Judith's Bridge (the Roman-built precursor to the Charles Bridge). Look for the touts in sailor suits right before the bridge; they will direct you to the ticket office. Cruises are offered daily from 10:30 to 6 from November through February, until 8 from March through June and September through October, and until 11 in July and August. Cruises cost 270 Kč.

Prague-Venice Cruises ☎ 776-776-779 ⊕ www.prague-venice.cz.

BUS TOURS

Čedok offers a 3½-hour "Prague Castle Tour," a combination bus and walking venture that covers the castle and major sights around town in English. The price is about 750 Kč. Stop by the main office for information on other tours and for information on tour departure points. You can also arrange a personalized walking tour. Times and itineraries are negotiable; prices start at around 500 Kč per hour.

Very similar tours by other operators also daily from náměstí Republiky Národní třída near Jungmannovo náměstí, and Wenceslas Square. Prices are generally a couple hundred crowns less than for Čedok's tours.

Čedok ☎ 224-197-242 ⊕ www.cedok.cz. **Martin Tour** ☎ 224-212-473 ⊕ www.martintour.cz. **Precious Legacy Tours** ☎ 222-320-398 ⊕ www.legacytours.cz. **Premiant City Tour** ☎ 296-246-070 ⊕ www.

premiant.cz. **Travel Plus** ☎ 224-227-989 ⊕ www.travel.cz. **Wittmann Tours** ☎ 222-252-472 ⊕ www.wittmann-tours.com.

PRIVATE GUIDES

Tours of Prague come under the supervision of Prague Information Service, which is reliable and always informative. The company organizes walking tours in Prague's city center and in the outskirts, including excursions from Prague. Arrangements can be made with them for many tailor-made tours. Nonregistered guides can also be found, but unless they come with a personal recommendation from someone you trust, their services cannot be guaranteed.

One private guide comes to us highly recommended. His name is Jaroslav "Jay" Pesta, and he's an informative and reliable guide who speaks good English. Jay offers a wide range of touring options, or he can design a personalized tour around your interests. He'll lead you around Prague on a full-day private walking tour for around 1,200 Kč per person (less if you want a half-day tour), and the experience is much more enjoyable than a bus tour with a large group. The best and easiest way to contact him is through his Web site. **Jay Pesta** ☎ 608-866-454 ⊕ www.prague-walks.com. **Prague Information Service** ☎ 236-002-569 ⊕ www.pis.cz.

WALKING TOURS

Theme walking tours are very popular in Prague. You can choose from tours on medieval architecture, "Velvet Revolution walks," visits to Communist monuments, and any number of pub crawls. Each year, four or five small operators do these tours, which generally last a couple of hours and cost 200 Kč to 300 Kč. Inquire at Prague Information Service or a major ticket agency for the current season's offerings. Most walks start at the clock tower on Old Town Square.

A special guide service is available in the Czech Republic, designed to examine and

...try's Jewish history. The ...mann Tours, offers several ...rs within Prague and also o... ...cluding the Terezín concentration c... ...p.

Wittmann Tours ☎ 222-252-472 ⊕ www.wittmann-tours.com.

■ ELECTRICITY

The electrical current in Eastern and Central Europe is 220 volts, 50 cycles alternating current (AC); wall outlets generally take plugs with two round prongs.

Consider making a small investment in a universal adapter, which has several types of plugs in one lightweight, compact unit. Most laptops and mobile phone chargers are dual voltage (i.e., they operate equally well on 110 and 220 volts), so require only an adapter. These days the same is true of small appliances such as hair dryers. Always check labels and manufacturer instructions to be sure. Don't use 110-volt outlets marked FOR SHAVERS ONLY for high-wattage appliances such as hair dryers.

Steve Kropla's Help for World Traveler's ⊕ www.kropla.com has information on electrical and telephone plugs around the world. **Walkabout Travel Gear** ⊕ www.walkabouttravelgear.com has good coverage about electricity under "adapters."

■ EMERGENCIES

Doctors & Dentists American Dental Associates ✉ V Celnici 4, Nové Město ☎ 221-181-121.
Foreign Embassy U.S. Embassy ✉ Tržiště 15, Malá Strana ☎ 257-530-663 ⊕ www.usembassy.cz.
General Emergency Contacts Ambulance ☎ 155. **Autoklub Bohemia Assistance** ☎ 1240. **Federal Police** ☎ 158. **Prague city police** ☎ 156. **ÚAMK Emergency Roadside Assistance** ☎ 1230 ⊕ www.uamk.cz.
Hospitals & Clinics Na Homolce Hospital ✉ Roentgenova 2, Motol ☎ 257-211-111 ⊕ www.homolka.cz.
Pharmacies Lékárna U Anděla ✉ Štefánikova 6, Smíchov ☎ 257-320-918.

Lékárna ✉ Belgická 37, Nové Město ☎ 222-513-396.

■ HEALTH

Make sure food has been thoroughly cooked and is served to you fresh and hot. If you have problems, mild cases of traveler's diarrhea may respond to Imodium (known generically as loperamide) or Pepto-Bismol. Be sure to drink plenty of fluids; if you can't keep fluids down, seek medical help immediately.

Infectious diseases can be airborne or passed via mosquitoes and ticks and through direct or indirect physical contact with animals or people. Some, including Norwalk-like viruses that affect your digestive tract, can be passed along through contaminated food. Condoms can help prevent most sexually transmitted diseases, but they aren't absolutely reliable and their quality varies from country to country. Speak with your physician and/or check the CDC or World Health Organization Web sites for health alerts, particularly if you're pregnant, traveling with children, or have a chronic illness.

For information on travel insurance, shots and medications, and medical-assistance companies *see* Shots & Medications *under* Things to Consider *in* Before You Go, *above*.

SPECIFIC ISSUES IN PRAGUE

There are no serious health hazards for travelers in the Czech Republic. The tap water is drinkable, but some of the pipes are old, so let the water run a bit before drinking. Bottled water is a plentiful and cheap alternative.

OVER-THE-COUNTER REMEDIES

Pharmacies in Prague are well-stocked with prescription and nonprescription drugs, though you may have trouble convincing a pharmacist to fill a foreign prescription. It's best to bring from home all of the prescribed medications you are likely to need. Pharmacies are generally open during regular business hours from 9 AM to 6 PM, with special weekend and nighttime service rotating among them. During off-hours, pharmacies will post the name and address of the nearest open pharmacy on their doors. Pharmacies sell not only prescription medicines but are the only licensed dealers of typical over-the-counter products like pain relievers and cough medicines. Most standard U.S. over-the-counter products have Czech equivalents. Aspirin is widely available. The most common nonaspirin pain reliever is Ibalgin (ibuprofen), sold in 200 mg and 400 mg doses.

■ TIP→ Pharmacists may not speak English or know a drug's non-Czech brand name, but will certainly know the drug's generic name ("acetaminophen" for "Tylenol," for example). Be sure to call a drug by its generic name when asking for it.

■ HOURS OF OPERATION

Though hours vary, most banks are open weekdays from 8 AM to 5 PM. Private currency exchange offices usually have longer hours, and some are open all night.

Gas stations on the main roads are open 24 hours a day.

In season (from May through September), most museums, castles, and other major sights are open daily—except Monday—from about 9 AM to 4 PM. Hours vary at other times during the year, and some attractions in smaller, off-the-beaten-track places shut down altogether from November to March.

Most pharmacies are open weekdays from about 9 AM to 6 PM, and are closed weekends. For emergencies, some pharmacies maintain weekend hours, though these can change from week to week. Ask someone locally for advice.

Most stores are open weekdays from 9 AM to 6 PM. Some larger grocery stores open as early as 6 AM, and a few of the hypermarkets in Prague (usually well outside of town along the metro lines) are open 24 hours. Department stores often stay open

until 7 PM. Outside Prague, most stores close for the weekend at noon on Saturday, although you may find a grocery store open at night or on the weekend.

HOLIDAYS

January 1; Easter Monday; May 1 (Labor Day); May 8 (Liberation Day); July 5 (Sts. Cyril and Methodius Day); July 6 (Jan Hus Day); September 28 (Day of Czech Statehood); October 28 (Czech National Day); November 17 (Day of a Struggle for Liberty and Democracy, aka "Velvet Revolution" Day); and December 24, 25, and 26 (Christmas Eve, Christmas Day, Boxing Day).

■ MAIL

It takes about a week for letters and postcards to reach the U.S. Remember to pay a little extra for airmail; otherwise your letters will be sent by ship. The opening hours of post offices vary—the smaller the place, the shorter the hours. Most large post offices are open from 8 AM to 7 PM on weekdays. The main post office in Prague is open 24 hours, with a 30-minute break after midnight. Orange post office boxes can be found around the city, usually attached to the side of a building.

At this writing, postcards to the United States cost 12 Kč, letters up to 20 grams in weight 14 Kč. You can buy stamps at post offices, hotels, newsstands, and shops that sell postcards.

If you don't know where you'll be staying, American Express mail service is a great convenience, available at no charge to anyone holding an American Express credit card or carrying American Express traveler's checks. There are several offices in Prague. You can also have mail held *poste restante* (general delivery) at post offices in major towns, but the letters should be marked *Pošta 1,* to designate the city's main post office; in Prague, the poste restante window is at the main post office. You'll be asked for identification when you collect your mail.

American Express ✉ Václavské nám. 56, Nové Město ☎ 234-711-711 ⊕ www. americanexpress.com.
Main Branch **Prague Main Post Office** ✉ Jindřišská ul. 14 ⊕ www.cpost.cz

SHIPPING PACKAGES

The Czech postal service, Česká pošta, runs an Express Mail Service (EMS). You can post your EMS parcel at any post office, and Česká pošta can supply forms for customs clearance. Delivery times vary between one and five days, though material is often delayed by American customs. You may not send currency, travel checks, precious metals, or stones through Express Mail. Not every post office offers a pickup service.

Many other private international express carriers also serve the Czech Republic.

Some major stores can make their own arrangements to ship purchases home on behalf of their customers. A number of freight and cargo services operate international delivery services, and these can generally be relied upon. An average shipping time to the U.S. is 21 days (4 days for air cargo). There's no reason not to use the reliable Česká pošta, which delivers anything up to 30 kg.

Express Services **DHL** ☎ 800-103-000 ⊕ www.dhl.cz. **EMS** ☎ 800-104-410 ⊕ www.cpost.cz. **Fed Ex** ☎ 800-133-339 ⊕ www.inspekta.cz/fedex. **UPS** ☎ 800-181-111 ⊕ www.ups.com.
Art Trans ✉ Podbabska 81/17/1, Bubeneč ☎ 233-336-076 ⊕ www.shipping.cz. **Fix Box Air Shipping** ✉ Sudoměřská 26, Žižkov ☎ 222-720-456.

I MONEY

Although the Czech Republic is still generally a bargain by Western standards, Prague remains the exception. Hotel prices in particular are often higher than the facilities would warrant, but prices at tourist resorts outside the capital are lower and, in the outlying areas and off the beaten track, very low. The story is similar for restaurants; with Prague being comparable to the U.S. and Western Europe, while outlying towns are much more reasonable. The prices for castles, museum, and other sights are rising, but still low by outside standards.

ATMs are common in Prague and most towns in the Czech Republic and more often than not are part of the Cirrus and Plus networks, meaning you can get cash easily. Outside of urban areas, machines can be scarce and you should plan to carry enough cash to meet your needs.

In Czech, an ATM is called a *bankomat,* and a PIN is also a PIN, just as in English.

Prices throughout this guide are given for adults. Substantially reduced fees are almost always available for children, students, and senior citizens.

■ TIP➔ **Banks in the U.S. never have every foreign currency on hand, and it may take as long as a week to order. If you're planning to exchange funds before leaving home, don't wait until the last minute.**

ATMS & BANKS

Your own bank will probably charge a fee for using ATMs abroad; the foreign bank you use may also charge a fee. Nevertheless, you'll usually get a better rate of exchange at an ATM than you will at a currency-exchange office or even when changing money in a bank. And extracting funds as you need them is a safer option than carrying around a large amount of cash.

■ TIP➔ **PIN numbers with more than four digits are not recognized at ATMs in many countries. If yours has five or more, remember to change it before you leave.**

ATMs are safe and reliable. Instructions are in English. If in doubt, use machines attached to established banks like Česká Spořitelna, Komerčni Banka, and ČSOB.

CREDIT CARDS

Throughout this guide, the following abbreviations are used: **AE**, American Express; **DC**, Diners Club; **MC**, MasterCard; and **V**, Visa.

It's a good idea to inform your credit-card company before you travel, especially if you're going abroad and don't travel internationally very often. Otherwise, the credit-card company might put a hold on your card owing to unusual activity—not a good thing halfway through your trip. Record all your credit-card numbers—as well as the phone numbers to call if your cards are lost or stolen—in a safe place, so you're prepared should something go wrong. Both MasterCard and Visa have general numbers you can call (collect if you're abroad) if your card is lost, but you're better off calling the number of your issuing bank, since MasterCard and Visa usually just transfer you to your bank; your bank's number is usually printed on your card.

If you plan to use your credit card for cash advances, you'll need to apply for a PIN at least two weeks before your trip. Although it's usually cheaper (and safer) to use a credit card abroad for large purchases (so you can cancel payments or be reimbursed if there's a problem), note that some credit-card companies *and* the banks that issue them add substantial percentages to all foreign transactions, whether they're in a foreign currency or not. Check on these fees before leaving home, so there won't be any surprises when you get the bill.

■ TIP→ **Before you charge something, ask the merchant whether he or she plans to do a dynamic currency conversion (DCC). In such a transaction the credit-card *processor* (shop, restaurant, or hotel, not Visa or MasterCard) converts the currency and charges you in dollars. In most cases you'll pay the merchant a 3% fee for this service in addition to any credit-card company and issuing-bank foreign-transaction surcharges.**

Dynamic currency conversion programs are becoming increasingly widespread. Merchants who participate in them are supposed to ask whether you want to be charged in dollars or the local currency, but they don't always do so. And even if they do offer you a choice, they may well avoid mentioning the additional surcharges. The good news is that you *do* have a choice. And if this practice really gets your goat, you can avoid it entirely thanks to American Express; with its cards, DCC simply isn't an option.

Visa, MasterCard, and American Express are widely accepted by major hotels, restaurants, and stores, Diners Club less so. Smaller establishments and those off the beaten track, unsurprisingly, are less likely to accept credit cards.

Reporting Lost Cards American Express
☎ 800/992-3404 in U.S., 336/393-1111 collect from abroad ⊕ www.americanexpress.com. **Diners Club** ☎ 800/234-6377 in U.S., 303/799-1504 collect from abroad ⊕ www.dinersclub.com. **MasterCard** ☎ 800/622-7747 in U.S., 636/722-7111 collect from abroad ⊕ www.mastercard.com. **Visa** ☎ 800/847-2911 in U.S., 410/581-9994 collect from abroad ⊕ www.visa.com.

CURRENCY & EXCHANGE

The unit of currency in the Czech Republic is the *koruna*, or crown (Kč), which is divided into 100 *haléřů*, or hellers. There are coins of 50 hellers; coins of 1, 2, 5, 10, 20, 50 Kč; and notes of 50, 100, 200, 500, 1,000, 2,000, and 5,000 Kč. Notes of 1,000 Kč and up may not always be accepted for small purchases.

Try to avoid exchanging money at hotels or private exchange booths, including the ubiquitous Chequepoint and Exact Change booths. They routinely take commissions of 8% to 10%. The best places to exchange money are at bank counters, where the commissions average 1% to 3%, or at ATMs. The koruna is fully convertible, which means it can be purchased outside the country and exchanged into other currencies. Of course, never change money with people on the street. Not only is it illegal, you will almost definitely be ripped off.

On arrival at the airport, the best bet for exchanging money are with one of the ATM machines lined up in the terminal just as you leave the arrivals area. The cur-

WORST-CASE SCENARIO

All your money and credit cards have just been stolen. In these days of real-time transactions, this isn't a predicament that should destroy your vacation. First, report the theft of the credit cards. Then get any traveler's checks you were carrying replaced. This can usually be done almost immediately, provided that you kept a record of the serial numbers separate from the checks themselves. If you bank at a large international bank like Citibank or HSBC, go to the closest branch; if you know your account number, chances are you can get a new ATM card and withdraw money right away. **Western Union** (☎ 800/325–6000 ⊕ www.westernunion. com) sends money almost anywhere. Have someone back home order a transfer online, over the phone, or at one of the company's offices, which is the cheapest option. The U.S. State Department's **Overseas Citizens Services** (☎ 202/647–5225) can wire money to any U.S. consulate or embassy abroad for a fee of $30. Just have someone back home wire money or send a money order or cashier's check to the state department, which will then disburse the funds as soon as the next working day after it receives them.

rency-exchange windows at the airport, happily, offer rates that are no worse than you will find anywhere in town, if not quite as good as those at banks.

At this writing the exchange rate was around 23 Kč to the U.S. dollar.

■ TIP➜ Even if a currency-exchange booth has a sign promising no commission, rest assured that there's some kind of huge, hidden fee. (Oh . . . that's right. The sign didn't say no *fee*). And as for rates, you're almost always better off getting foreign currency at an ATM or exchanging money at a bank.

Exchange Services **Exchange** ✉ 2 nám. Franze Kafka.

Some consider this the currency of the cave man, and it's true that fewer establishments accept traveler's checks these days. Nevertheless, they're a cheap and secure way to carry extra money, particularly on trips to urban areas. Both Citibank (under the Visa brand) and American Express issue traveler's checks in the United States, but Amex is better known and more widely accepted; you can also avoid hefty surcharges by cashing Amex checks at Amex offices. Whatever you do, keep track of all the serial numbers in case the checks are lost or stolen.

American Express now offers a stored-value card called a Travelers Cheque Card, which you can use wherever American Express credit cards are accepted, including ATMs. The card can carry a minimum of $300 and a maximum of $2,700, and it's a very safe way to carry your funds. Although you can get replacement funds in 24 hours if your card is lost or stolen, it doesn't really strike us as a very good deal. In addition to a high initial cost ($14.95 to set up the card, plus $5 each time you "reload"), you still have to pay a 2% fee for each purchase in a foreign currency (similar to that of any credit card). Further, each time you use the card in an ATM you pay a transaction fee of $2.50 on top of the 2% transaction fee for the conversion—add it all up and it can be considerably more than you would pay when simply using your own ATM card. Regular traveler's checks are just as secure and cost less.

American Express ☎ 888/412–6945 in U.S., 801/945–9450 collect outside of U.S. to add value or speak to customer service ⊕ www. americanexpress.com.

▌RESTROOMS

Public restrooms are more common, and cleaner, than they used to be in the Czech Republic. You nearly always have to pay 5 Kč to 10 Kč to the attendant. Restaurant and bar toilets are generally for customers only, but if you're discreet no one will care if you just drop by to use the facilities.

Find a Loo The Bathroom Diaries ⊕ www.thebathroomdiaries.com is flush with unsanitized info on restrooms the world over—each one located, reviewed, and rated.

▌SAFETY

Crime rates are relatively low in Prague, but travelers should be wary of pickpockets in crowded areas, especially on metros and trams, and at railway stations. Trams that are popular with tourists, such as the number 22 tram, which circumnavigates most of the major sites, is popular with pickpockets. In general, always keep your valuables on your person—purses, backpacks, or cameras are easy targets if they are hung on or placed next to chairs.

Violent crime is extremely rare, and you shouldn't experience any problems of this sort. That said, you should certainly take the typical precautions you would take in any large city.

Although nothing is likely to happen, it is not wise for a woman to go alone to a bar or nightclub or to wander the streets late at night. When traveling by train at night, seek out compartments that are well populated.

As with any city popular with tourists, Prague has its share of scams. The most common rip-offs are dishonest taxi drivers, pickpockets in the trams and metros, and the ubiquitous offers to "change money" on the street. All of these are easily avoided if you take precautions. If you have to hail a cab on the street, ask the driver what the approximate fare will be before you get in (if he can't tell you, that's a bad sign), and ask for a receipt (*paragon*) at the end of the ride. In trams and metros watch your valuables carefully. And never exchange money on the street unless you want to end up with a handful of fake and worthless bills.

▌ TIP→ **Distribute your cash, credit cards, IDs, and other valuables between a deep front pocket, an inside jacket or vest pocket, and a hidden money pouch. Don't reach for the money pouch once you're in public.**

▌TAXES

Taxes are usually included in the prices of hotel rooms, restaurant meals, and items purchased in shops. The price on the tag is what you'll pay at the register. The airport departure tax, about 600 Kč, is usually included in the price of airline tickets.

The Czech V.A.T. is called DPH (daň z přidané hodnoty), and there are two rates. The higher one (19%) covers nearly everything—gifts, souvenirs, clothing, and food in restaurants. Food in grocery stores and books are taxed by 5%. Exported goods are exempt from the tax, which can be refunded. All tourists outside the EU are entitled to claim the tax back if they spend more than 2,500 Kč in one shop on the same day. Global Refund processes V.A.T. refunds in the Czech Republic and will give you your refund in cash (U.S. dollars or euros) from a booth at the airport; be aware that the Czech Republic does *not* provide a postage-paid mailer for V.A.T. refund forms, unlike most other European countries.

When making a purchase, ask for a V.A.T. refund form and find out whether the merchant gives refunds—not all stores do, nor are they required to. Have the form stamped like any customs form by customs officials when you leave the country or, if you're visiting several European Union countries, when you leave the EU. After you're through passport control, take the form to a refund-service counter for an on-the-spot refund (which is usually the quickest and easiest option), or mail it to the address on the form (or the envelope with it) after you arrive home. You receive the total refund stated on the form, but the processing time can be long, especially if you request a credit-card adjustment.

EFFECTIVE COMPLAINING

Things don't always go right when you're traveling, and when you encounter a problem or service that isn't up to snuff, you should complain. But there are good and bad ways to do so.

Complain in person when it's serious. In a hotel, serious problems are usually better dealt with in person, at the front desk; if it's something quick, you can phone.

Complain early rather than late. Whenever you don't get what you paid for (the type of hotel room you booked or the airline seat you pre-reserved) or when it's something timely (the people next door are making too much noise), try to resolve the problem sooner rather than later. It's always going to be harder to deal with a problem or get something taken off your bill after the fact.

Be willing to escalate, but don't be hasty. Try to deal with the person at the front desk of your hotel or with your waiter in a restaurant before asking to speak to a supervisor or manager. Not only is this polite, but when the person directly serving you can fix the problem, you'll more likely get what you want quicker.

Say what you want, and be reasonable. When things fall apart, be clear about what kind of compensation you expect. Don't leave it to the hotel or restaurant or airline to suggest what they're willing to do for you. That said, the compensation you request must be in line with the problem. You're unlikely to get a free meal because your steak was undercooked or a free hotel stay if your bathroom was dirty.

Do it in writing. If you discover a billing error or some other problem after the fact, write a concise letter to the appropriate customer-service representative. Keep it to one page, and as with any complaint, state clearly and reasonably what you want them to do about the problem. Don't give a detailed trip report or list a litany of problems.

Global Refund is a Europe-wide service with 225,000 affiliated stores and more than 700 refund counters at major airports and border crossings. Its refund form, called a Tax Free Check, is the most common across the European continent. The service issues refunds in the form of cash, check, or credit-card adjustment.

V.A.T. Refunds Global Refund ☎ 800/566-9828 ⊕ www.globalrefund.com.

▌TIME

The Czech Republic is on Central European Time (CET), one hour ahead of Greenwich Mean Time and six hours ahead of the Eastern time zone of the United States.

▌TIPPING

Service is not usually included in restaurant bills. In pubs or ordinary places, simply round up the bill to the next multiple of 10 (if the bill comes to 83 Kč, for example, give the waiter 90 Kč); in nicer places, 10% is considered appropriate for good food and service. Tip porters who bring bags to your rooms 40 Kč–50 Kč total. For room service, a 20 Kč tip is enough. In taxis, round the bill up by 10%. Give tour guides and helpful concierges between 50 Kč and 100 Kč for services rendered.

INDEX

PHOTO CREDITS

Cover Photo (Charles Bridge): *David Zimmerman/Masterfile*. 7, *Sergio Pitamitz/age fotostock*. 10, *Doug Scott/age fotostock*. 11 (left), *Miroslav Krob/age fotostock*. 11 (right), *Jon Arnold/age fotostock*. 12, *Danita Delimont/Alamy*. 14, *Pixonnet.com/Alamy*. 15, *Hemis/Alamy*. 16, *Doug Scott/age fotostock*. 17 (left), *czechtourism.com*. 17 (right), *David Crausby/Alamy*. 18, *czechtourism.com*. 19, *Doug Scott/age fotostock*. 20, *Vaclav Ostadal/age fotostock*. 21 (left), *P. Narayan/age fotostock*. 21 (right), *czechtourism.com*. 82, *Profimedia International s.r.o./Alamy*. 162, *PCL/Alamy*.

NOTES

NOTES

NOTES

NOTES

NOTES

NOTES

NOTES

NOTES

NOTES

NOTES

ABOUT OUR WRITERS

Mark Baker is a longtime journalist and writer who came to Prague in 1991 to write a book on politics and so far has found it too pleasant to leave. He was the original author of *Fodor's Czechoslovakia* in 1991. For eight years, he was a newsroom editor at the Prague-based international broadcaster *Radio Free Europe*. Currently, he's at work on a series of travel books on Eastern Europe.

Mindy Kay Bricker is a freelance journalist based in Prague, where, since 2002, she's made a career out of writing about shopping and travel for books and magazines in the U.S. and Europe. She also reports on regional women's issues for Women's eNews, a New York-based news Web site.

Evan Rail moved to Prague in 2000 and stayed there primarily because of the kvas-nicové pivo. For many years he reviewed restaurants and covered food and drink for the *Prague Post* until he left to write the *Good Beer Guide to Prague and the Czech Republic* for CAMRA, a UK beer consumers' organization. His stories have been included in *Best Food Writing* and *Travelers' Tales* anthologies and appear frequently in the *New York Times* travel section.

Raymond Johnston has worked in media for all of his professional career, hosting a popular radio show in the Midwest in the early 1990s before moving to New York to work for a company that published critical guidebooks on the Internet. In 1996 he moved to Prague where he has worked as a film critic, historical and linguistic consultant for TV programs, and a magazine editor.